MW01631213

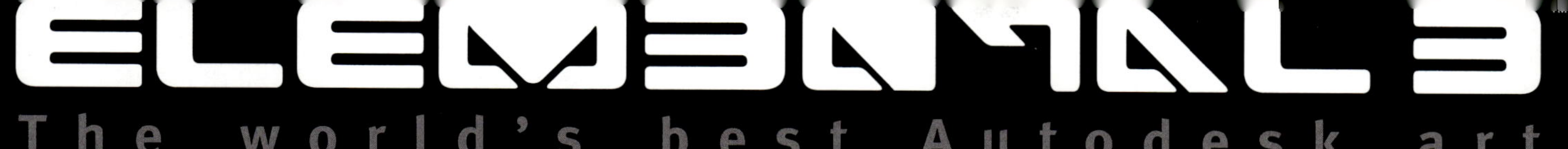

The world's best Autodesk art

Edited by

Daniel Wade & Paul Hellard

Publishers

Mark Snoswell & Daniel Wade

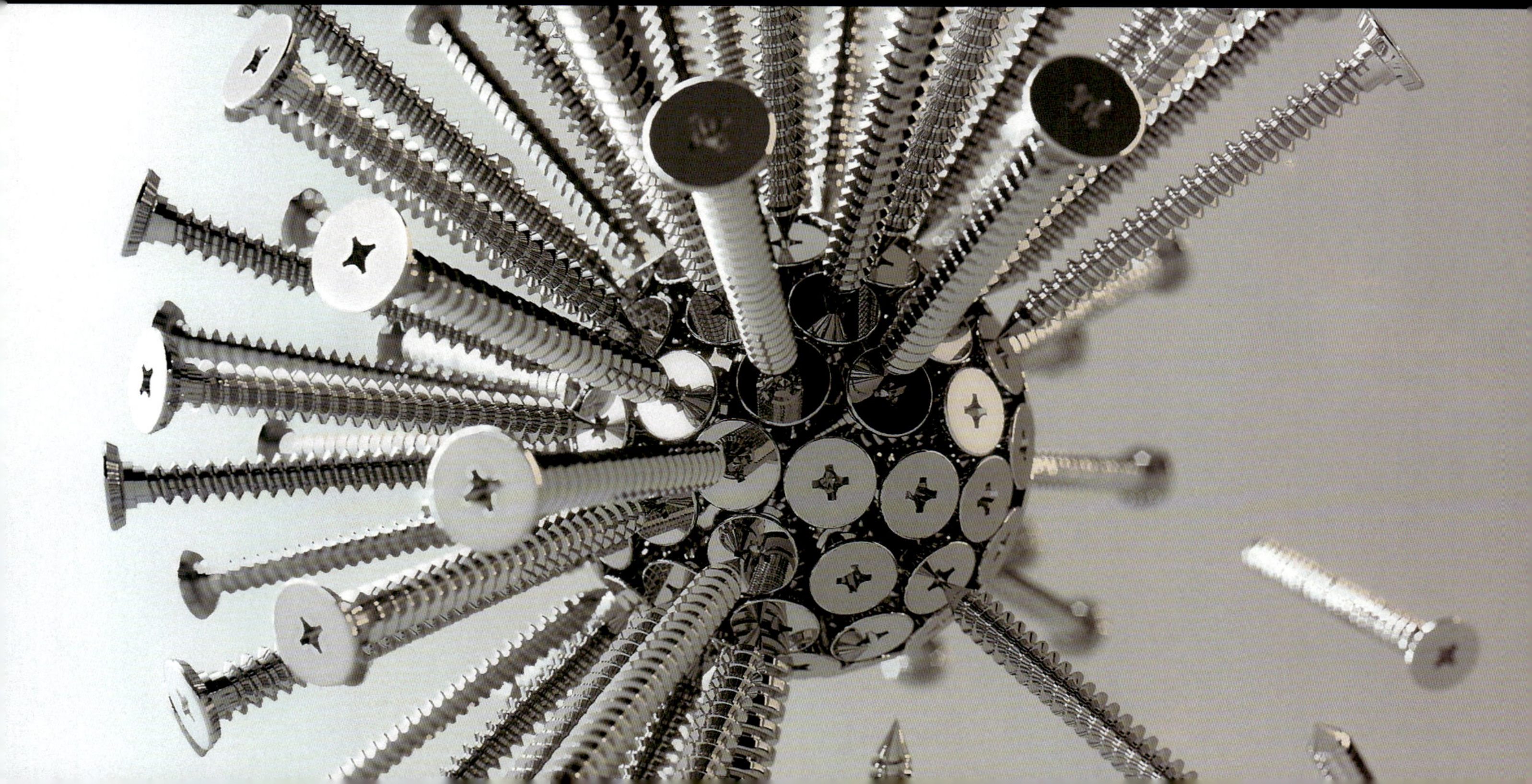

ELEMENTAL 3™

Published
by
Ballistic Publishing
Publishers of digital works for the digital world
134 Gilbert St
Adelaide, SA 5000
Australia
www.BallisticPublishing.com
Correspondence:
info@BallisticPublishing.com

First Edition published in Australia 2008 by Ballistic Publishing

Hardcover Edition ISBN 978-1-921002-53-3
Limited Edition ISBN 978-1-921002-52-6

Managing Editor/Co-Publisher
Daniel Wade

Assistant Editor
Paul Hellard

Art Director
Mark Snoswell

Design & Image Processing
Lauren Stevens, Daniel Cox

Printing and binding
Everbest Printing (China)
www.everbest.com

Partners
The CGSociety (Computer Graphics Society)
www.CGSociety.org

Also available from Ballistic Publishing
EXPOSÉ 6 Softcover ISBN 978-1-921002-50-2
d'artiste Character Modeling 2 ISBN 978-1-921002-35-9
Creative ESSENCE: The Face ISBN 978-1-921002-36-6
EXOTIQUE 3 Softcover ISBN 978-1-921002-45-8

Visit www.BallisticPublishing.com
for our complete range of titles.

Cover image credits

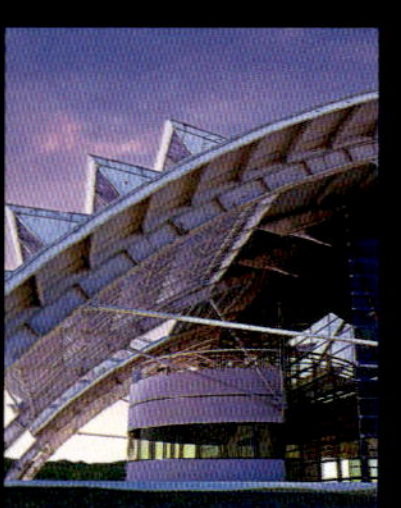

Homage to Sidonio Porto
AutoCAD, 3ds Max,
mental ray, Photoshop
Marcelo Eder, BRAZIL
[Front cover: ELEMENTAL 3 Softcover edition], 56-57

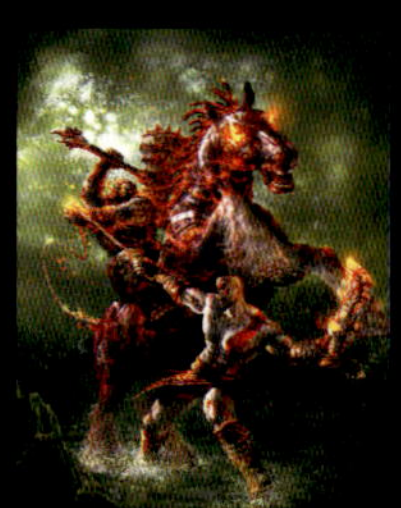

God of War 2: Kratos vs. Barbarian King
Photoshop, Maya
Andy Park, SCEA, USA
[Back cover: ELEMENTAL 3 Softcover edition], 21
'God of War 2'
© Sony Computer Entertainment America Inc.

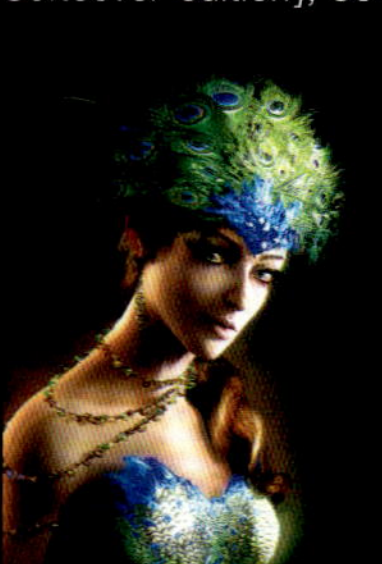

Peacock woman
3ds Max, Photoshop
Jiri Adamec,
CZECH REPUBLIC
[Cover: ELEMENTAL 3 Limited Edition], 18

/ BALLISTIC /

EDITORIAL

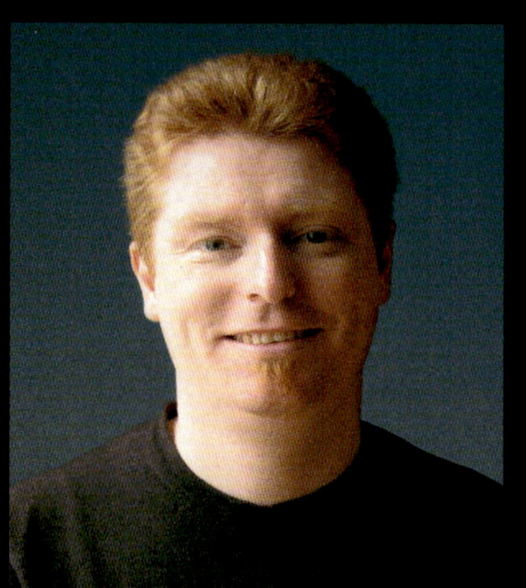
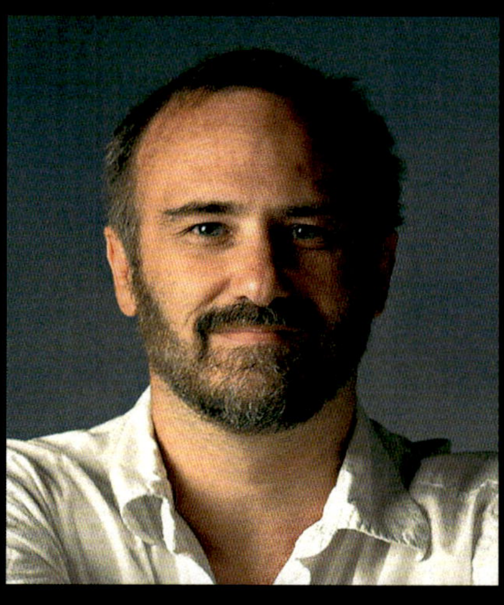

Daniel Wade | Co-Publisher & Mark Snoswell | Co-Publisher

The first ELEMENTAL book was launched in partnership with Autodesk in mid-2004, and its sequel was released one year later. Both books showcased the world's best images created with Autodesk 3D visualization and animation software. Two years on, Autodesk has grown at a remarkable rate with acquisitions of companies like Alias (creators of Maya), and Skymatter (creators of Mudbox) to name only two. With the Alias acquisition particularly, Autodesk moved to the forefront of automotive design and 3D film effects, both significant fields in addition to the CAD, games, TV, film effects and product design—areas Autodesk has dominated.

The success of the original ELEMENTAL books not only made this book possible, but also guaranteed an even larger selection of superbly realized artwork from some of the best-known artists and companies across the gaming, architectural visualization, and visual effects fields. ELEMENTAL 3 builds on the success of the first two editions with a growing number of architectural works—the field that Autodesk continues to lead. With ELEMENTAL 3 we are proud to celebrate the artistic talents of the diverse and growing community of Autodesk artists.

ELEMENTAL 3 is a completely independent production of Ballistic Publishing, with images being selected solely on their artistic merit. We appointed an independent advisory board of high profile artists in the fields of visual effects, game development, architecture, and software development. With the advisory board's help we then sorted through 1,800 entries (the highest number of entries for an ELEMENTAL book) to select just 246 images from 170 artists in 43 different countries.

Images were allocated to one of 13 categories: Architecture Exterior (Public); Architecture Exterior (Residential); Architecture Interior (Public); Architecture Interior (Residential); Architecture Reconstruction; Characters; Creatures; Robotic/Cyborg; Product Design; Still Life; Transport; Abstract; and Environment. By category, the best images were awarded Master Awards and depending on merit 1-3 images received Excellence Awards.

As with our EXPOSÉ series, the hardest part of the whole process was agonizing over all the fantastic images entered that we just did not have room to print. The quality of the entries was great with less than one in seven images making it to print. We encourage you to visit our website to see all the images entered for this and other books from Ballistic Publishing.

Finally, thanks also go out to Autodesk team and in particular Rick Champagne, Alexandre-Simon Labelle, Annie Belanger, Roohi Saeed, and Bill O'Connor for their help with ELEMENTAL 3.

ELEMENTAL 3 CATEGORIES

CHOOSING CATEGORIES

A total of 1,800 images were entered for ELEMENTAL 3 covering a wide range of genres. Images were collected into categories which best described the subject matter. With entries growing significantly over the previous ELEMENTAL books, it was necessary to choose categories that reflected these increased entries. Like the original ELEMENTAL books, the architectural entries continued to dominate for ELEMENTAL with five categories: Architecture Exterior (Public); Architecture Exterior (Residential); Architecture Interior (Public); Architecture Interior (Residential); and Architecture Reconstruction. The character-based entries saw a sharp increase which required the creation of the Creatures and Robotic/Cyborg categories in addition to the Characters category. Environment, Product Design, Transport and Abstract remained popular for ELEMENTAL 3. The other category addition was Still Life which received a healthy number of entries compared to previous books.

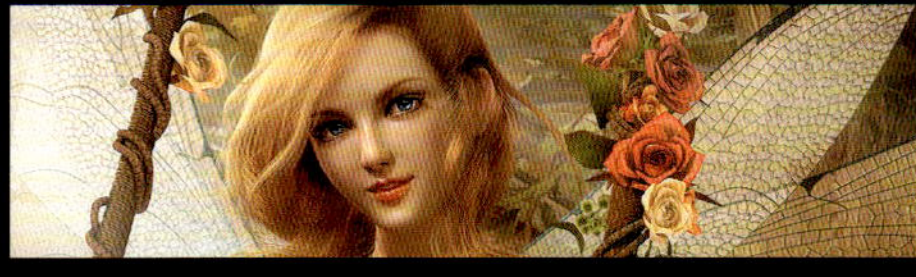

CHARACTERS

This category recognized the greatest talent in bringing a 3D character to life. The defining criterion for the category was the ability that the artist demonstrated in bringing the subject to life, particularly with texturing and lighting. Successful entries encompassed technical skill, believability, composition, and, most of all, emotion.

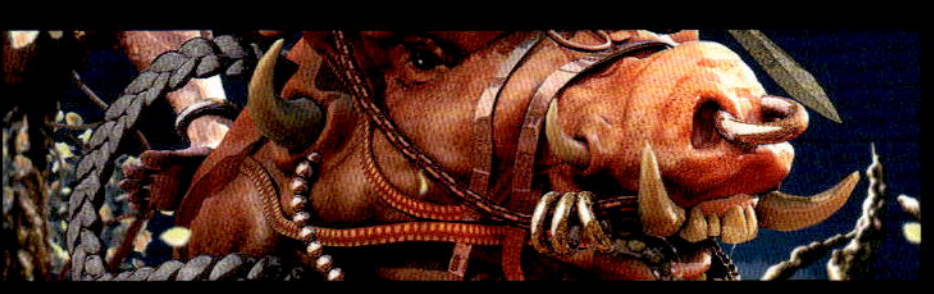

CREATURES

This category recognized the greatest talent in bringing a creature (real or mythical) to life. This was independent of style or of the organic nature of the creature. The defining criterion was the artist's ability to create a living creature. This encompassed technical skill, believability, and composition.

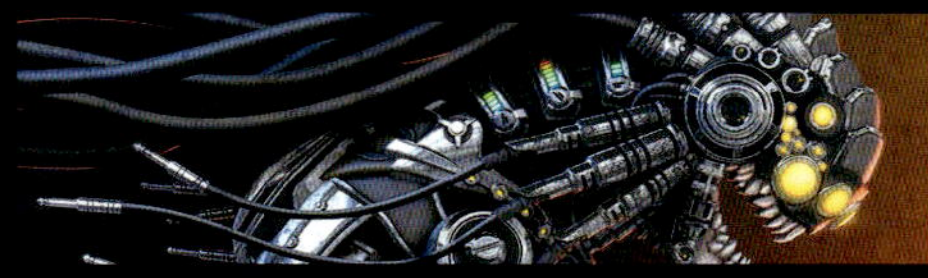

ROBOTIC/CYBORG

The Robotic/Cyborg category recognizes the highest achievement in bringing a robotic or mechanical character into existence. The defining criterion was the artist's ability to create a believable being either totally mechanical, or a composite of organic being and machine. This encompasses technical skill, believability, composition, and emotion.

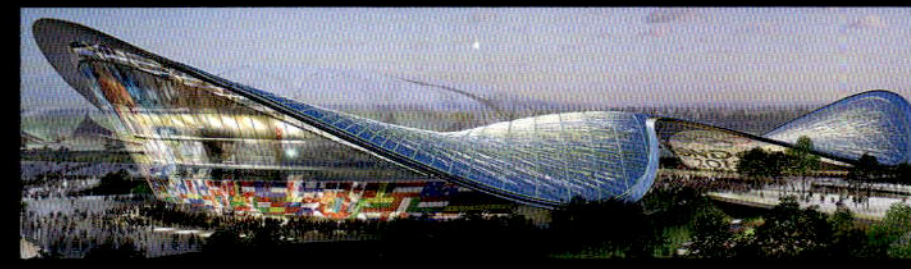

ARCHITECTURE EXTERIOR (PUBLIC)

This category awarded the best exterior architectural visualization of a public space, independent of style, or setting. The category tested the artist's ability to create a space that was not just believable (lighting, scale and perspective), but inspirational and evoked a desire to visit the location/building/space.

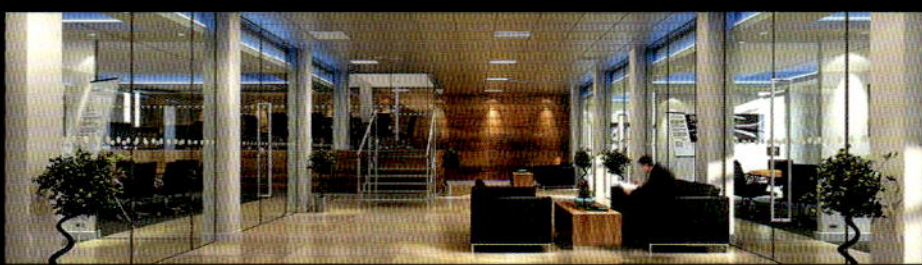

ARCHITECTURE INTERIOR (PUBLIC)

This category awarded the best interior architectural visualization of a public space, independent of style, or setting. The category tested the artist's ability to create a space that was not just believable (lighting, scale and perspective), but inspirational and evoked a desire to visit the location/building/space.

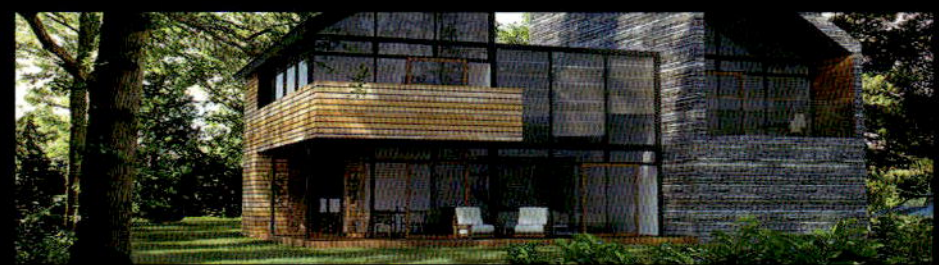

ARCHITECTURE EXTERIOR (RESIDENTIAL)

This category awarded the best exterior architectural visualization of a residential space, independent of style, or setting. The category tested the artist's ability to create a space that was not just believable (lighting, scale and perspective), but inspirational and evoked a desire to visit the location/building/space.

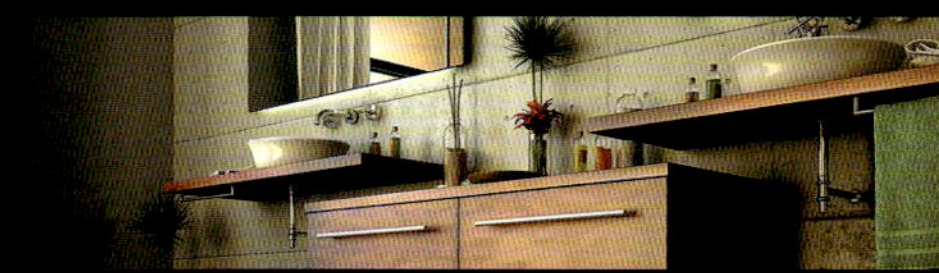

ARCHITECTURE INTERIOR (RESIDENTIAL)

This category awarded the best interior architectural visualization of a residential space, independent of style, or setting. The category tested the artist's ability to create a space that was not just believable (lighting, scale and perspective), but inspirational and evoked a desire to visit the location/building/space.

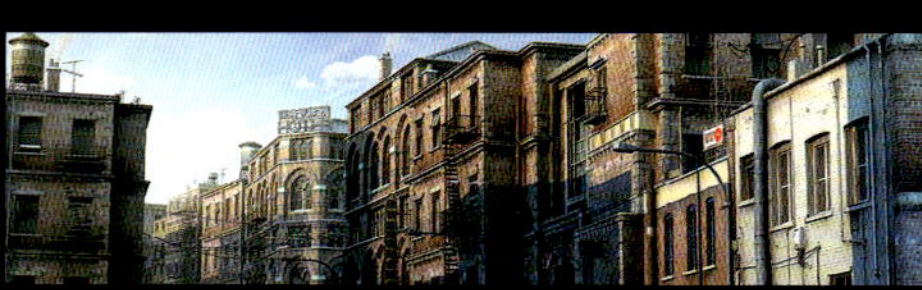

ARCHITECTURE RECONSTRUCTION

This new category recognized the best examples of built architecture which were not visualizations of new buildings. The judging criterion was to capture the feel of a structure built long ago that has weathered the years and its occupants. Composition, modeling, texturing, and lighting were all crucial factors in successful entries.

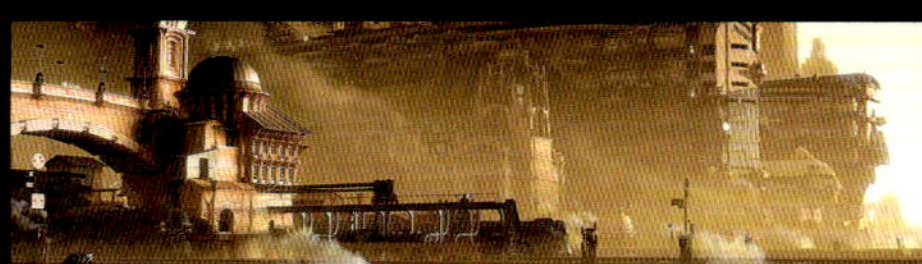

ENVIRONMENT

This category honored the best landscape or location (indoors, outdoors, underwater, or in space). The artist's ability to evoke a sense of wonder and a wish to see more was paramount. The category demanded a combination of artistic interpretation, detail, and lighting to create a believable and evocative environment.

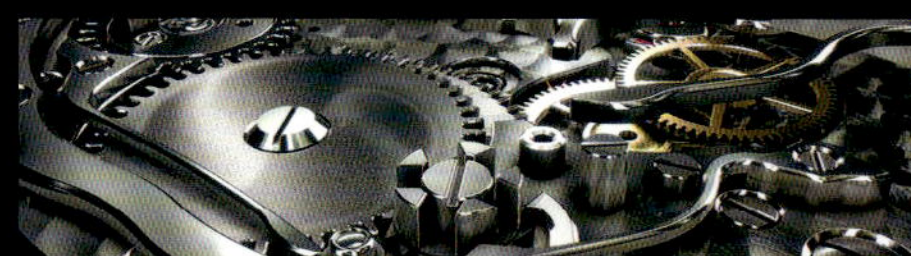

PRODUCT DESIGN

This category awarded the best examples of still life and product designs that demonstrated excellence in technical design and execution. The judging criterion for this category was a combination of the intricacy of the design and the technical excellence of the modeling, texturing, and lighting.

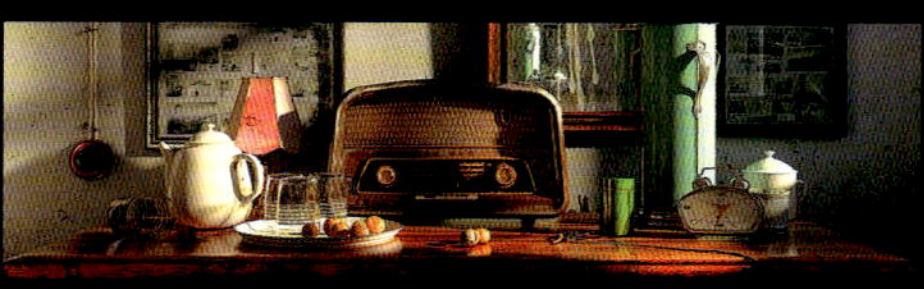

STILL LIFE

This category awarded the best examples of still life and product designs that demonstrated excellence in technical design and execution. The judging criterion for this category was a combination of the intricacy of the design and the technical excellence of the modeling, texturing, and lighting.

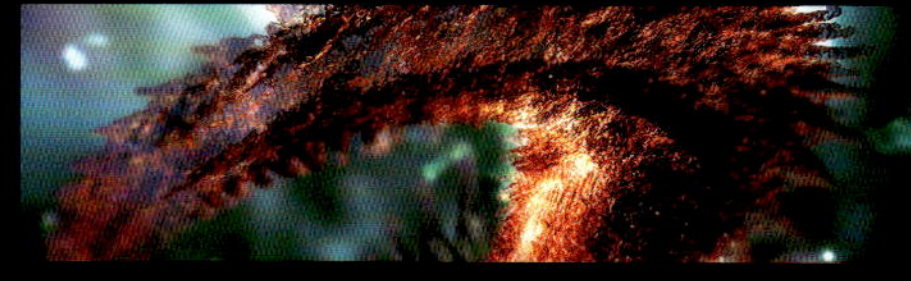

ABSTRACT

This category recognized the most outstanding image that was abstract or predominantly abstract (fractal-generated or 3D). Here, the artist's design and artistic expression were paramount in creating a piece of artwork that defied categorization and excelled in its pure design and visual appeal.

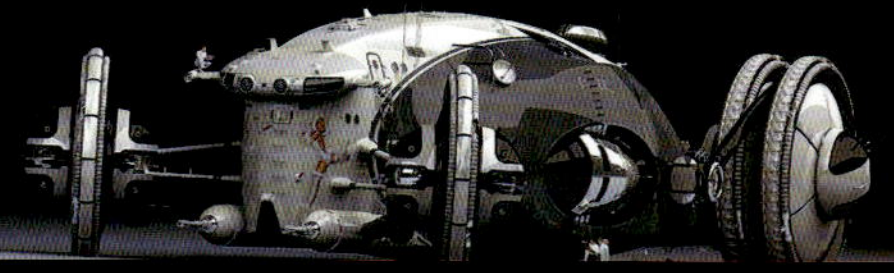

TRANSPORT

This category recognized the best vehicle for moving about in. Whether exotic vehicle, vintage aircraft, or futuristic oceangoing vessel, this category sought out the best examples of transportation. The defining quality was the artist's ability to capture and evoke the desire to travel to a place, or by a mode of transport.

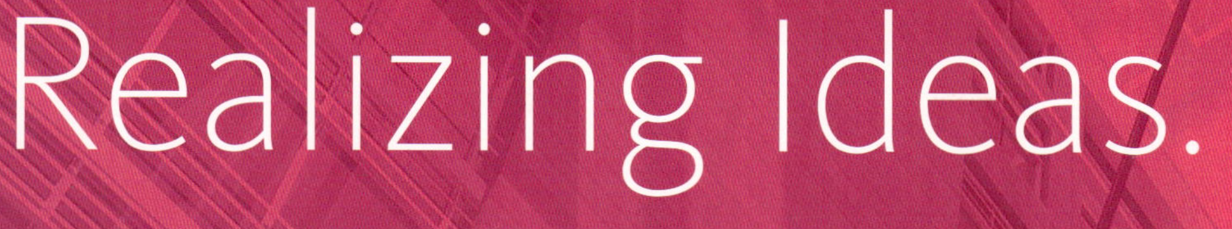

Realizing Ideas.

If you were to ask me what I like best about my job as Autodesk CEO, one of the answers would be that I get to see so many of the amazing things that our customers create with our software.

This book is a great example of the imaginative genius of some of our most exciting customers in the fields of visual effects, animation, game development, and design visualization.

From stunning digital artistry in films, games, television shows, and advertising to beautiful visualizations of manufacturing and architectural projects, the selections gathered here represent the world's best Autodesk-created art.

We think of our tools as instruments of imagination, and we are proud of the fact that our customers are using our technology to shape and change the world.

We applaud and congratulate everyone who submitted their work to this book for their creativity and passion. We are dedicated to delivering the best solutions to help creative professionals realize their boldest visions.

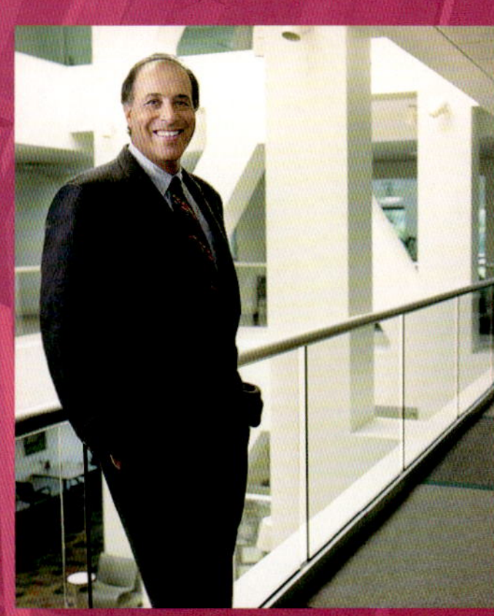

Carl Bass
CEO
Autodesk, Inc.

Carl Bass

Autodesk®

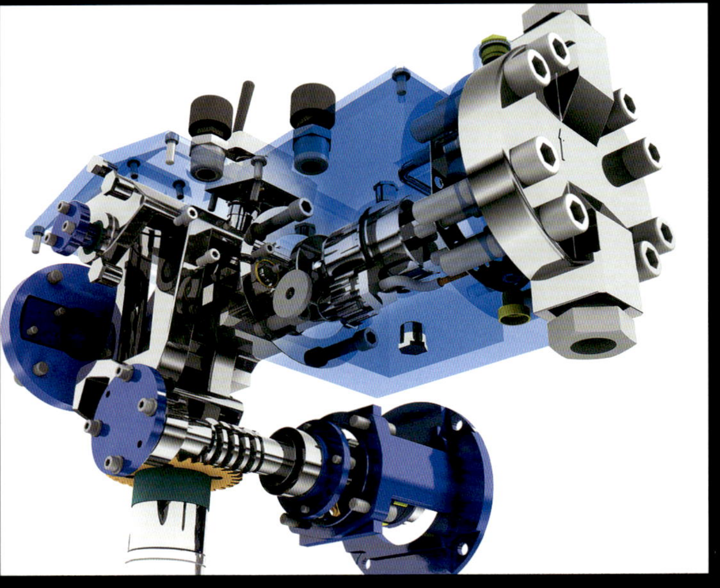

Image courtesy of Haskel International Inc.
Created with Autodesk® Inventor® software.

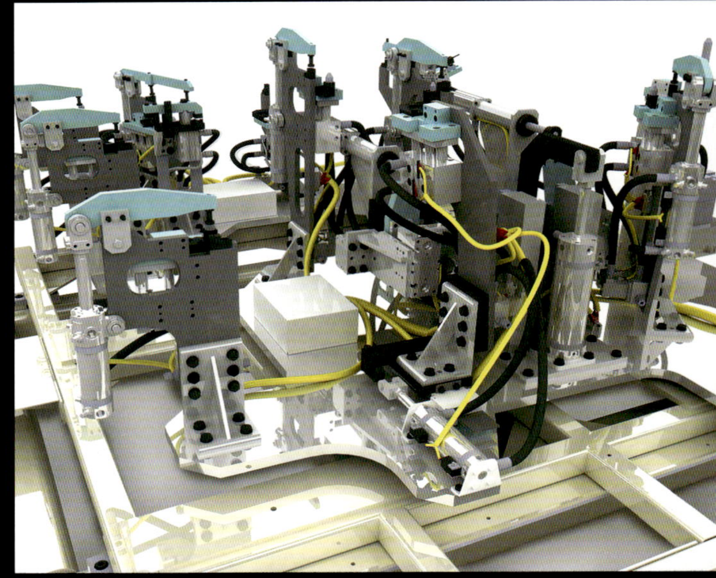

Image courtesy of Aska International.
Created with Autodesk® Inventor® software.

Manufacturing

In Manufacturing, Autodesk helps customers experience their ideas before they're real by providing state-of-the-art, interoperable, 2D and 3D model-based design technologies that are redefining the product development process. With Digital Prototyping, manufacturers can optimize and validate their ideas before actually creating a product, helping to remove time and costs from the product development process, and get the "right" product to market faster.

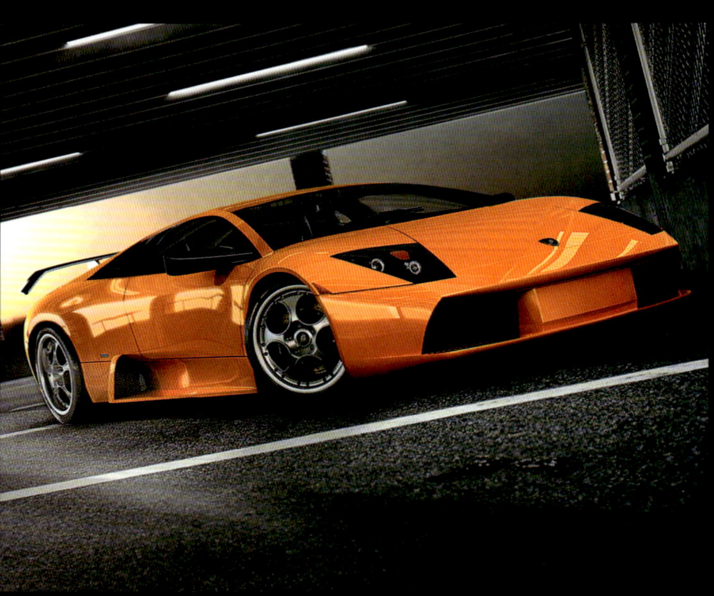

Image courtesy of With A Twist Studio.
Created with Autodesk® 3ds Max®.

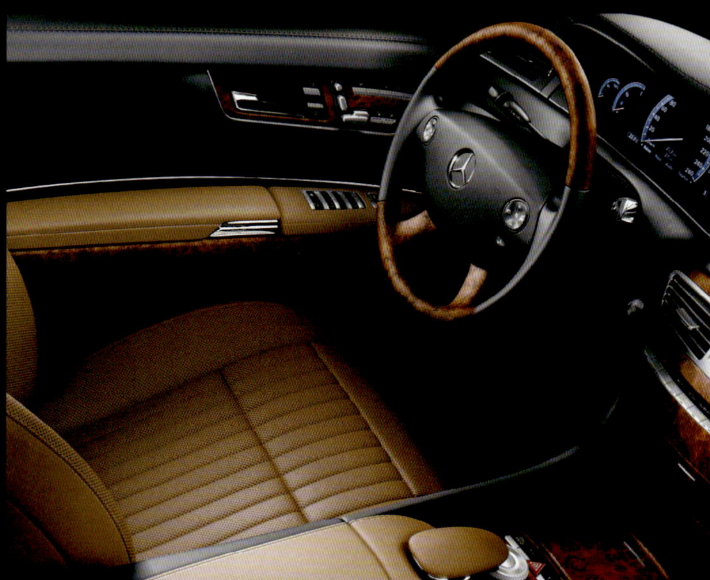

Image courtesy of Mackevision.
Created with Autodesk® 3ds Max®.

Automotive & Transportation

Autodesk provides powerful applications to help automotive and transportation manufacturers design the next market-leading transportation product with tools and services that enable communication, collaboration, and visualization of the entire product development process.

Autodesk manufacturing solutions for transportation drive results—efficiently and effectively—for the entire network of manufacturers and suppliers. Customers stay ahead of the competition with solutions from a world leader in transportation design, manufacturing, and collaboration.

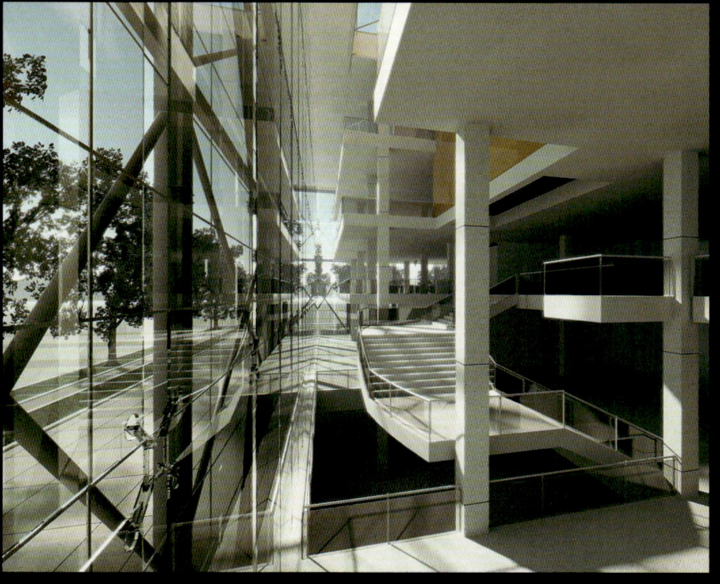

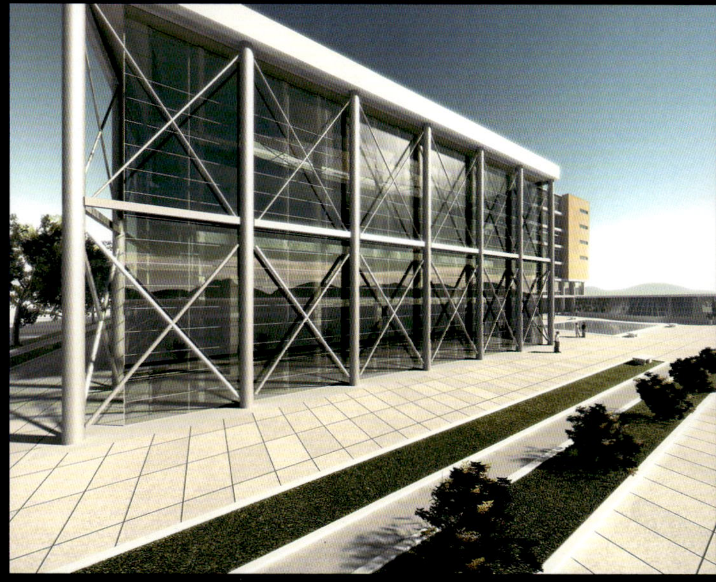

Image courtesy of Delta Tracing.
Created with Autodesk® 3ds Max®.

Image courtesy of Delta Tracing.
Created with Autodesk® 3ds Max®.

Architecture, Engineering & Construction

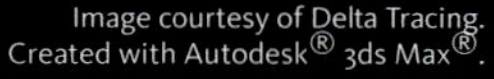

Architecture, Engineering, and Construction (AEC) Solutions from Autodesk enable AEC firms and the clients they serve to create and profit from digital design data and streamlined communications across extended teams. By adopting Building information modeling (BIM), architects, engineers, construction firms, and building owners can benefit from increased profitability, reduced risk, and minimized inefficiencies in building design, civil engineering, construction, and operation.

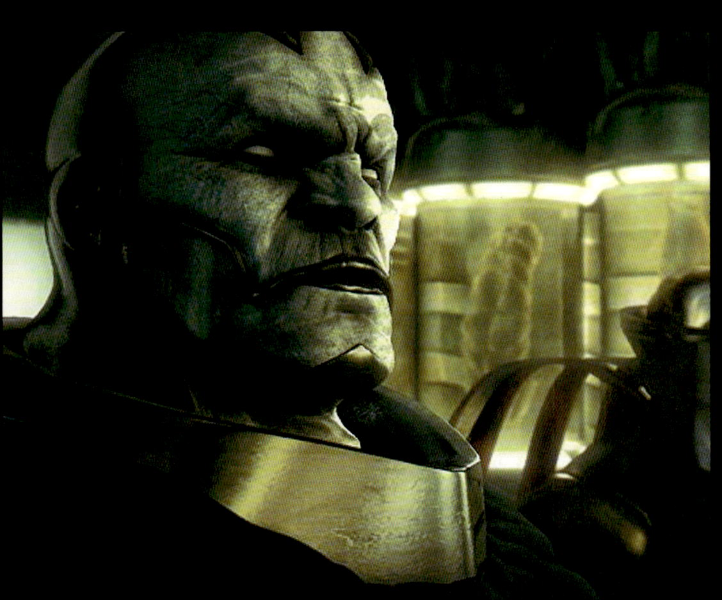

Image courtesy of Blur.
Created with Autodesk® 3ds Max®.

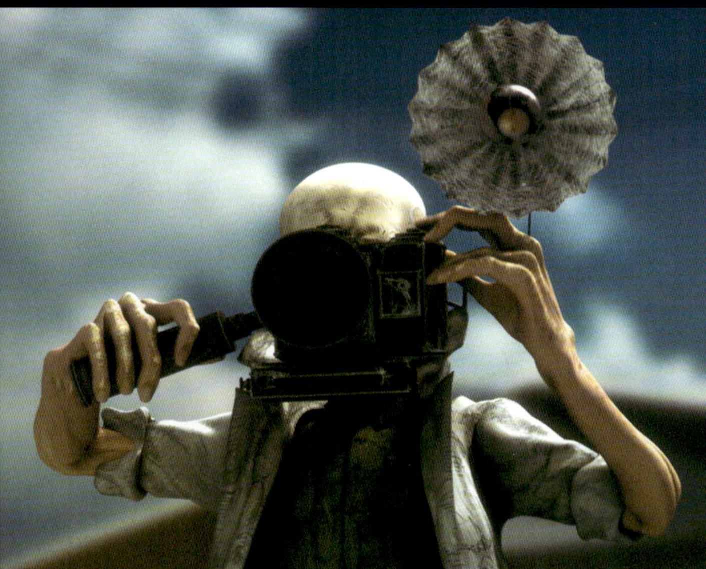

Image courtesy Platige Image
Created with Autodesk® 3ds Max®

Media & Entertainment

In Media & Entertainment, Autodesk helps digital artists and animators experience their ideas before they're real by providing end-to-end, state-of-the-art 2D and 3D technologies that are redefining digital content creation. With the most advanced, creative toolset, customers can not only create the most innovative images and tell the most compelling stories, but they can also move data faster and streamline their pipeline efficiency.

Imagination unleashed!

Around the world, hundreds of thousands of digital artists use Autodesk's Media & Entertainment products. Regardless of their age, background and industry, what all these artists have in common is passion. They're passionate about our products, and they're passionate about great storytelling and great design. At Autodesk, we feel fortunate to be part of such a wonderful 3D community. Thank you to all the artists.

I also want to thank all the developers who have shaped our 3D products over the years, working hand-in-hand with the community. Delivering on the needs of the most creative minds on earth is no small feat. The future is about better 3D tools; tools that are easier to use, eliminating barriers between artists and imaginations.

This book is a celebration of digital art. It's the magic that happens when great imaginations are paired with great technology. Like its predecessor, ELEMENTAL 3 features the best-of-the-best Autodesk 3ds Max art. We're excited that Autodesk Maya and Autodesk Mudbox artwork is included for the first time.

Congratulations to everyone whose work is featured in ELEMENTAL 3.

Prepare to be amazed!

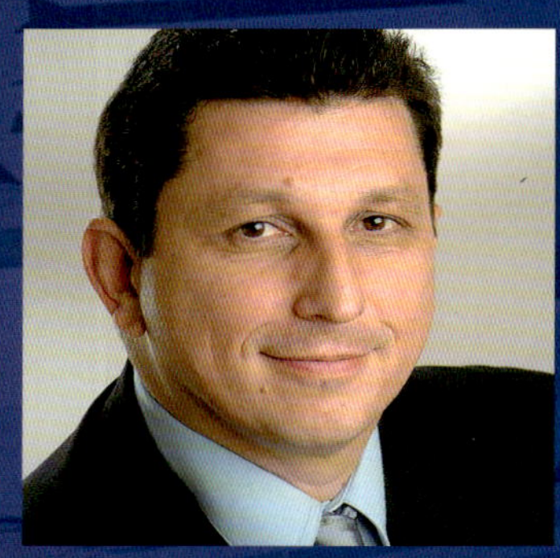

Marc Petit
Senior Vice President
Autodesk Media & Entertainment

About Autodesk

Autodesk is a world leader in design innovation technology.

Customers use our products to create digital models and workflows that allow them to visualize, simulate, and analyze their designs, and to experience them before they are real.

This enables them to explore many design alternatives, and to make early improvements to the way their projects and products will look, perform, and be used in the real world.

Autodesk offers a portfolio of 2D and 3D products that serve a wide range of industries, giving designers, architects, engineers, and digital artists the tools they need to create the skyscrapers, bridges, products, games, and films that make up our modern world.

ADVISORY BOARD AND JURY

For the third edition of ELEMENTAL, we appointed an advisory board to assist in nominating and judging images for the ELEMENTAL 3 awards. All of these people are either leading artists in their own right or are experienced and respected members of the Autodesk product team.

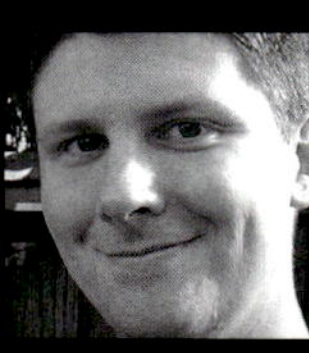

Neil Blevins is a Technical Director for Pixar Animation Studios, primarily creating Environments and FX. He started off painting and drawing traditionally, then shifted into 3D graphics. After getting a BFA in Design Art at Concordia University, he moved to Los Angeles where he worked for Blur Studio, creating graphics for video games, commercials, TV, feature and ride films. He was also a tester for the Brazil Rendering System. In his spare time, he creates 3D/2D hybrid artwork depicting creatures, robots and alien landscapes, author tools and writes art-related tutorials to give back to the community who he feels has been so gracious in helping him get to where he is today.

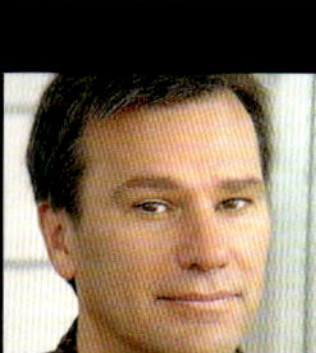

Jeff Kleiser is Visual Effects Supervisor and co-founder of Synthespian Studios. He has contributed to films with groundbreaking visual effects including 'Tron', 'Stargate', 'Judge Dredd', 'Clear and Present Danger', 'Mortal Kombat Annihilation', 'X-Men', 'X-Men United', and 'X-Men: The Last Stand'. He serves on the board of directors of the Visual Effects Society and the board of trustees of The Norman Rockwell Museum. He is also a founder and trustee of the Williamstown Film Festival and a member of the Academy of Motion Picture Arts and Sciences.

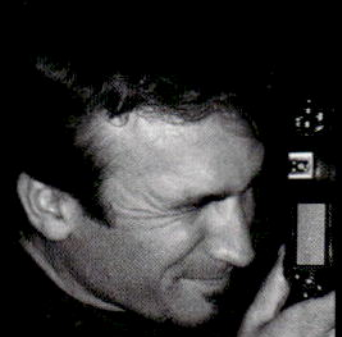

Raphael Lacoste is a matte painter and production designer at RodeoFX in Montreal. He was previously an Art director on Videogames and Cinematics (CG) for more than seven years at Ubisoft where he worked on such licenses as 'Prince of Persia' and 'Assassin's Creed'. He won a VES Award in February 2006 for his work as Art Director on 'Prince of Persia the Two Thrones' high-resolution cinematics. His focus now is to work as matte painter and production designer for film. Raphael prefers to work on environments, moods, picture composition and lighting.

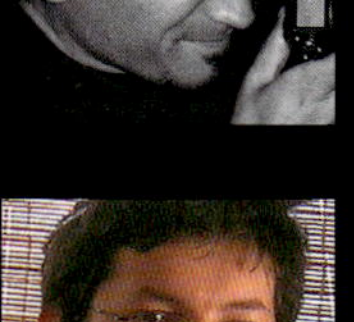

Pascal Blanché is Art Director at one of the world's biggest gaming companies, Ubisoft Canada based in Montreal. His most recent game project was 'Naruto: Rise of a Ninja', based on the Naruto anime series. Pascal started on the path towards a career in art/design for games at the Art School of Luminy, Marseille. Following art school, he freelanced for TILT magazine, an early video games magazine and then worked in modeling, concept art, texturing, lighting and animation for various French gaming companies.

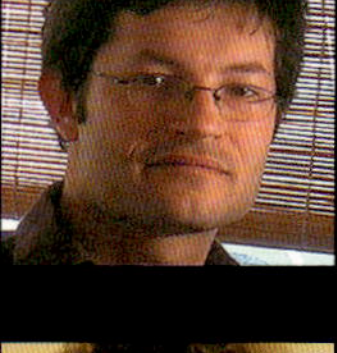

Sebastian Sylwan is the Senior Industry Manager Film and Television for Autodesk. In this role he helps shape the strategic direction of all Autodesk products for the Film and TV industries. Before joining Autodesk, Sebastian was the Director of Technology at Digital Domain where he renewed the technology infrastructure and led the development for its first Stereoscopic rendition of a CG-animated movie. Sebastian was previously the Principal Technology Advisor at USC's Institute for Creative Technologies Graphics Lab and also built Lumiq, Italy's largest TV, VFX, and Animation studio.

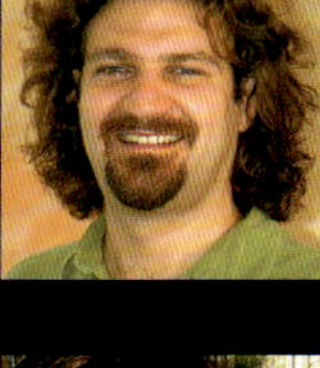

Shawn Hendriks is a Special Projects manager for Autodesk and has worked in the 3D industry for 14 years. His early work in the industry included commercial animation, design visualization, and even accident reconstruction. Shawn's first job with Autodesk was as a 3D and compositing demo artist. Recently he has been responsible for creating feature videos, customer video profiles as well as demos and presentations, and has taken over managing the AREA (Autodesk's web community). Thanks to the nature of his job, Shawn spends a lot of time visiting and talking with top production companies and artists in many fields about their work, problems and successes. Shawn is based in Toronto, Canada.

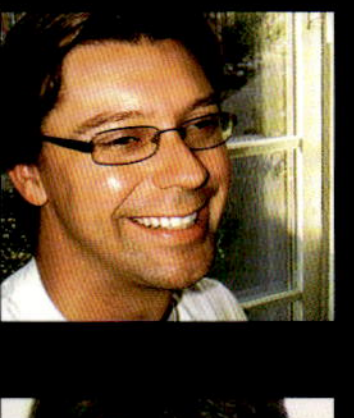

Vlad Bina is the founder of xyBlue Design based in Los Angeles. He was trained and worked as an architect before turning to feature film design projects. He has contributed to the design and execution of several full CG digital sets as well as set extensions for the following motion pictures: '13 Ghosts'; 'Matrix Reloaded'; 'Matrix Revolutions'; 'Catwoman'; 'Sin City'; 'The Da Vinci Code'; 'Spider-Man 3'; and 'Shine a Light'. Vlad considers digital set design as an intricate part of production design, and hopes that in a near future there will be a convergence of the two fields in terms of tools and pipelines.

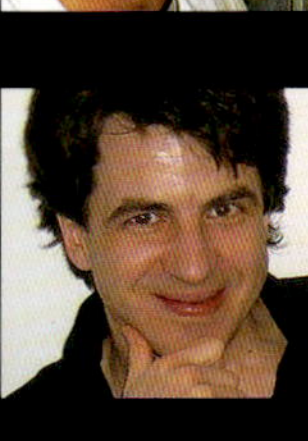

Francisco Cortina is founder of Cortina Digital providing high-quality character development and licensing to companies. He joined the Japanese video game giant Square USA in 1996, where he worked on several game titles such as 'Parasite Eve' and 'Final Fantasy IX', the animated feature film 'Final Fantasy: The Spirits Within' and the animated short 'Animatrix: Final Flight of the Osiris'. He then moved to Dreamworks Animation and Digital Domain working on 'Sharktale', 'Aeon Flux', and 'My Super Ex-Girlfriend'. He is currently working with Digital Domain as the Modeling/Character Supervisor for 'Mummy 3: Tomb of the Dragon Emperor'.

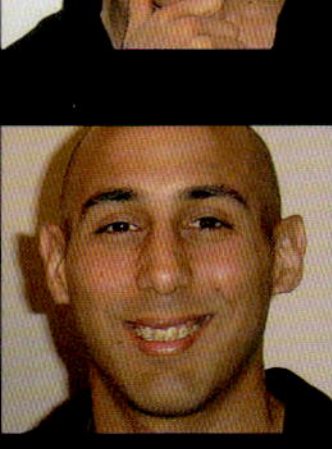

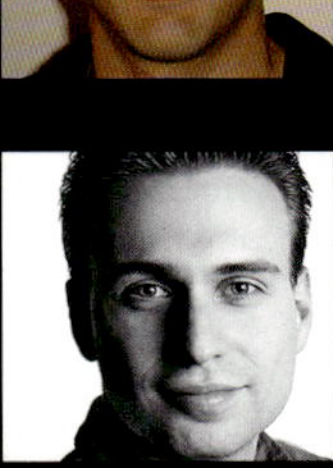

Jeff Mottle is the President and Founder of CGarchitect.com, the leading online architectural visualization magazine. He has worked for the past 12 years in the field of architectural visualization, including for the London based design communications firm, Smoothe, as North American Production Director. Jeff also helped develop and manage the visualization department for one of the largest office solutions providers in the world. Having since left production, Jeff currently works as business development manager for VisMasters, an online software marketing and resource company for design visualization professionals.

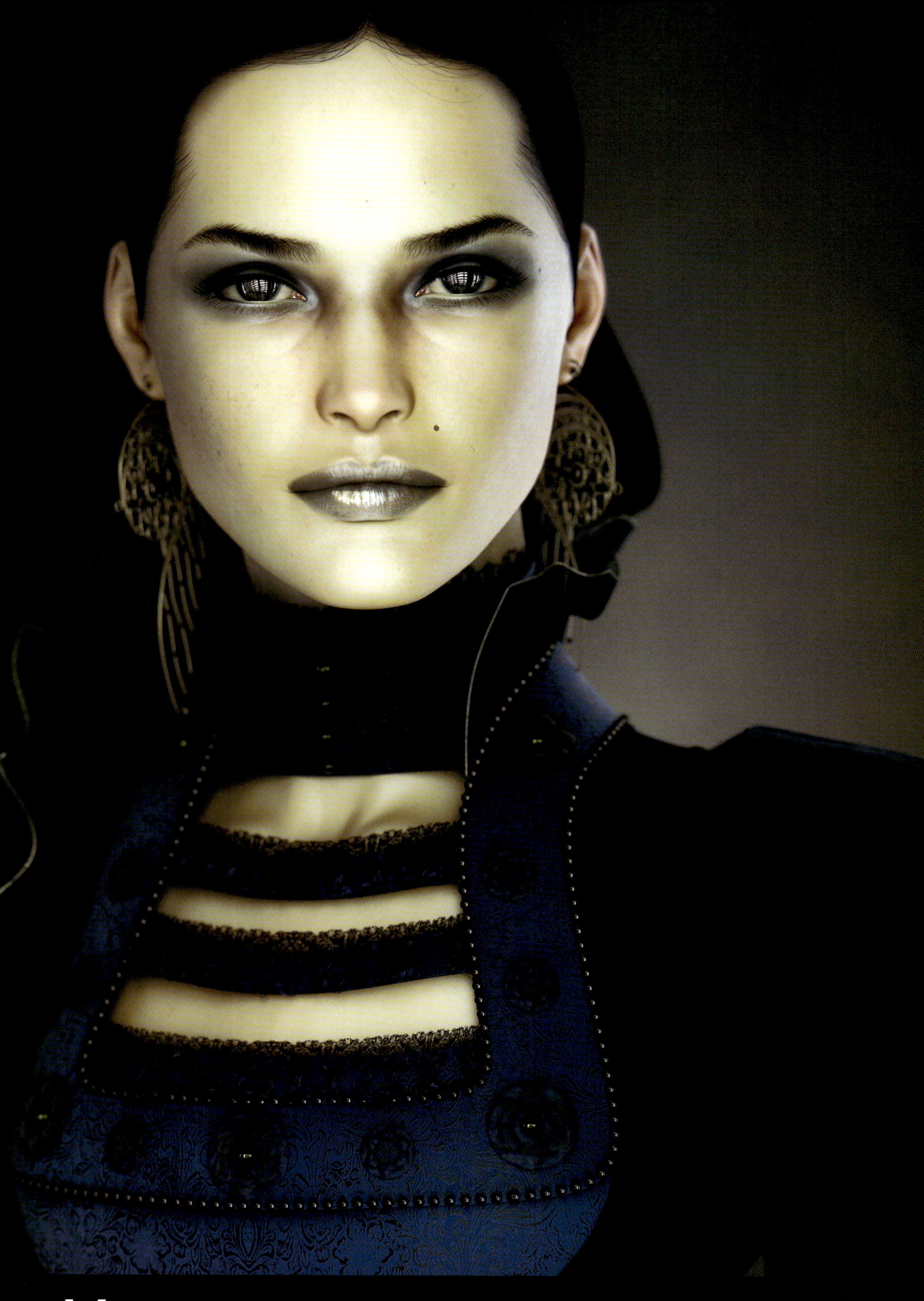

Master

Characters

Cold Blue
3ds Max
Olivier Ponsonnet
FRANCE

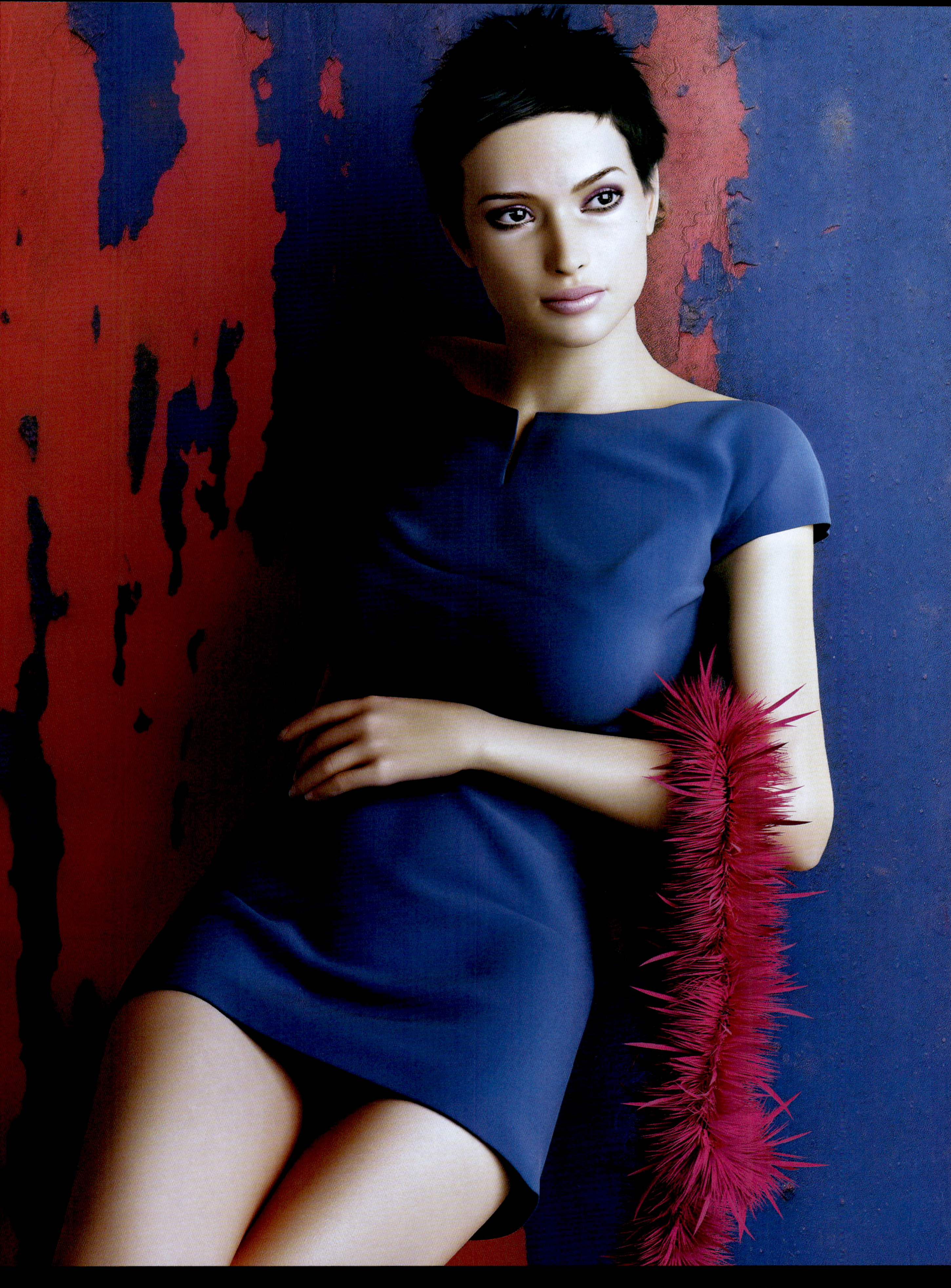

Natalie
3ds Max, Photoshop
Jan Jureczko,
POLAND

Excellence
Characters

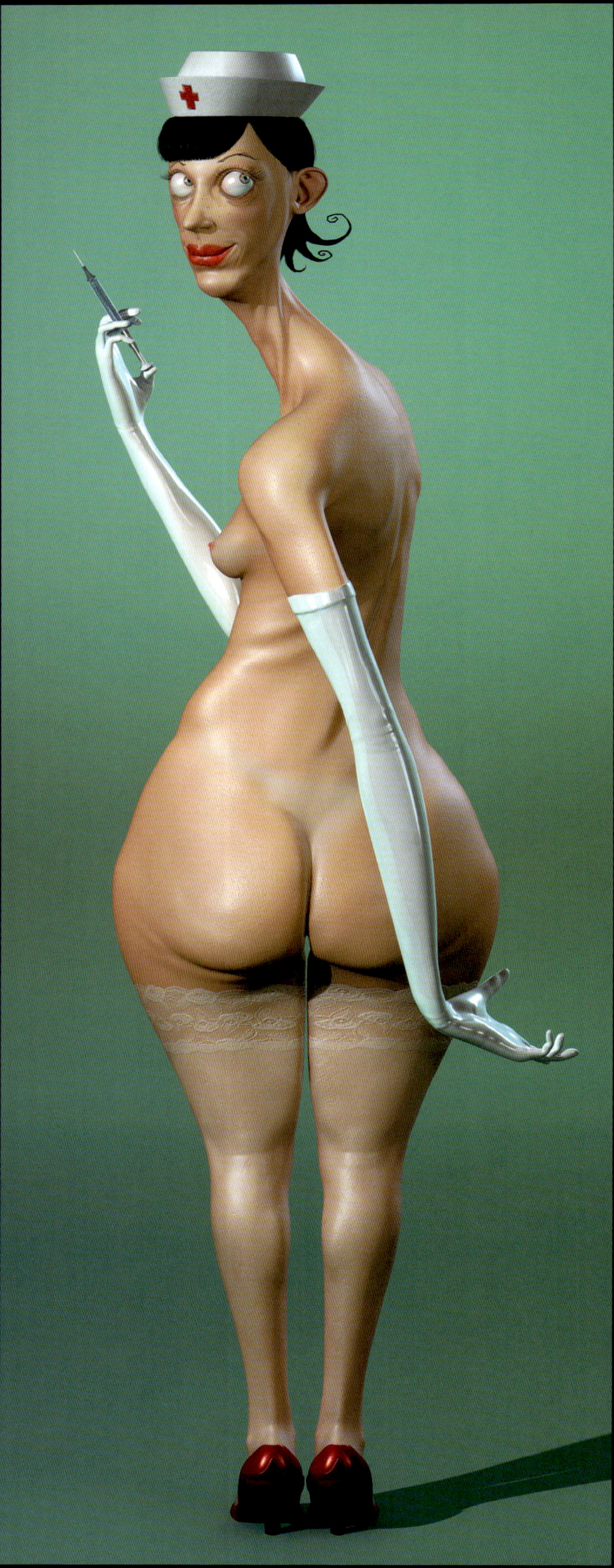

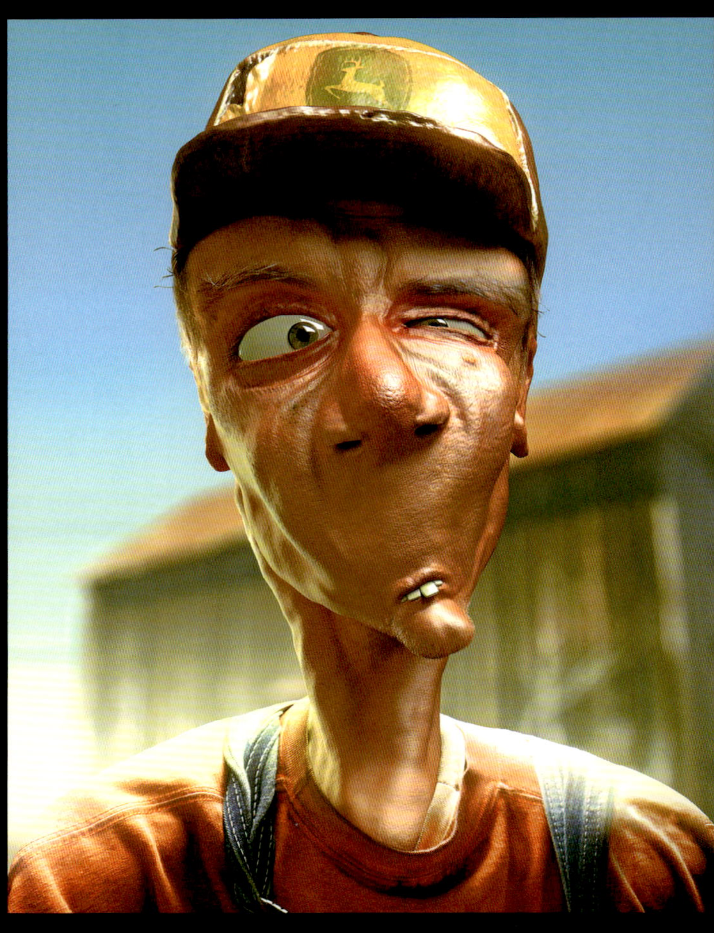

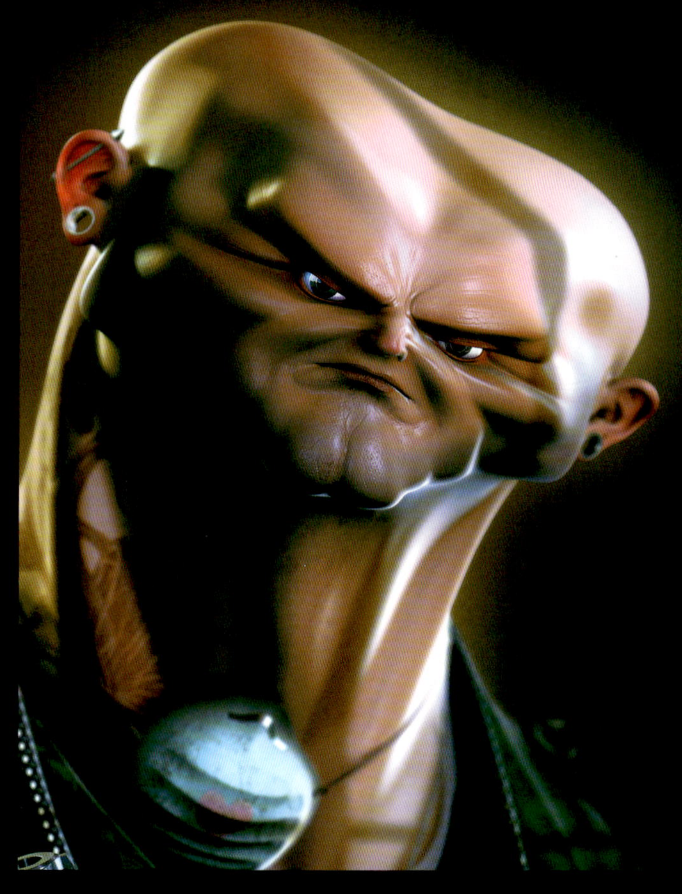

Flu Shot Anyone?
Maya, mental ray, Photoshop, ZBrush
Eric Provan, USA
[above]

Billy Bob Boone
3ds Max, ZBrush, Photoshop, V-Ray
Richard Rosenman, CANADA
[top]

Anton
3ds Max, Photoshop, ZBrush
Jonathan Simard, CANADA
[above]

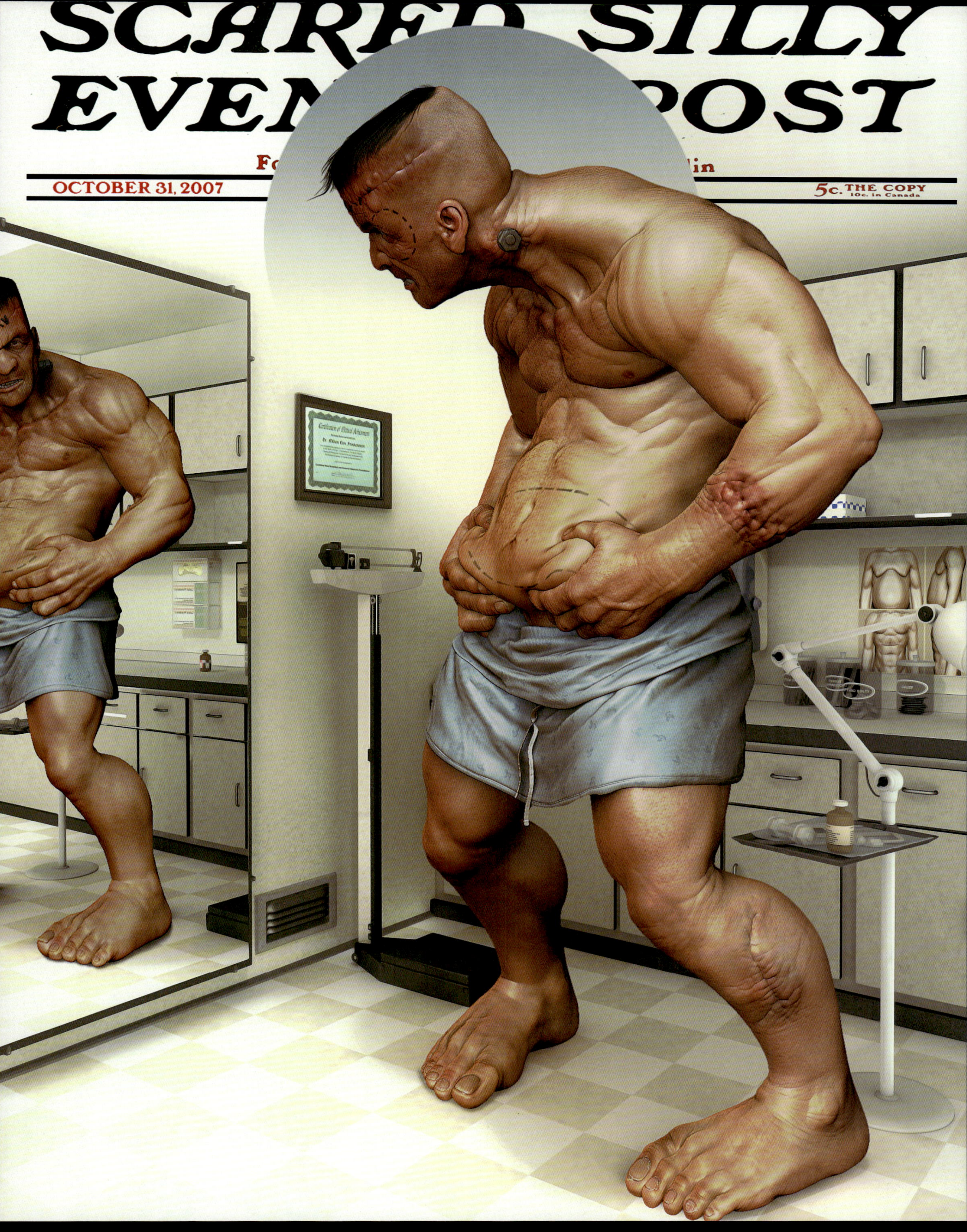

Dr. Frankenstein 90210
ZBrush, 3ds Max, Photoshop
Alex Velazquez, Ravensoft, USA

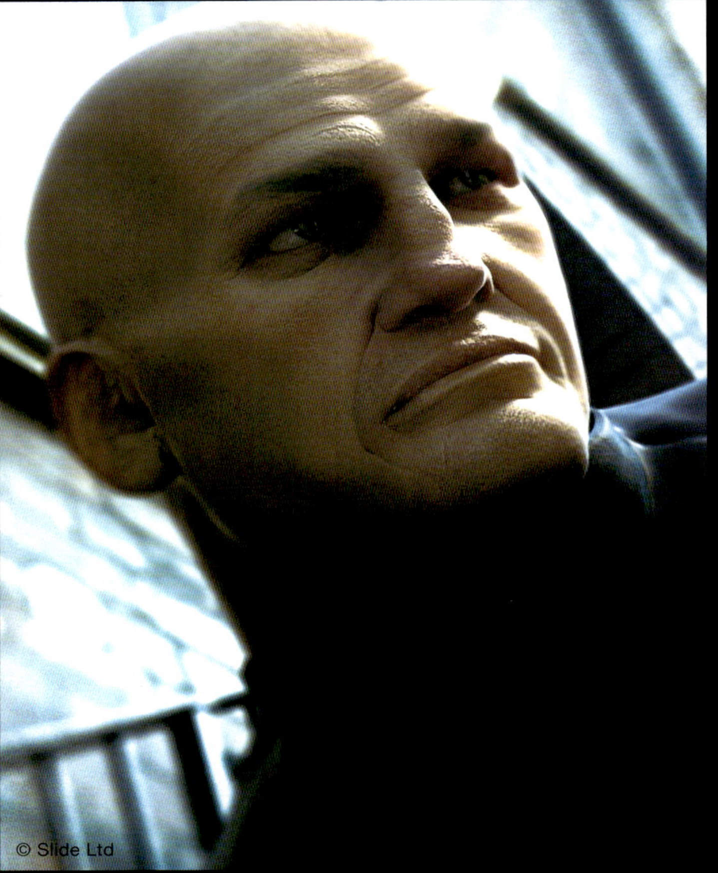

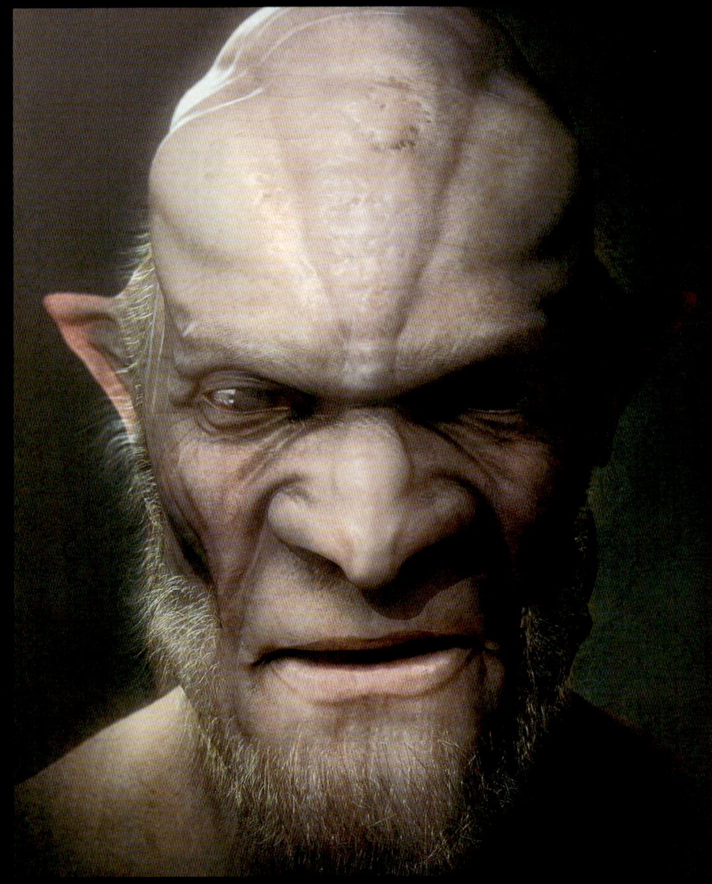

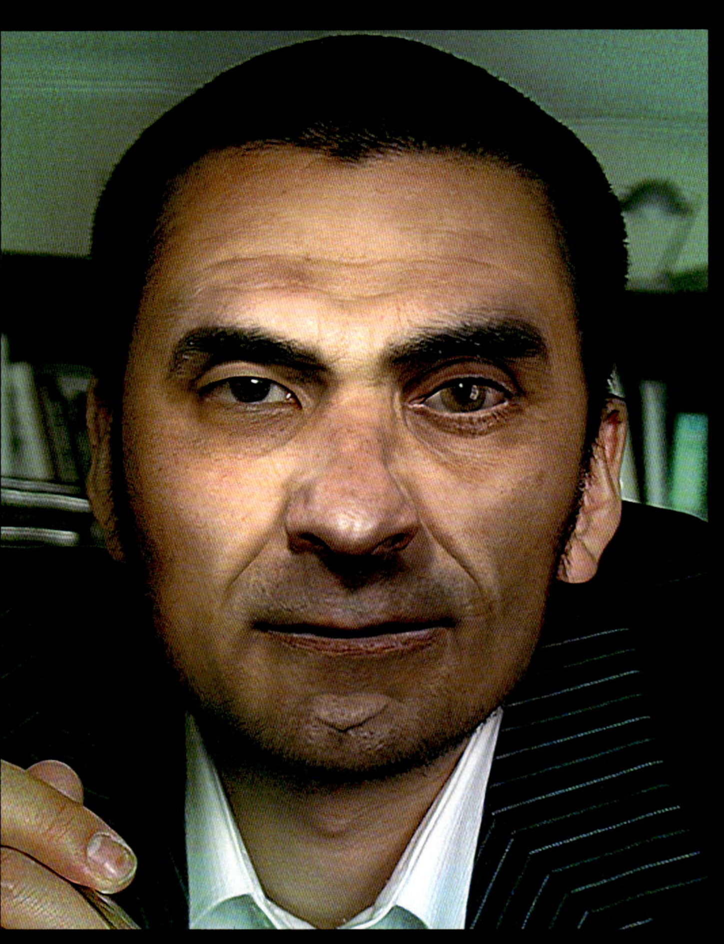

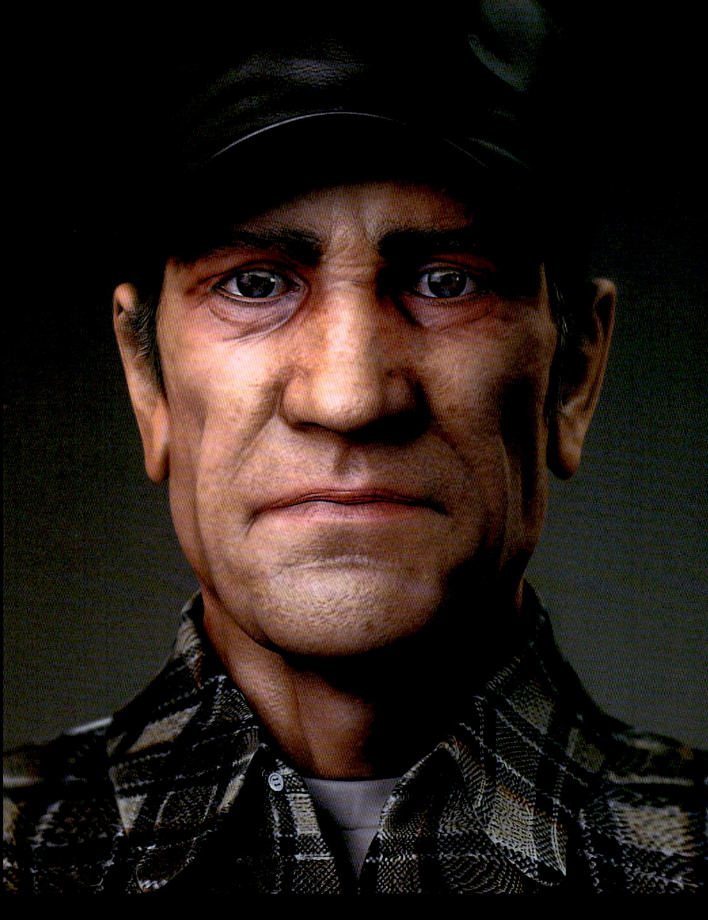

Marek
3ds Max, mental ray,
ZBrush, Photoshop
Etienne Jabbour, Slide Ltd,
GREAT BRITAIN *[top]*

Thinker2
Maya, ZBrush,
mental ray, Photoshop
Jung Rock Hwang, USA
[above]

The Mirror
3ds Max, Mudbox,
Photoshop
Sergio Santos, SPAIN
[top]

Old Hunter
3ds Max, ZBrush, Photoshop
Ricardo Rocha, Southlogic
Studios, BRAZIL
[above]

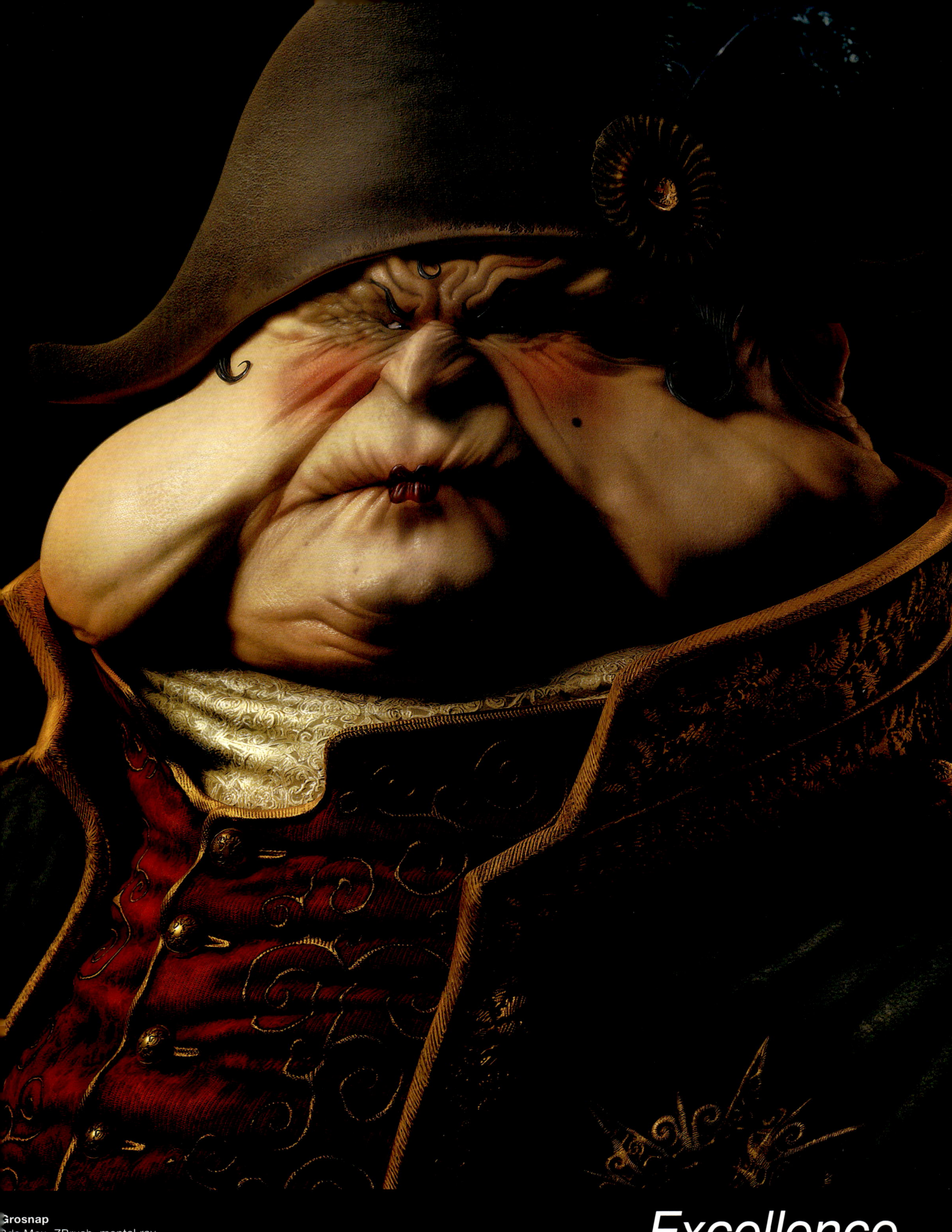

Grosnap
3ds Max, ZBrush, mental ray, Photoshop
Laurent Pierlot, Blur Studio Inc., USA

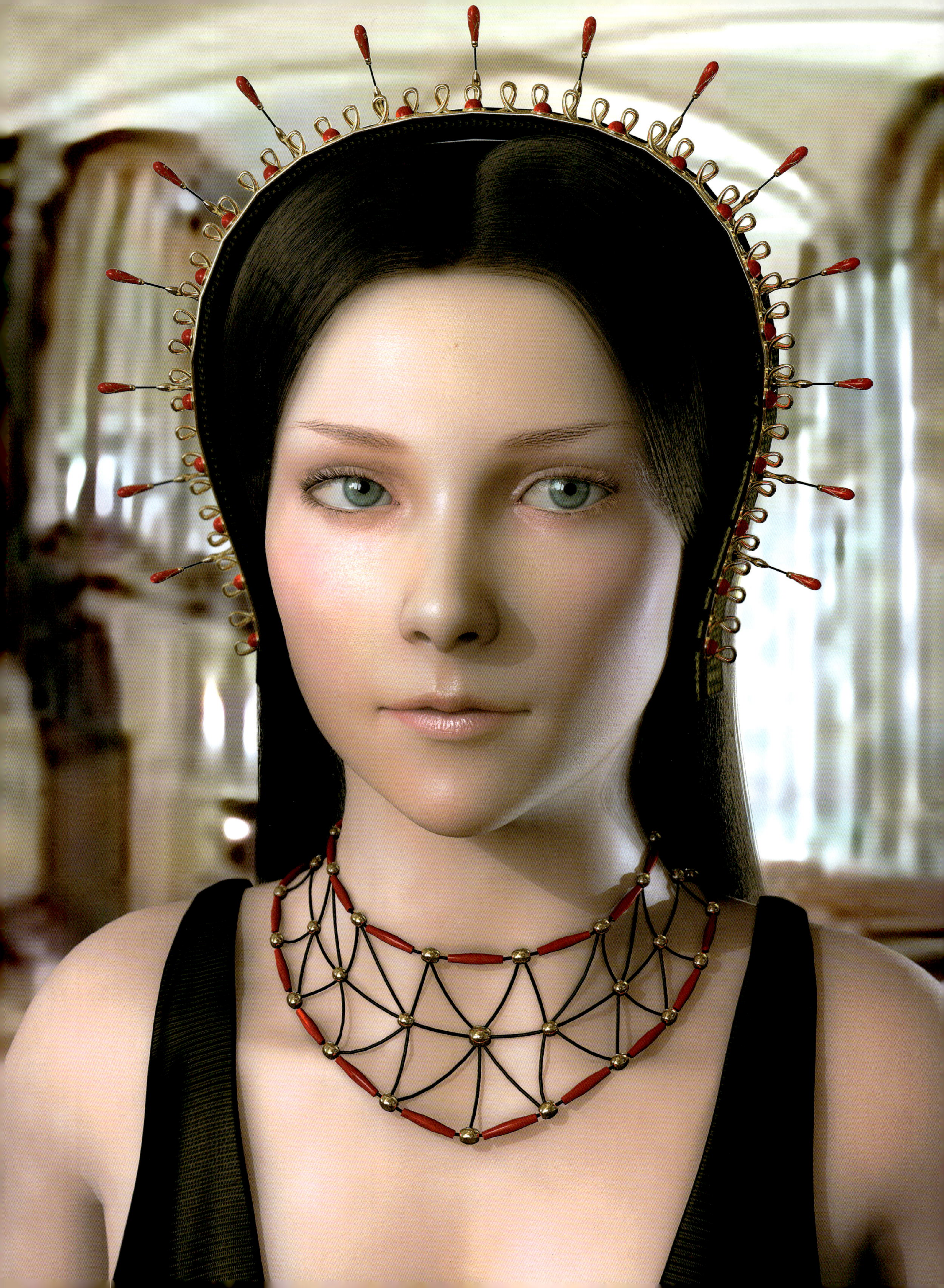

Lady Mary
Maya, ZBrush,
BodyPaint 3D, Photoshop
Zhang Zili, CHINA
[left]

The Butterfly Dancer
Maya, Softimage|XSI,
mental ray, Photoshop
Jeen Lih Lun,
GREAT BRITAIN
[right]

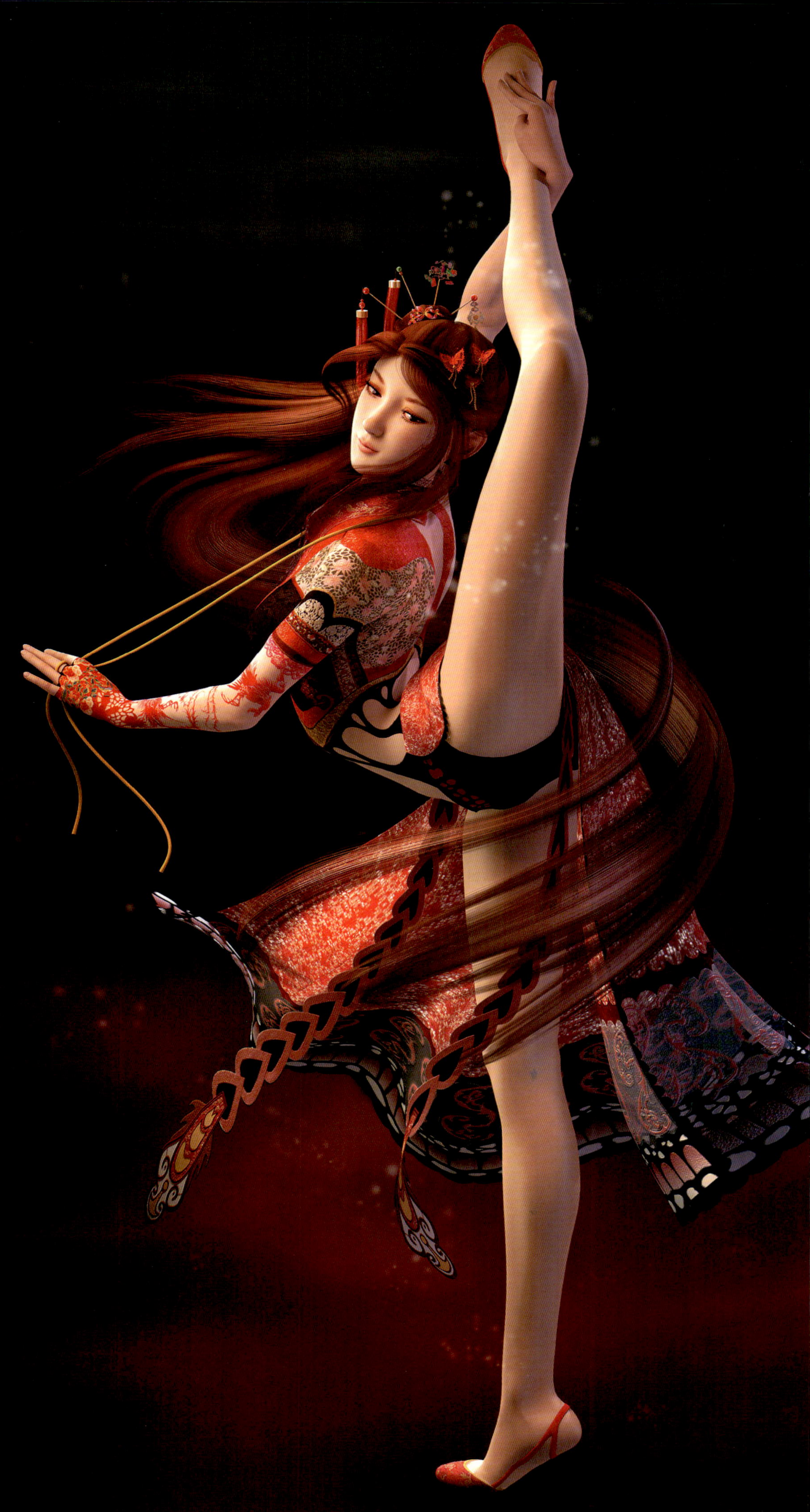

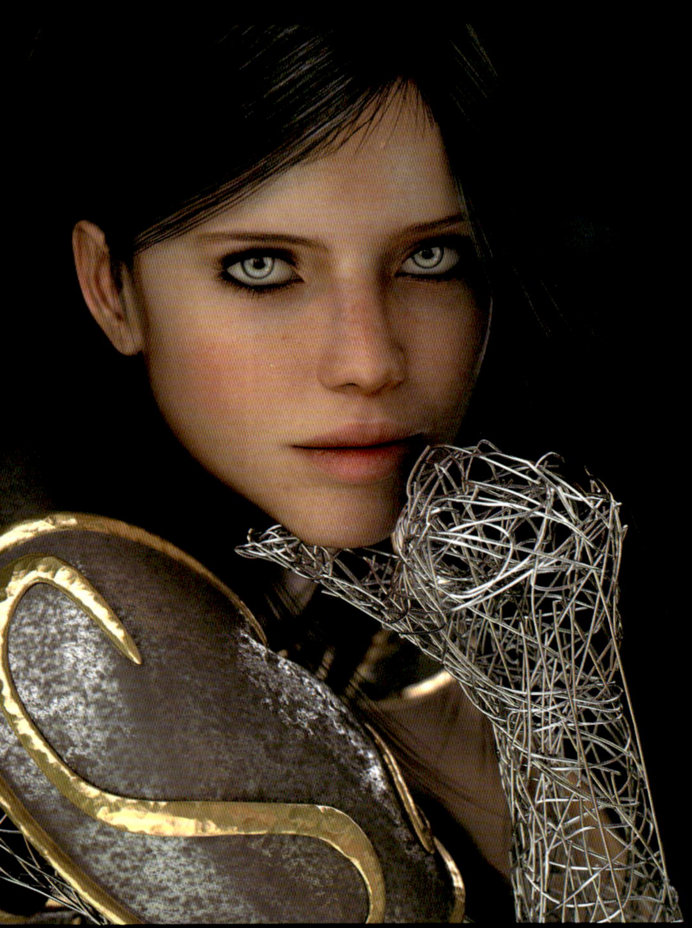

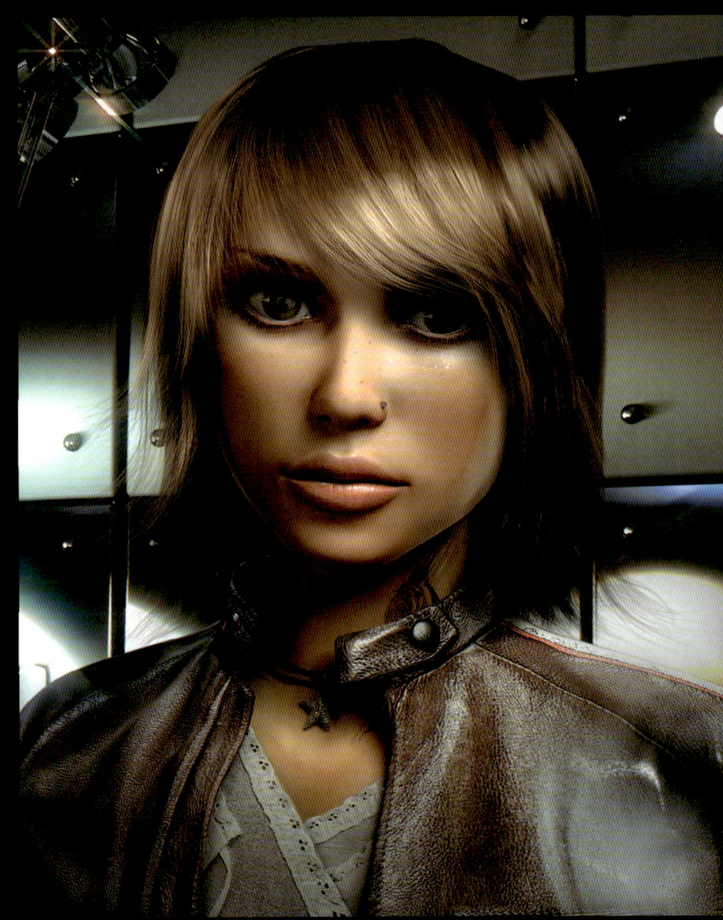

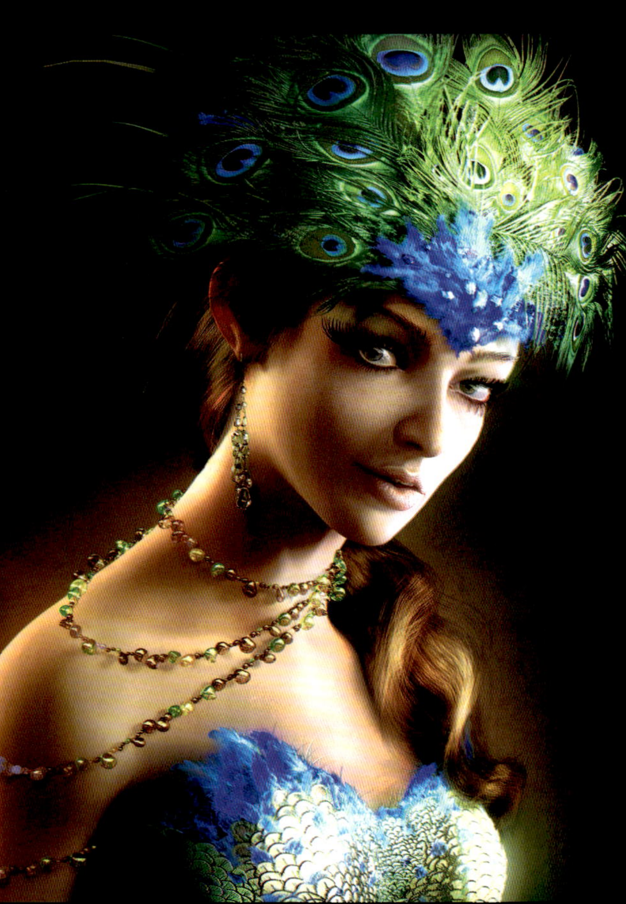

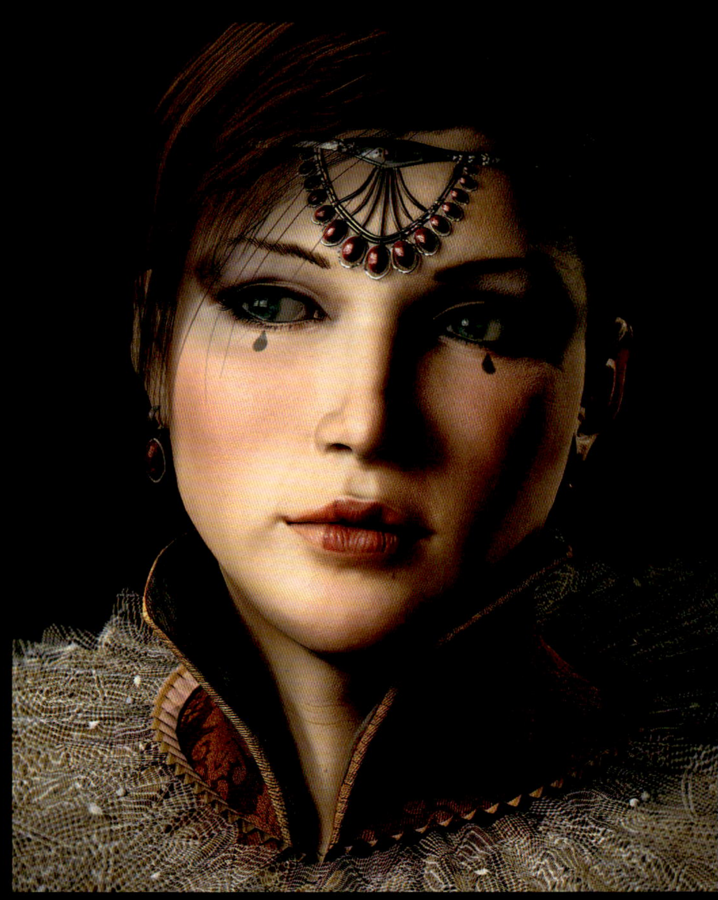

Unfinished
3ds Max, Poser, V-Ray, pFlow
Adam Potter, AUSTRALIA
[top]

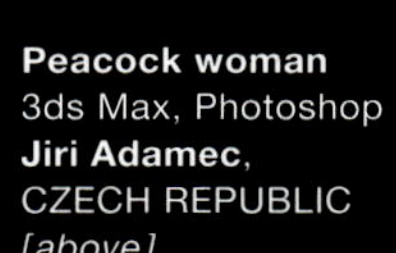

Peacock woman
3ds Max, Photoshop
Jiri Adamec,
CZECH REPUBLIC
[above]

Scarlett
After Effects, Photoshop,
3ds Max, mental ray
Mauro Baldissera, ITALY
[top]

Harlequin
Maya, Photoshop, ZBrush
Camila Davila,
USA
[above]

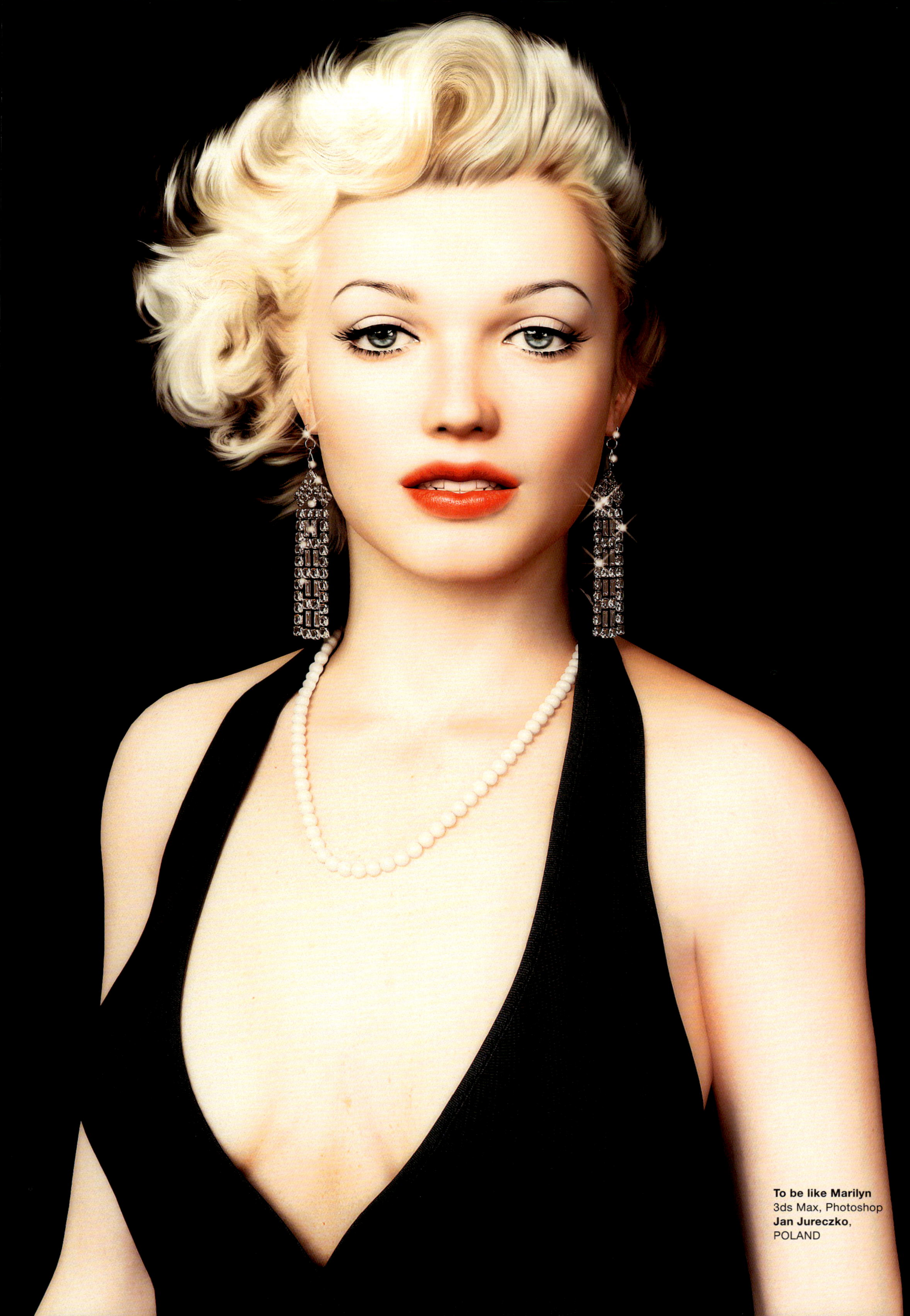

To be like Marilyn
3ds Max, Photoshop
Jan Jureczko,
POLAND

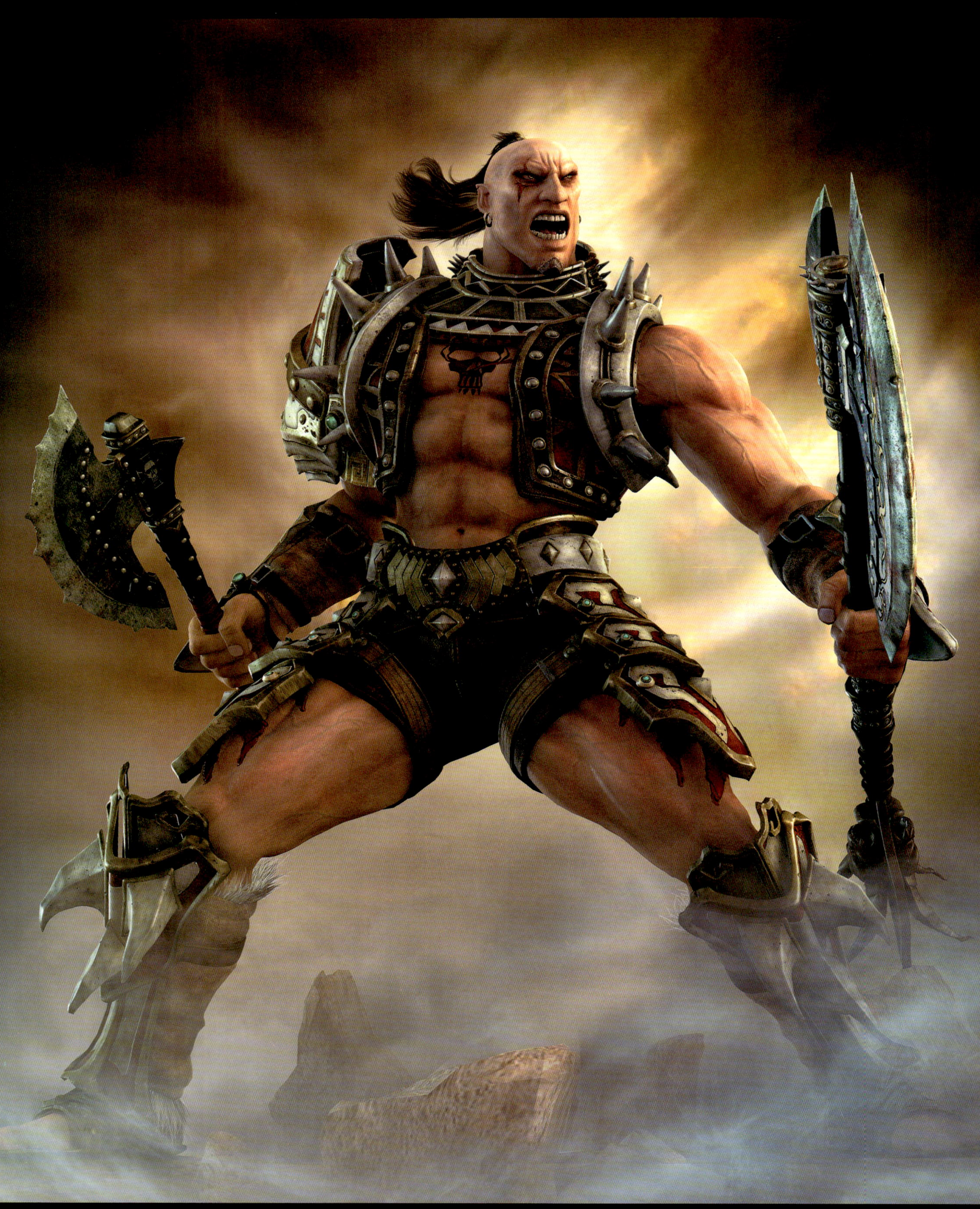

Titan
Maya, mental ray, Photoshop
Seokchan Yoo,
NAKO Interactive, KOREA
[above]

God of War 2: Kratos vs. Barbarian King
Photoshop, Maya
Andy Park, SCEA, USA
[right]

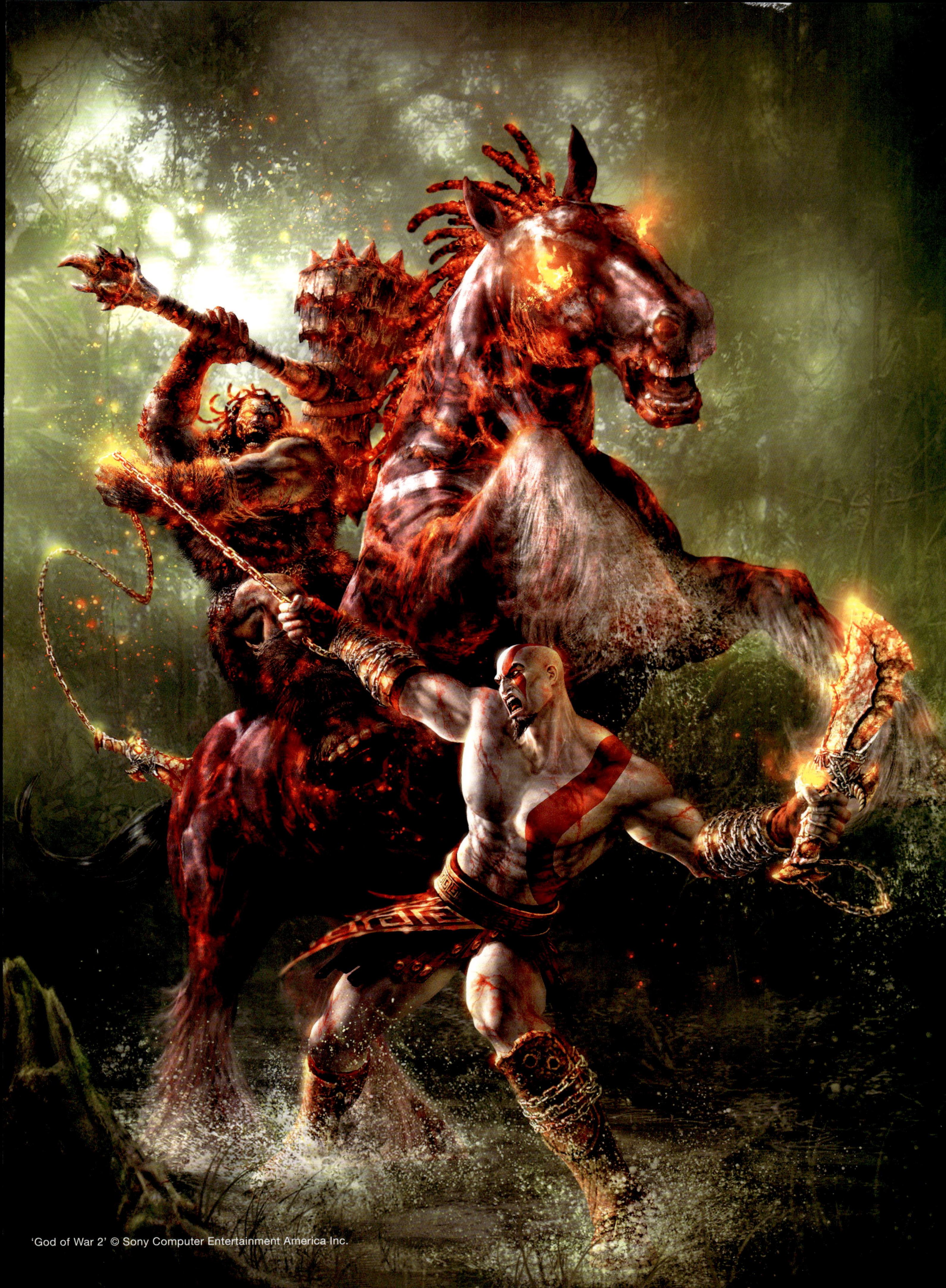

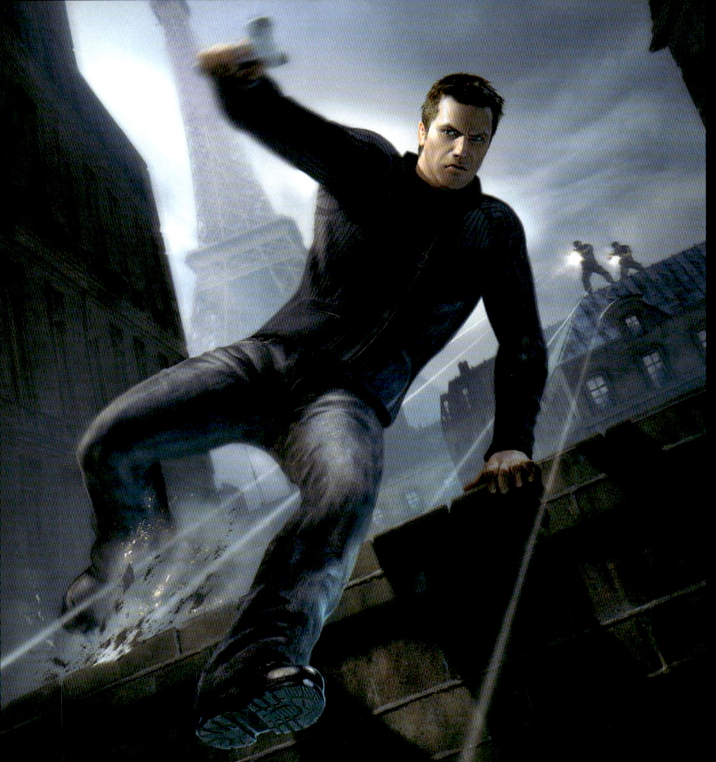

'Robert Ludlum's The Bourne Conspiracy' © High Moon Studios

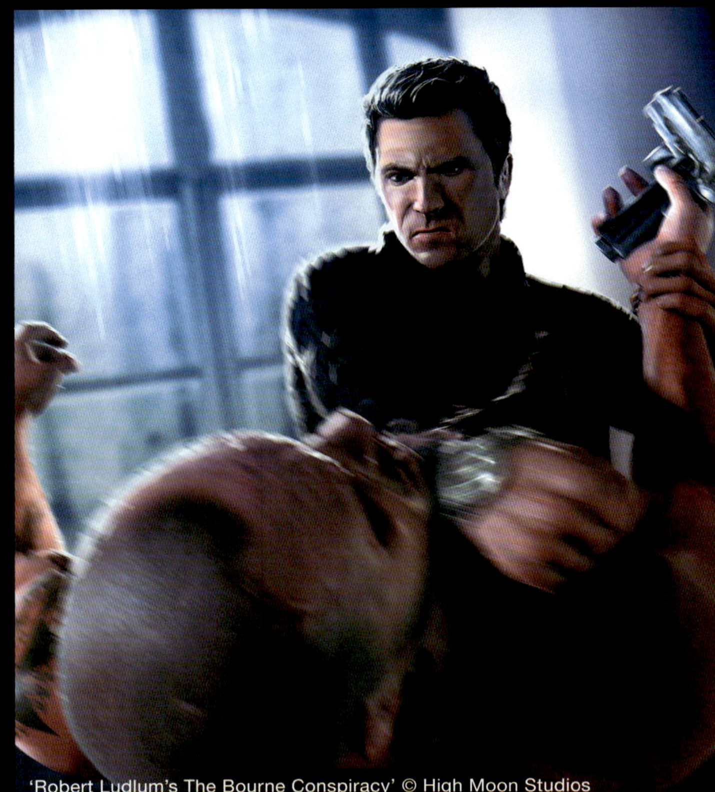

'Robert Ludlum's The Bourne Conspiracy' © High Moon Studios

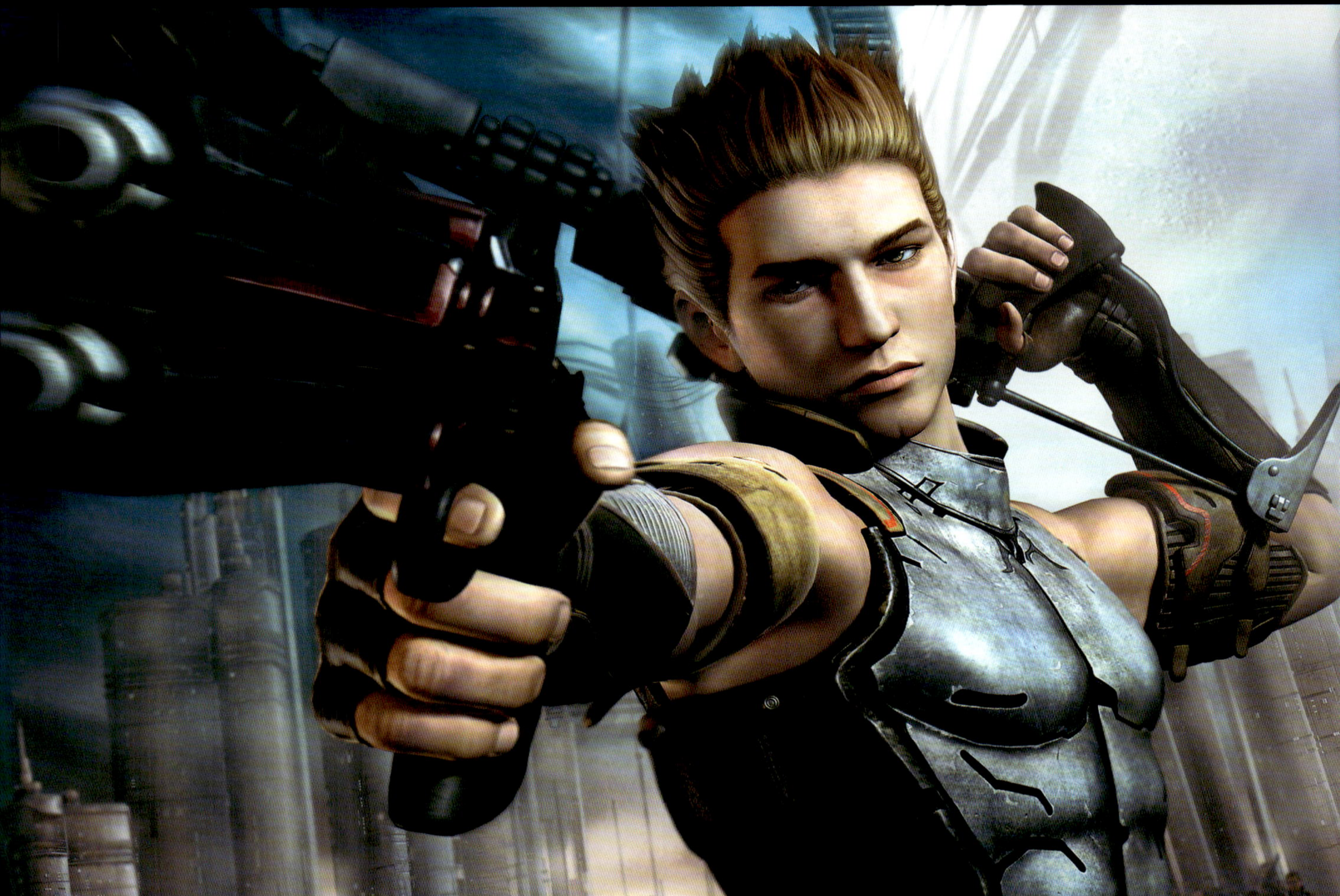

Robert Ludlum's The Bourne Conspiracy: Paris Snipers
3ds Max, Photoshop
Art Director: Sean Miller
Aaron Limonick and **Mike Brown**, High Moon Studios, USA
[top]

Gun man
Maya, mental ray, Photoshop
Seokchan Yoo,
NAKO Interactive, KOREA
[above]

Robert Ludlum's The Bourne Conspiracy: O'Connor
3ds Max, Photoshop
Art Director: Sean Miller
Billy King and **Mike Brown**, High Moon Studios, USA
[top]

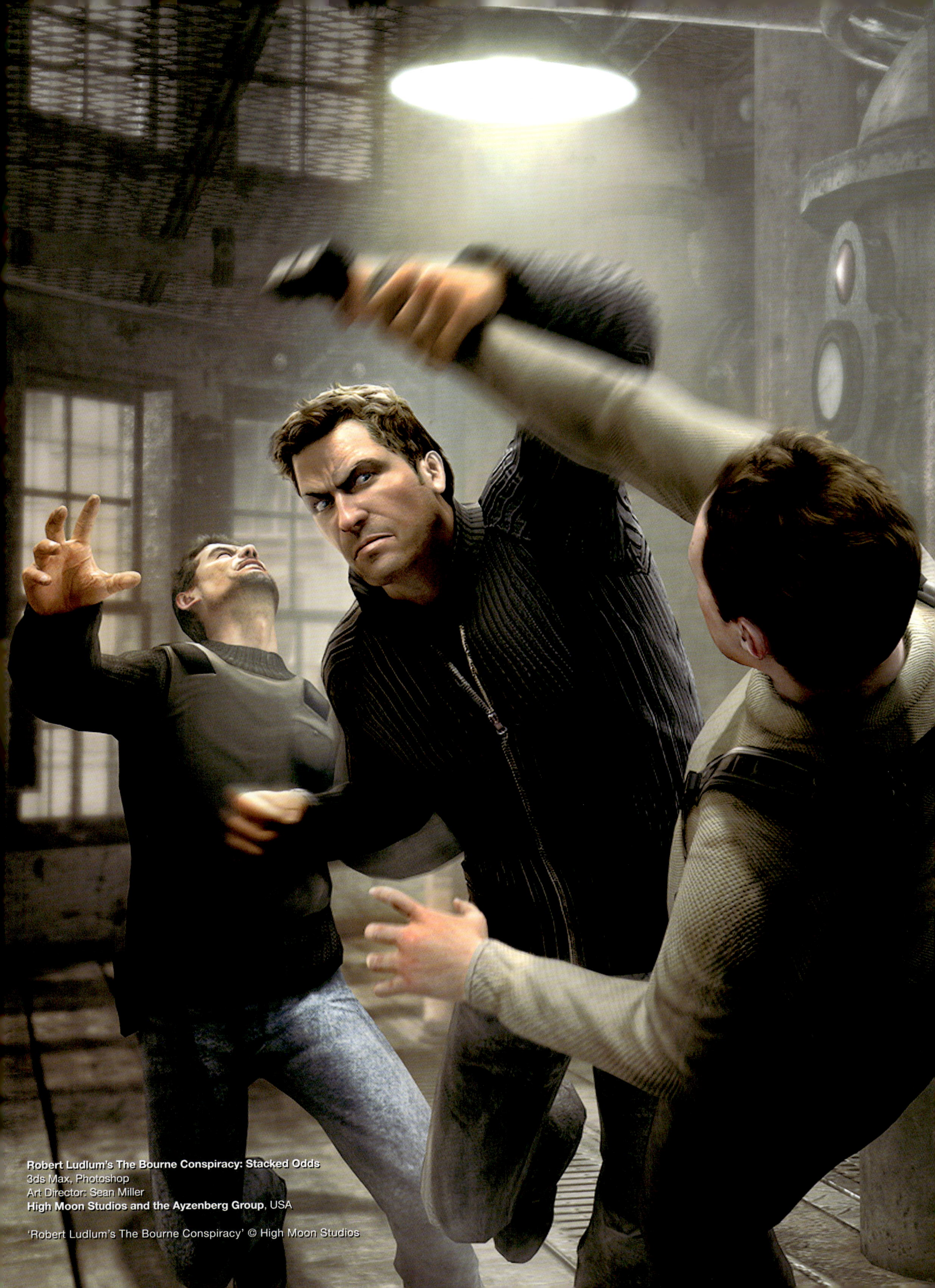

Robert Ludlum's The Bourne Conspiracy: Stacked Odds
3ds Max, Photoshop
Art Director: Sean Miller
High Moon Studios and the Ayzenberg Group, USA

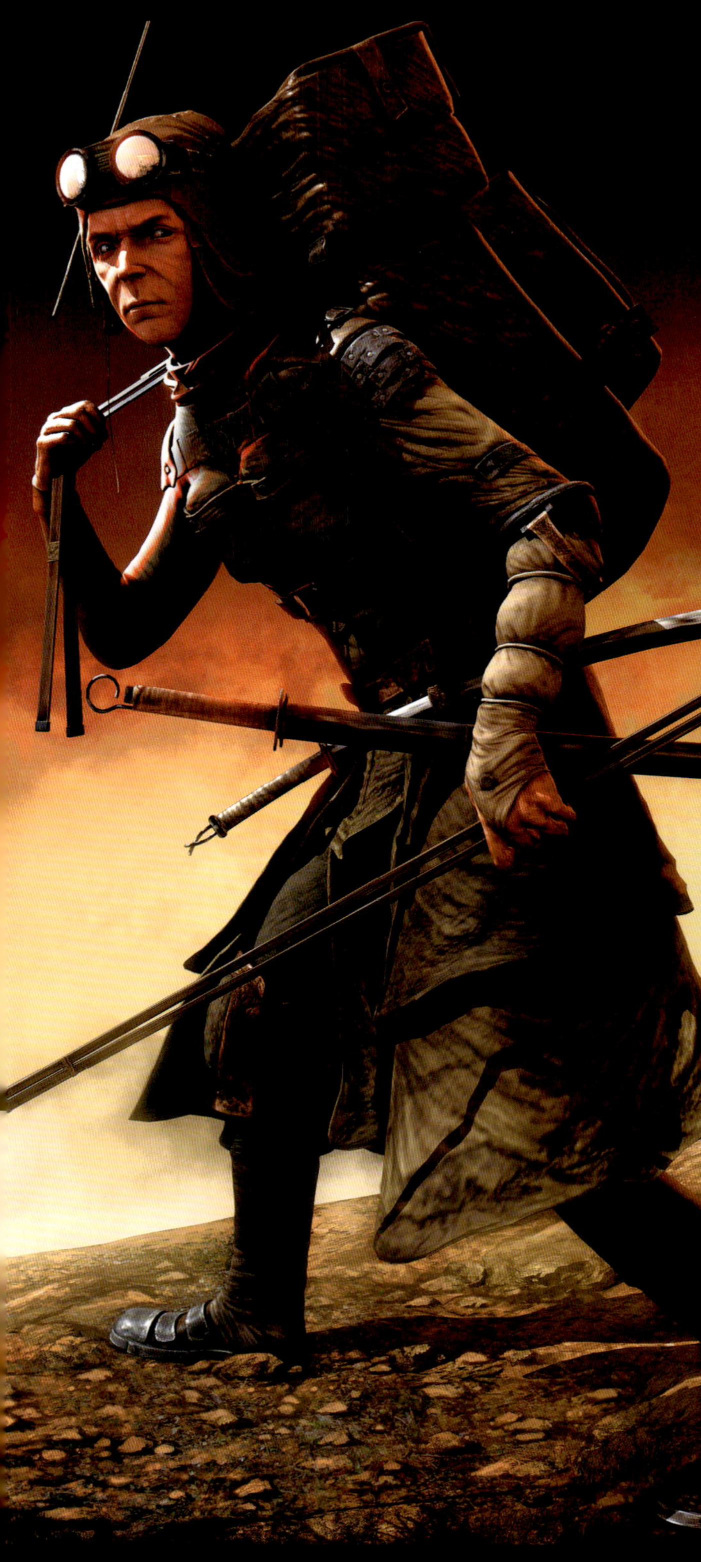

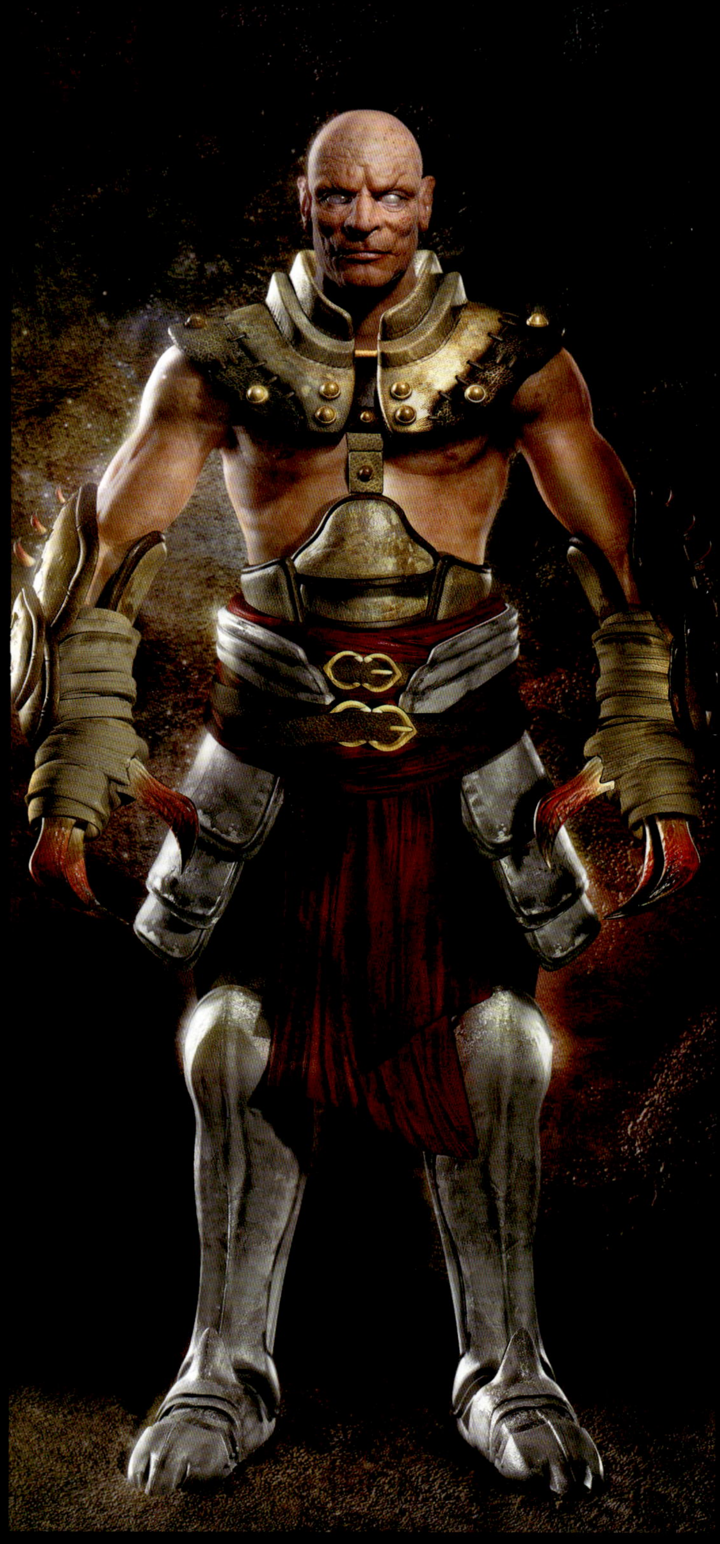

The Scavenger
Maya, ZBrush, BodyPaint 3D, Photoshop
Inspired by: Keith Thompson
Antonio Jose Gonzalez Benitez, SPAIN
[above]

Laplace's Demon
Maya, mental ray, Mudbox, Photoshop
Daniel Crossland, GREAT BRITAIN
[above]

The Last Kraken
3ds Max, Photoshop
Thibaut Claeys, CANADA
[right]

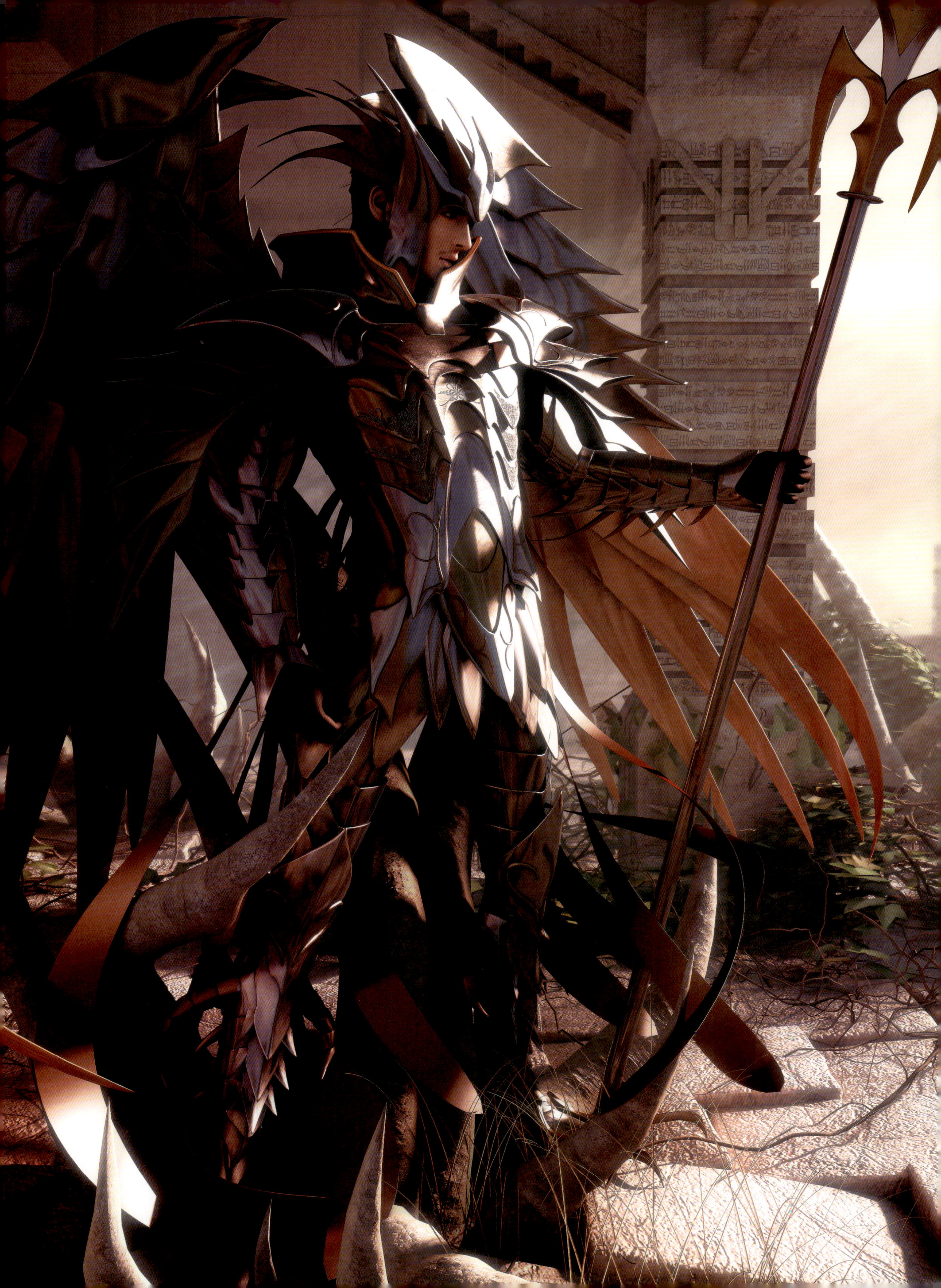

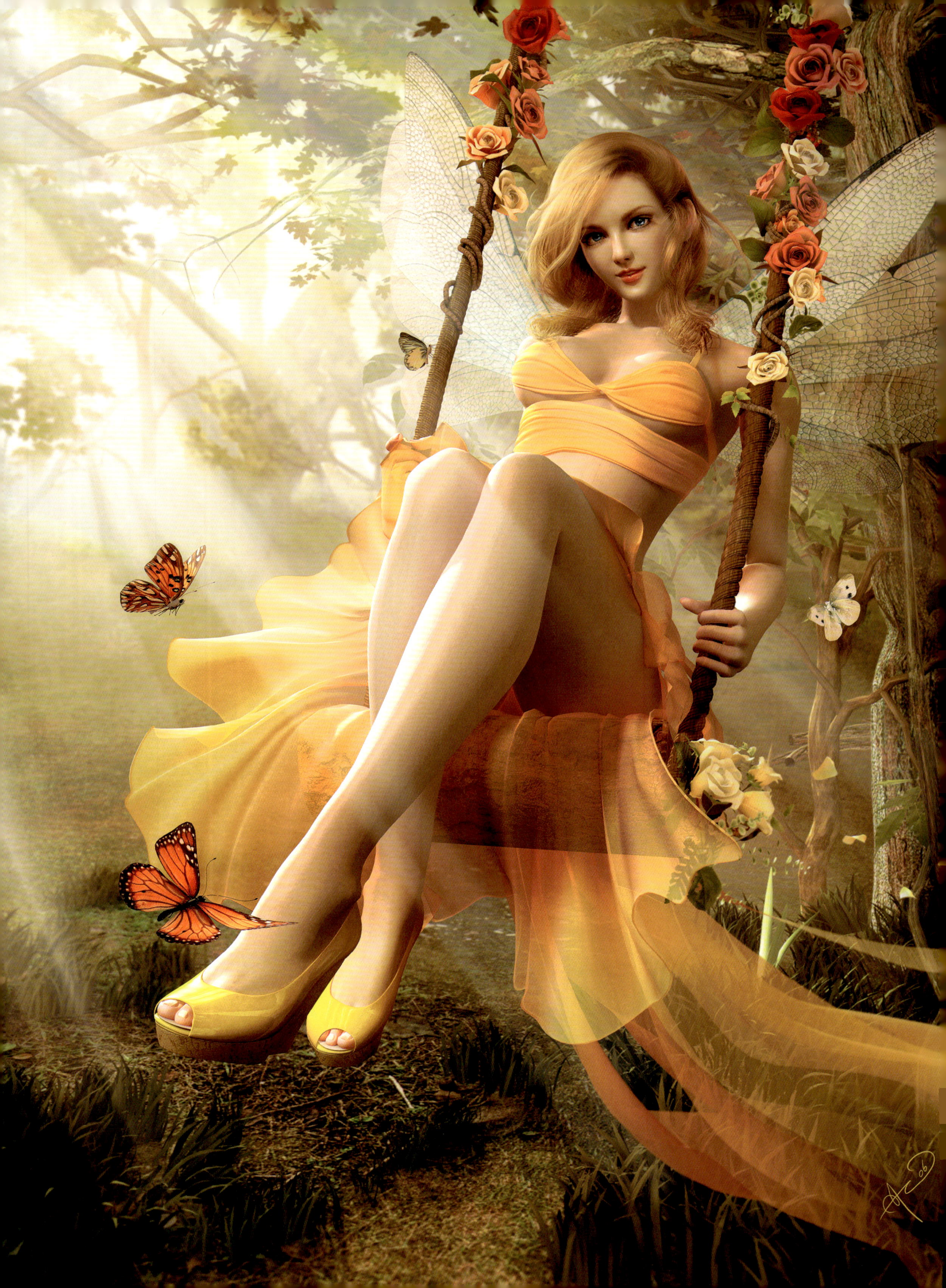

In the golden forest
3ds Max
Soa Lee, KOREA
[left]

Gun and Sword
3ds Max, V-Ray, Photoshop
Choe Byung-hee, KOREA
[right]

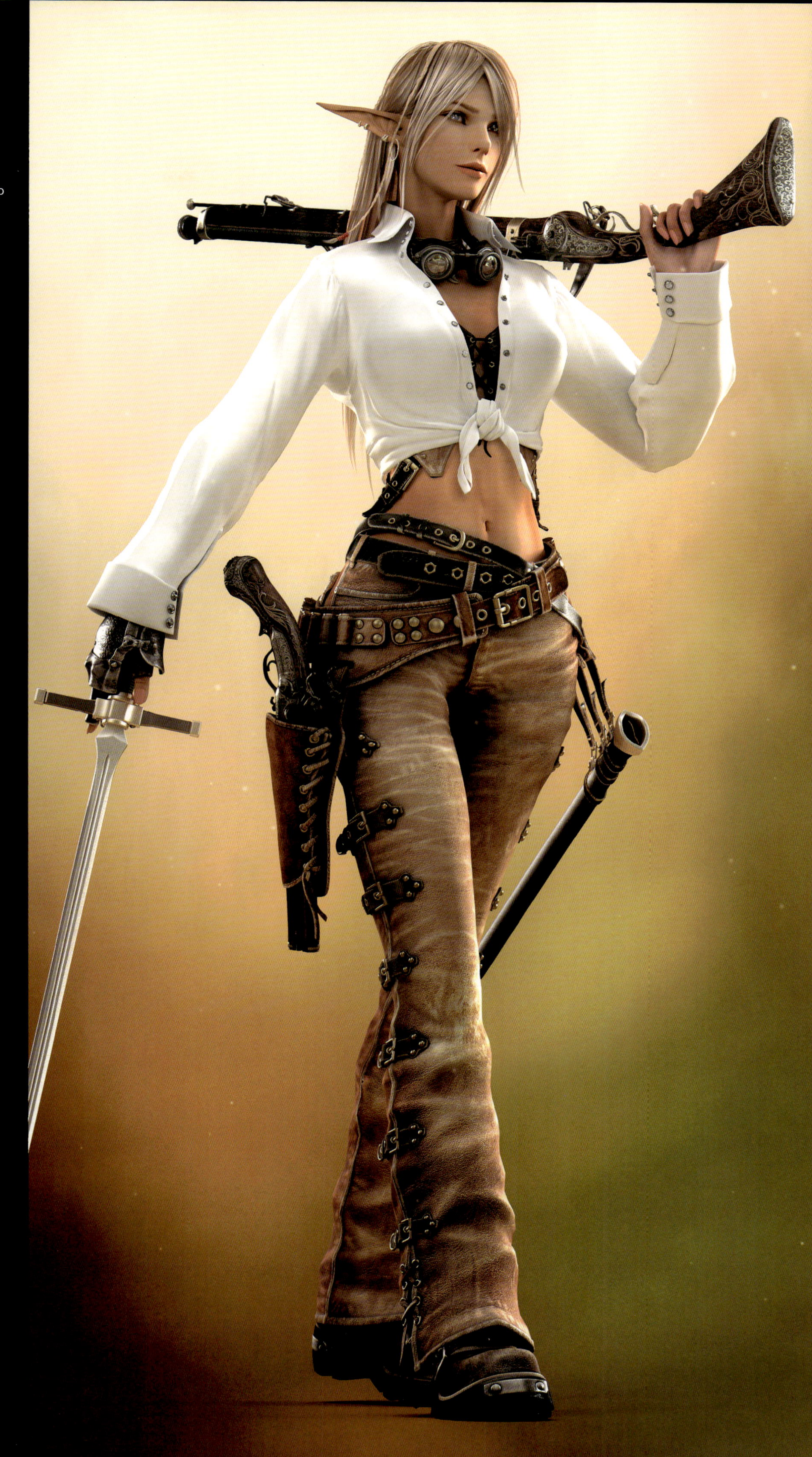

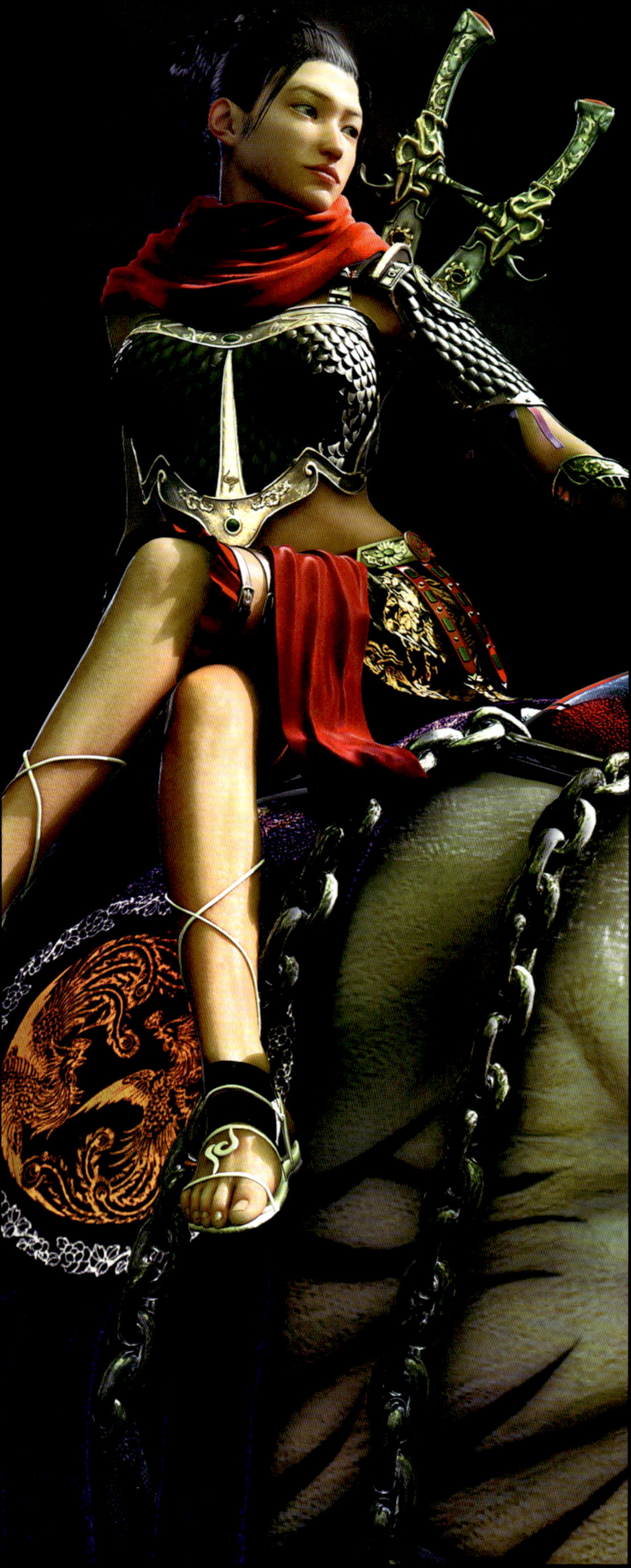

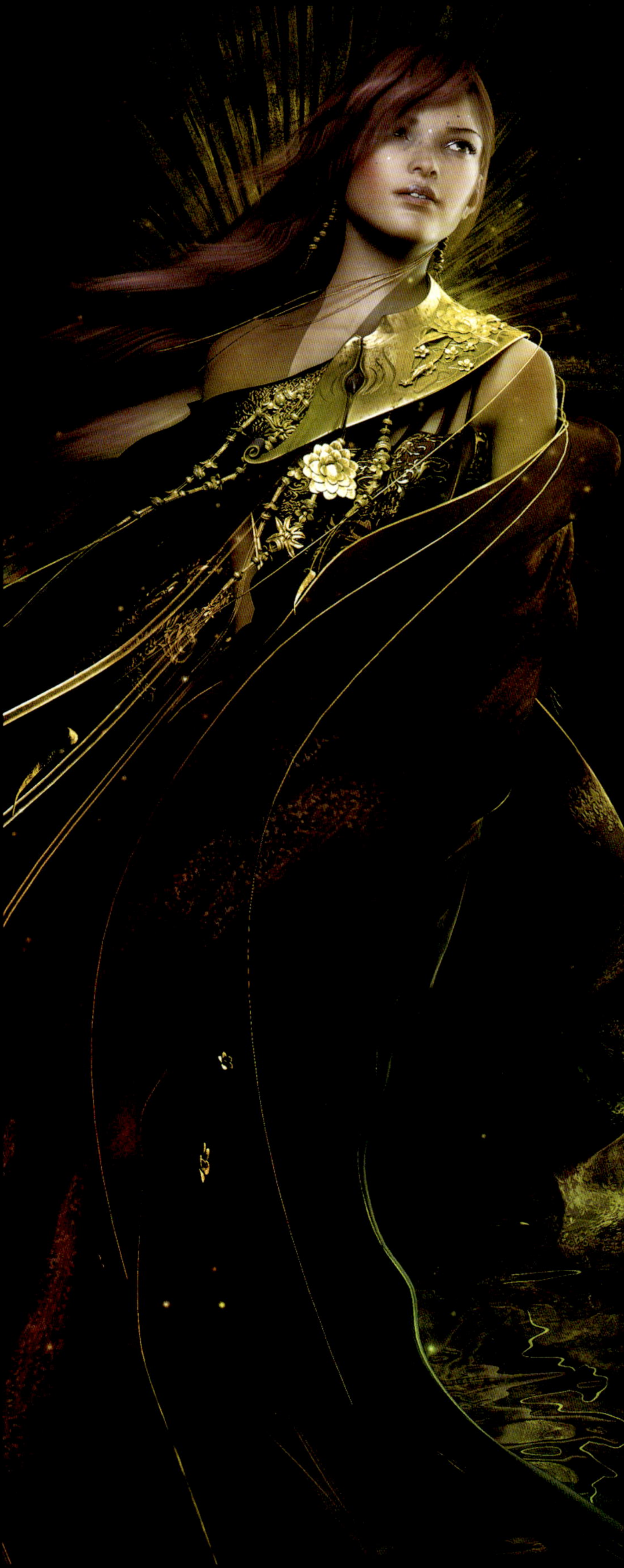

Dark Phoenix
Maya, mental ray
Wang Xiaoyu, Beijing Perfect World Co. Ltd, CHINA
[above]

Golden Flow
3ds Max
Olivier Ponsonnet, FRANCE
[above]

Nimhoa
Maya, Photoshop
Daniele Scerra, ITALY
[right]

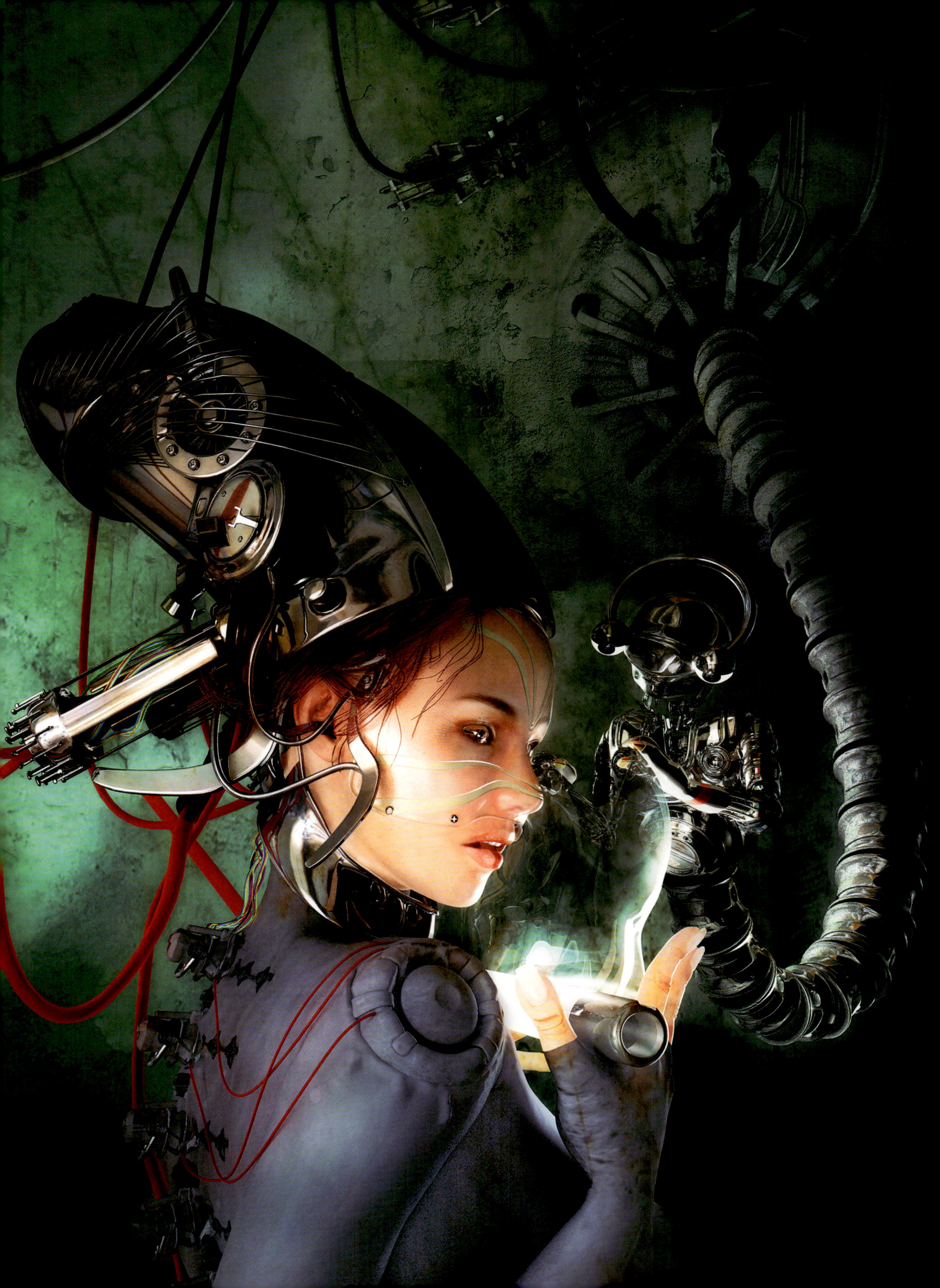

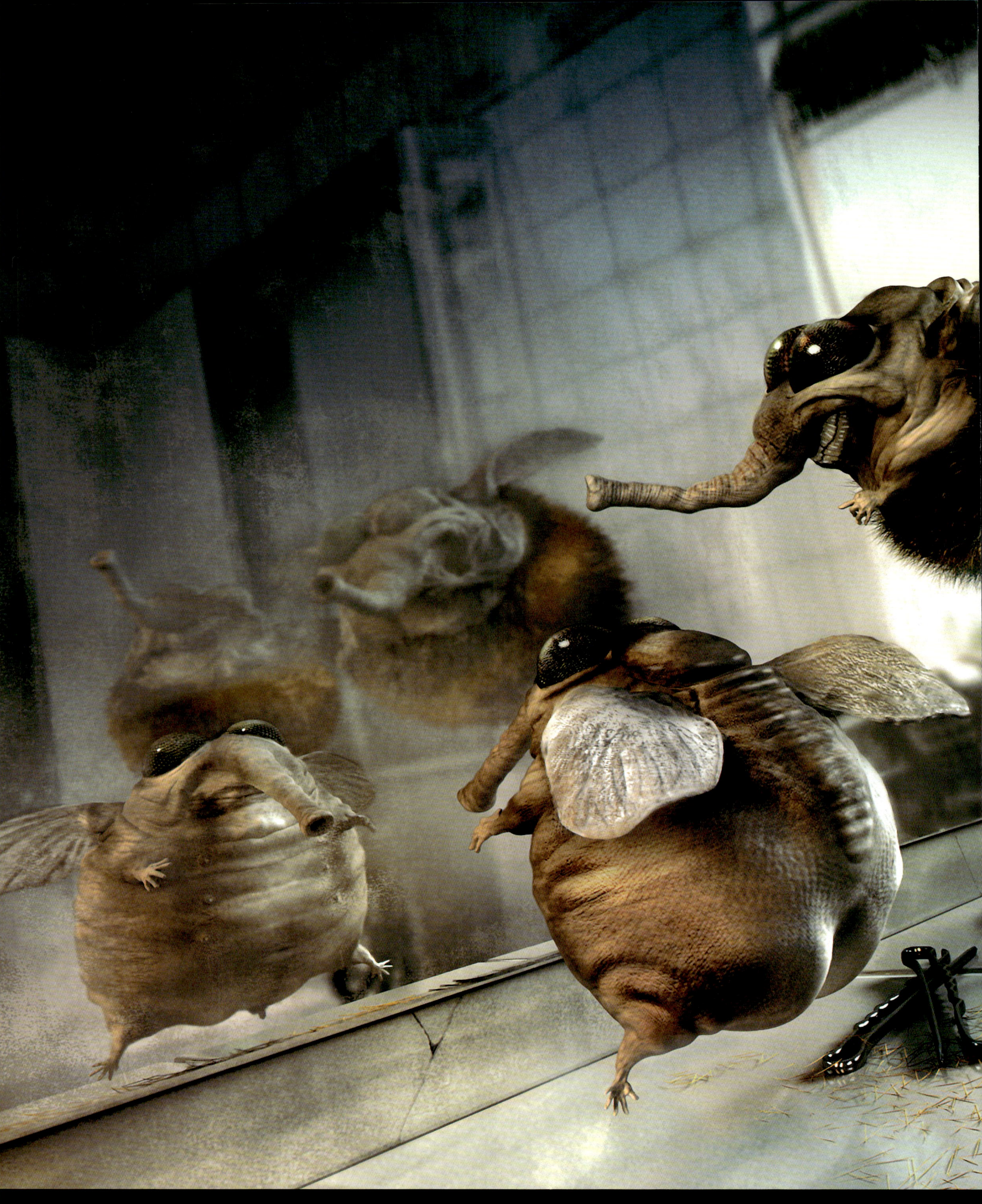

Master
Creatures

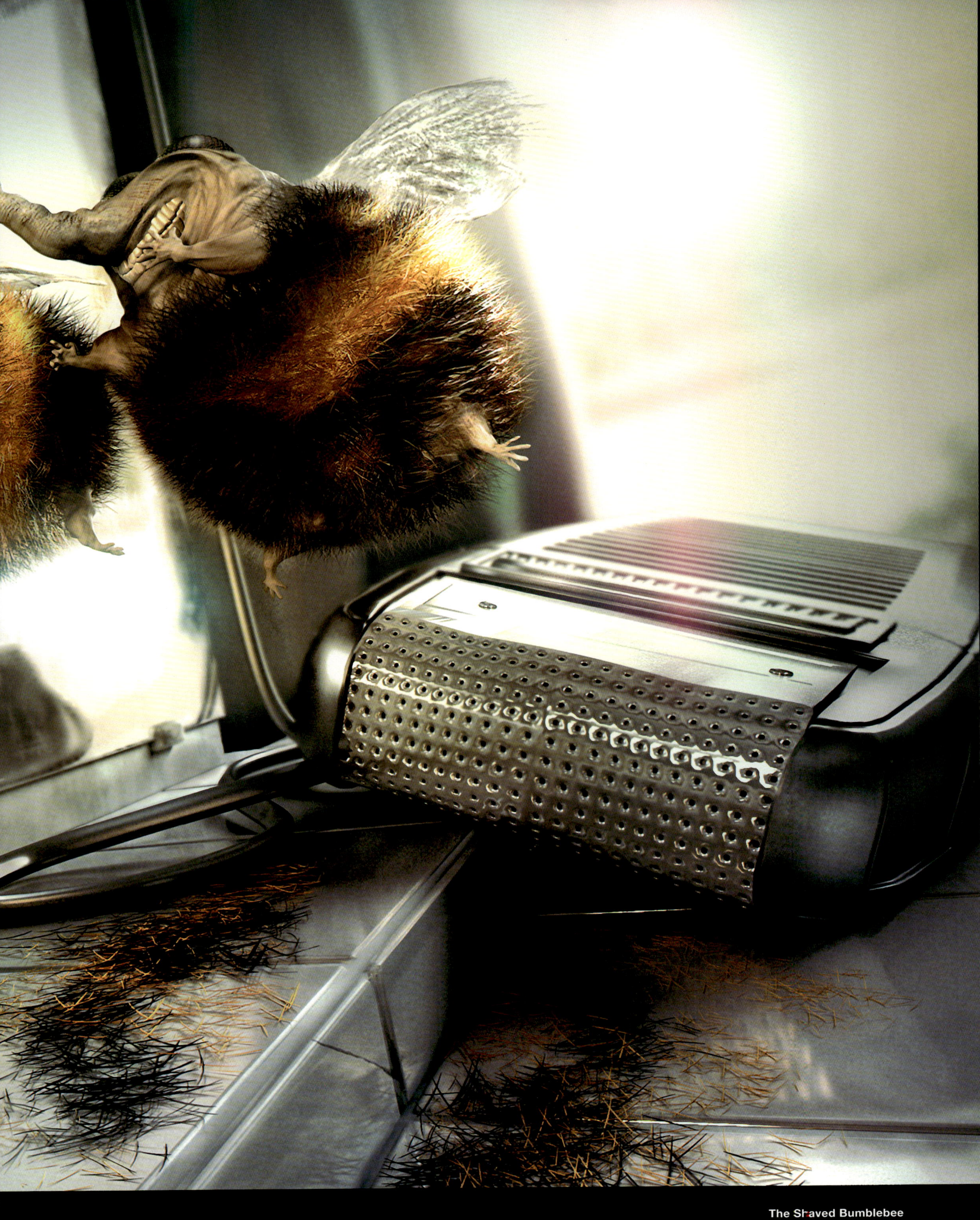

The Shaved Bumblebee
3ds Max, Photoshop, ZBrush
Till Nowak, GERMANY

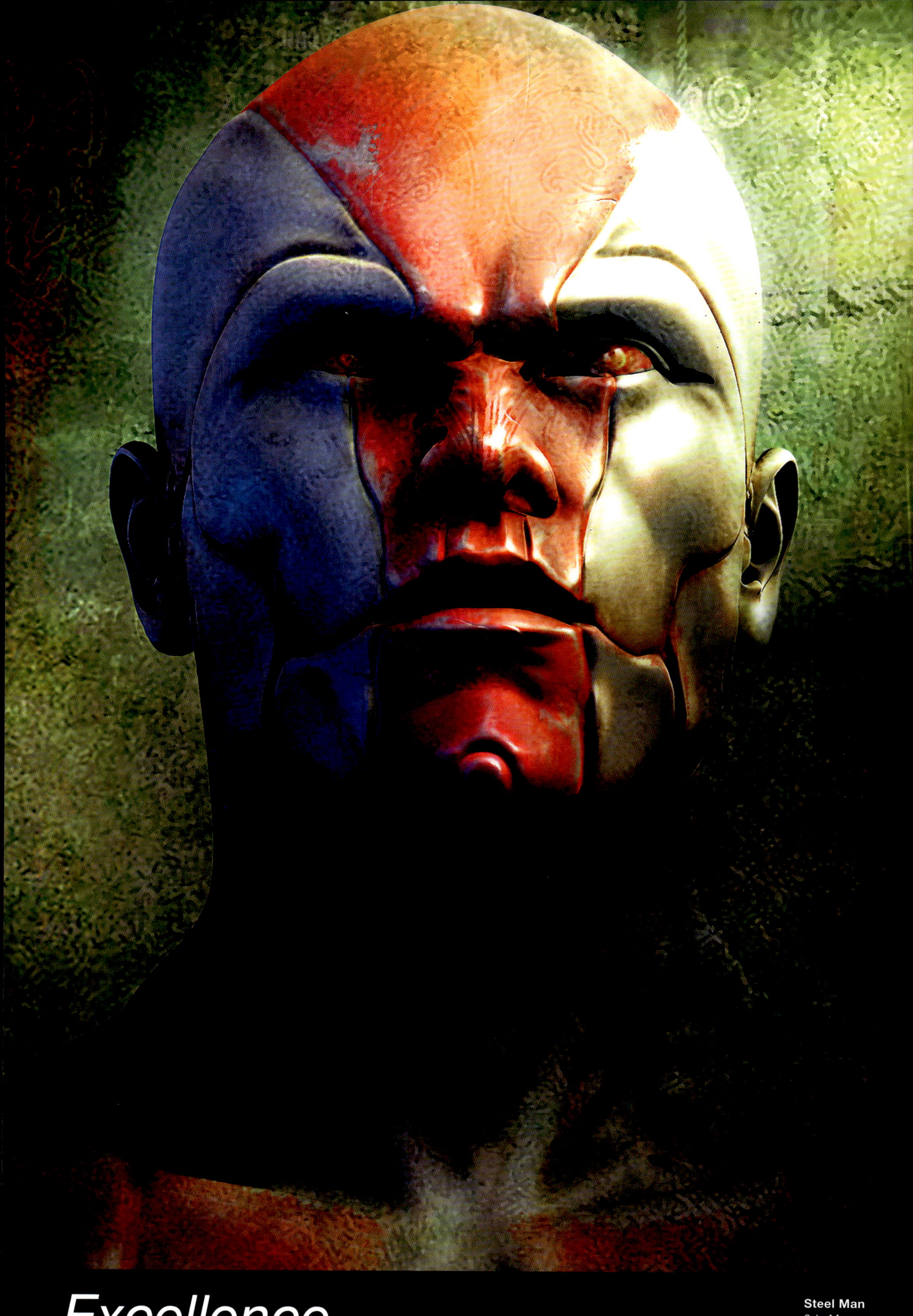

Excellence

Creatures

Steel Man
3ds Max
Weiye Yin, CHINA

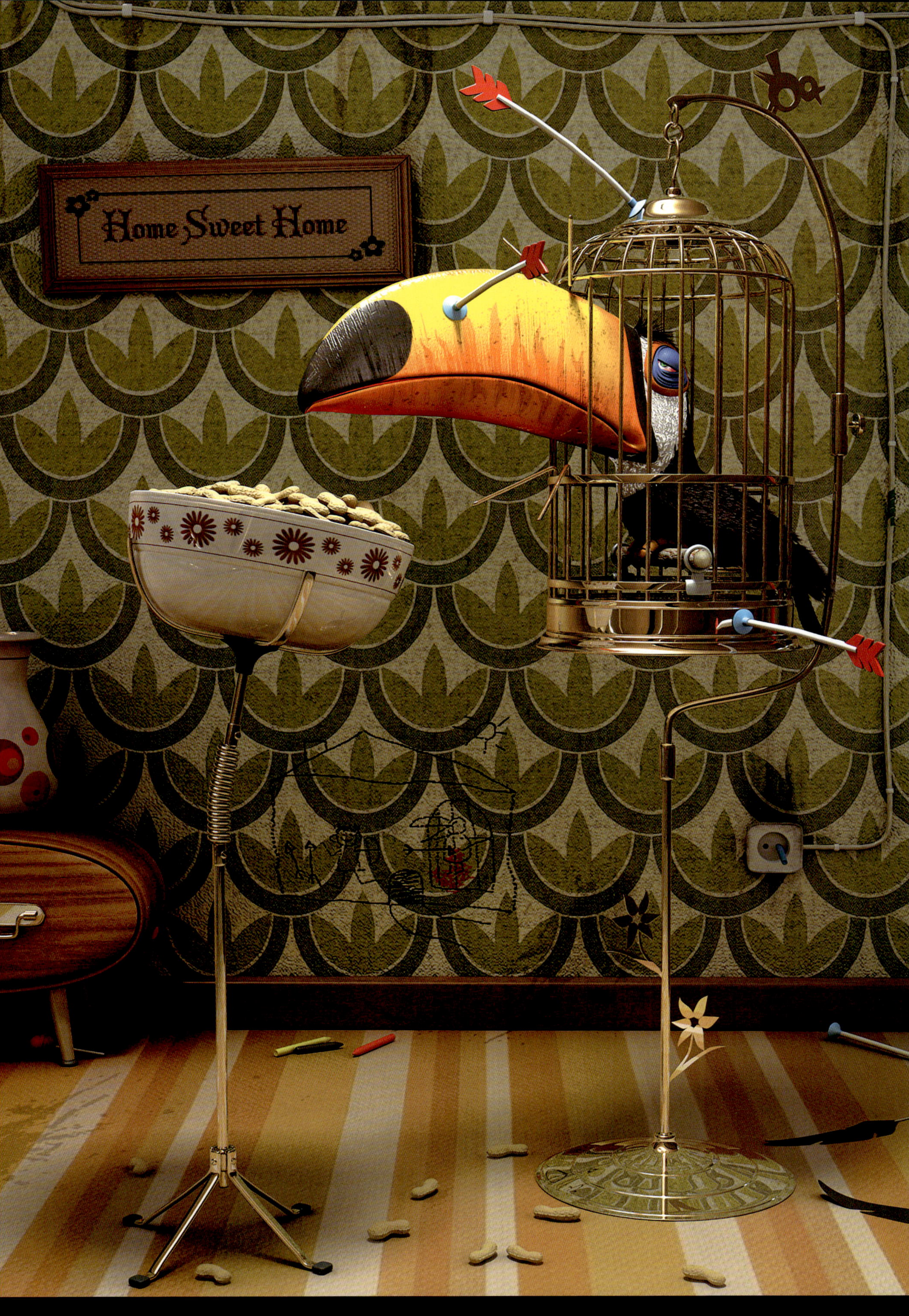

Home Sweet Home
Maya, mental ray, Photoshop
Iker Cortazar, SPAIN

Excellence
Creatures

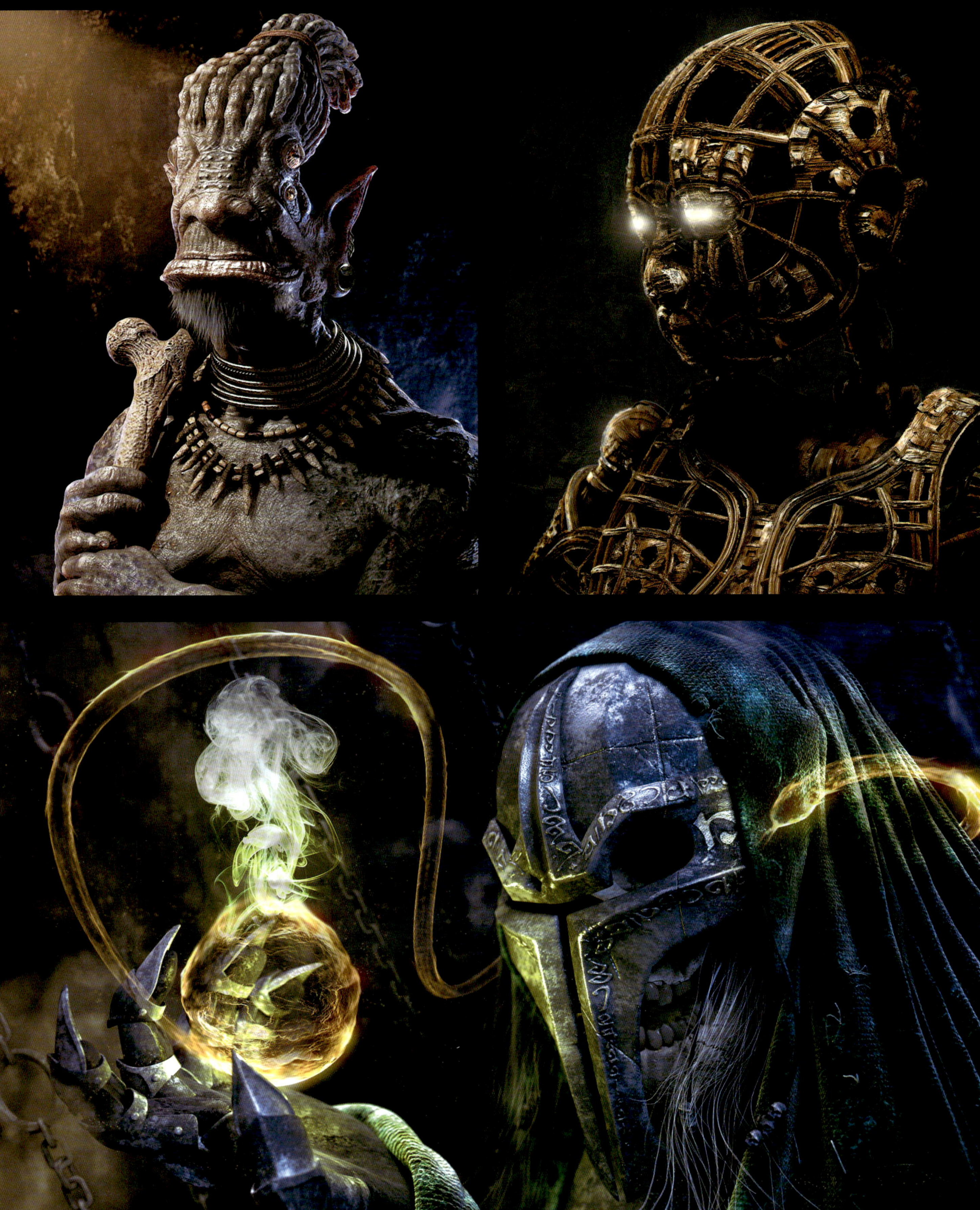

Alien Shaman
3ds Max, mental ray, ZBrush
Mark Skelton, USA
[top]

Undead wizard
3ds Max, Photoshop, V-Ray
Balázs Pápay, HUNGARY
[above]

Rust
Maya, Painter
Daniel Arnold-Mist, GREAT BRITAIN
[top]

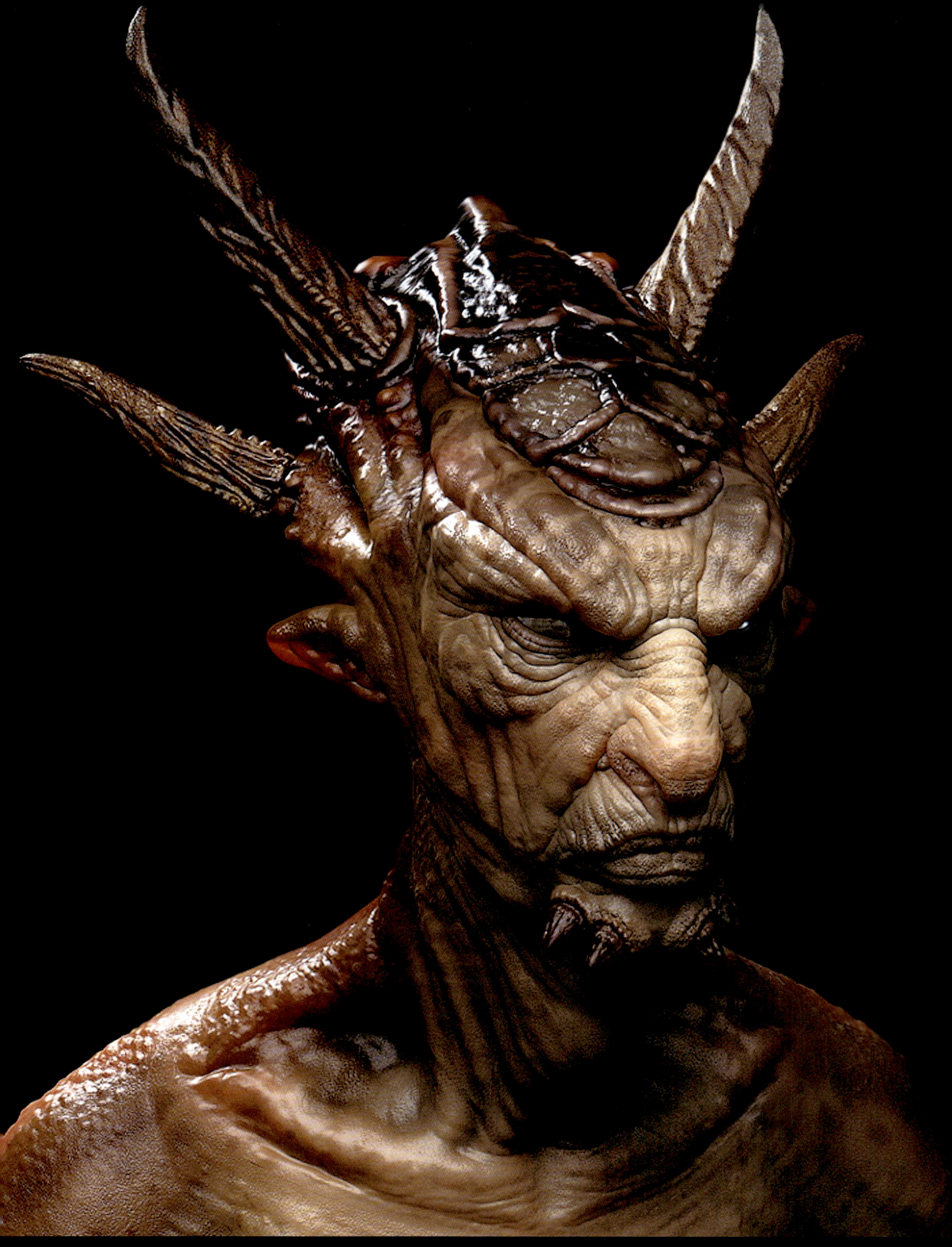

Creature concept 02
3ds Max, ZBrush
Mathieu Aerni, CANADA

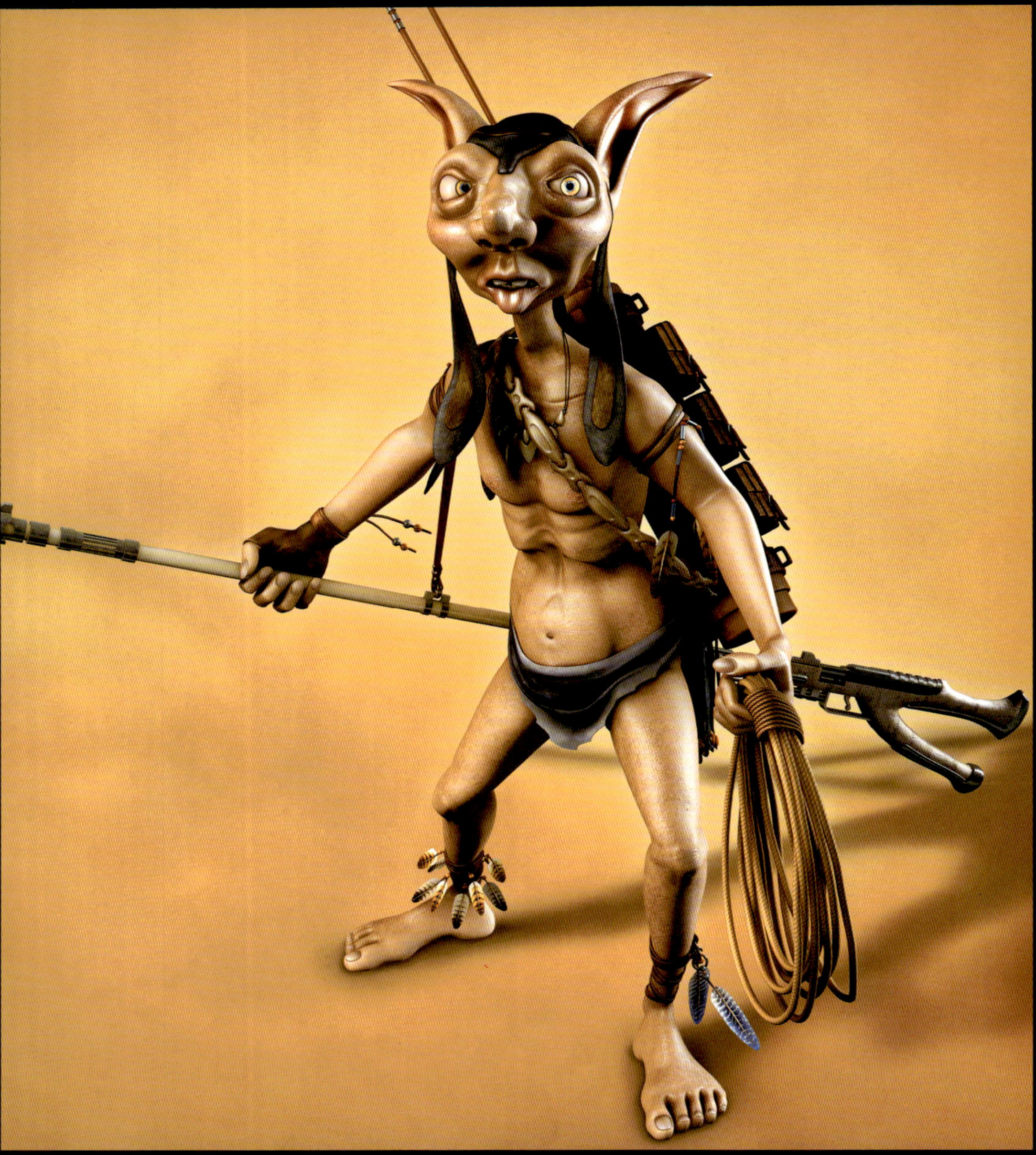

The Gatherer
3ds Max, Photoshop
Matthew Coombe, CANADA
[left]

Hell yeah!
3ds Max, Brazil r/s, ZBrush
Vaclav Krivanek,
CZECH REPUBLIC
[right]

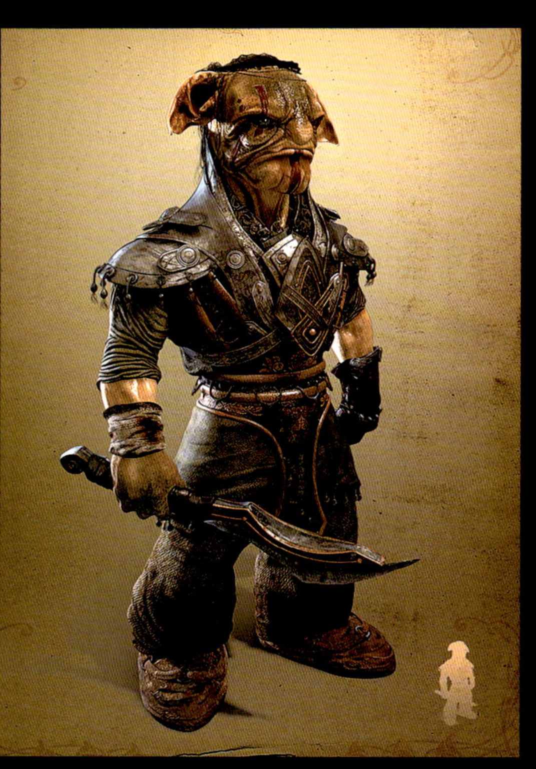

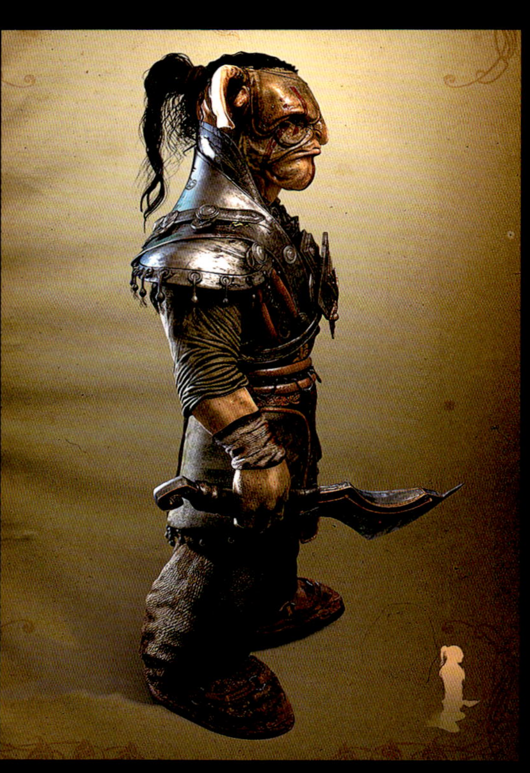

Prince Ný Tael's ID
3ds Max, Brazil r/s, V-Ray,
Photoshop
Miguel Ângelo Carvalho
Bernardo Teixeira,
PORTUGAL
[far left, left]

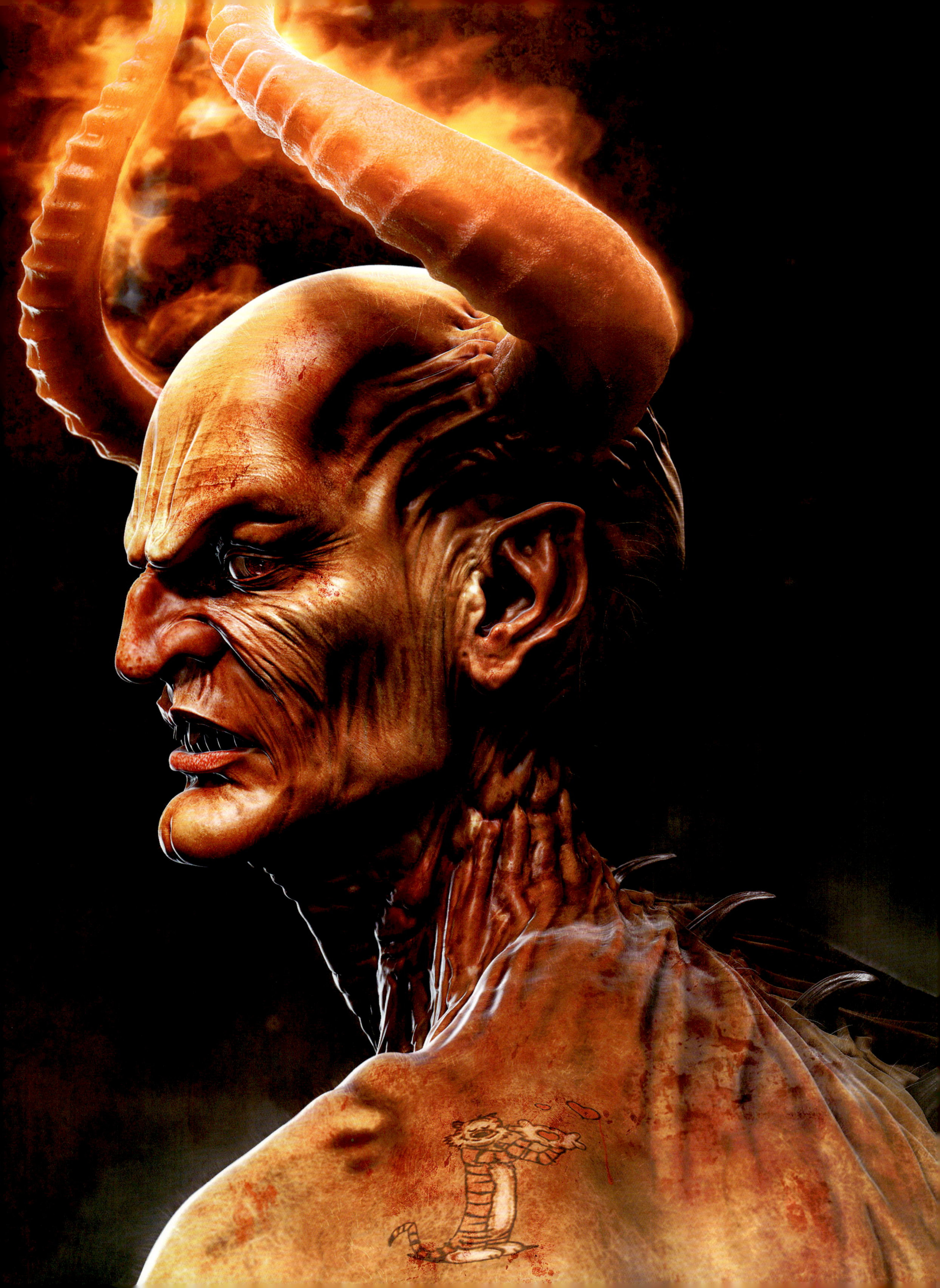

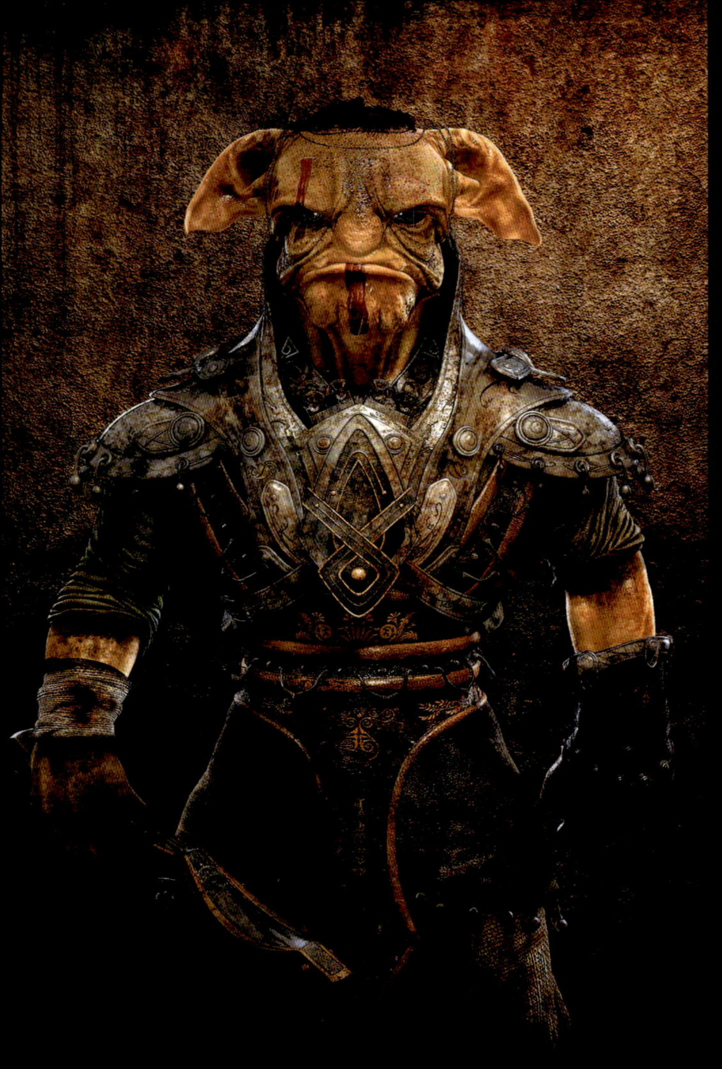

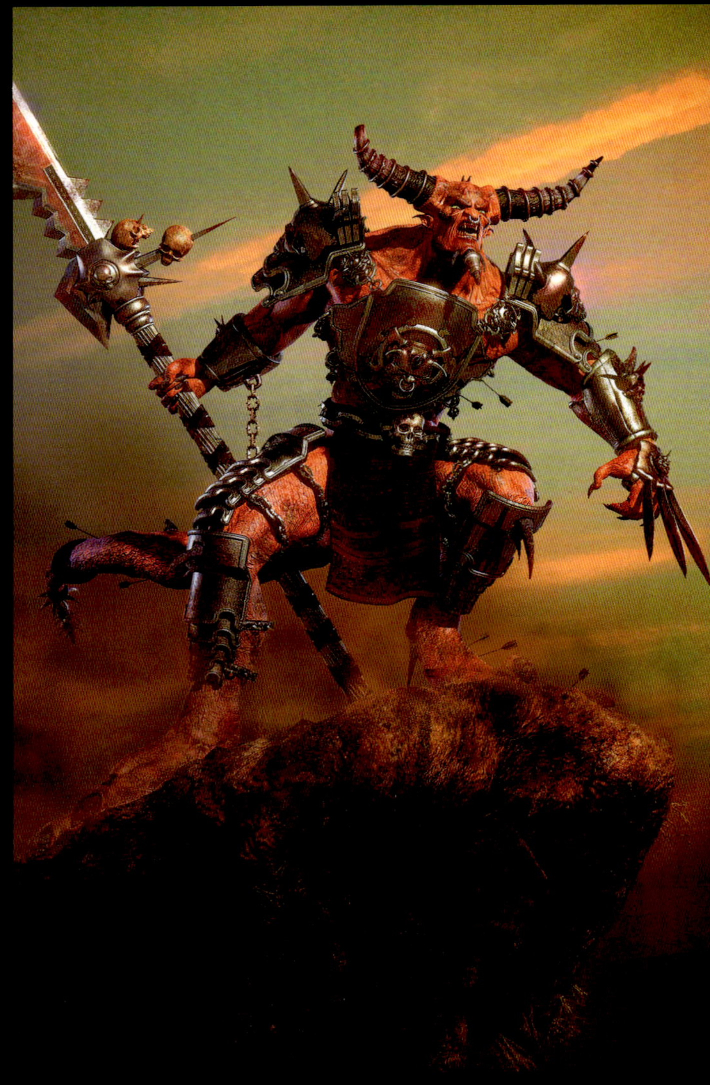

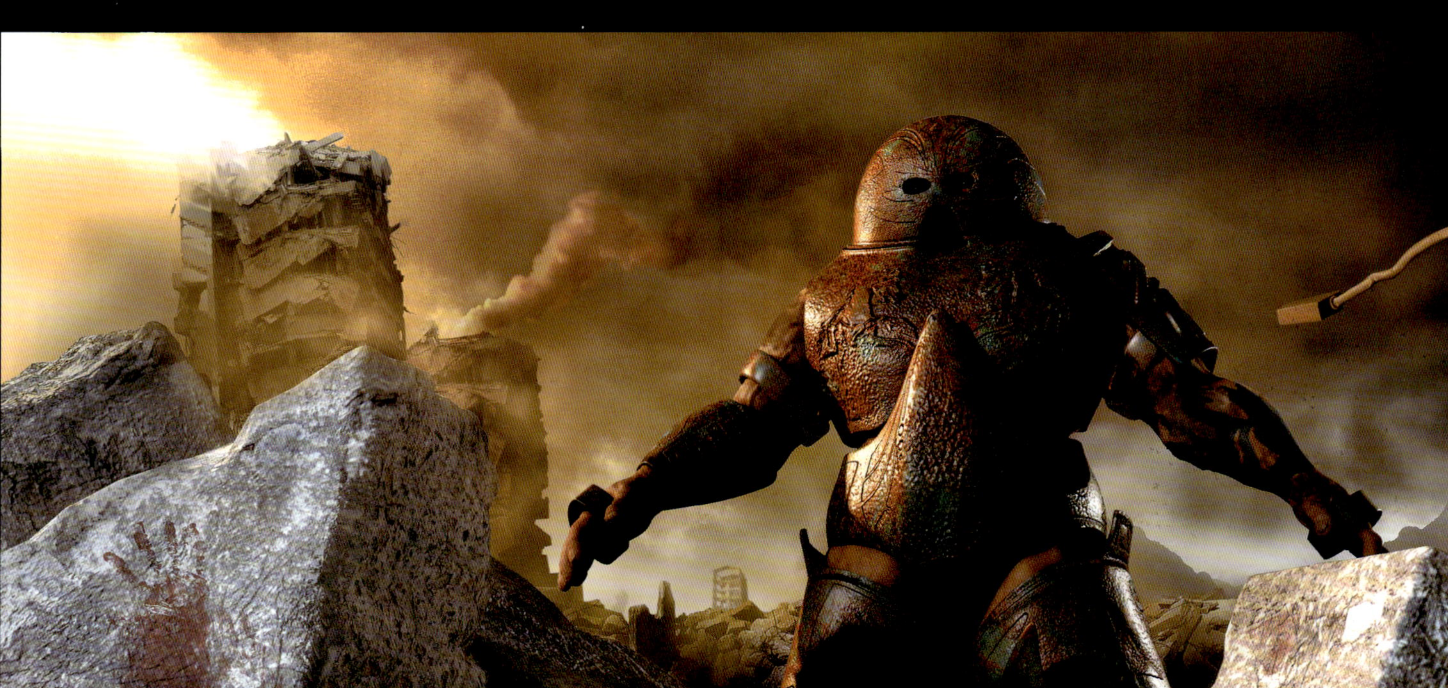

Prince Ný Tael
3ds Max, Brazil r/s, V-Ray, Photoshop
Miguel Ângelo Carvalho Bernardo Teixeira, PORTUGAL
[top]

Ready the Cyttorak
Maya, ZBrush, Photoshop, mental ray
Inspired by: Marvel Comics' supervillian, "The Juggernaut"
Eric Butts, USA
[above]

Demon War
3ds Max, ZBrush, Photoshop
Moayad Fahmi, TRUEMAX, DENMARK
[top]

Lobo: Chained!
3ds Max, Mudbox, V-Ray, Photoshop
Dedicated in loving memory to Zdenka Klabíková
Stanislav Klabík, CZECH REPUBLIC
[right]

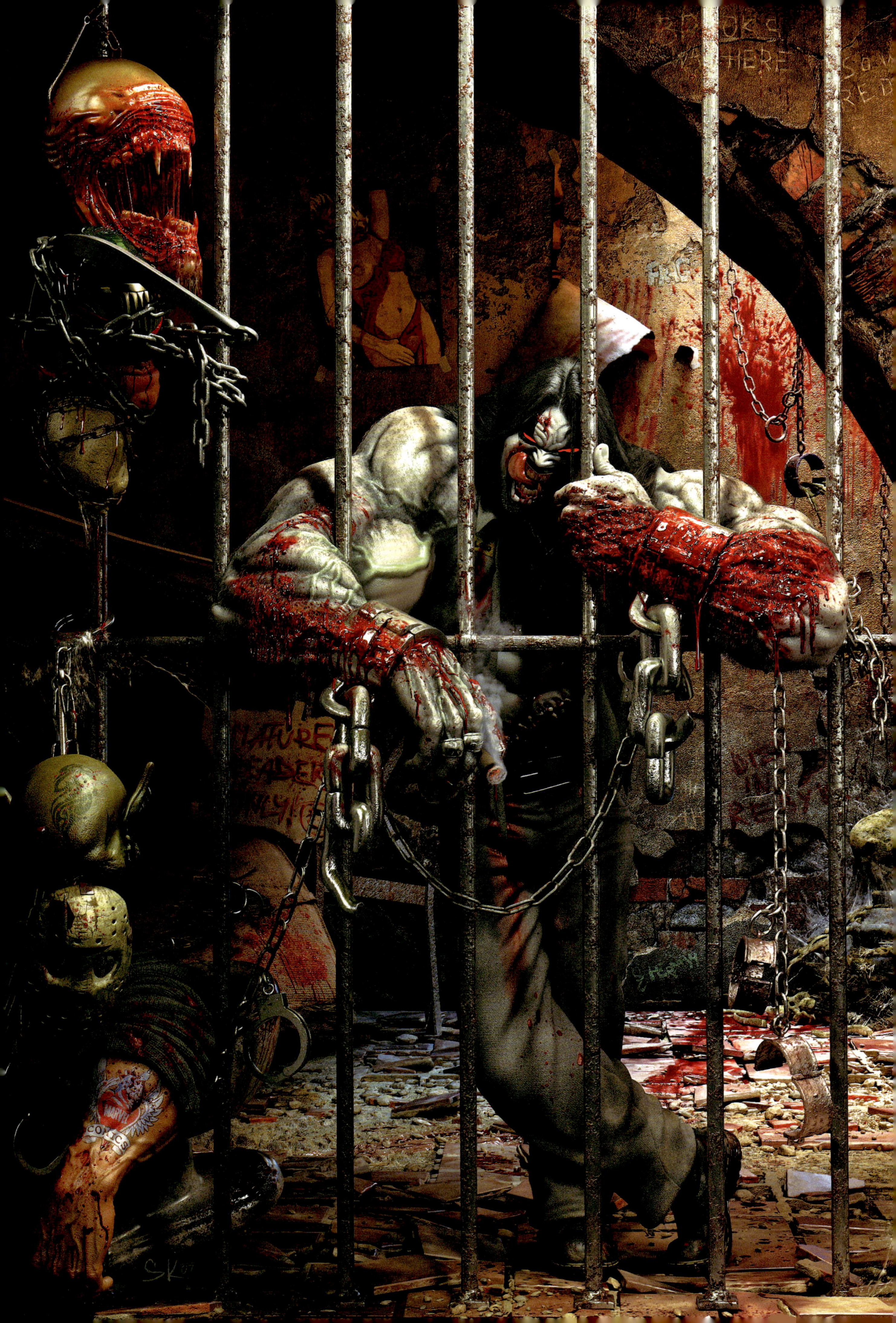
HERE

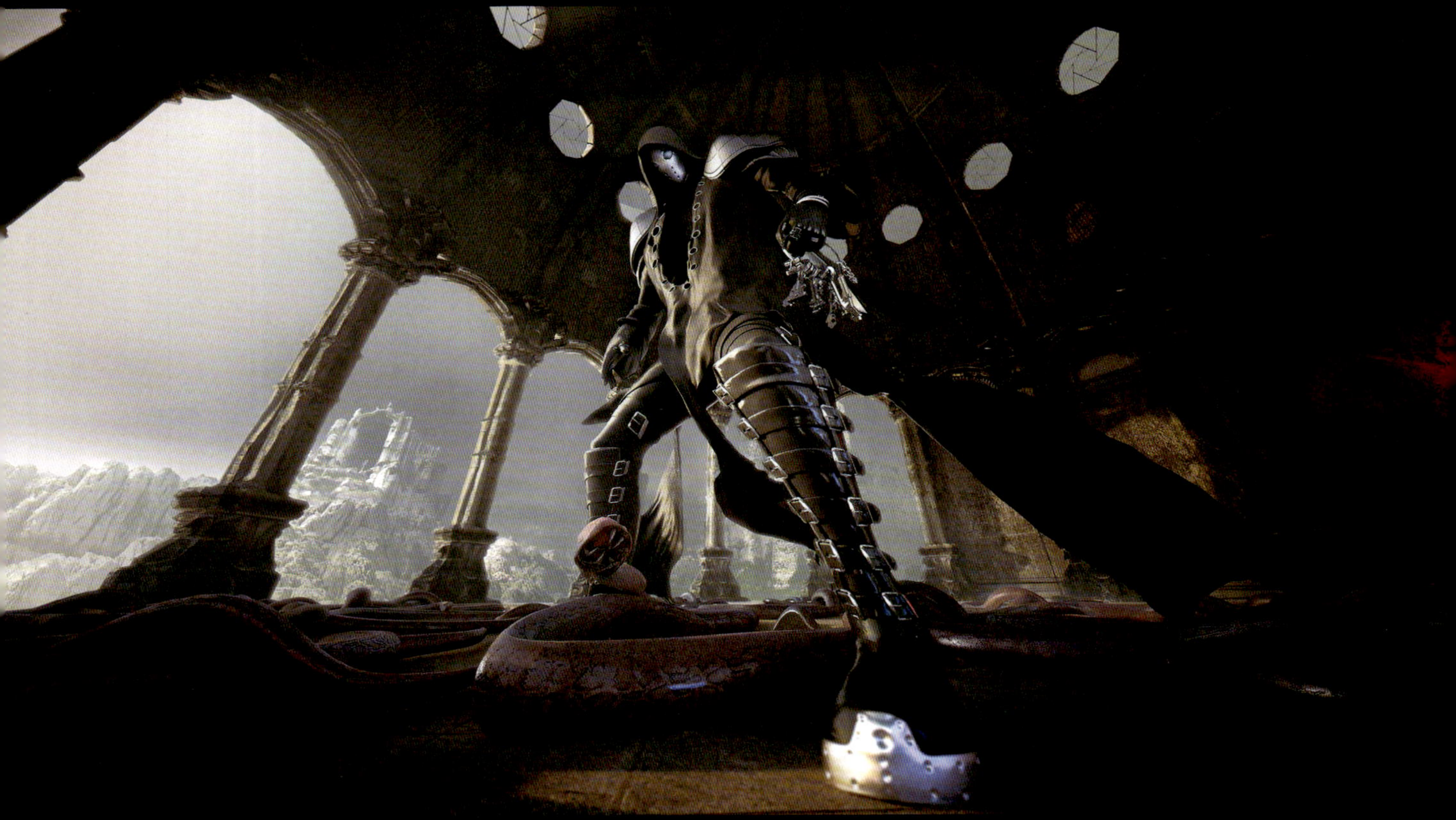

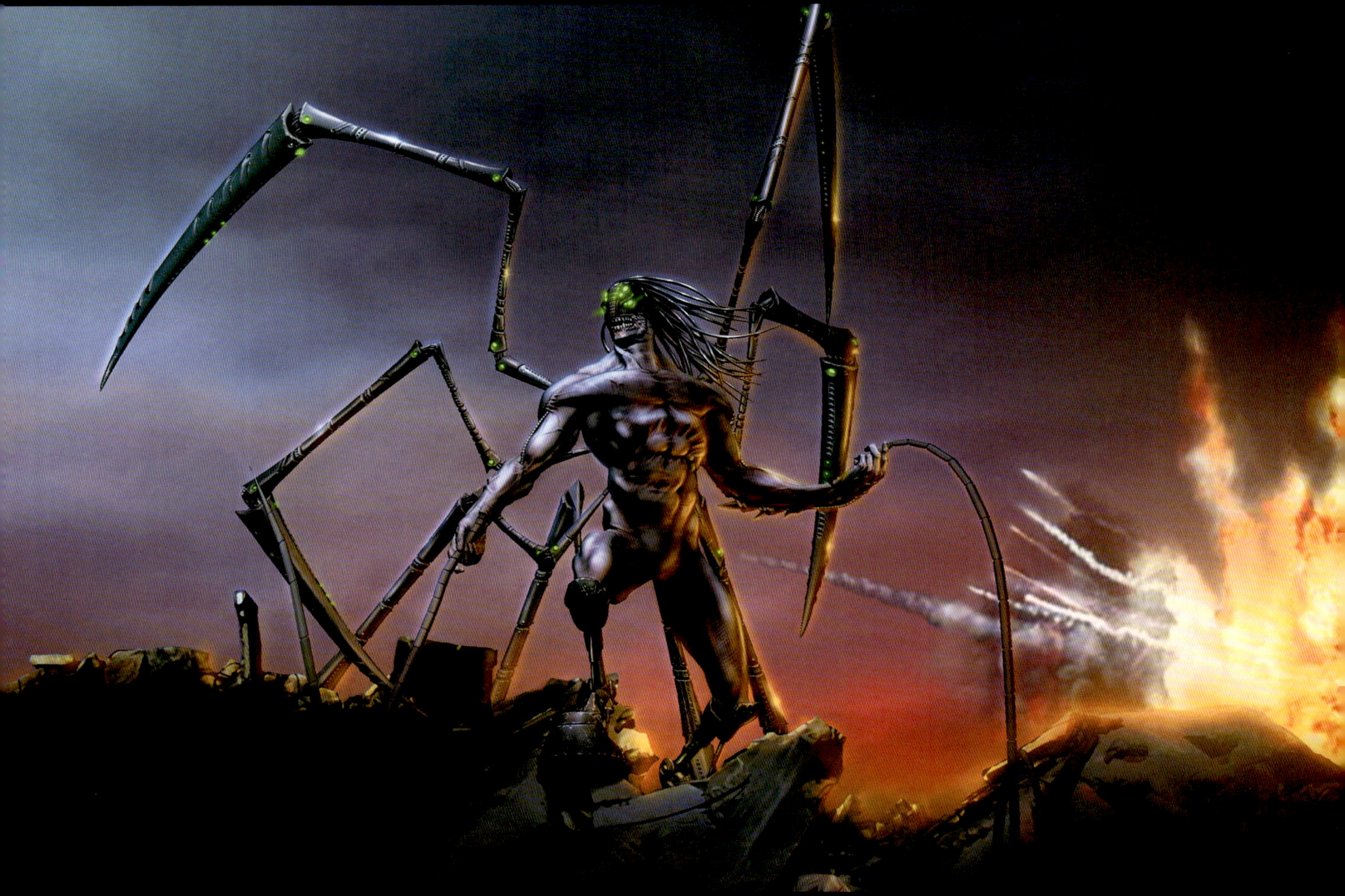

The Keyholder
3ds Max, Mudbox, BodyPaint 3D,
Photoshop, Maxwell Render
Gieanu Dragos, HotShotsVFX, ROMANIA
[top]

Invasion
Maya, ZBrush, Photoshop
Adam McMahon,
USA
[above]

Dark Corner of the Earth
Photoshop, 3ds Max, ZBrush
Inspired by: H.P Lovecraft
Petar Milivojevic, SERBIA
[right]

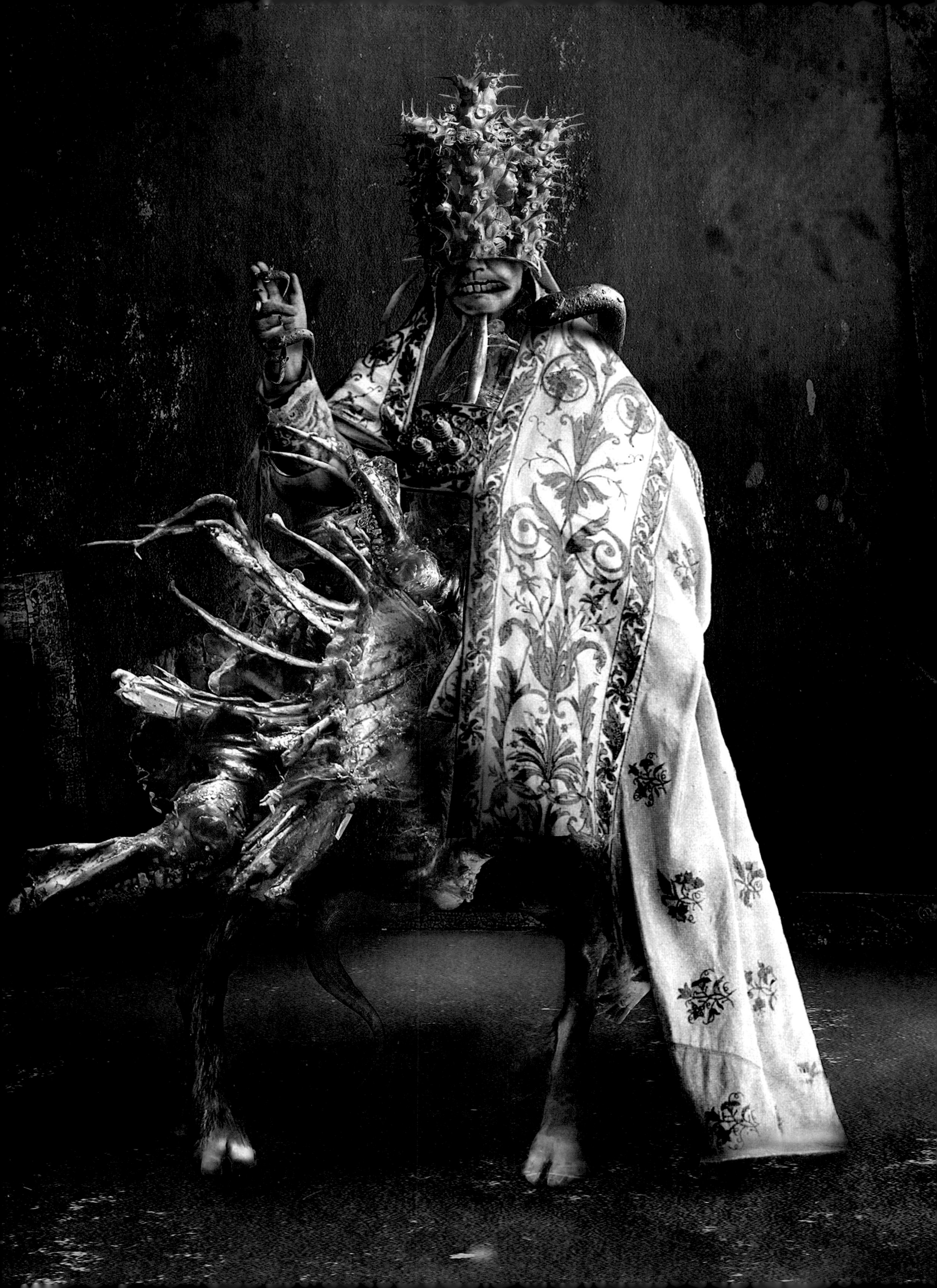

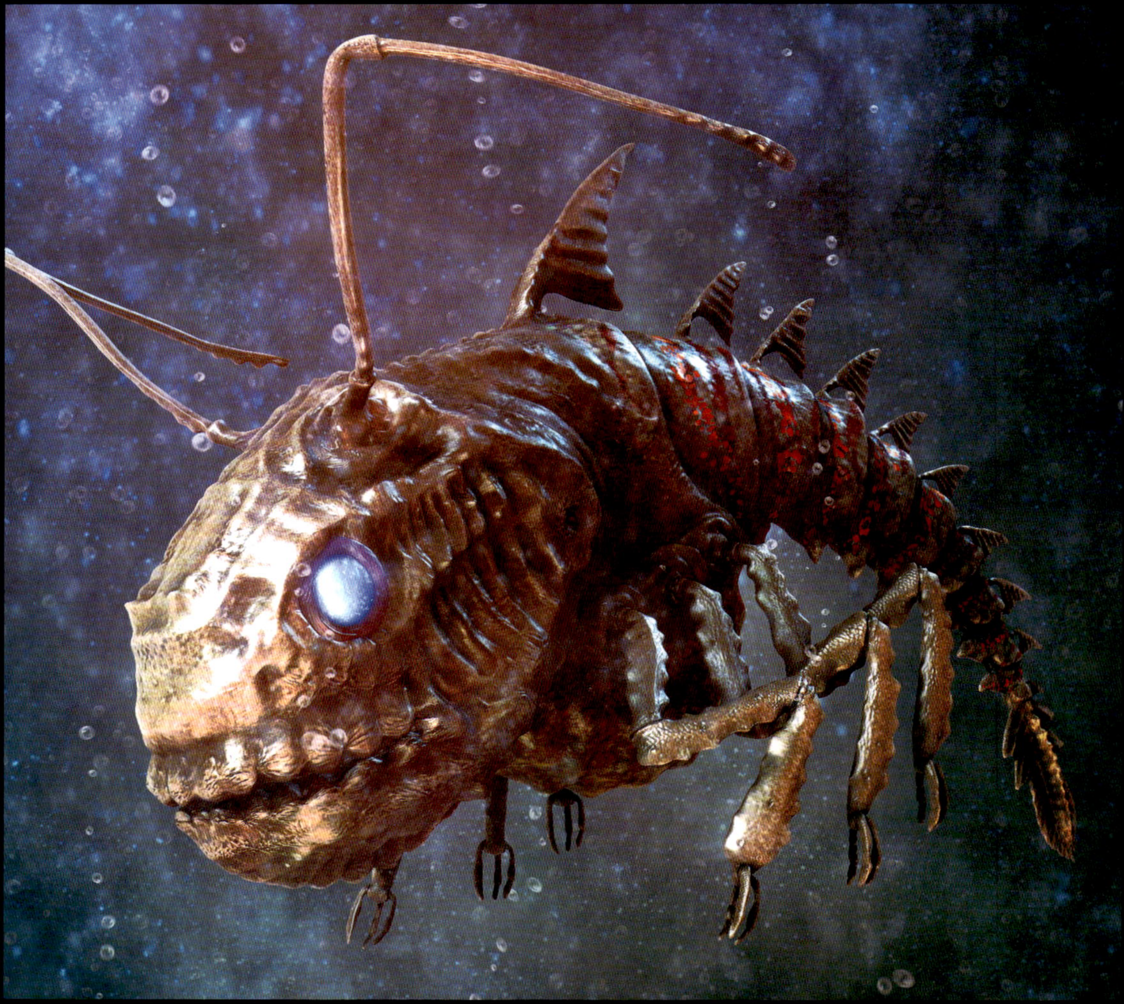

Alien Shrimp
SoftimageIXSI, Maya, Mudbox, ZBrush
Nick Gizelis, GREECE
[left]

Hanuman
Maya, ZBrush, Photoshop
Monsit Jangariyawong, THAILAND
[right]

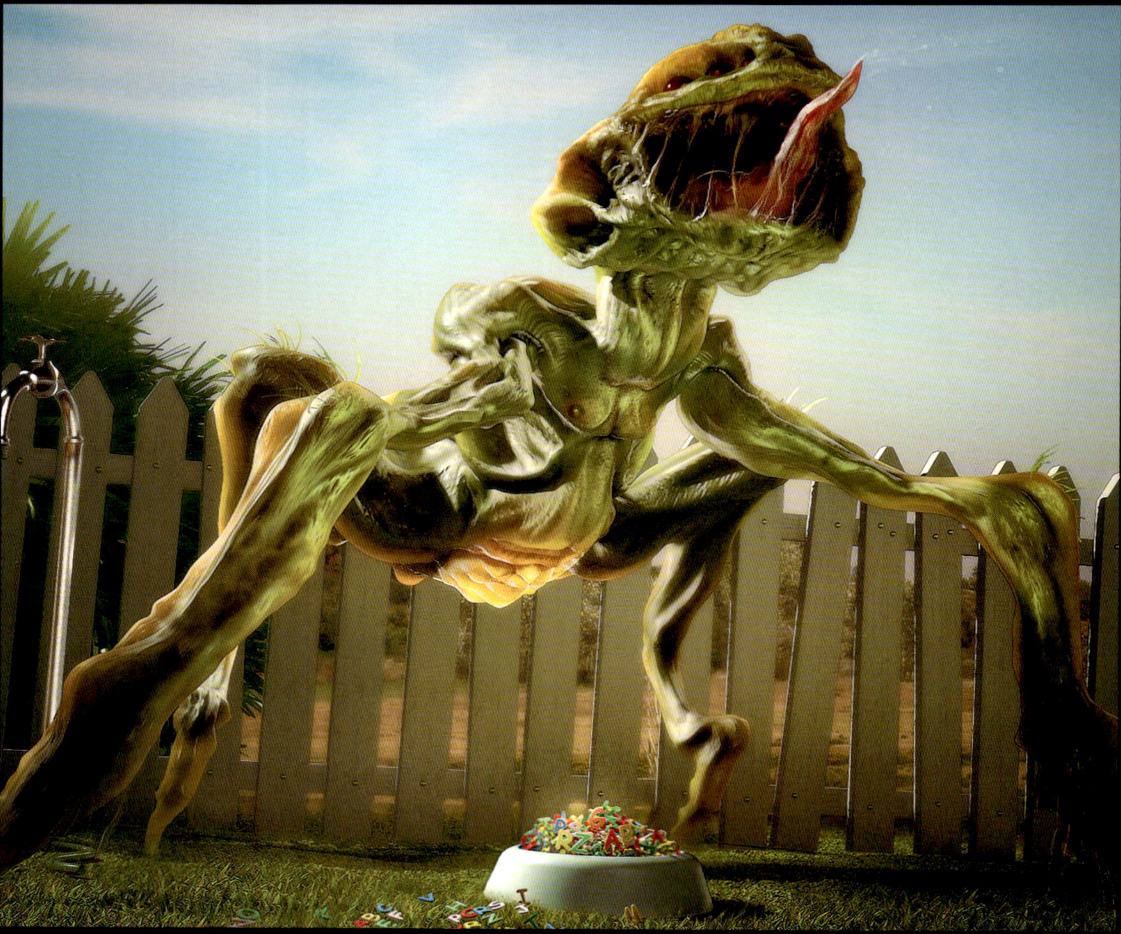

My Suburban Pet
3ds Max, ZBrush, Photoshop, mental ray
Roy Stein, GREAT BRITAI
[left]

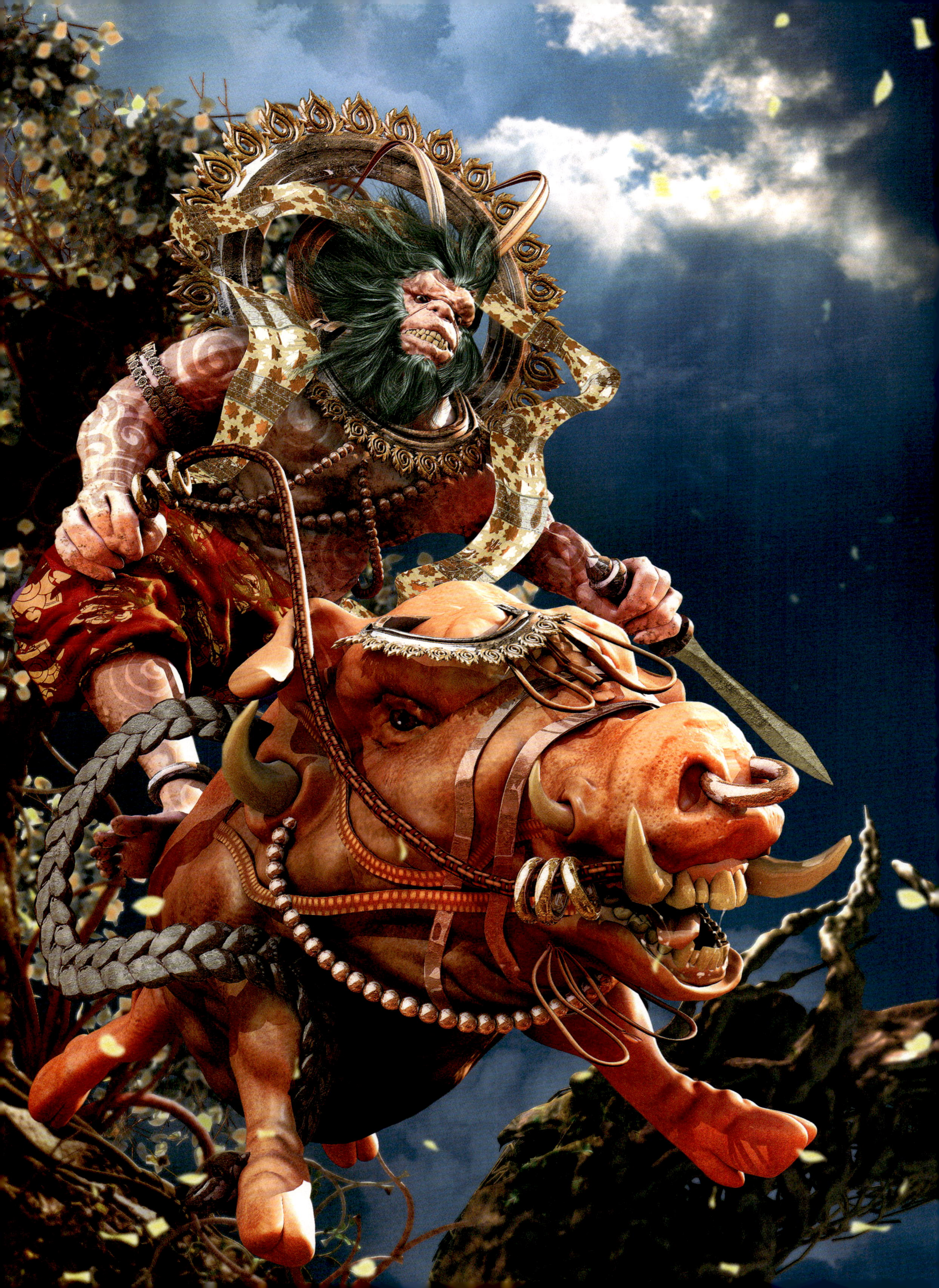

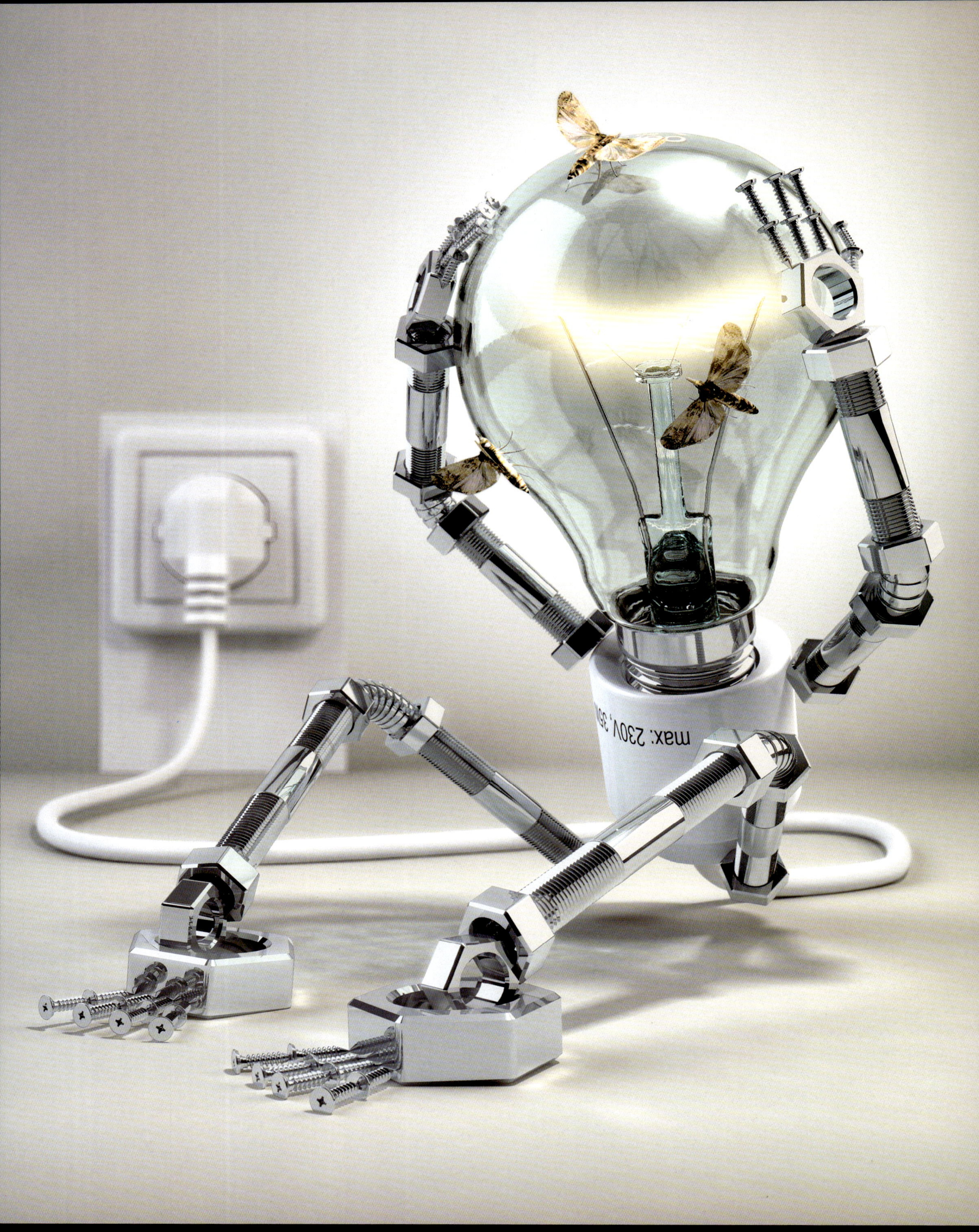

Master

Robotic/Cyborg

Selfillumination 2
3ds Max, mental ray, Photoshop, Rhino
Andre Kutscherauer, GERMANY

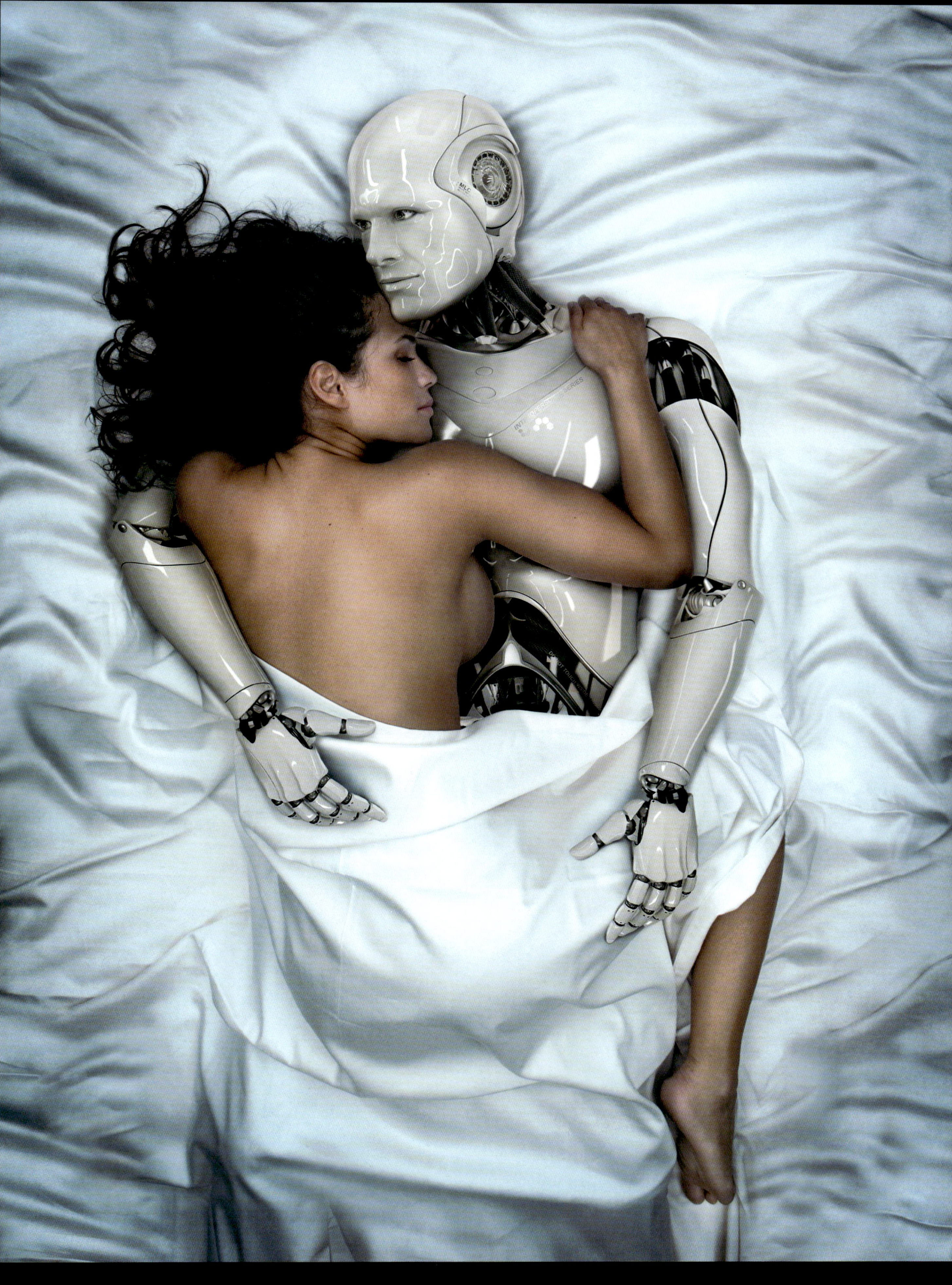

Personal Robot 03
3ds Max, Photoshop
Franz Steiner, Blutsbrueder Design,
GERMANY

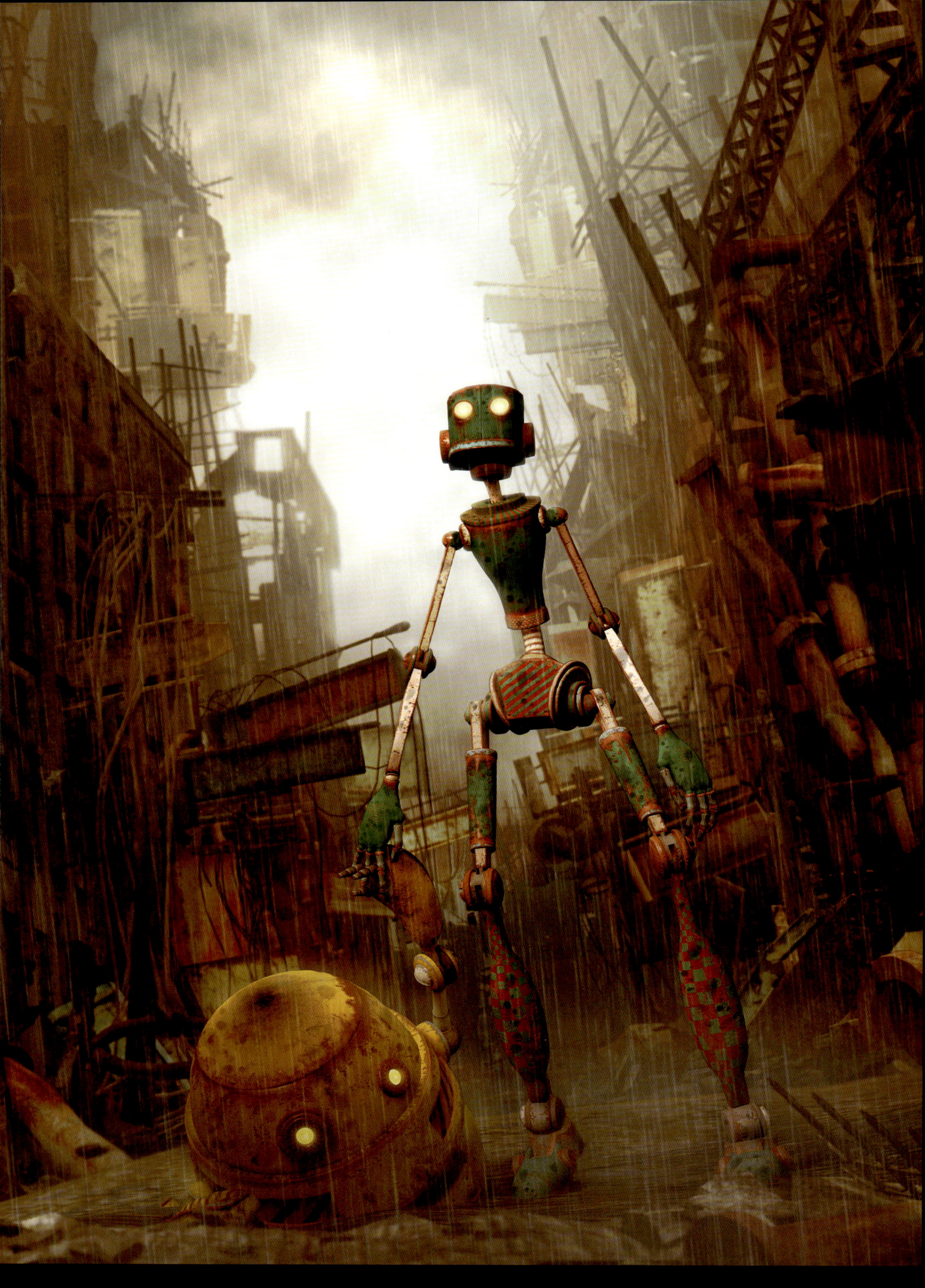

Excellence

Robotic/Cyborg

Watchers
Maya, Photoshop
Ruidan Lv, Beijing Film Academy,
CHINA

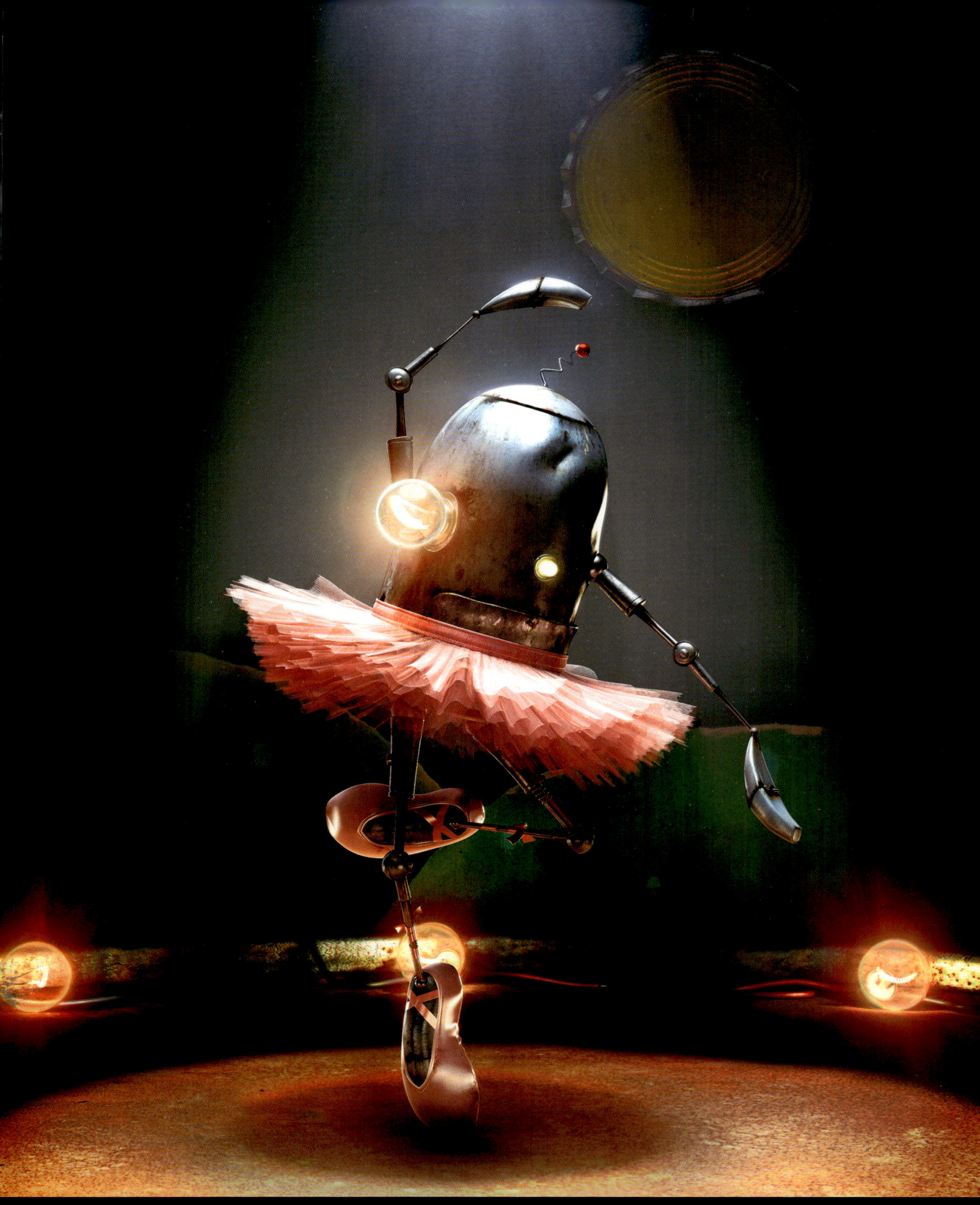

Ballet-bot
3ds Max, Photoshop, V-Ray
Alex Jefferies, GREAT BRITAIN

Excellence
Robotic/Cyborg

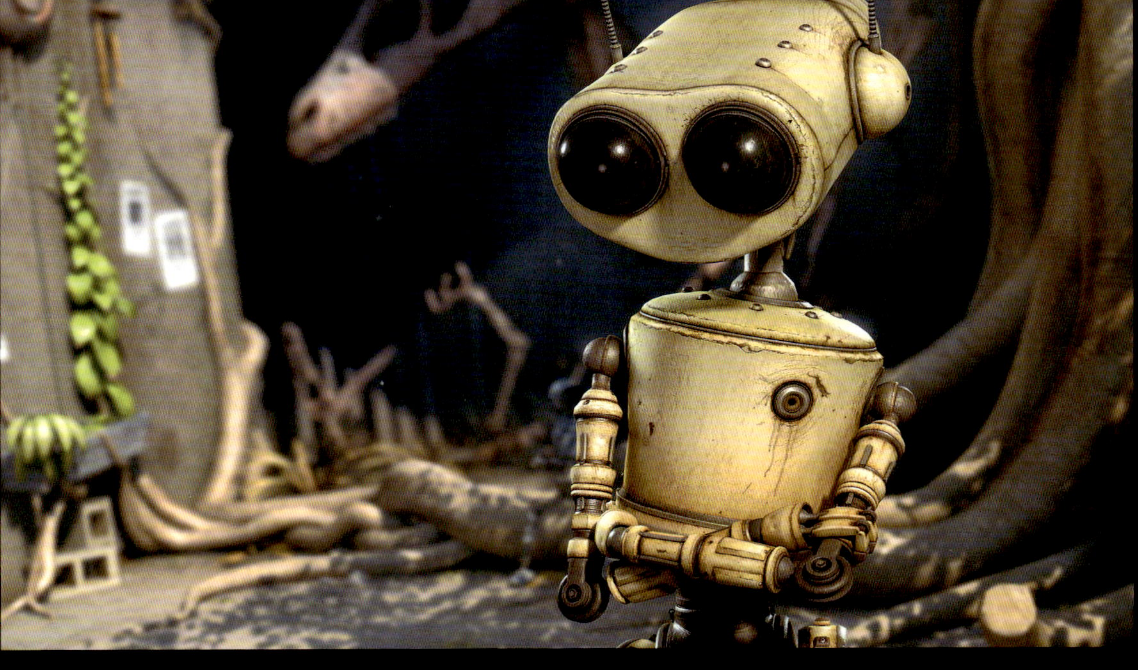

Nerm
3ds Max, V-Ray, Photoshop
Chris Wilson, USA
[left]

Dr. Grordbort: Automaitre D (Automated Man)
Maya, Photoshop
Client: Weta Workshop
Modeling: Tim Gibson
Greg Broadmore, Weta Workshop, NEW ZEALAND
[right]

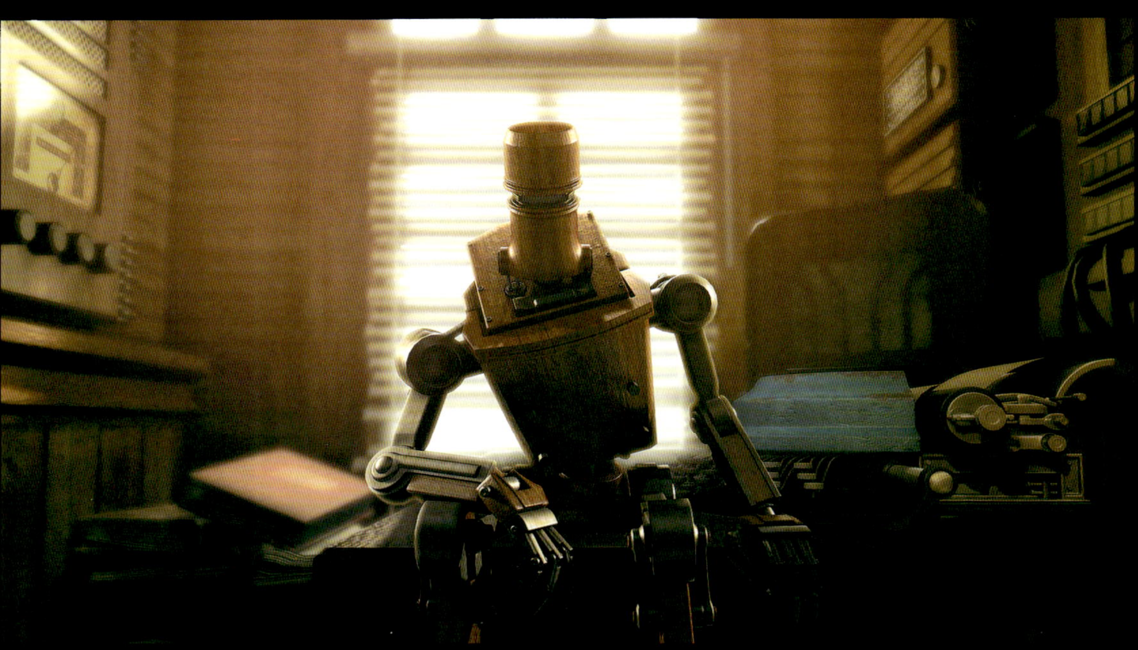

Philosopher 3
Maya, Shake, Photoshop
Tey ChengChan, SINGAPORE
[left]

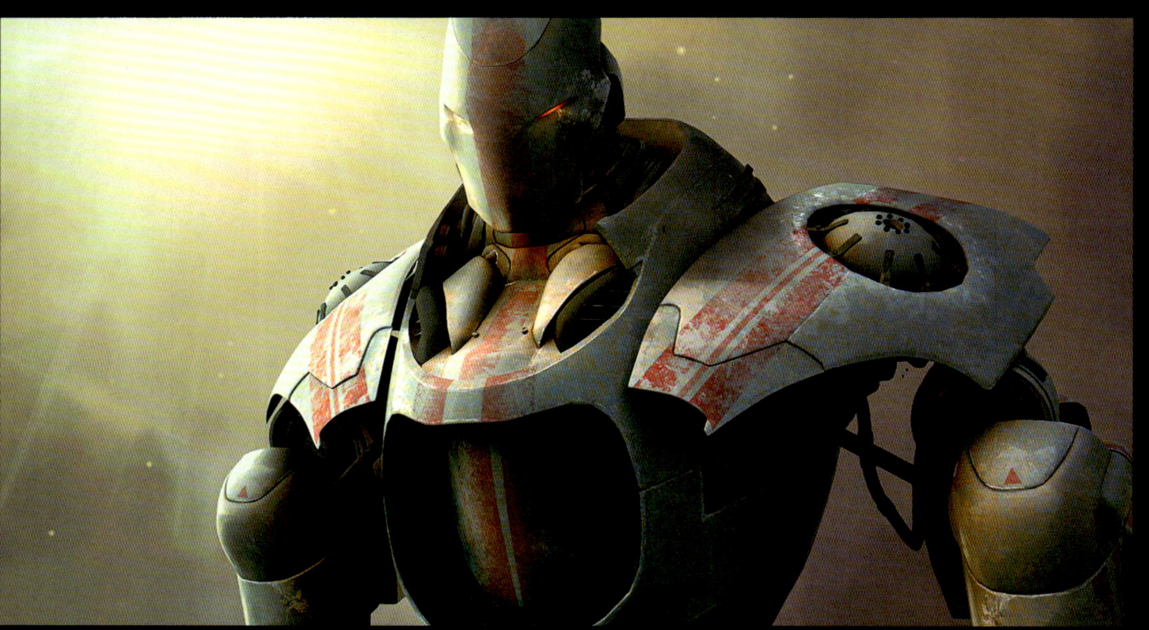

The Singularity
3ds Max, Photoshop
Mehran Khan, ittrango, PAKISTAN
[left]

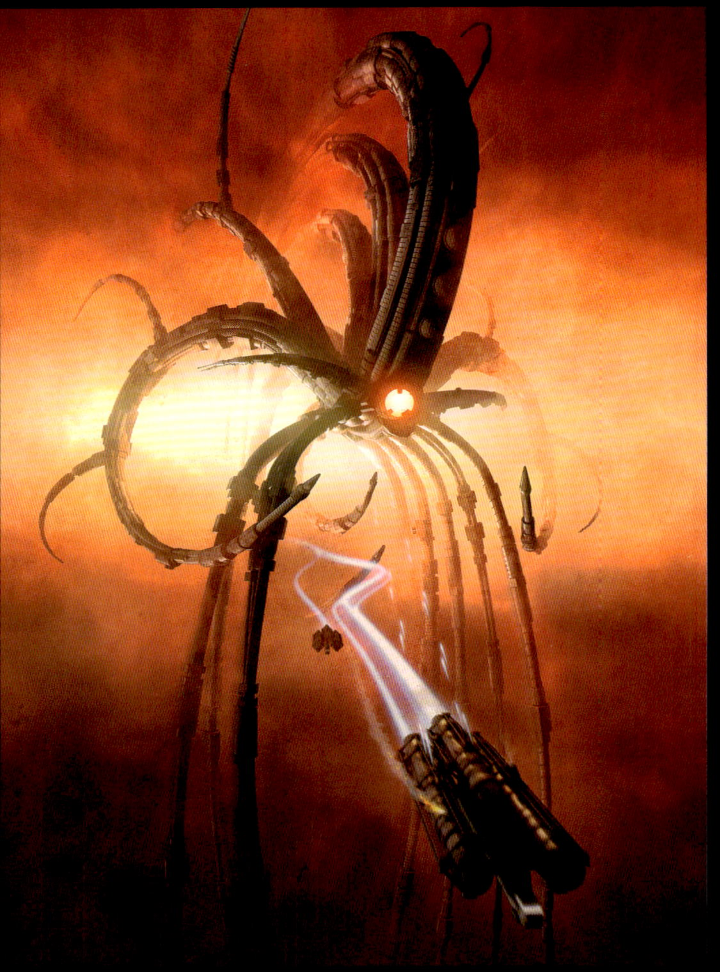

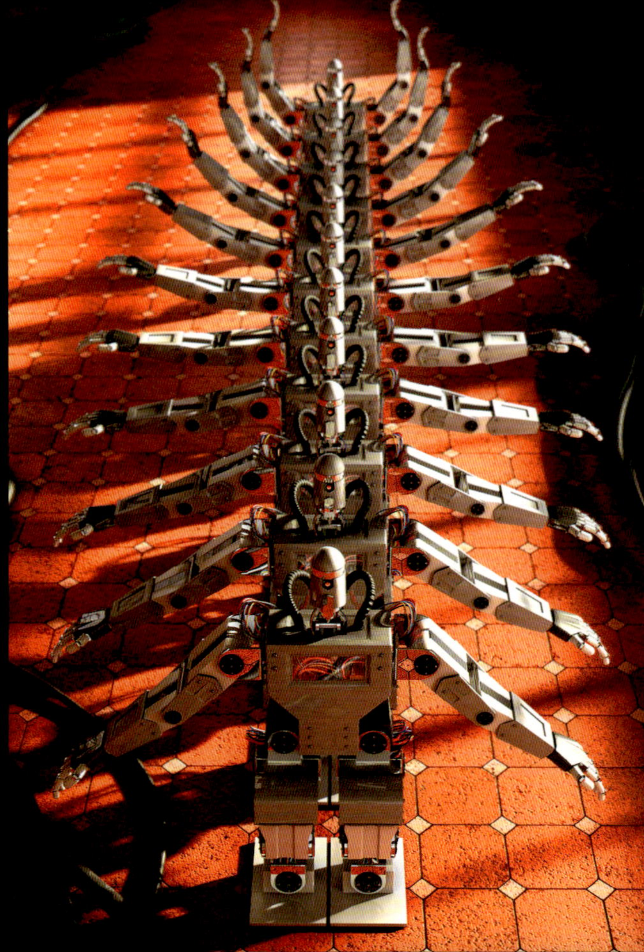

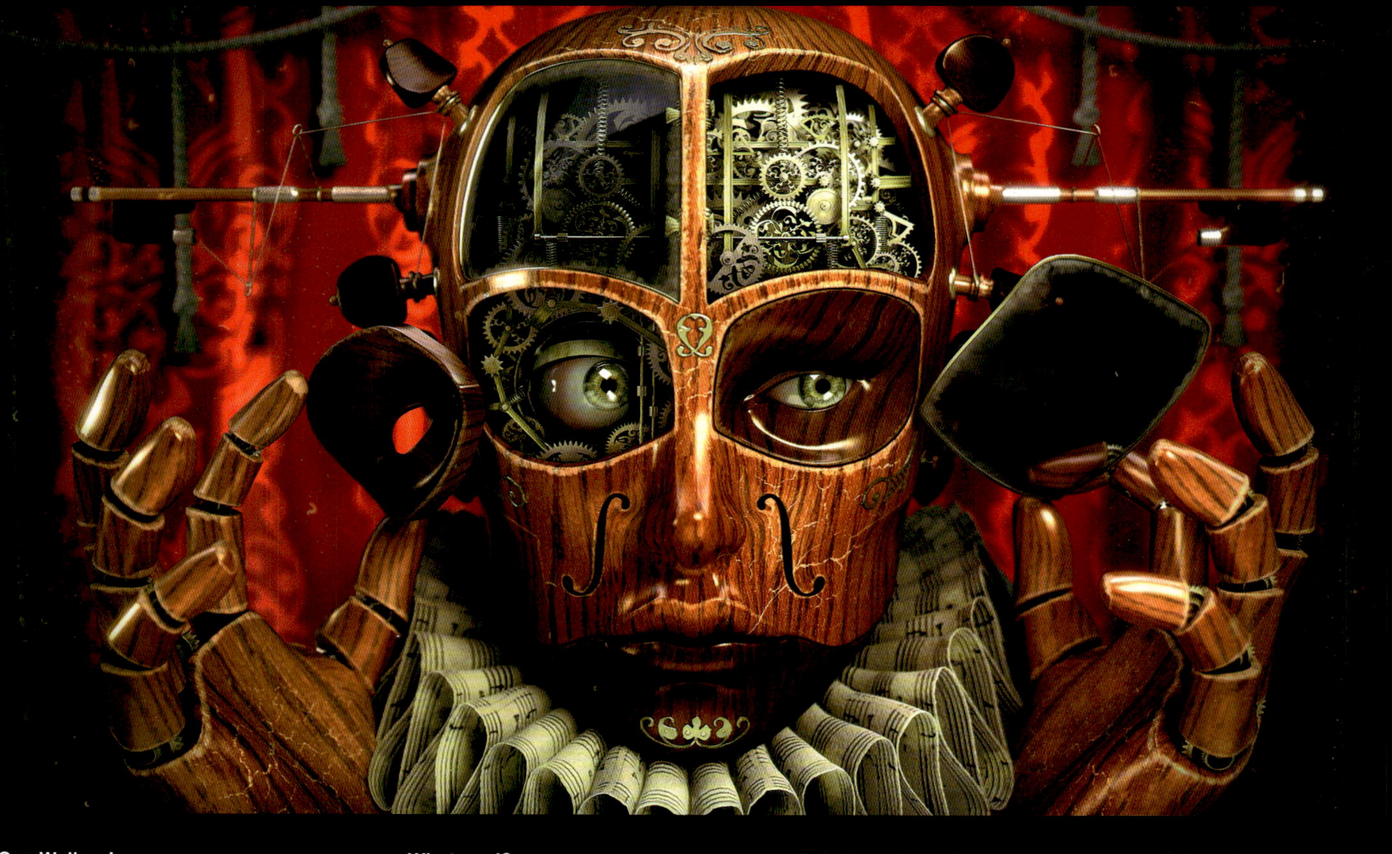

Gas Walker I
3ds Max, Brazil r/s, Photoshop
Neil Blevins,
USA
[top]

What am I?
3ds Max, Photoshop, V-Ray
Balázs Pápay,
HUNGARY
[above]

Roboticized Rhythm
Maya, Photoshop
Rui Xu, USA
[top]

Robot Rock
3ds Max, ZBrush,
Photoshop, mental ray
Jonathan Simard, CANADA
[right]

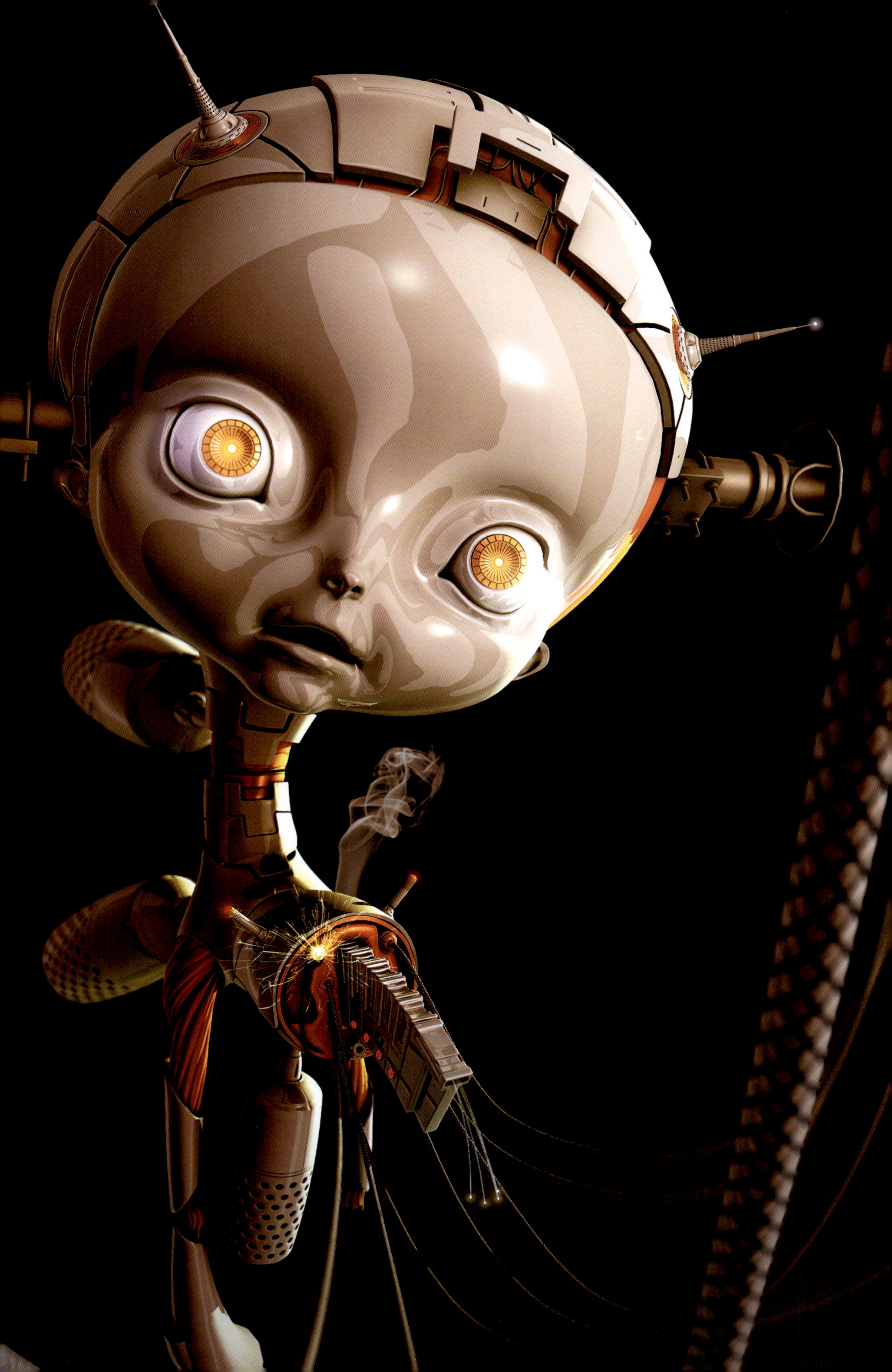

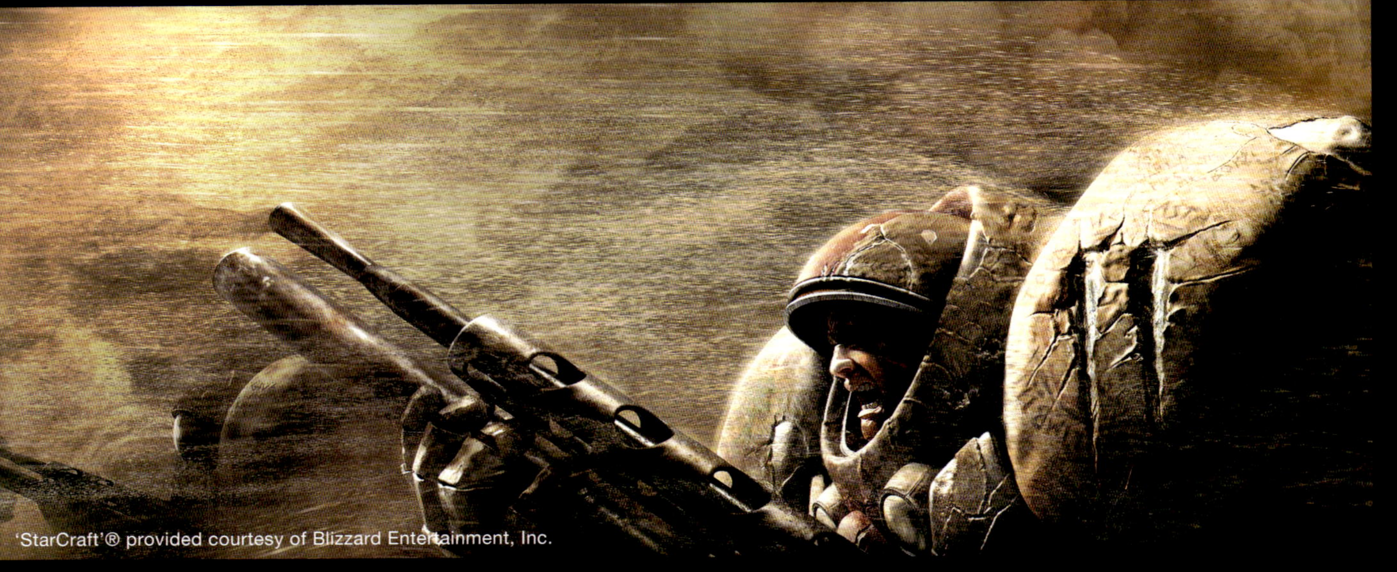

'StarCraft'® provided courtesy of Blizzard Entertainment, Inc.

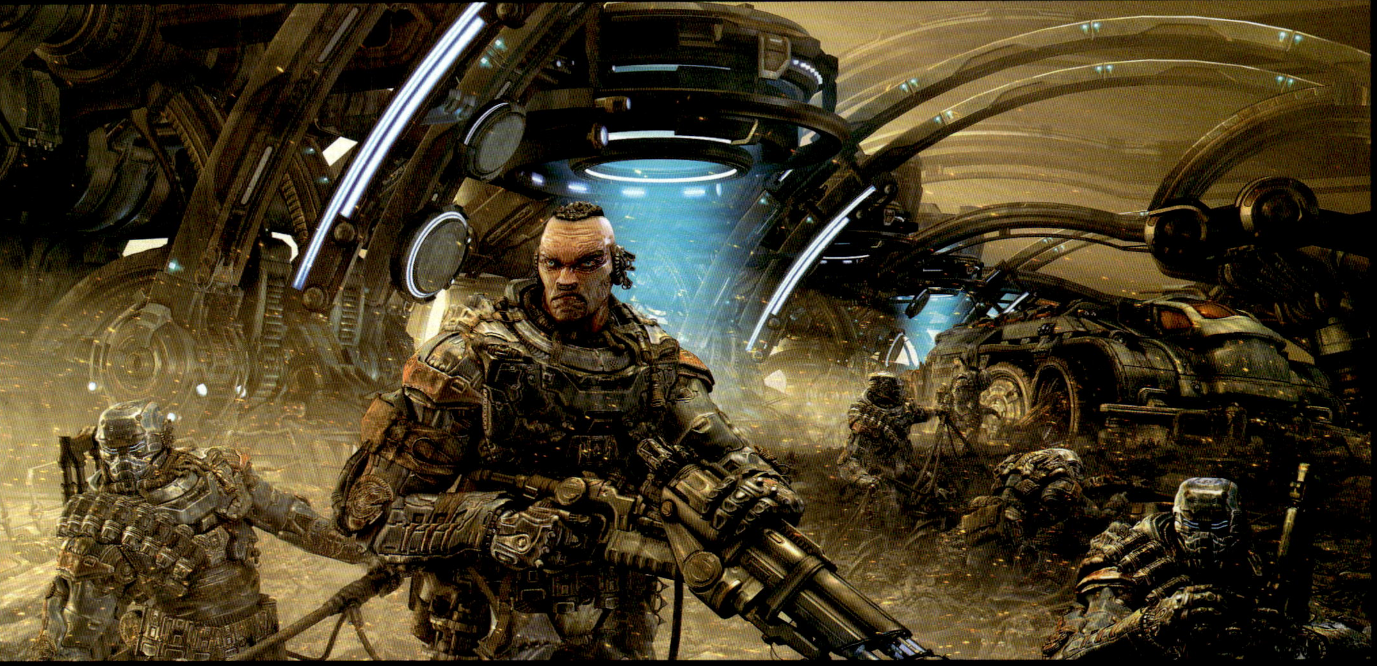

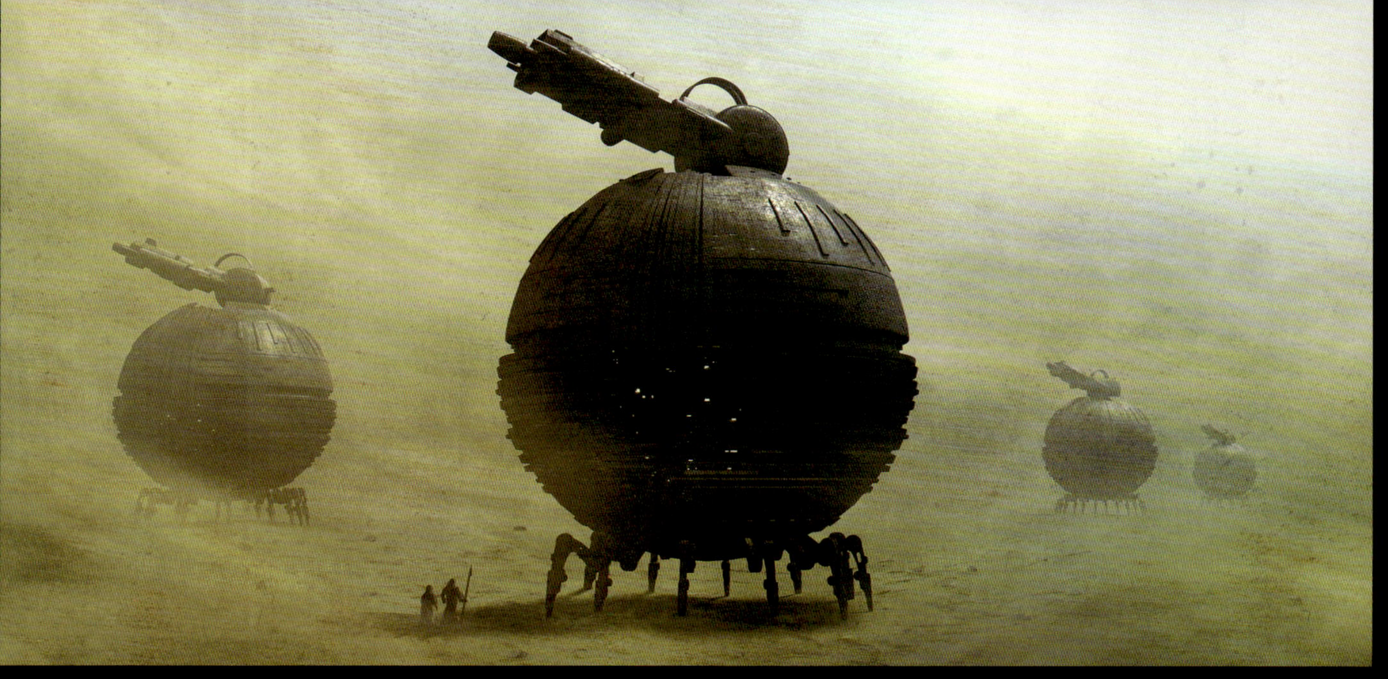

Sunday afternoon at Augustgrad
3ds Max, Photoshop, V-Ray, ZBrush
Inspired by: Blizzard Entertainment's 'Starcraft Terran'
David Levy, snowball I VFX, ISRAEL
[left]

Cyclone interceptor
3ds Max, V-Ray, Photoshop
Miao He, GERMANY
[right]

Storm is coming
3ds Max, Photoshop
Jan Harcarik, SLOVAKIA
[left]

Planetary Defense
3ds Max, Brazil r/s, Photoshop
Neil Blevins, USA
[left]

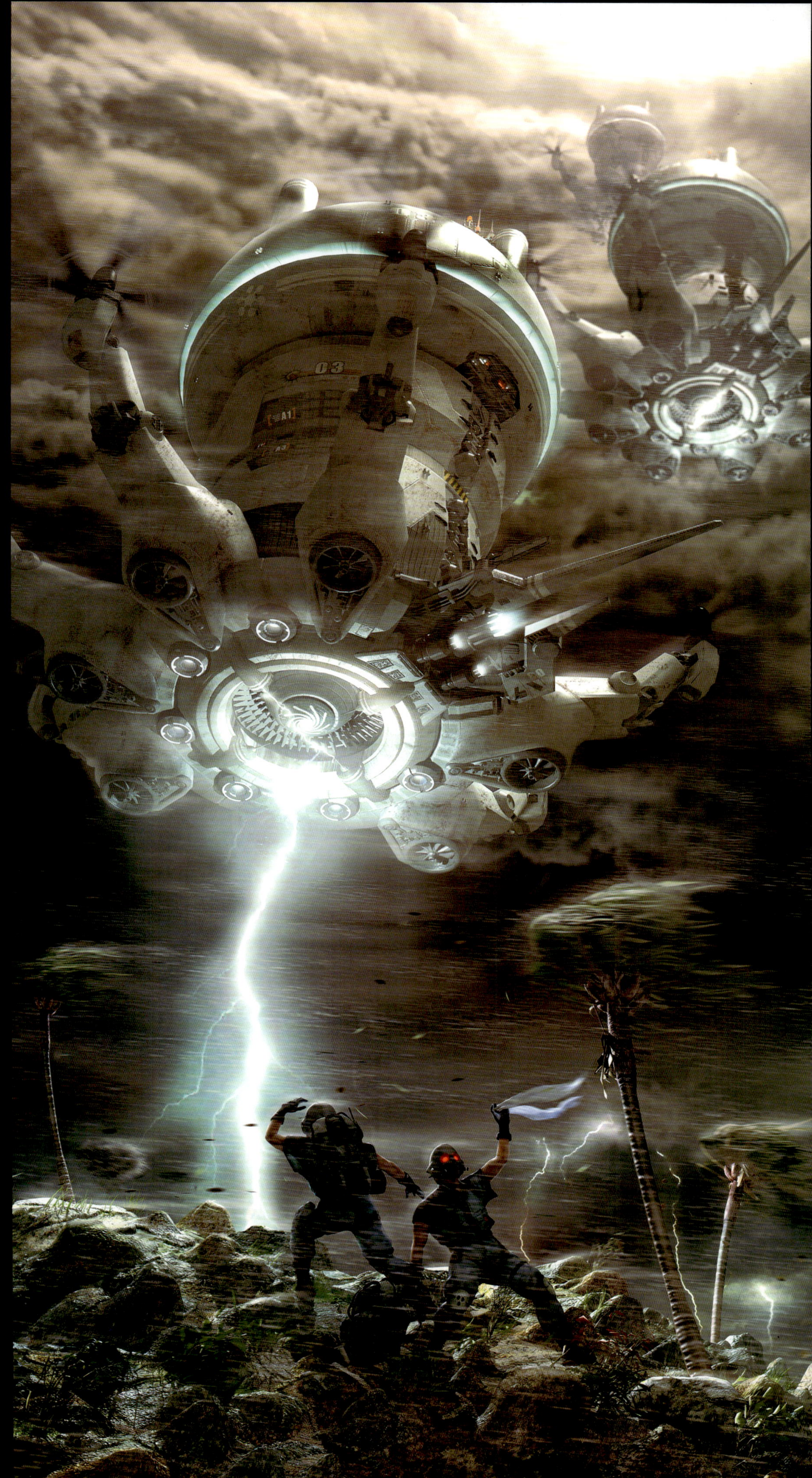

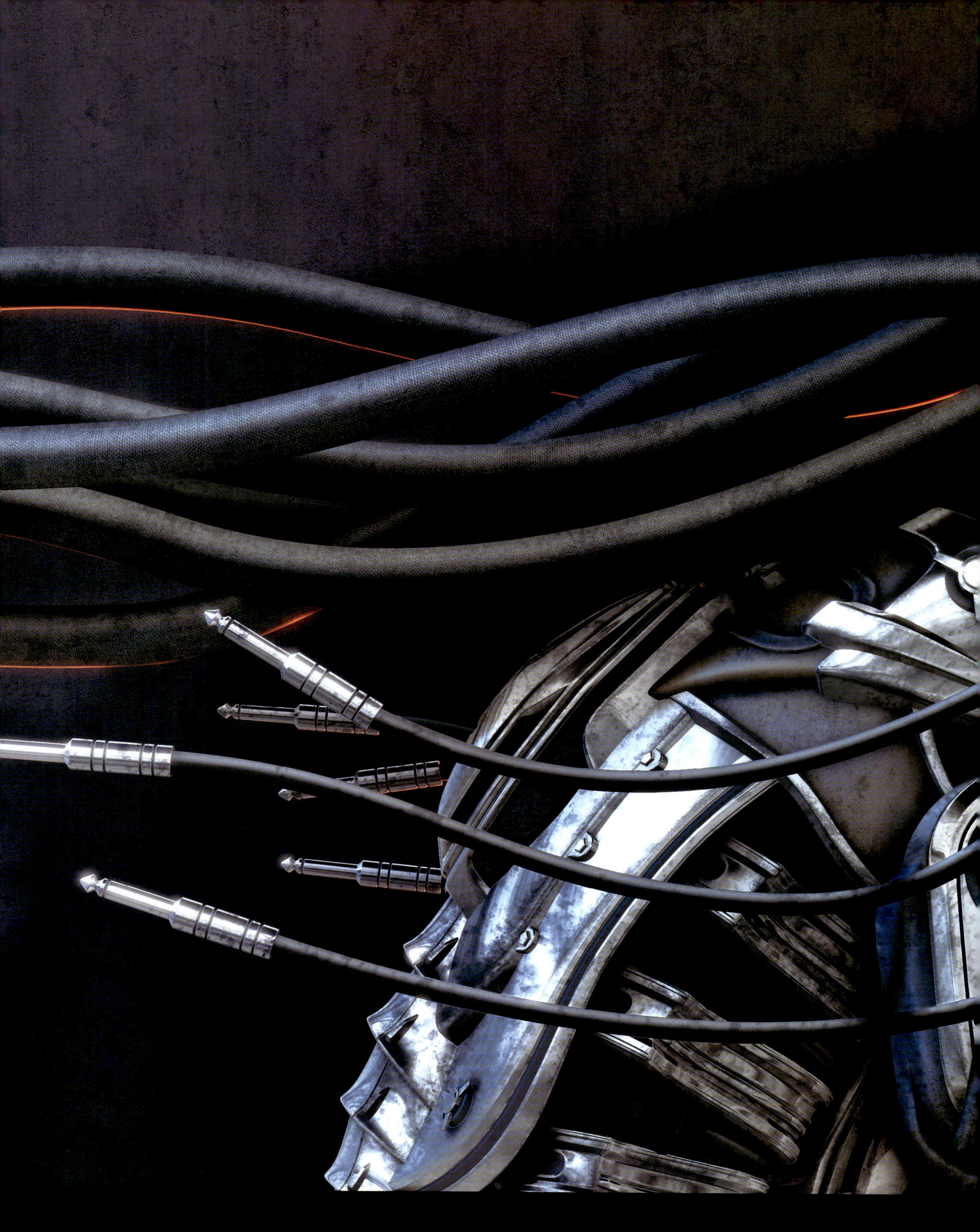

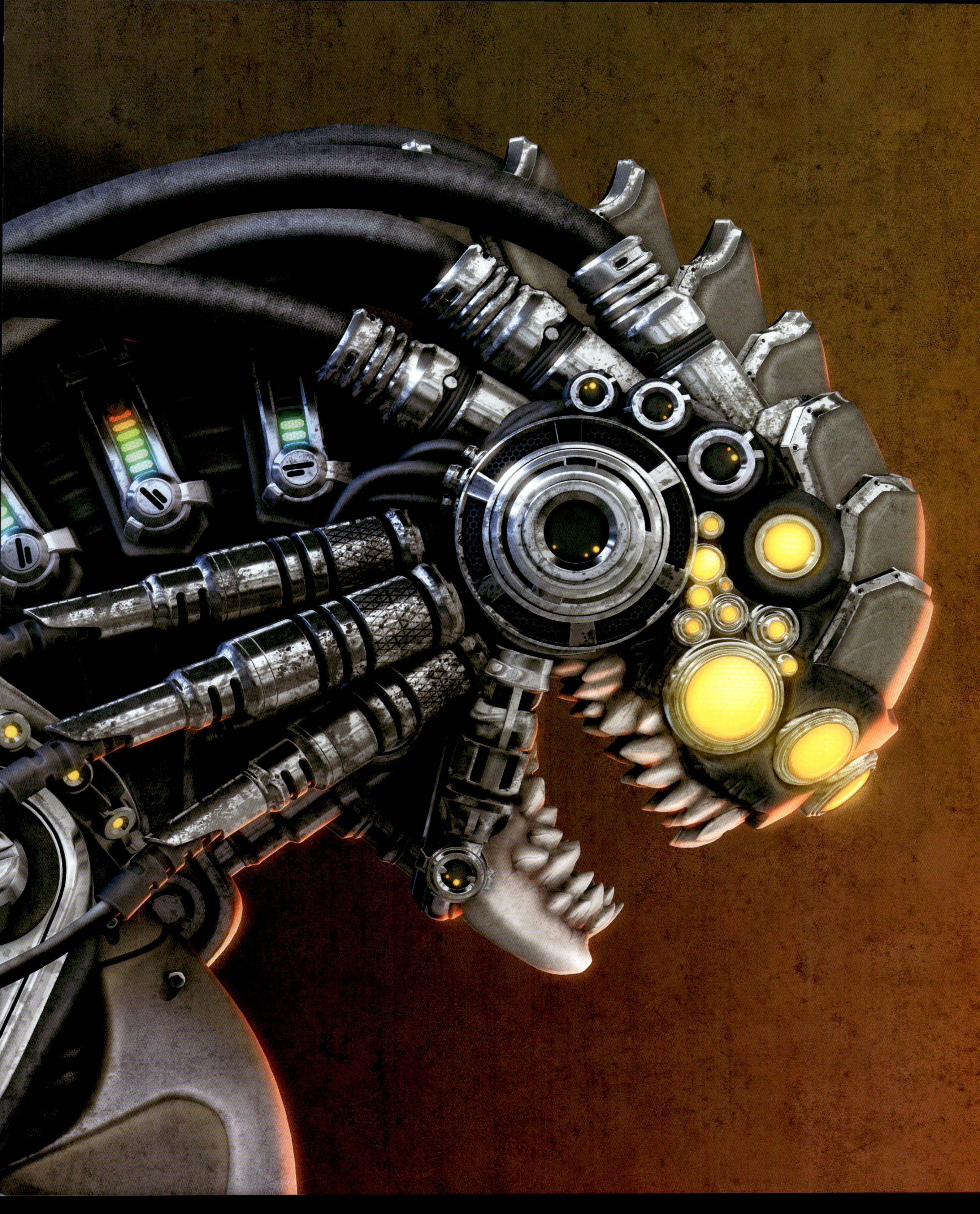

2084
3ds Max, Photoshop
Mark Van Haitsma, USA

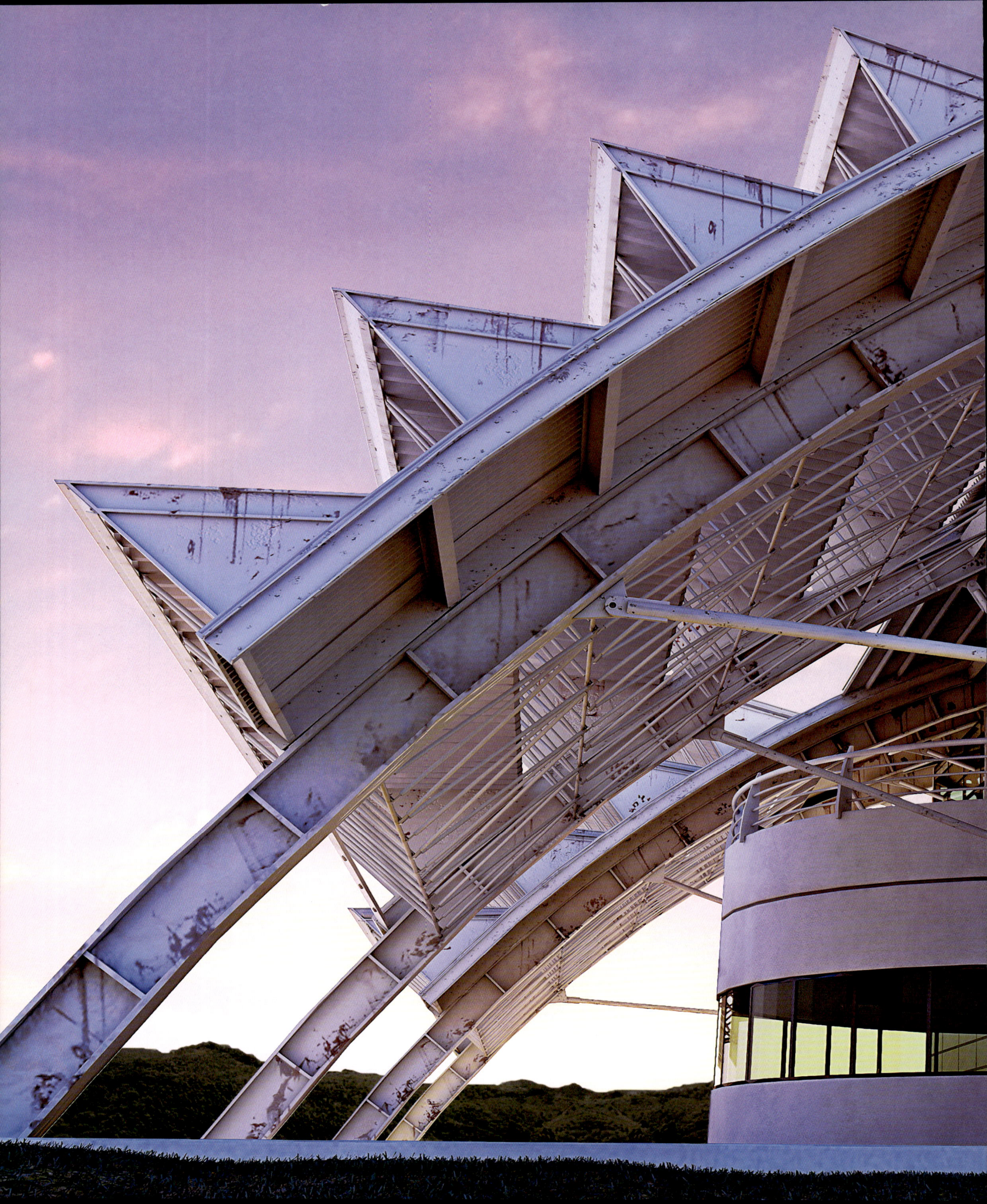

Master

Architecture Exterior (Public)

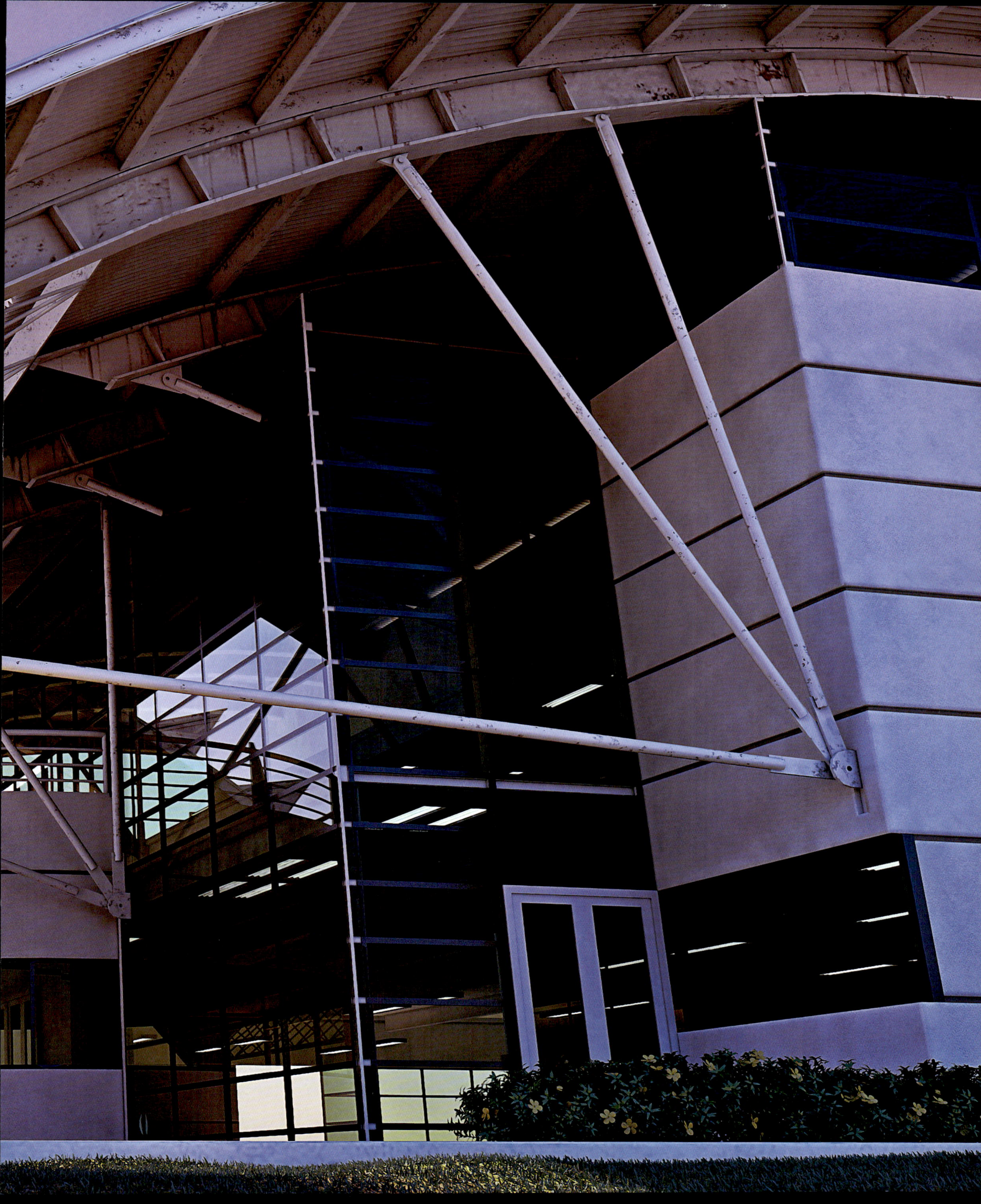

Homage to Sidonio Porto
AutoCAD, 3ds Max,
mental ray, Photoshop
Marcelo Eder, BRAZIL

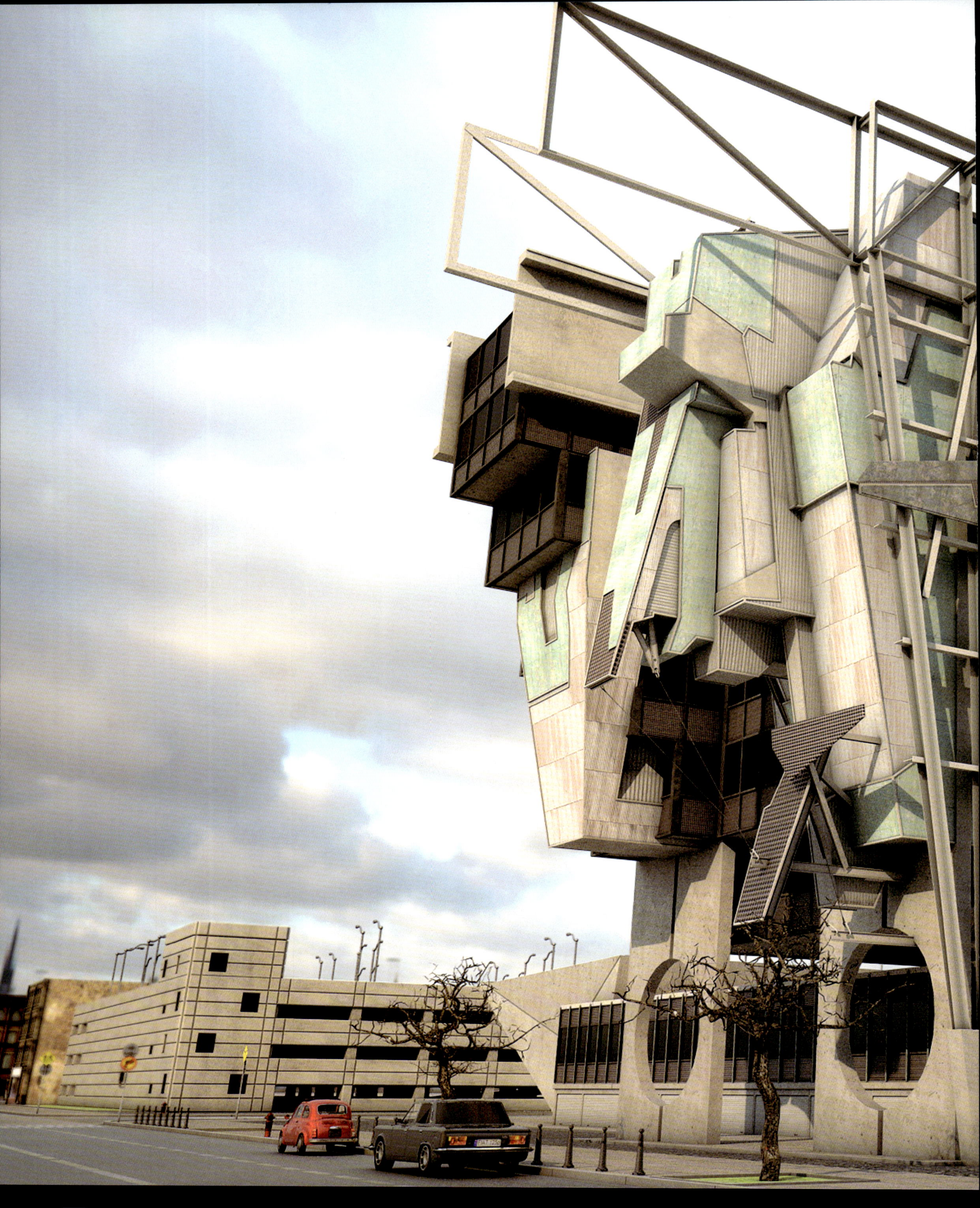

Excellence

Architecture Exterior (Public)

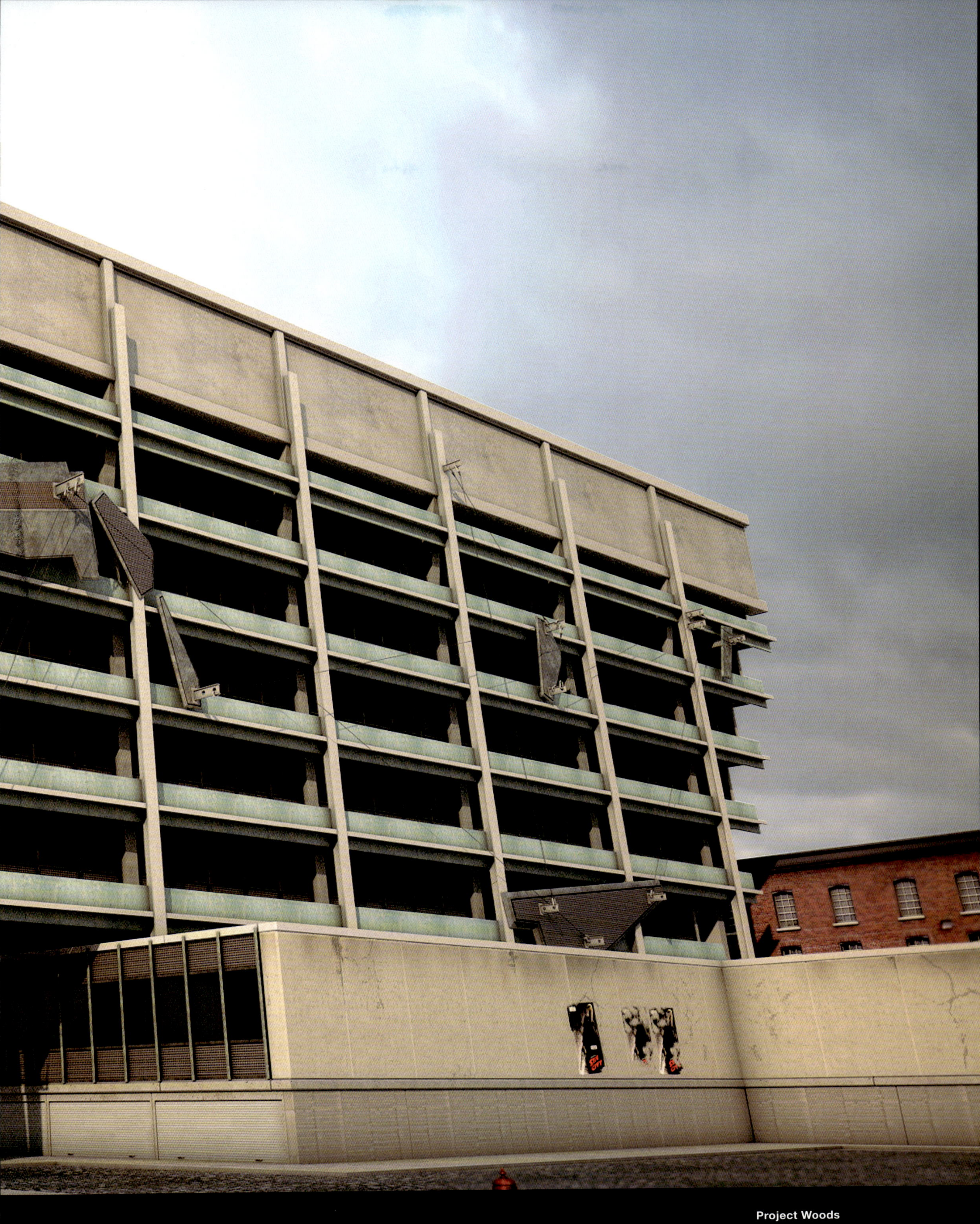

Project Woods
3ds Max
Inspired by: Lebbeus Woods
Carlos Fueyo, Insomnia3d LLC, USA

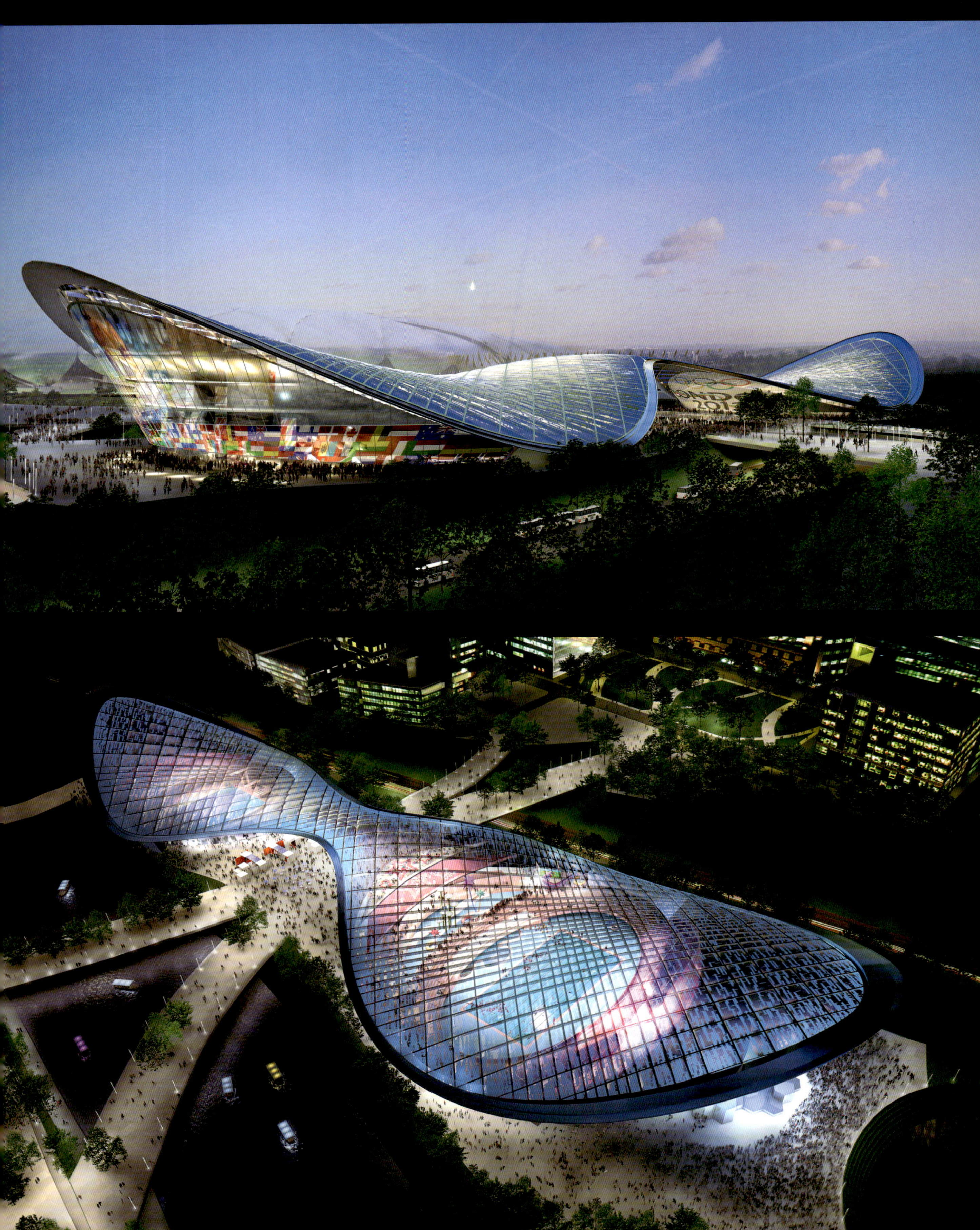

London 2012 Olympic Aquatic Centre
3ds Max, V-Ray, Photoshop
Client: Make Ltd.
GMJ Visualisation, GREAT BRITAIN
[top, above]

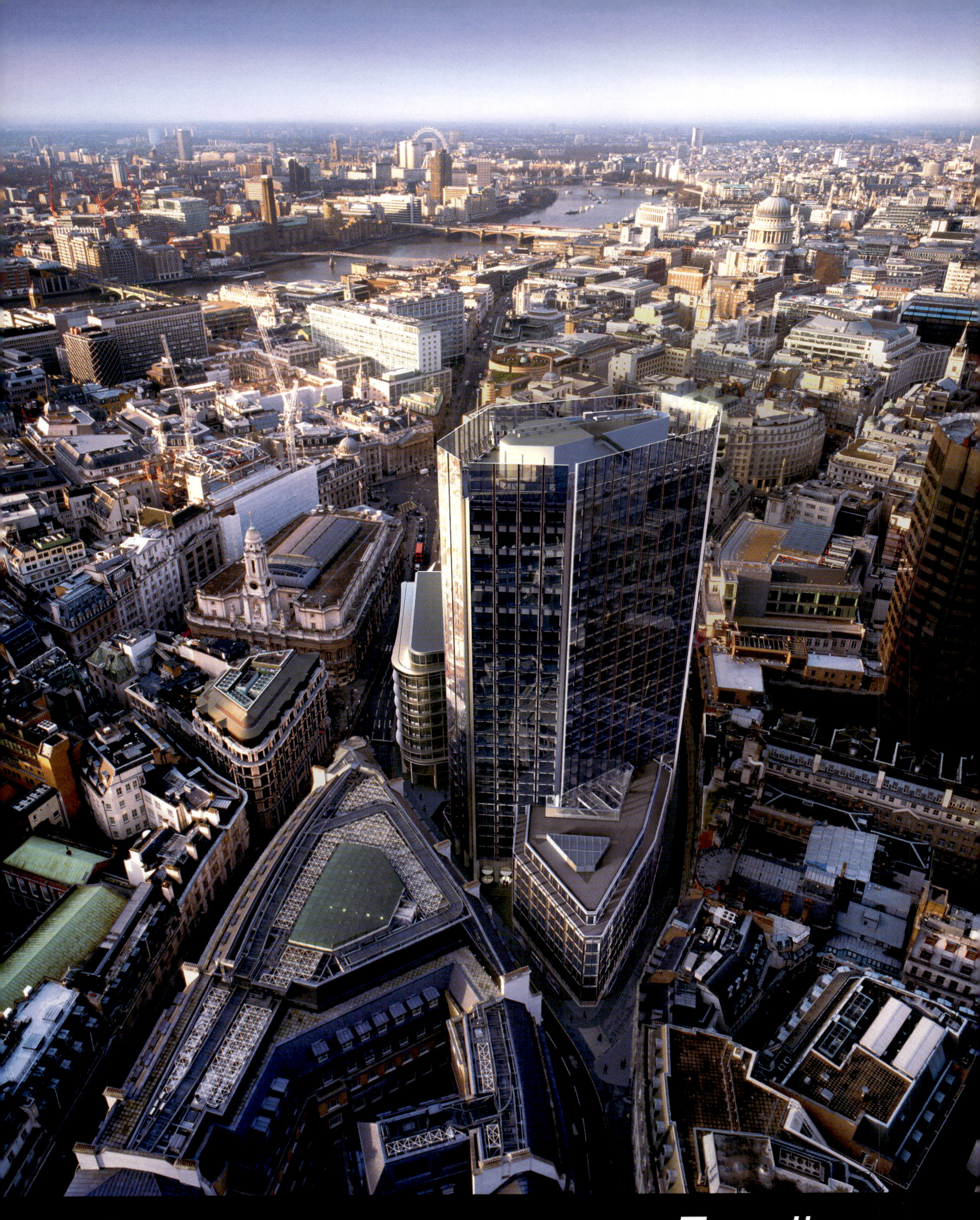

125 Old Broad Street
3ds Max, V-Ray, Photoshop
Client: Hammerson PLC
Mark Glazier and **Paul Ingram**,
Smoothe Ltd., GREAT BRITAIN

Excellence

Architecture Exterior (Public)

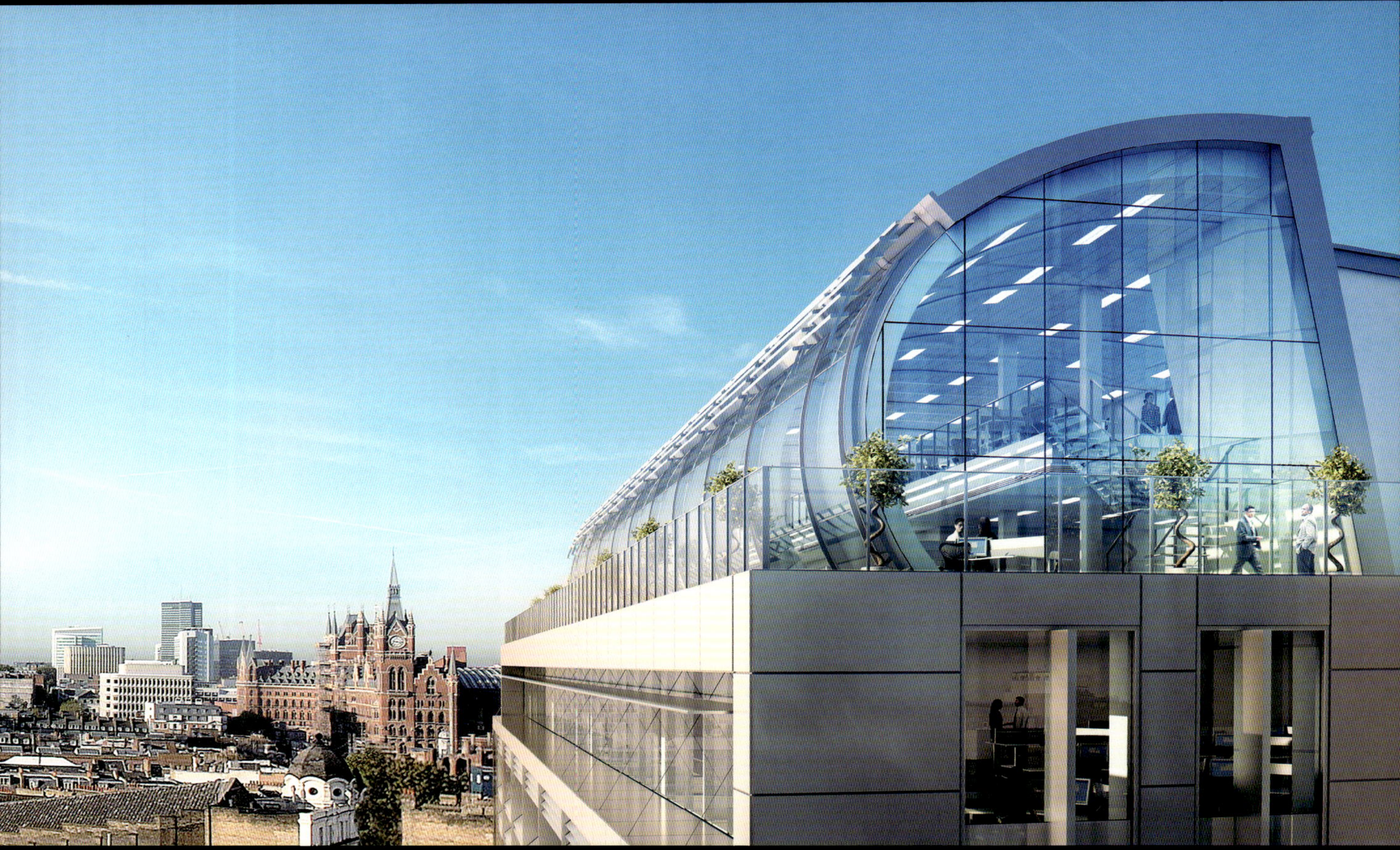

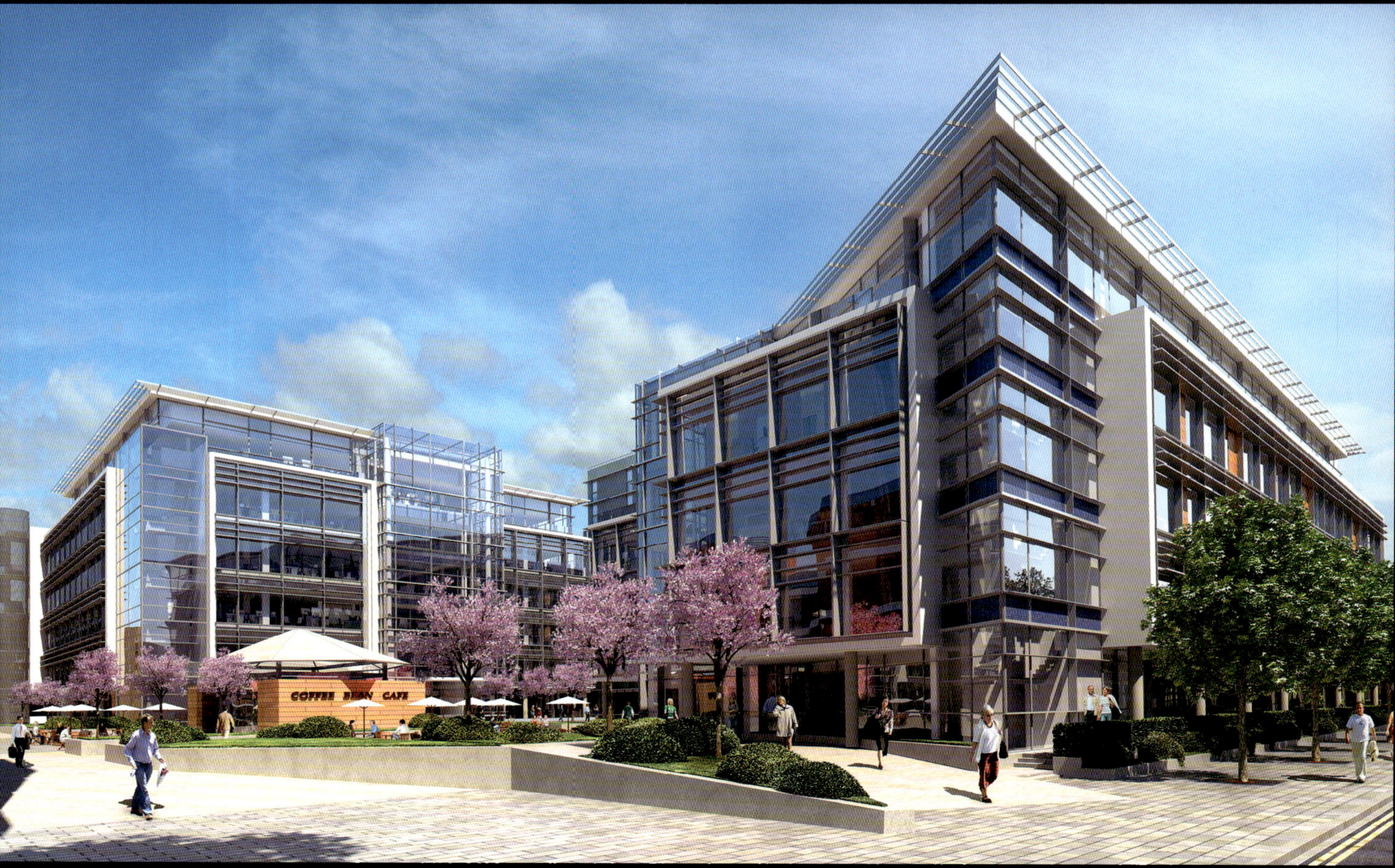

Pentonville Road
3ds Max, V-Ray, Photoshop
John Crighton, Visualisation One Ltd,
GREAT BRITAIN
[top]

No. 51 London Road
3ds Max, V-Ray, Photoshop
Architect: TP Bennett LLP
Troy Pearse, Preconstruct, GREAT BRITAIN
[above]

Duja 2
3ds Max, AutoCAD, Photoshop, V-Ray
Client: His Excellency Nassir Hussain lootah
Maryam Nademi, ZAS Architects, UAE
[right]

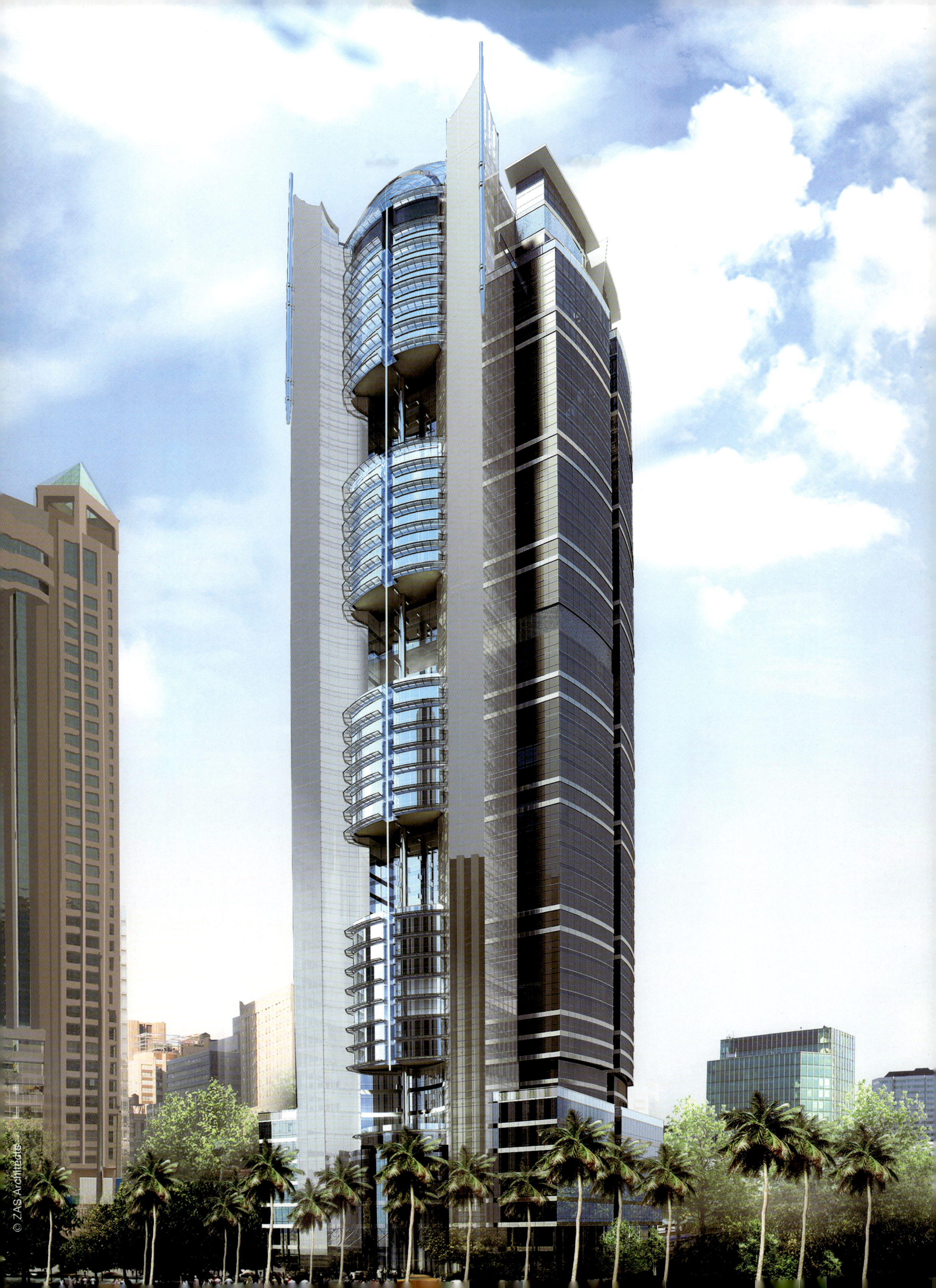

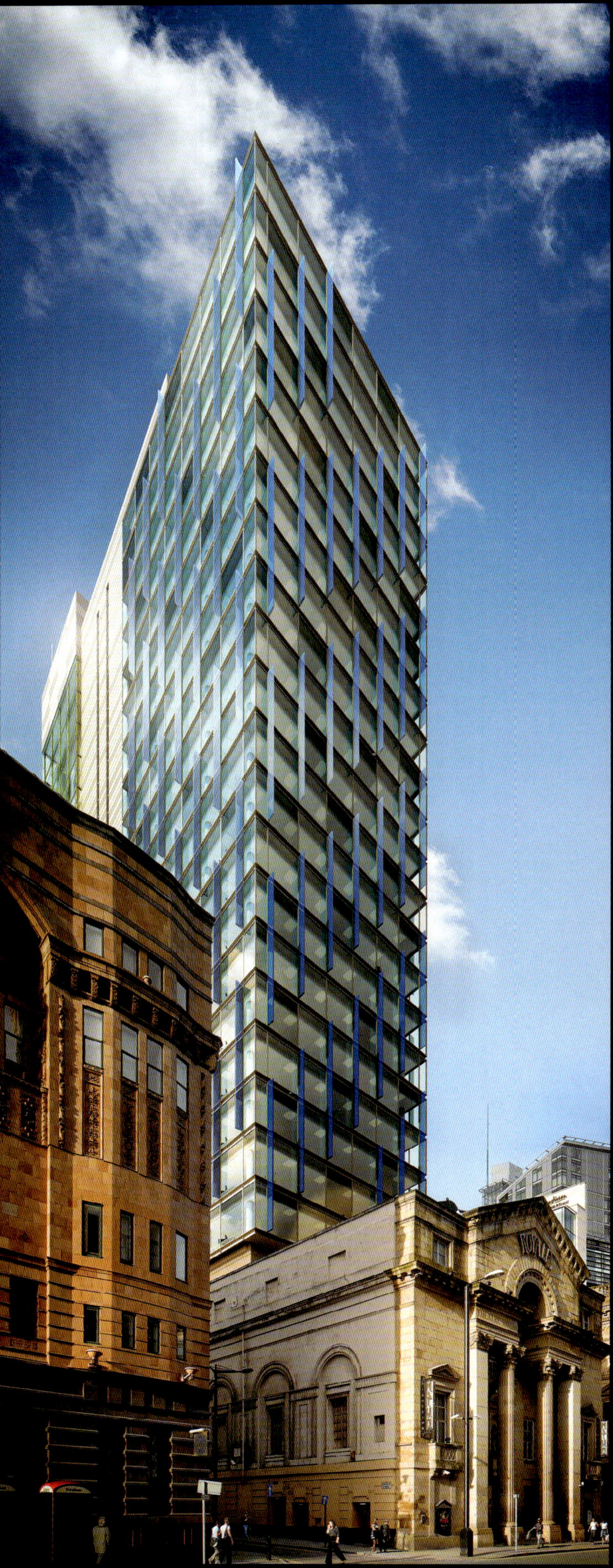

Theatre Royal
3ds Max, V-Ray, Photoshop
John Crawshaw, AHD-Imaging,
GREAT BRITAIN
[above]

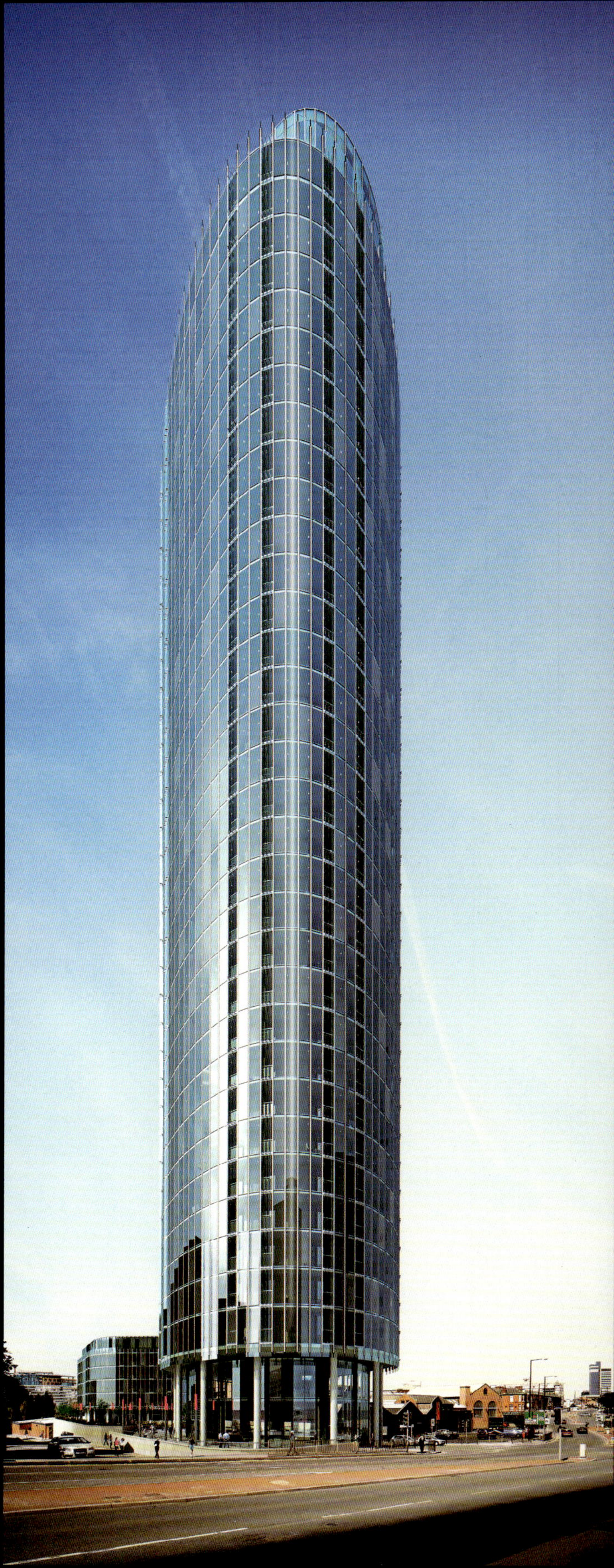

Store Street External Day
3ds Max, V-Ray, Photoshop
Phil Greaves, AHD-Imaging,
GREAT BRITAIN
[above]

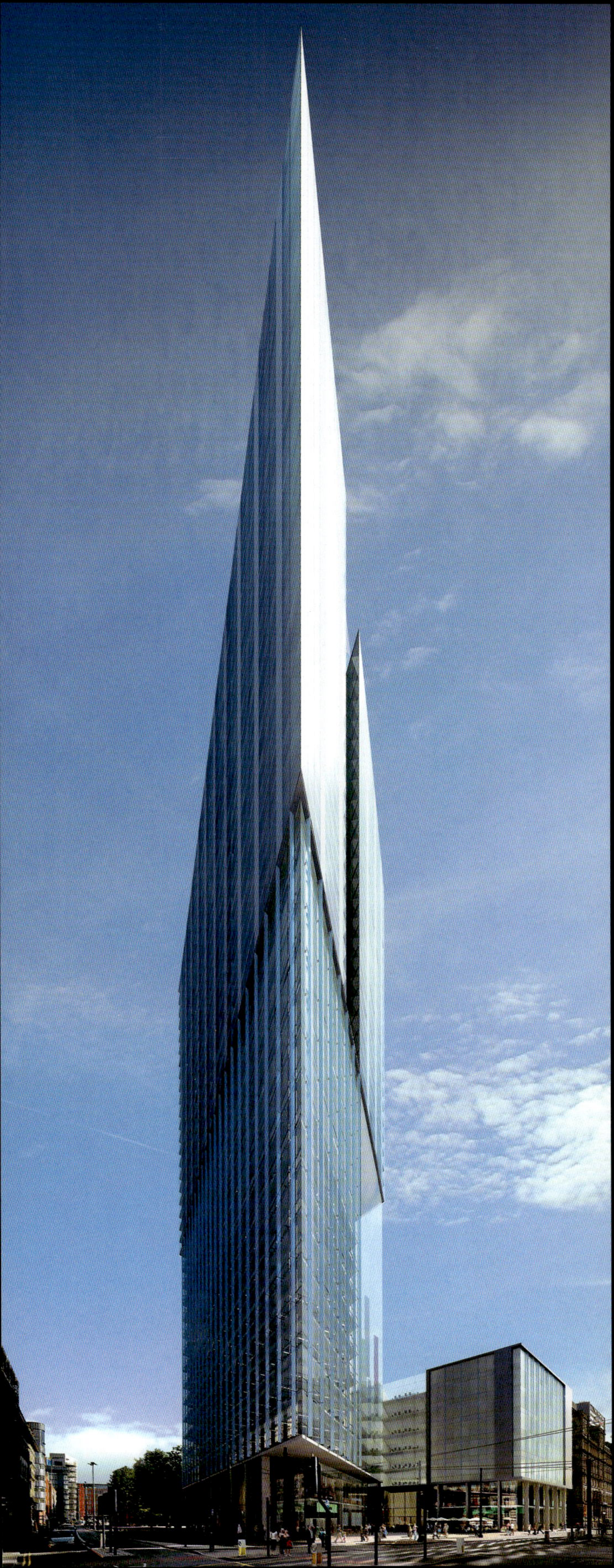

Aytoun Street Day Shot
3ds Max, V-Ray, Photoshop
Matthew Clayton,
AHD-Imaging, GREAT BRITAIN
[above]

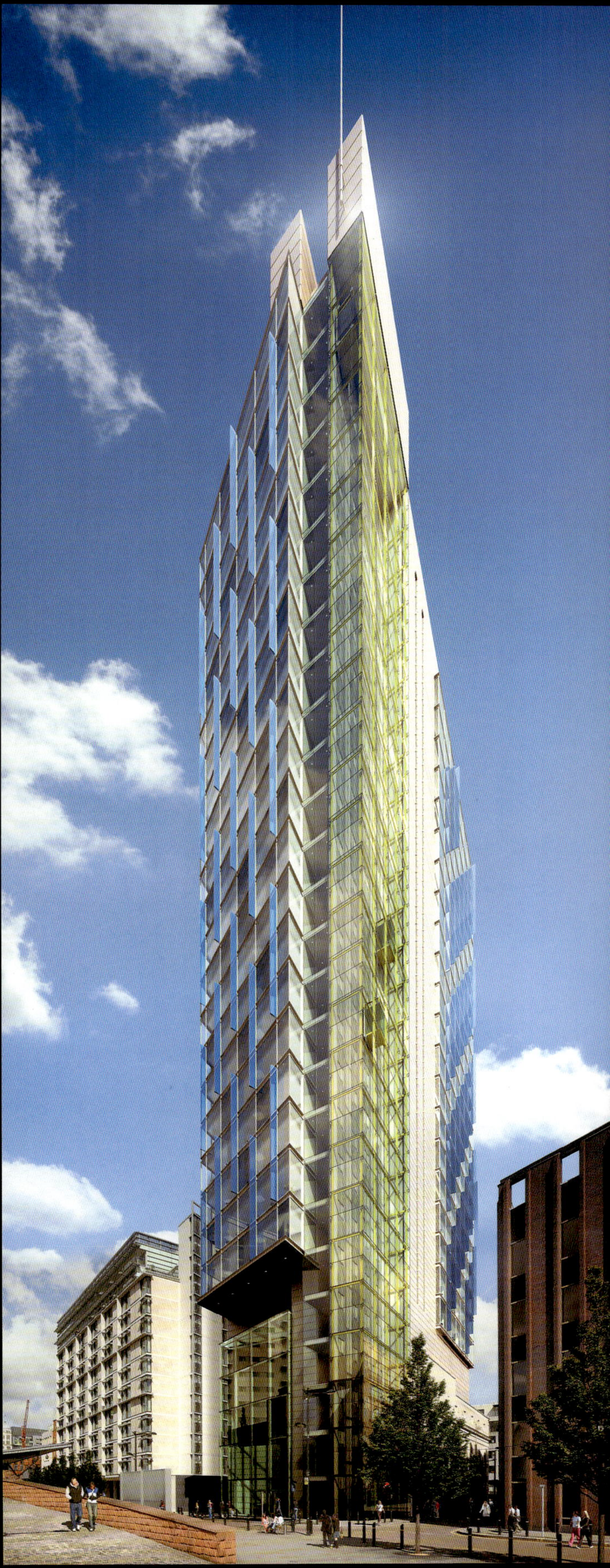

Theatre Royal Tower
3ds Max, V-Ray, Photoshop
Matthew Clayton, AHD-Imaging,
GREAT BRITAIN
[above]

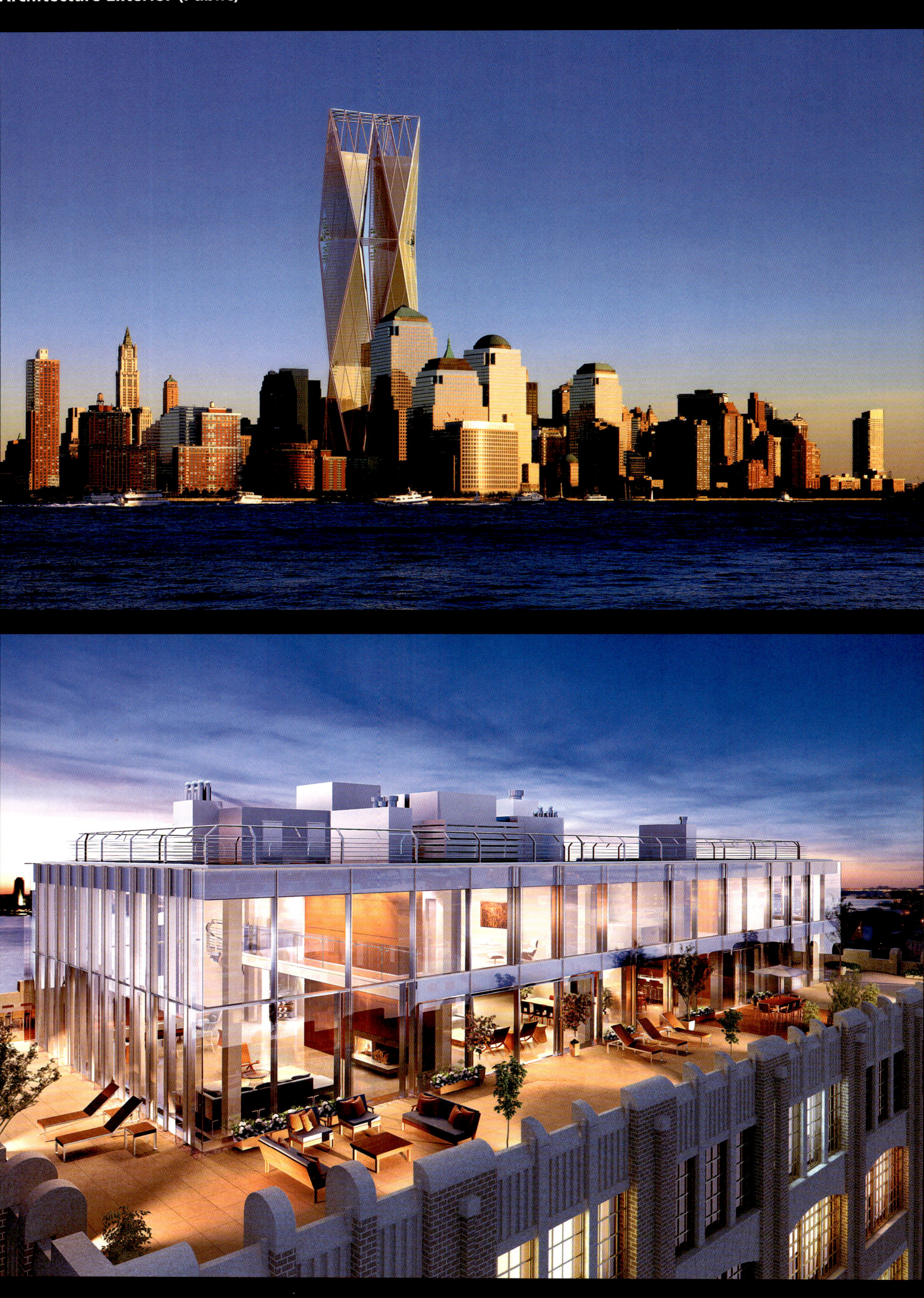

World Trade Center (Dusk)
3ds Max, Photoshop
Architect: Foster and Partners
GMJ Visualisation, GREAT BRITAIN
[left]

Trump SoHo
3ds Max, Photoshop
Client: Bayrock/Sapir Organization
Spine3D, USA
[right]

Skylofts Night Aerial
3ds Max, V-Ray, Photoshop
Client: 145 Hudson Street
Associates, Stanley D. Scott
Lon Grohs and **Victor Erthal**,
Neoscape, Inc., USA
[left]

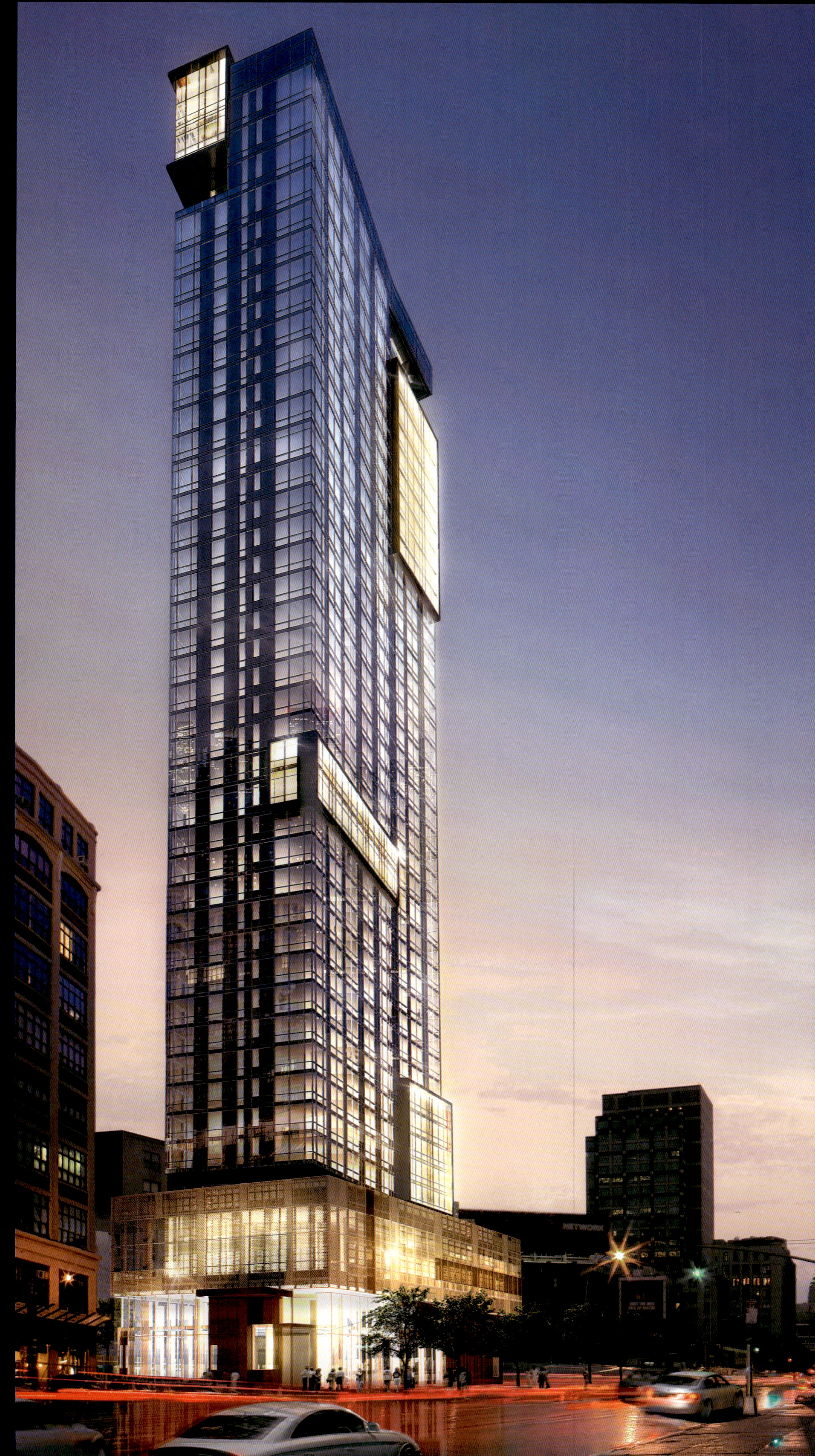

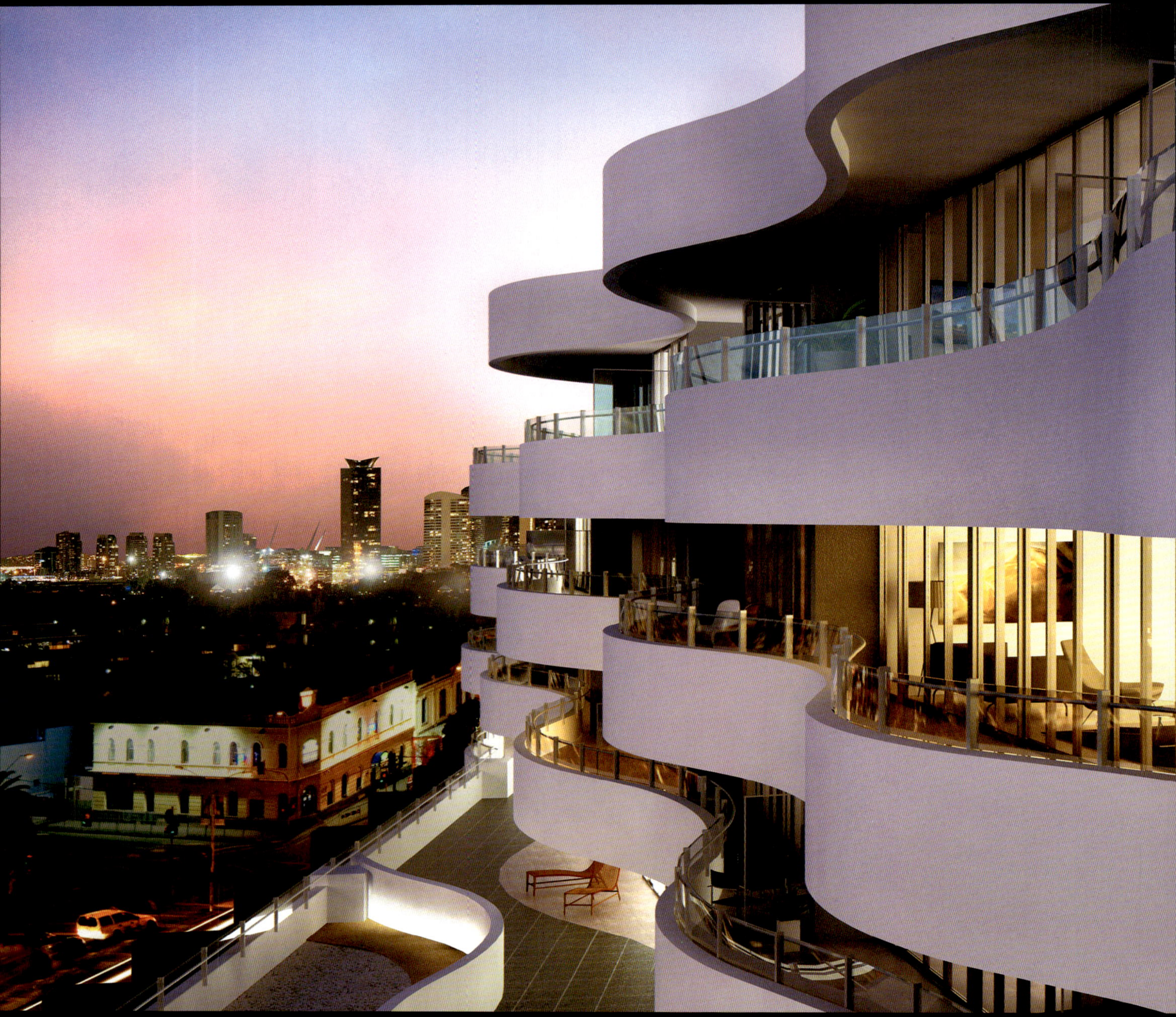

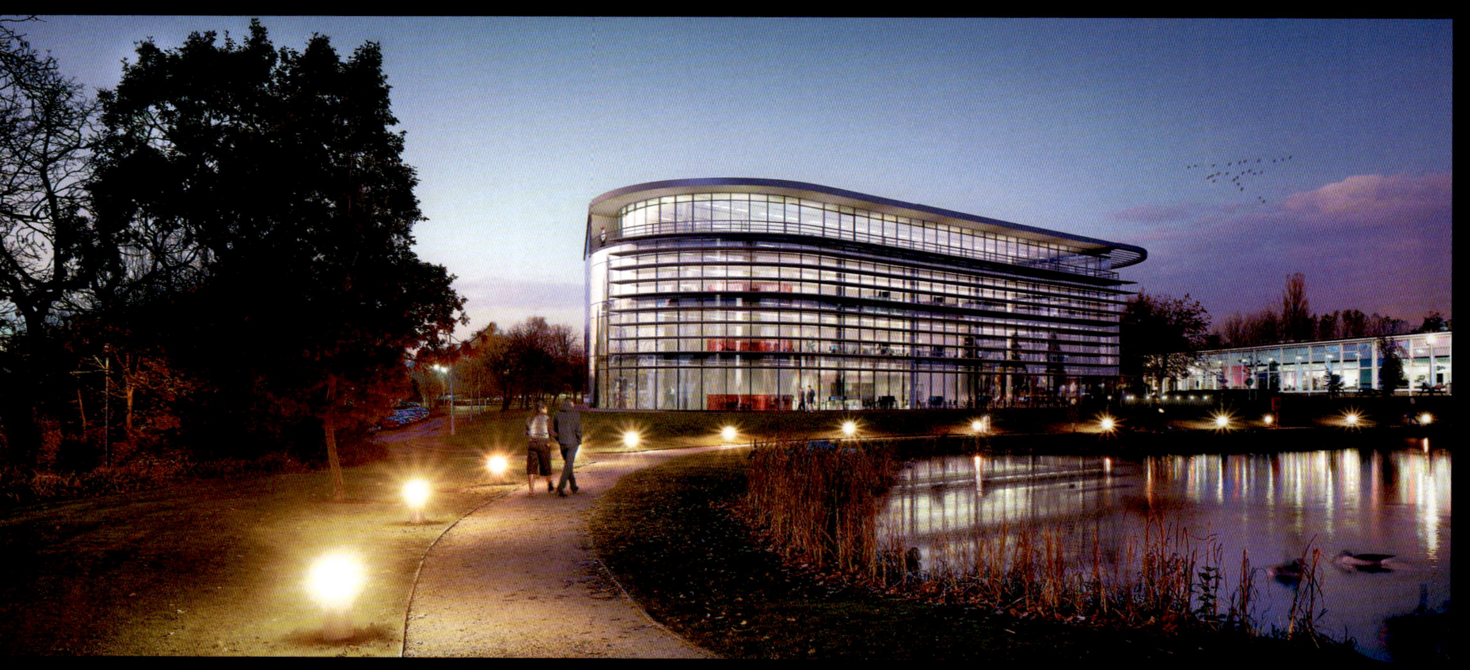

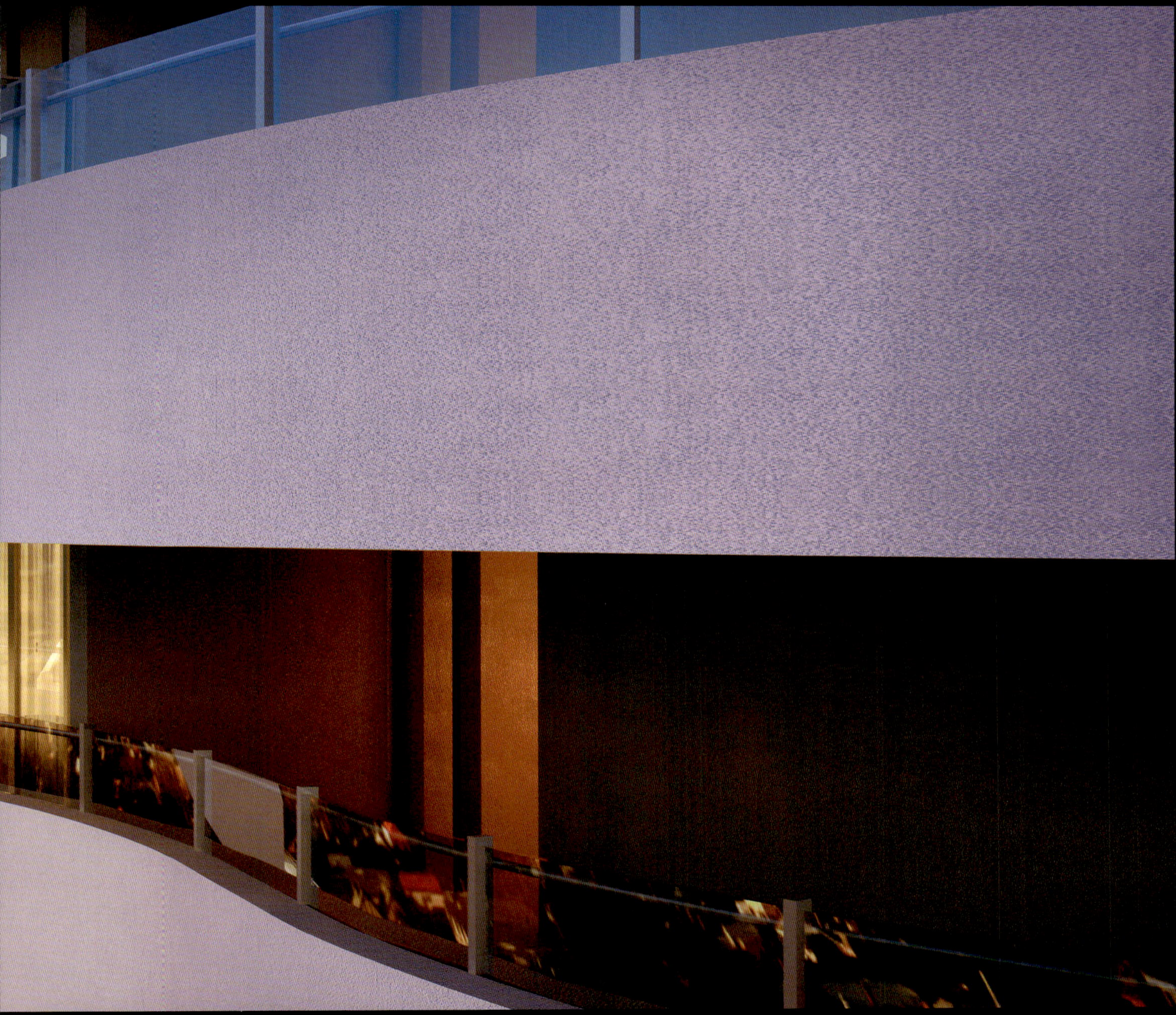

Bianca
3ds Max, V-Ray, Photoshop
Client: Peter Sexty Design
Sam Slicer, AUSTRALIA
[above]

Birchwood Park (Dusk)
3ds Max, V-Ray, Photoshop
Matthew Clayton,
AHD-Imaging,
GREAT BRITAIN
[left]

W Hotel Boston
3ds Max, mental ray,
Photoshop
Client: William Rawn Arch.
Carlos Cristerna,
Neoscape, Inc., USA
[right]

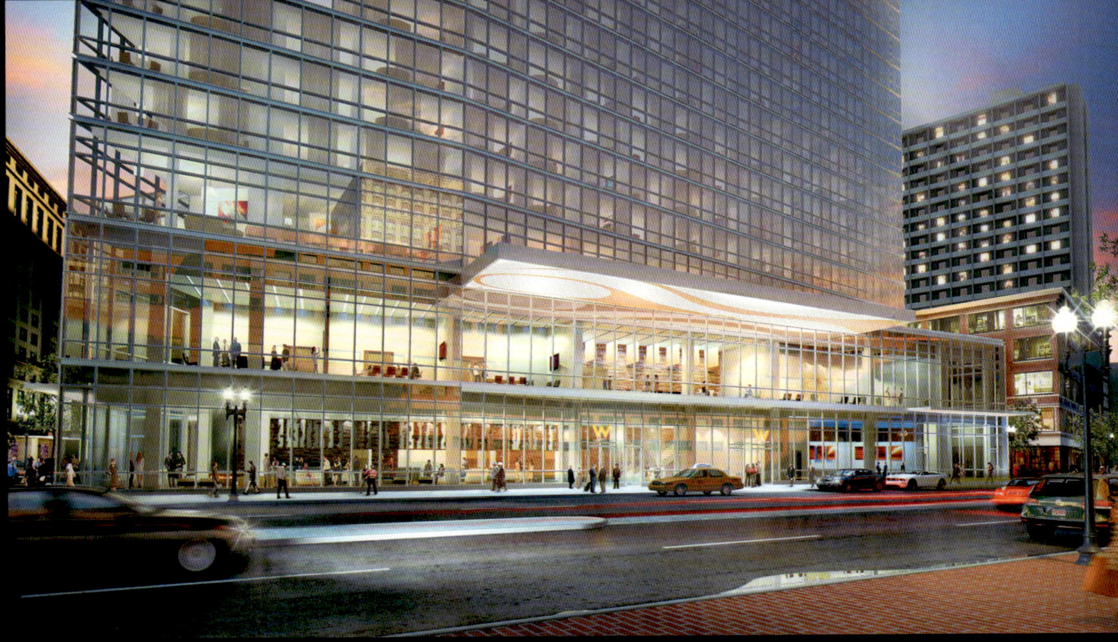

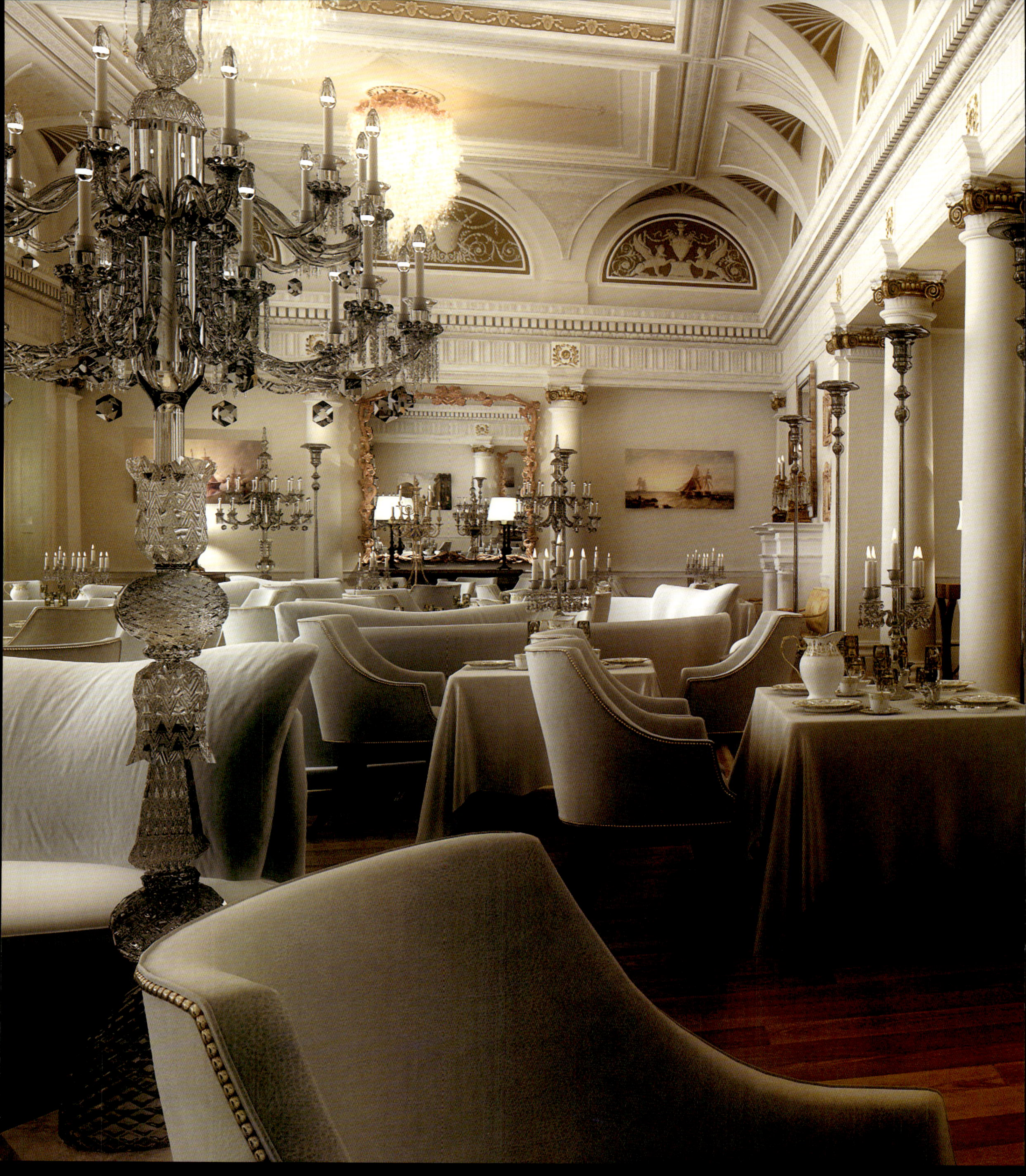

Master
Architecture Interior (Public)

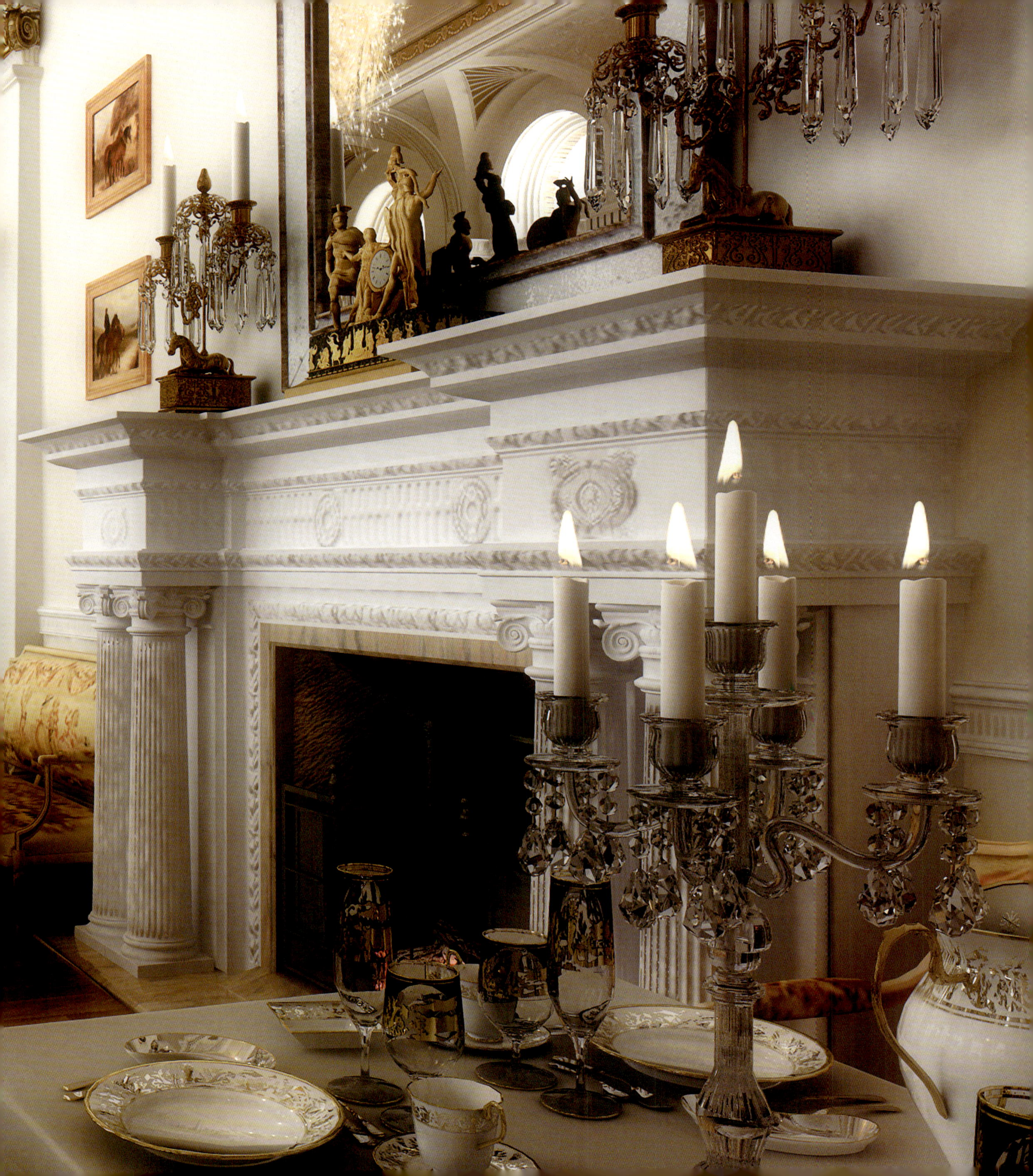

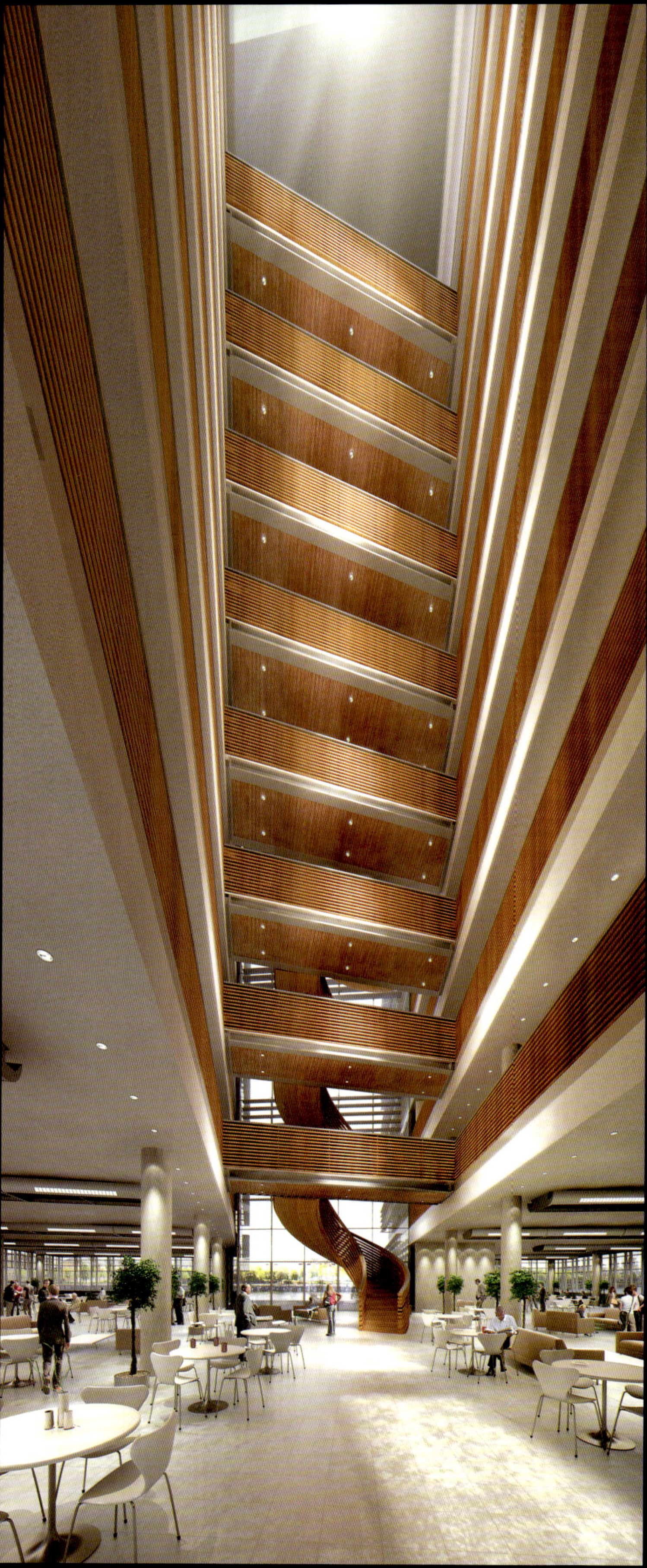

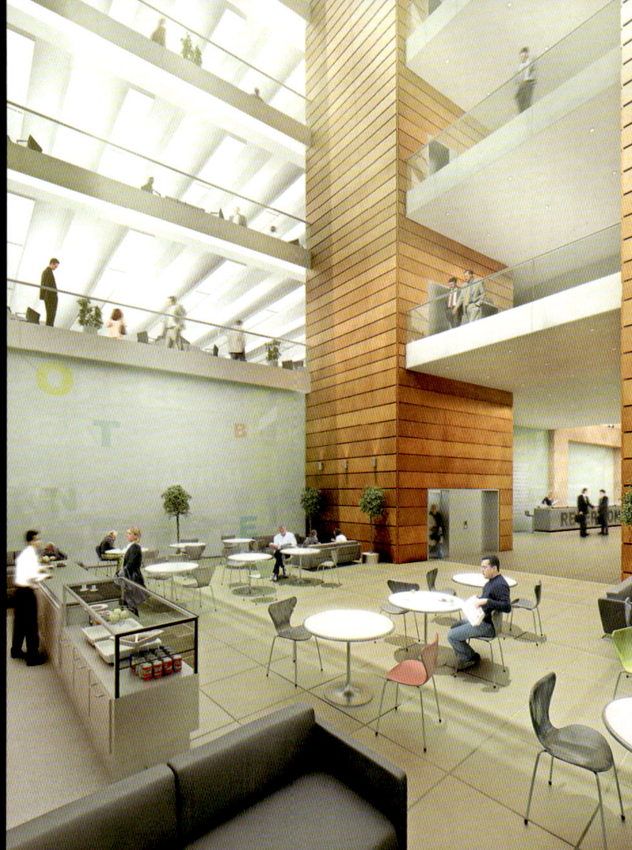

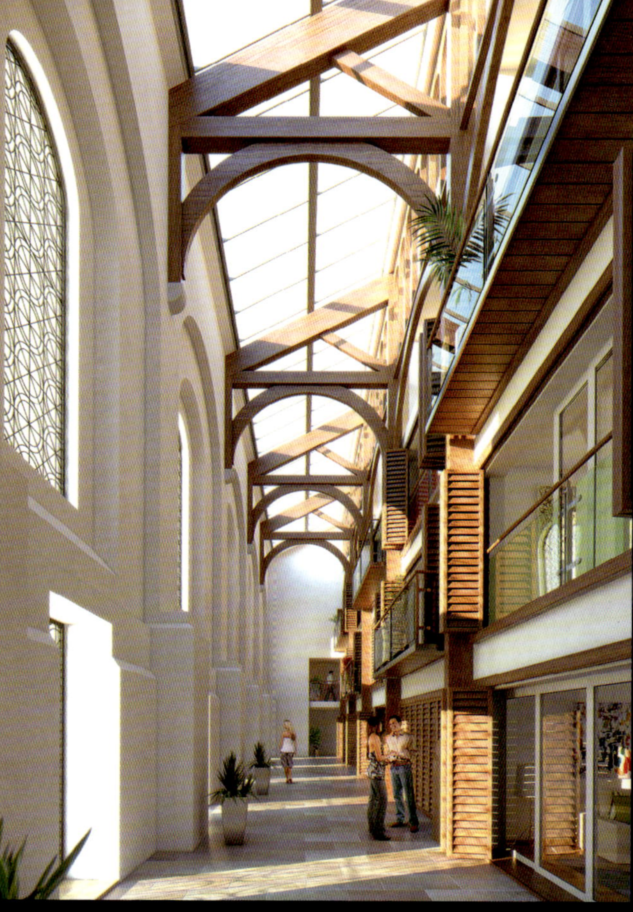

Erie Basin Internal
3ds Max, V-Ray, Photoshop
John Crawshaw, AHD-Imaging,
GREAT BRITAIN
[above]

Cafe Atrium
3ds Max, V-Ray, Photoshop
Gareth Thatcher,
AHD-Imaging, GREAT BRITAIN
[top right]

The Cathedral
3ds Max, V-Ray, Photoshop
Client: Urban Creation
Architect: AWW
Martin Drake, Preconstruct, GREAT BRITAIN *[above]*

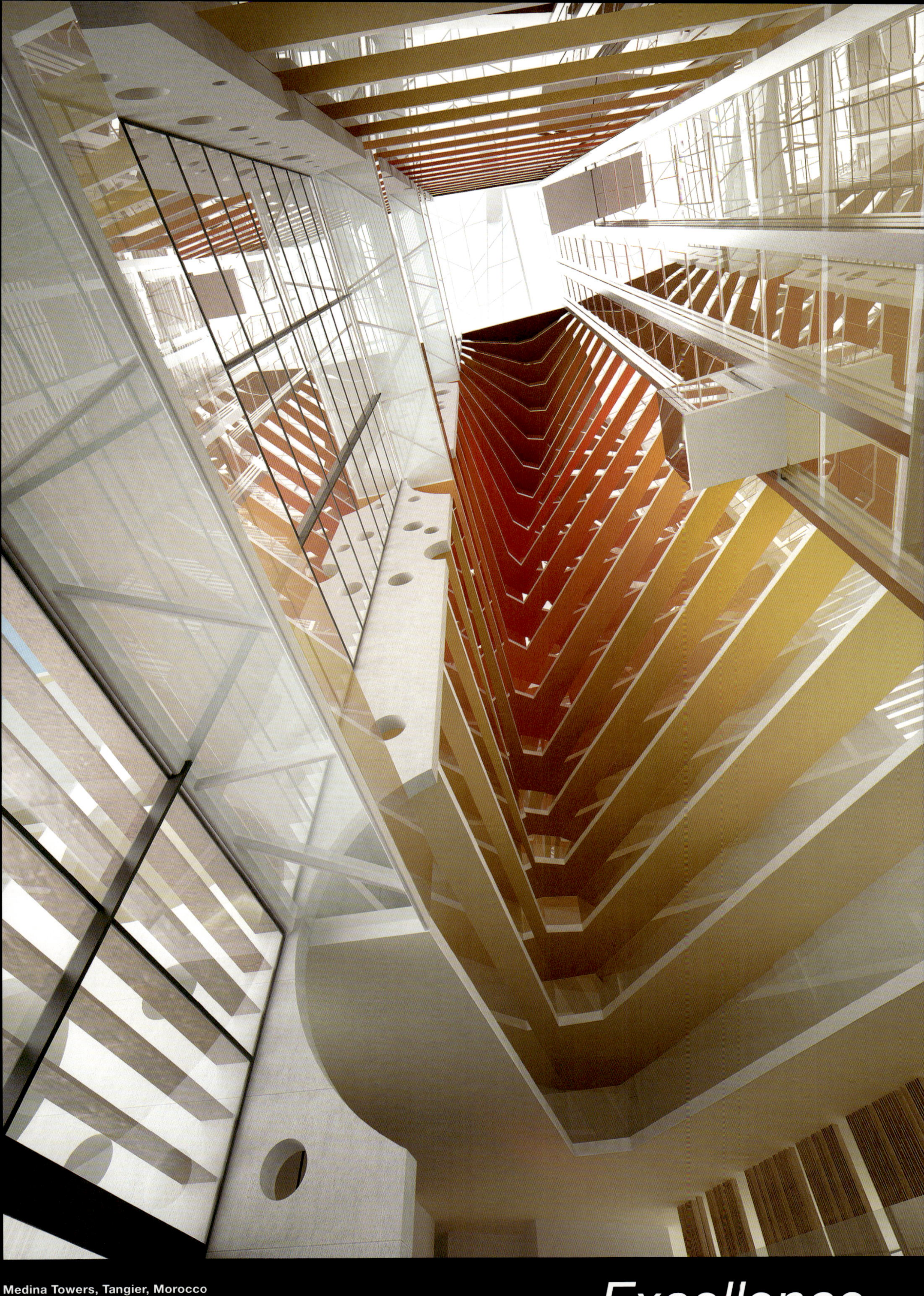

Medina Towers, Tangier, Morocco
3ds Max, V-Ray, Photoshop
Client: LD2 Architects
Christophe Landrain and **Robert Ivanov**, BELGIUM

Excellence
Architecture Interior (Public)

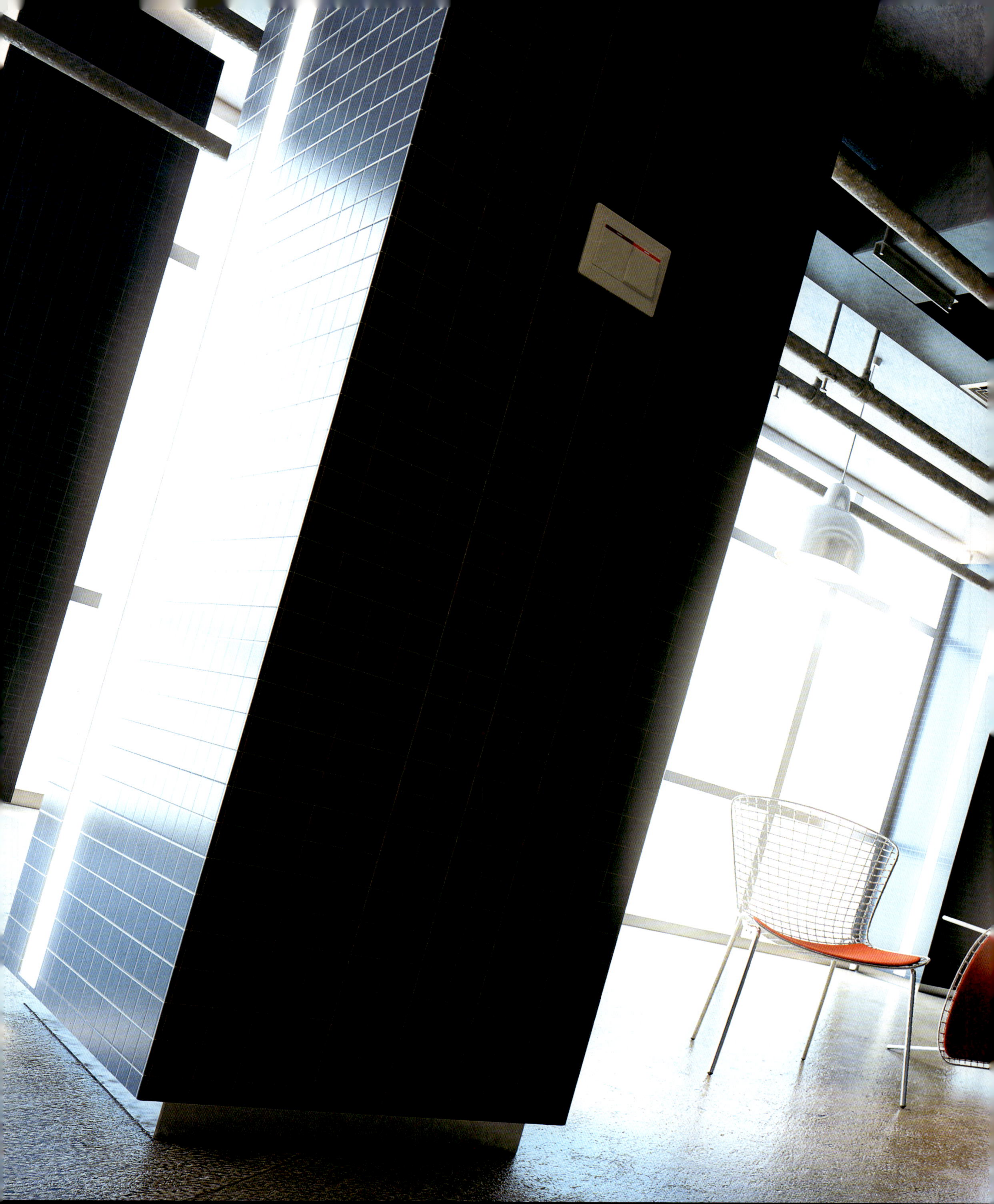

Excellence

Architecture Interior (Public)

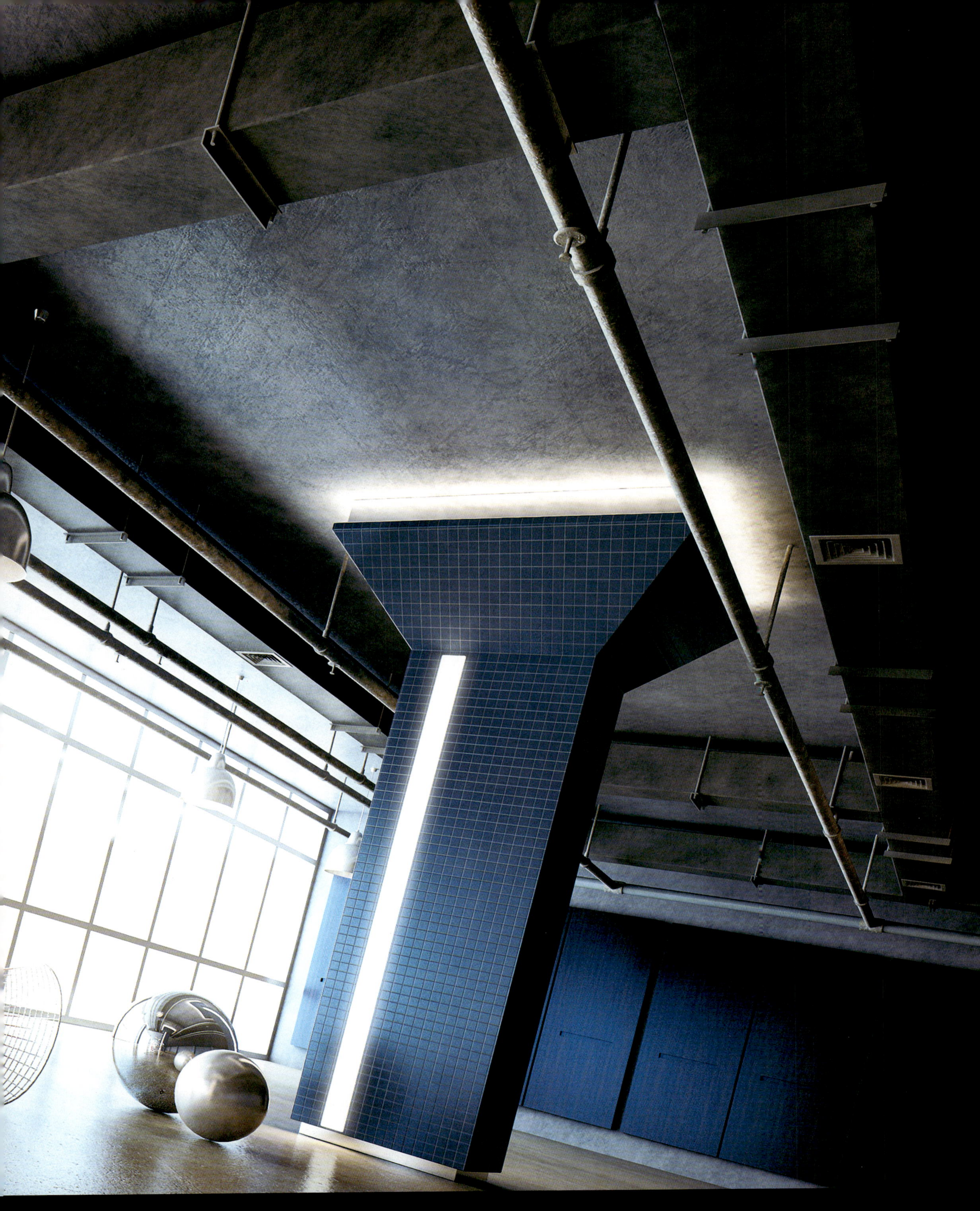

Capital at Brickell
3ds Max, Photoshop, After Effects
Client: CABI Developers
Spine3D, USA

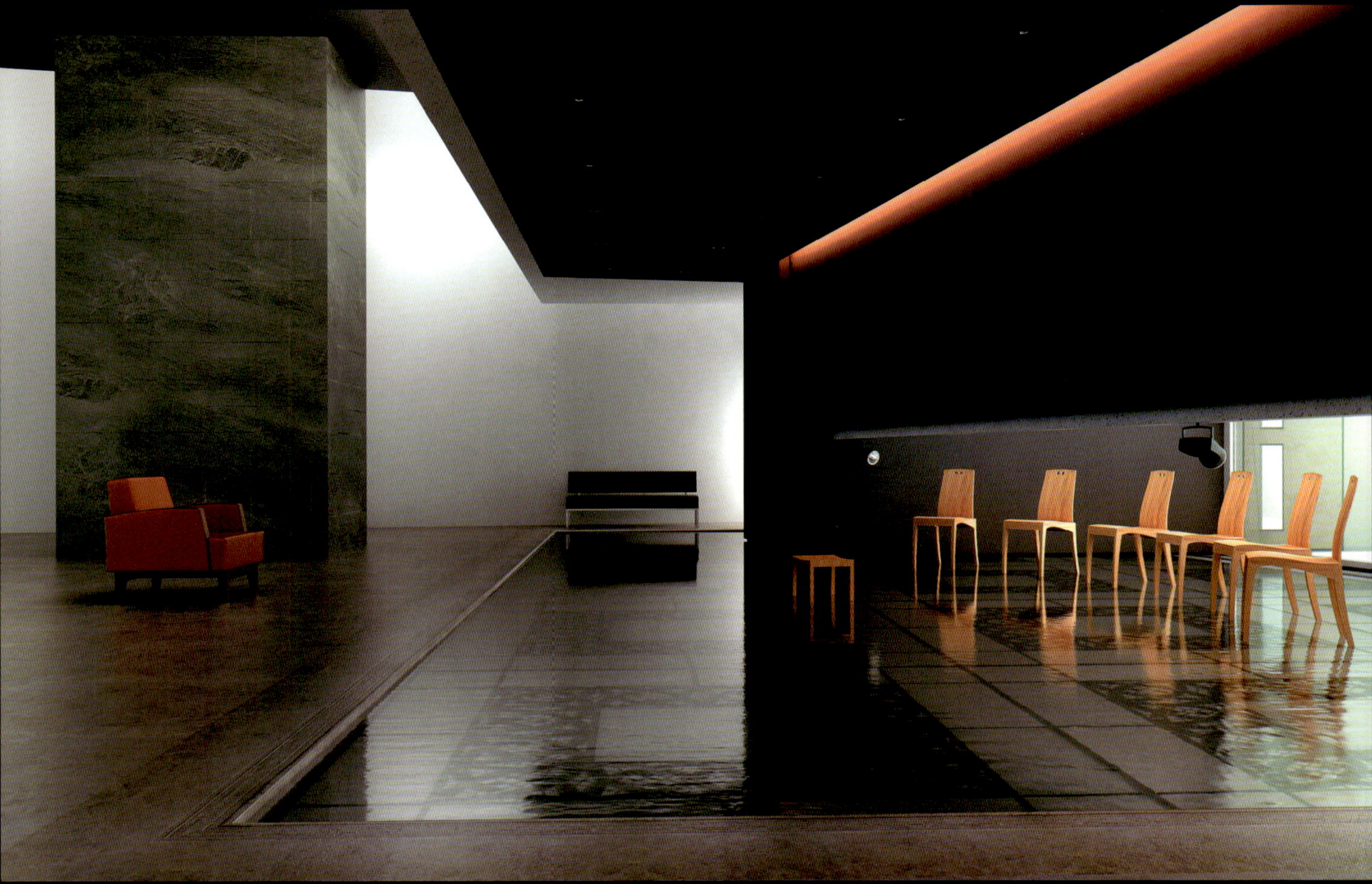

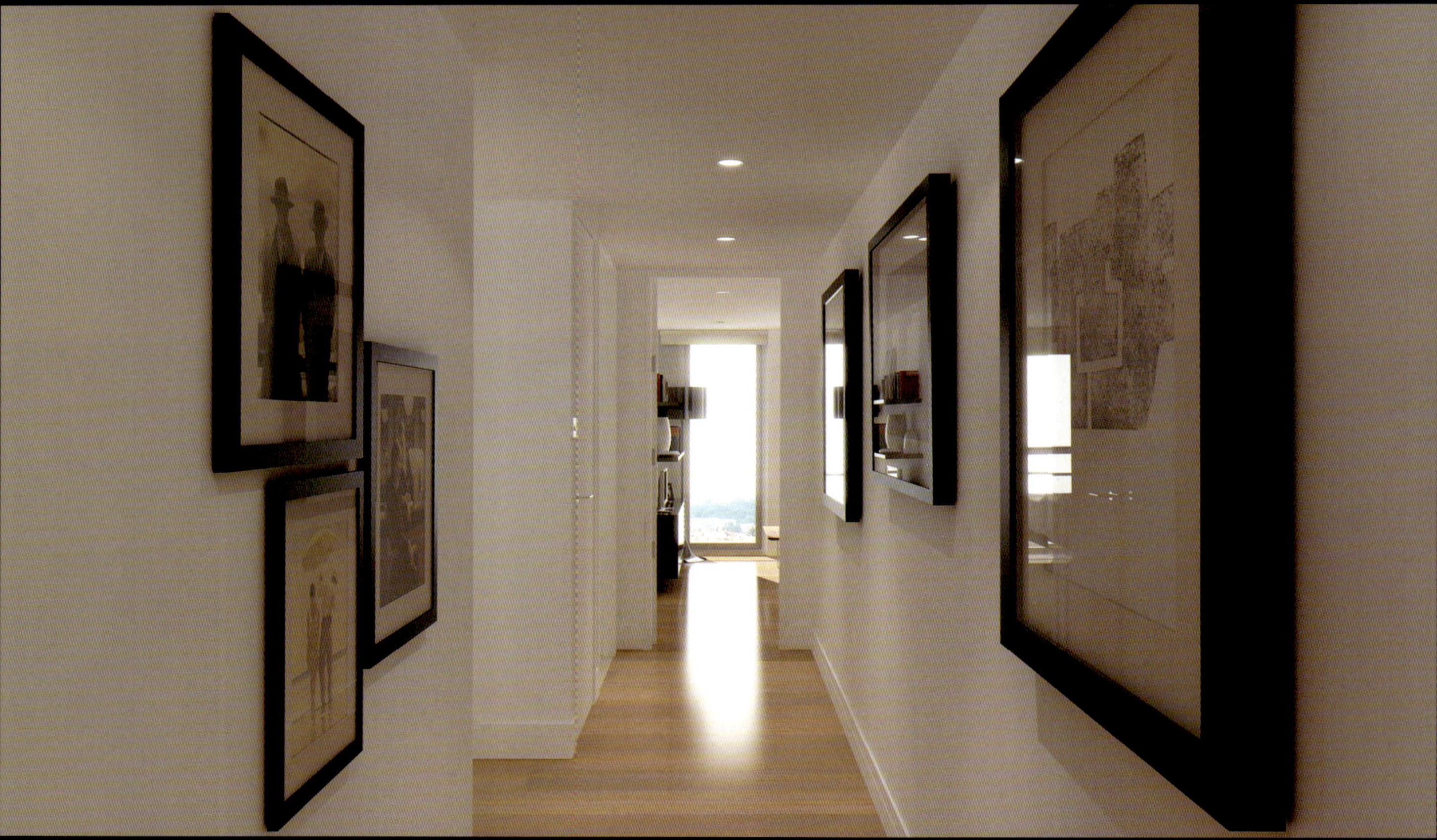

Furniture concert
3ds Max, Photoshop
Zoltán Kovács, ZOA Architects,
HUNGARY
[top]

Airpoint Hallway
3ds Max, V-Ray, Photoshop
Uniform,
GREAT BRITAIN
[above]

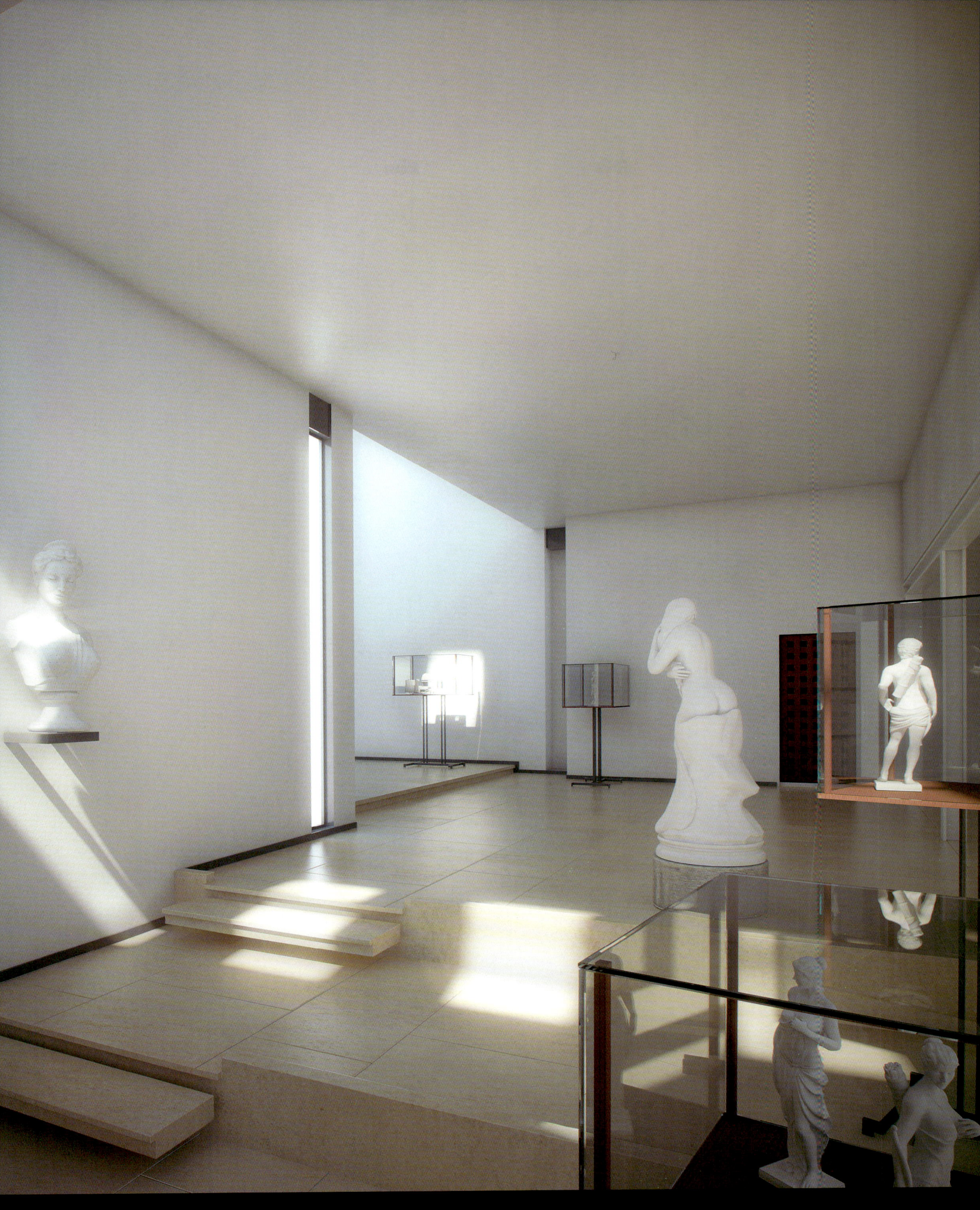

Museo Canoviano 2
3ds Max, SketchUp,
Photoshop, V-Ray
Peter Guthrie,
GREAT BRITAIN

Excellence
Architecture Interior (Public)

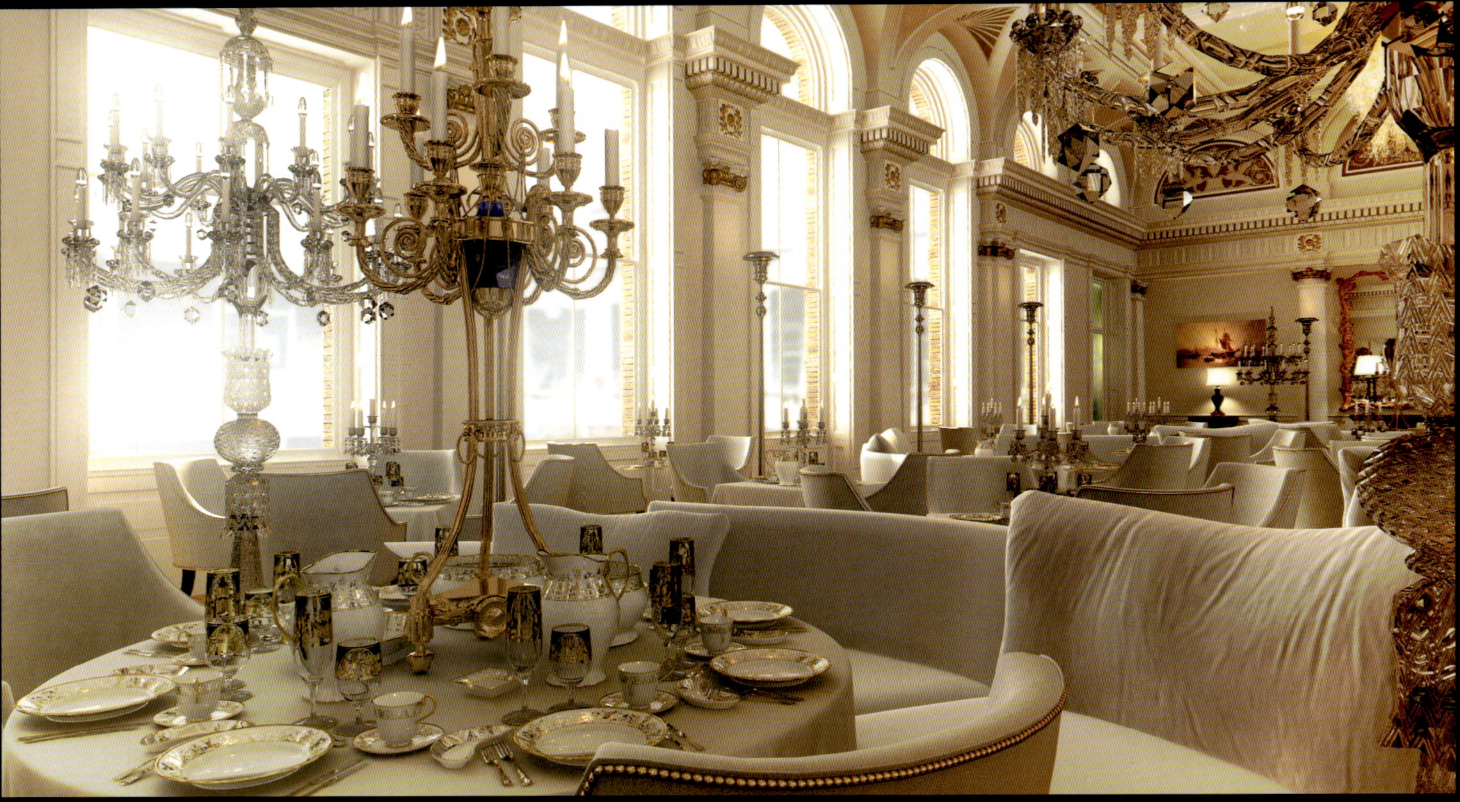

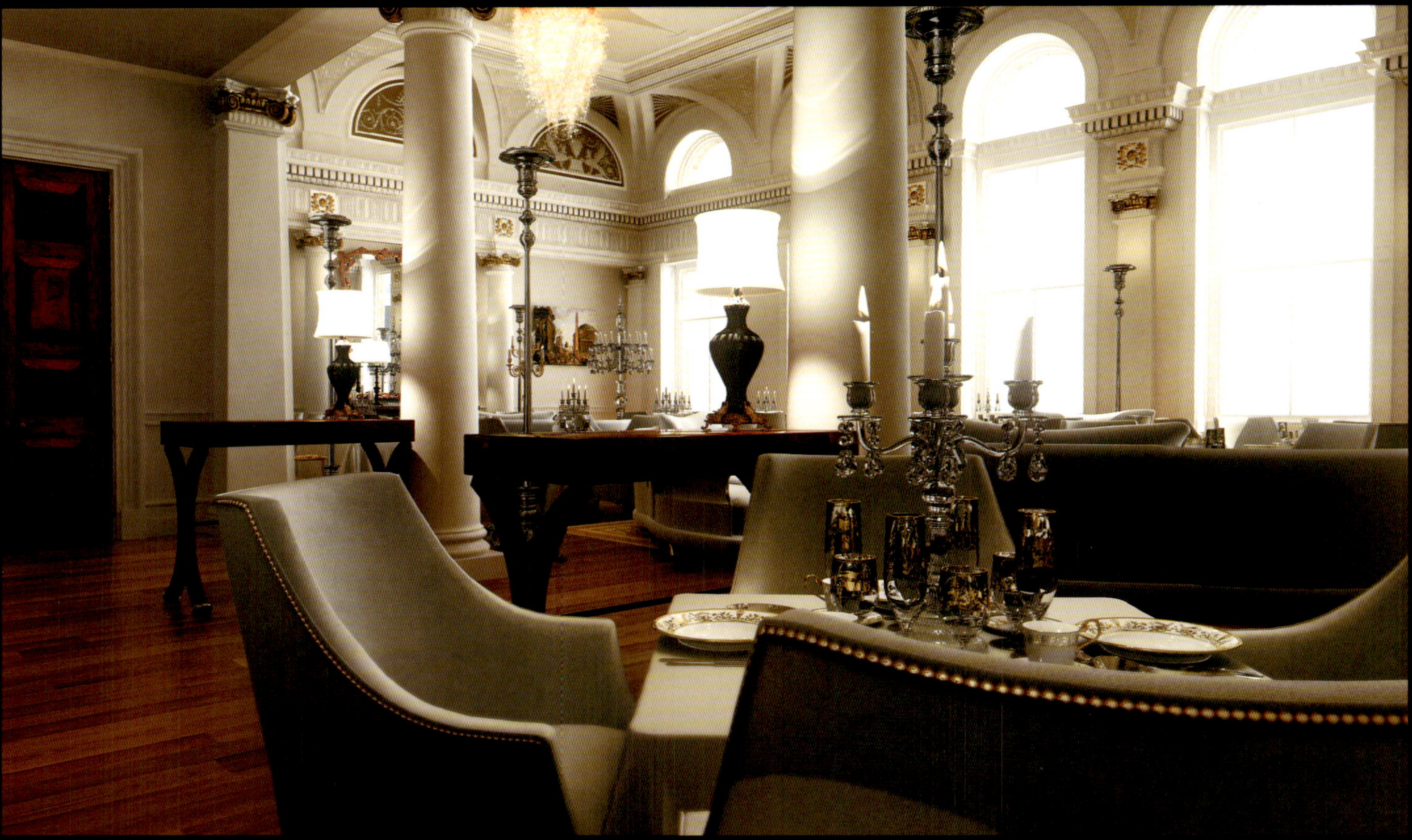

Ballroom
3ds Max, V-Ray, Photoshop
SPLITT Ltd/3D Helps,
GREAT BRITAIN
[top, above]

Entrance Hall
3ds Max, V-Ray, Photoshop
Maryam Nademi, IRAN
[right]

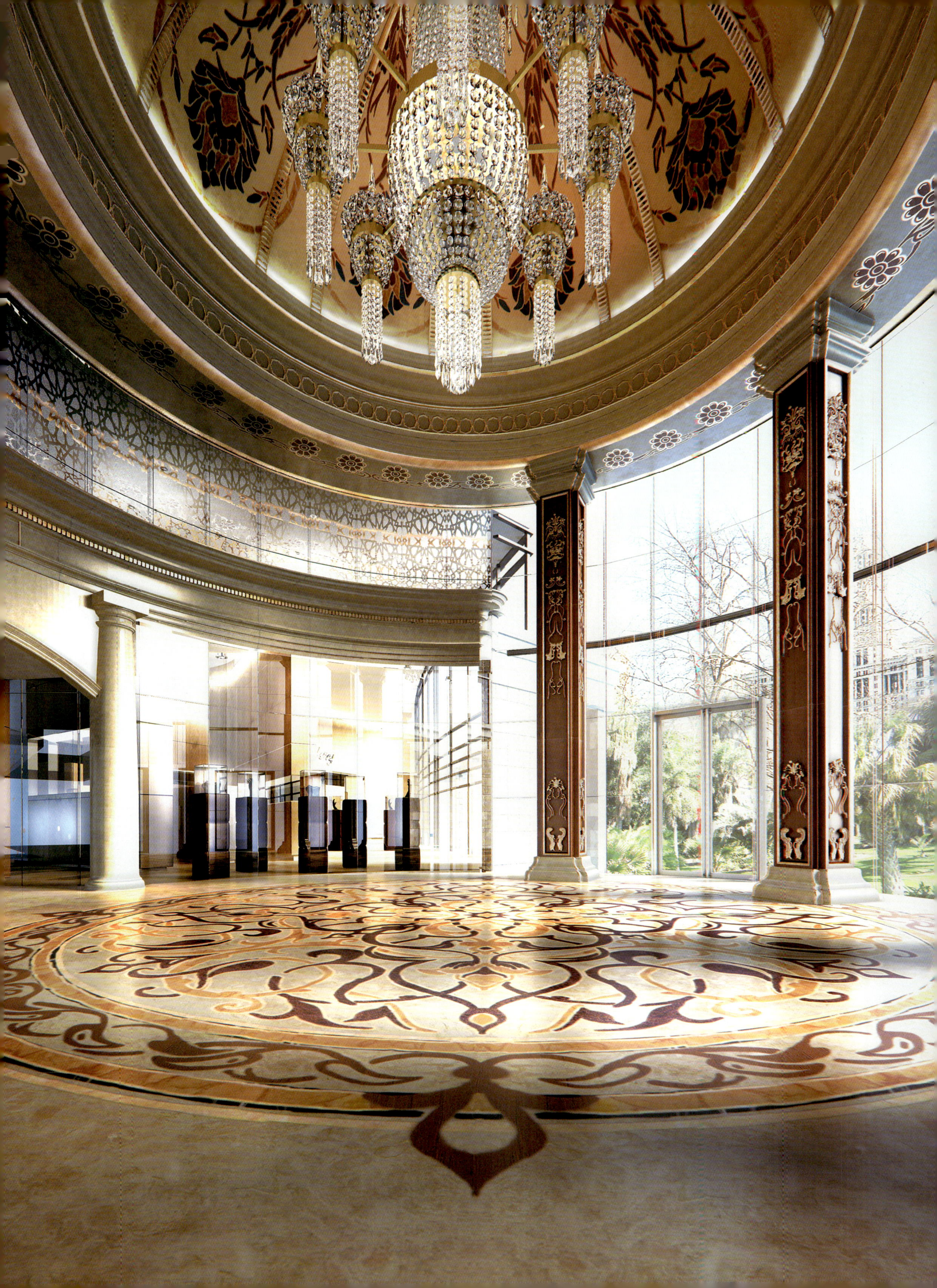

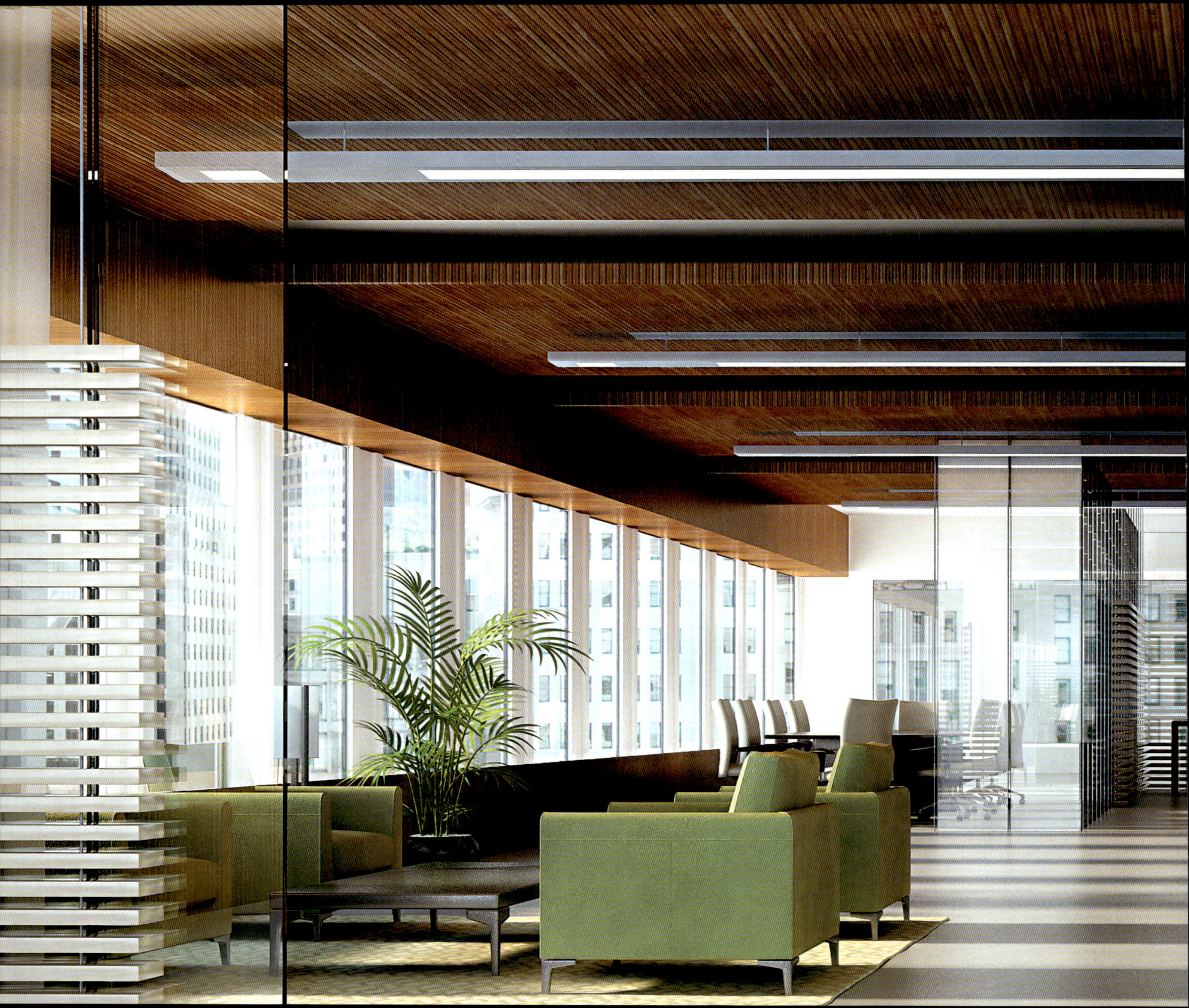

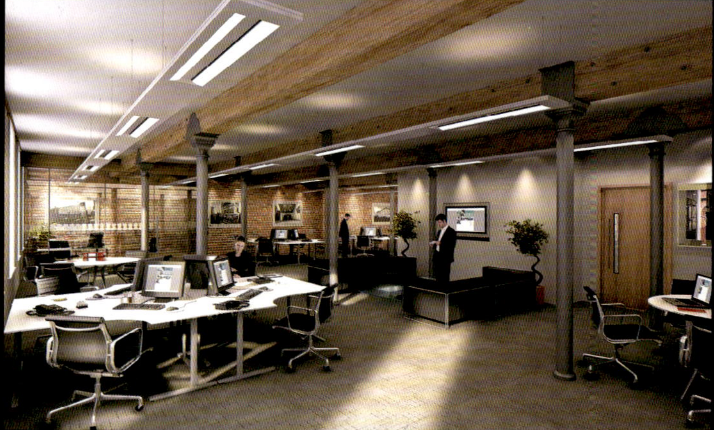

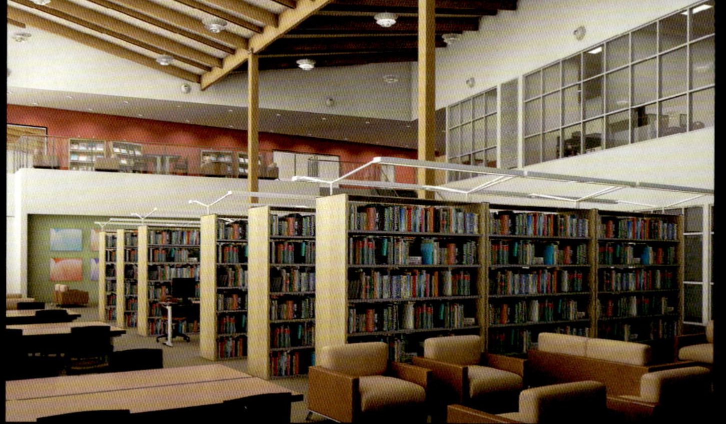

Boston Office
3ds Max, V-Ray, Photoshop
Nensi Karanxha, Neoscape, Inc., USA
[top]

61 Oxford Street Office
3ds Max, V-Ray, Photoshop
Phil Greaves, AHD-Imaging, GREAT BRITAIN
[above]

San Louis Library
3ds Max, V-Ray
Client: Yuma County
Timothy Saunders, VCBO Architecture, USA
[above]

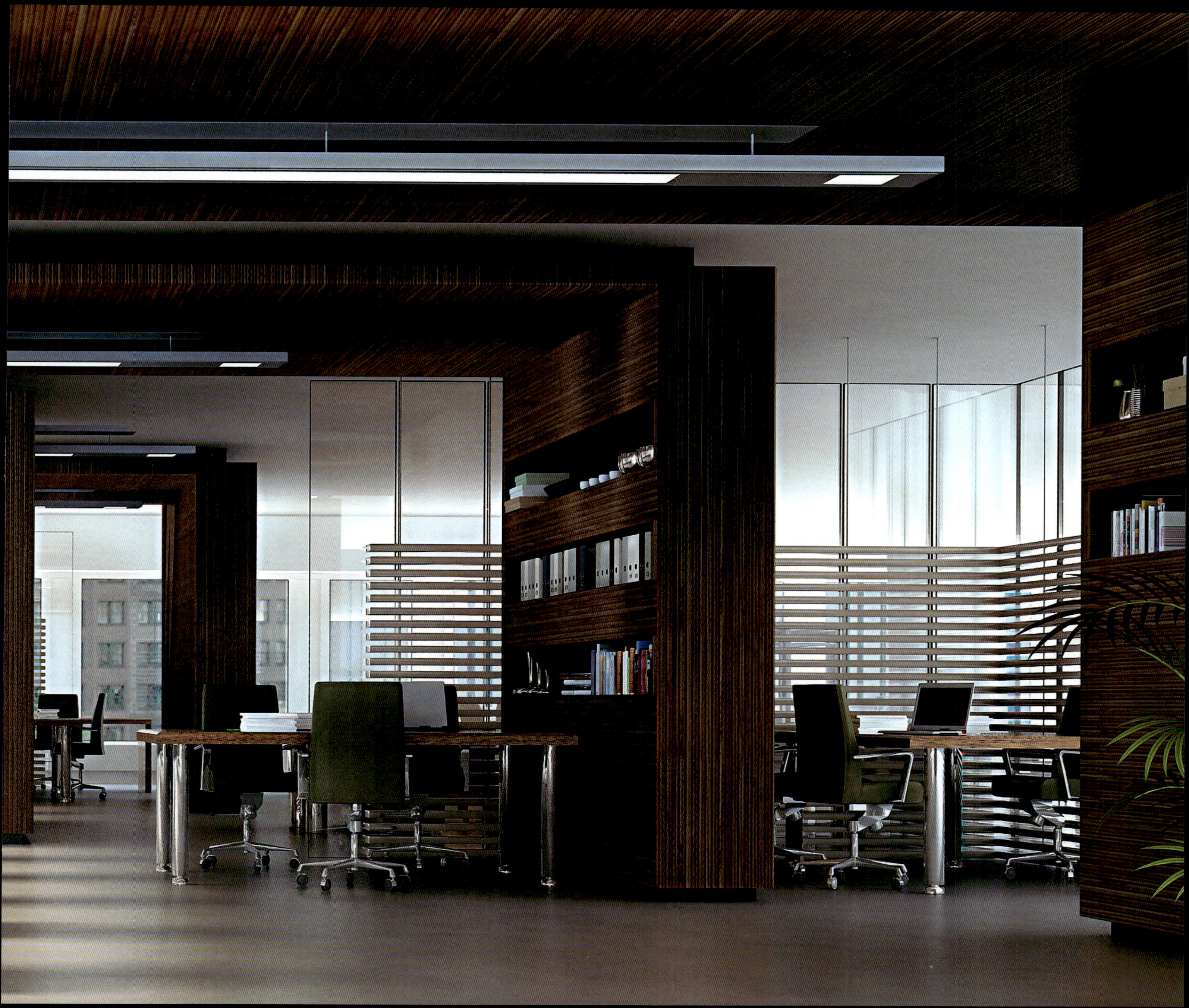

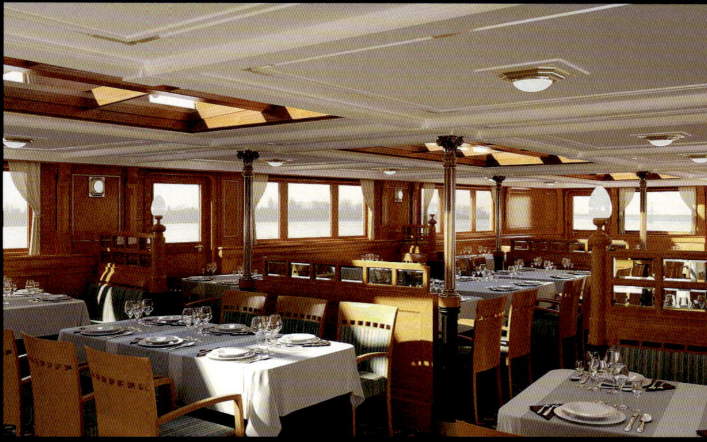

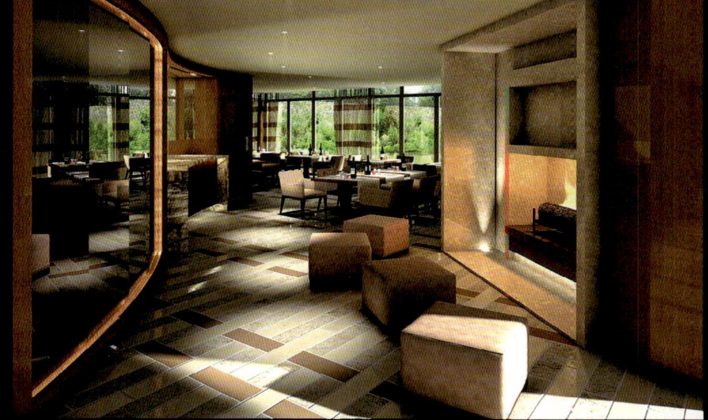

Ship Restaurant
3ds Max, Photoshop
Architect, Interior Designer: Sándor Csepregi
Zoltán Kovács, ZOA Architects, HUNGARY
[above]

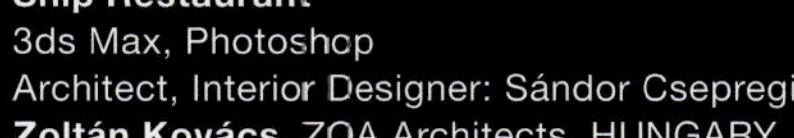

Before Service
CINEMA 4D, AutoCAD, SketchUp, Photoshop
Client: Lucknam Park Spas
Stephen Leworthy and **Holder Mathias Architects**, GREAT BRITAIN
[above]

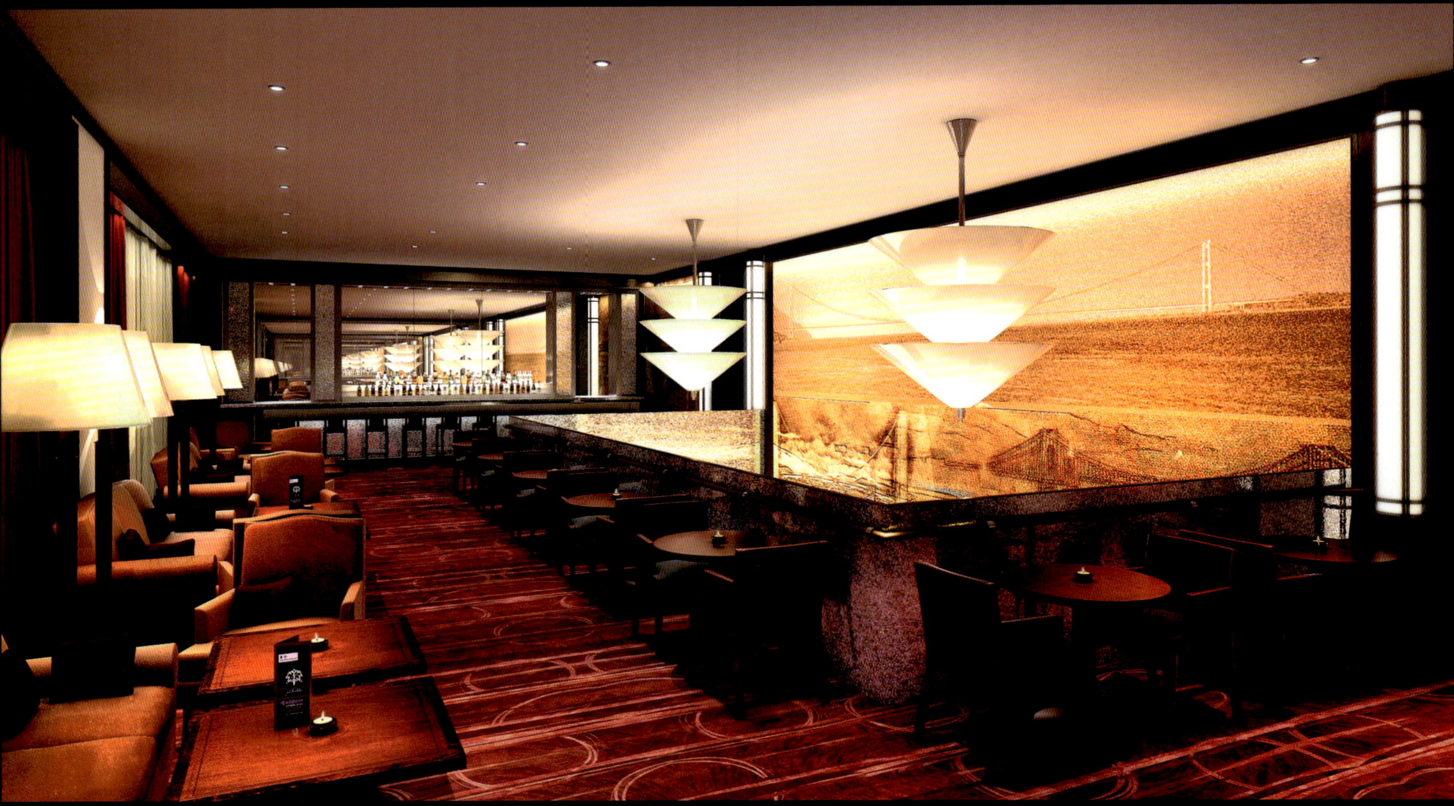

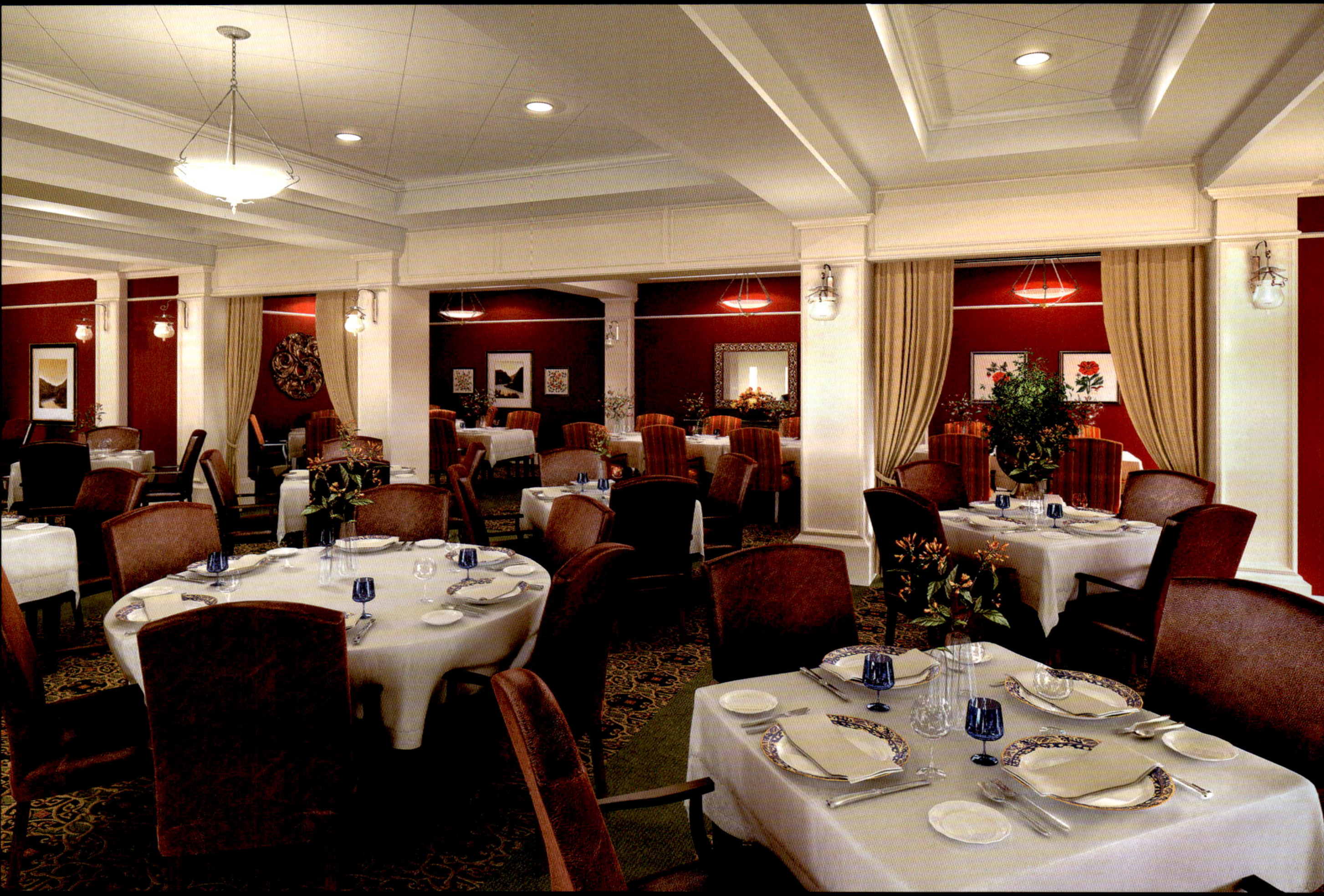

NYC Hotel Lounge Design
3ds Max, mental ray, Photoshop
Anthony Cortez, Arup,
USA
[top]

Cypress of Raleigh
3ds Max, Photoshop
Client: THW Design
Spine3D, USA
[above]

Highland Park Methodist Transept
3ds Max, Photoshop, V-Ray
Client and Architect: Selzer Associates, Inc.
Green Grass Studios, USA
[right]

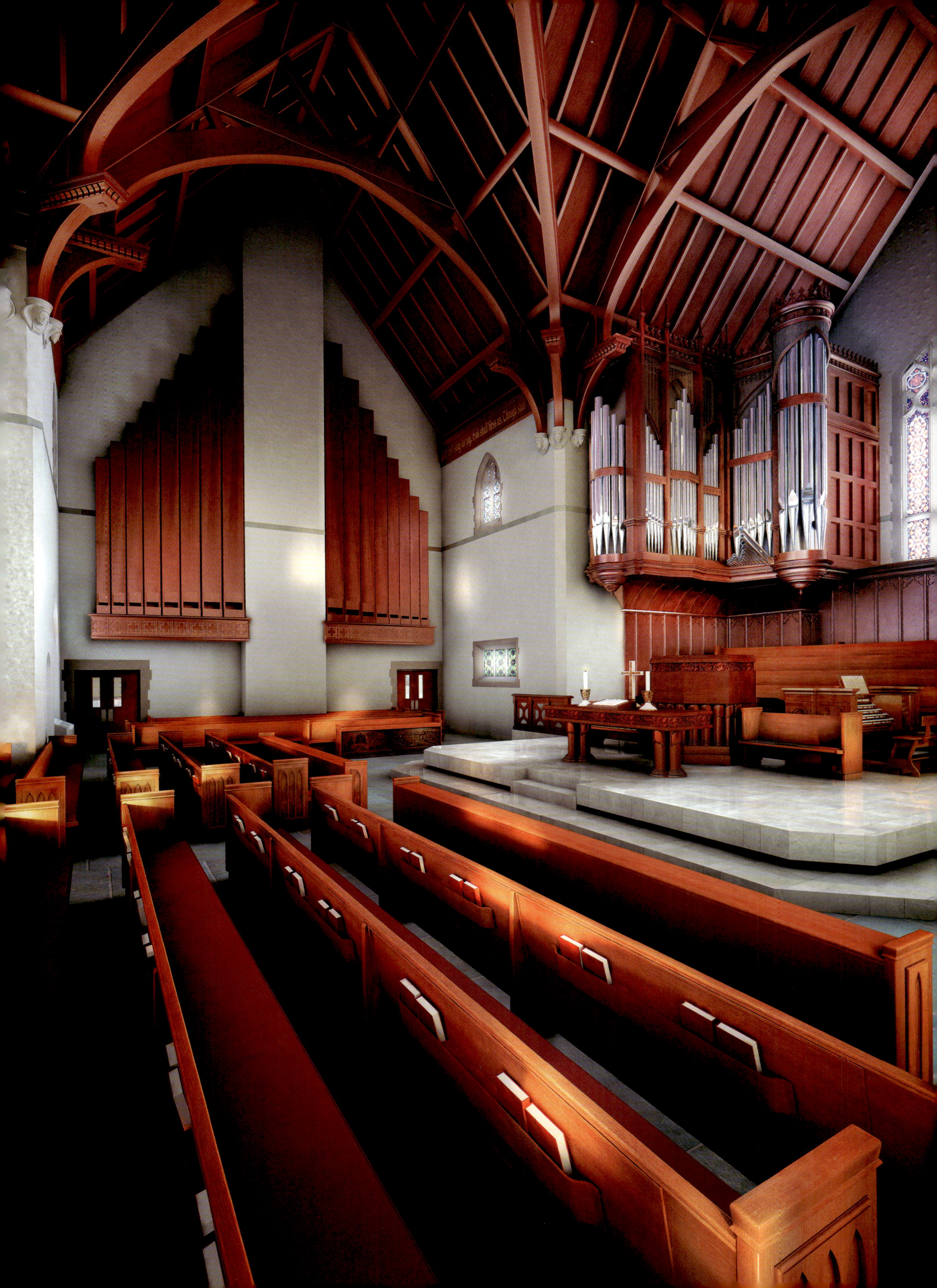
God shall bless us. Through

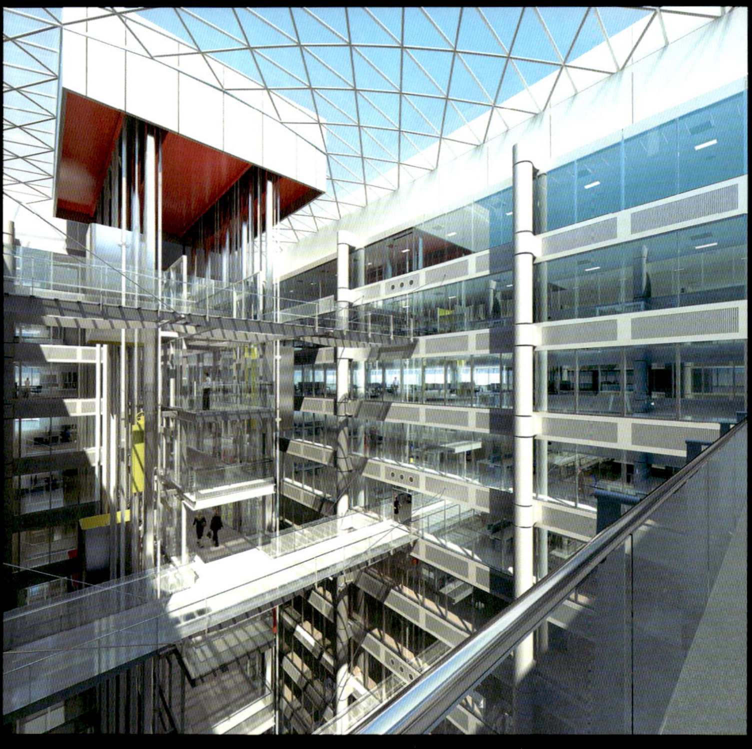

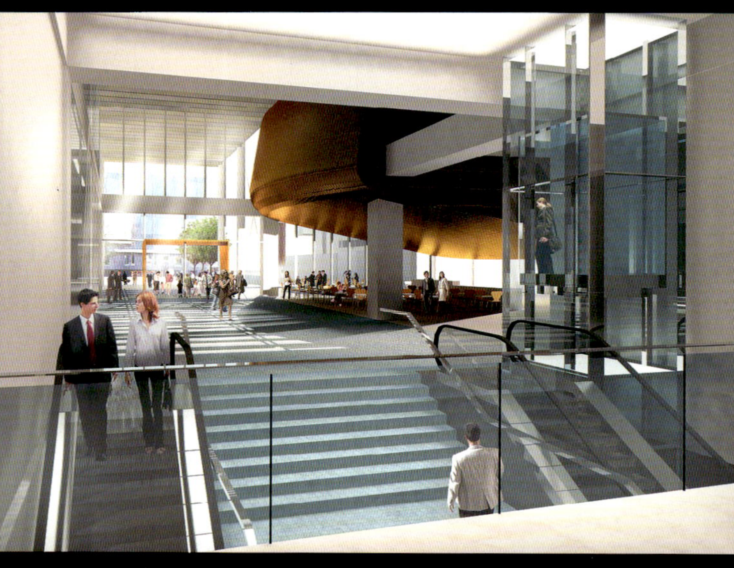

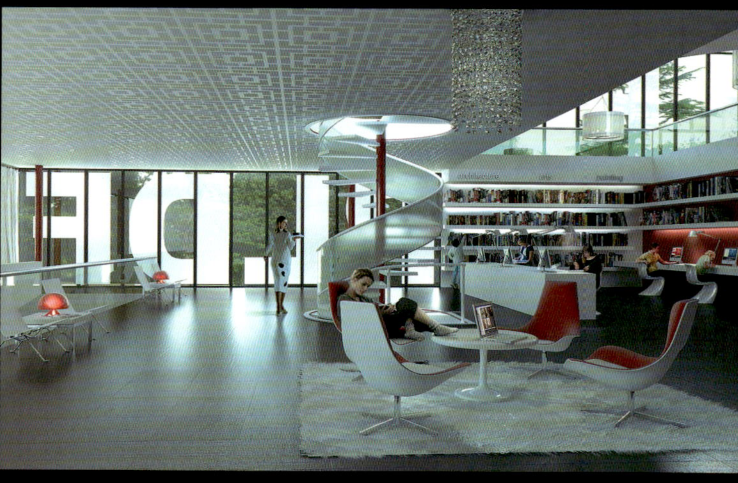

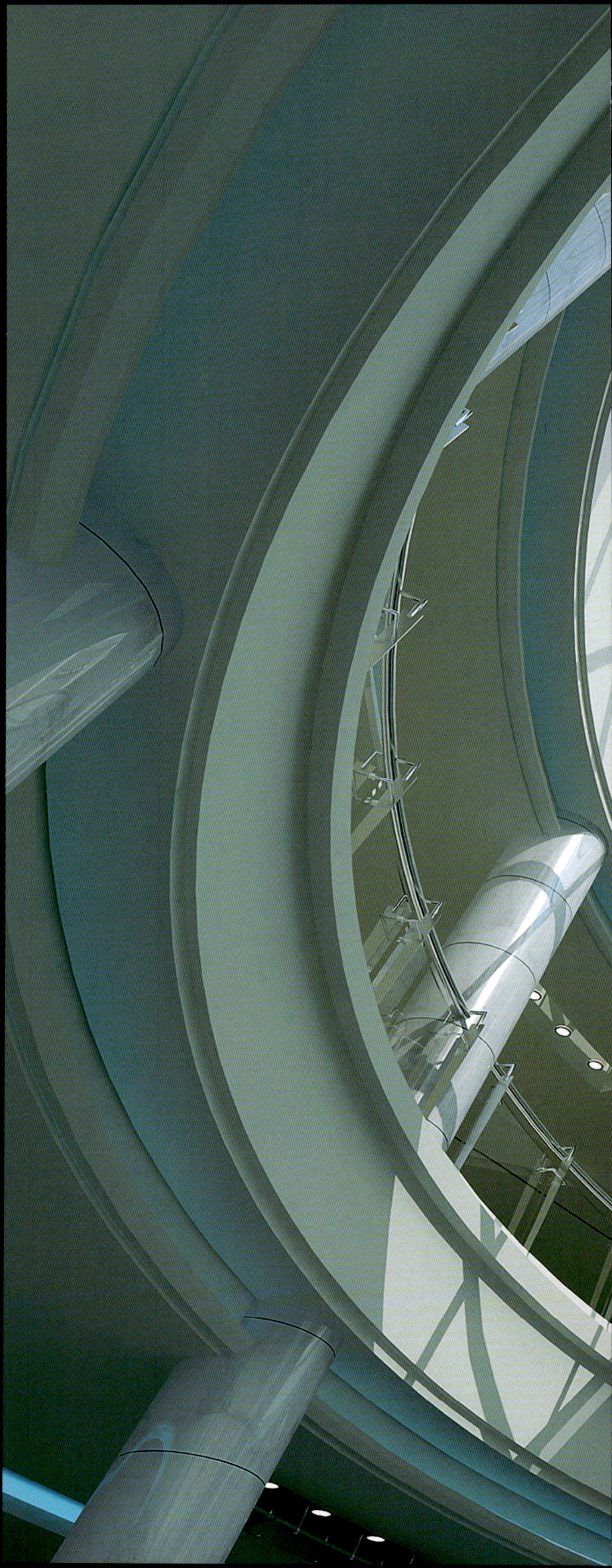

St. Botolphs Atrium
3ds Max, V-Ray, Photoshop
Uniform,
GREAT BRITAIN
[top]

Entrance Interior 01
3ds Max, mental ray, Photoshop
Architects: Athfield
Caroline Boetzelen,
NEW ZEALAND *[center]*

Bibliotheque
3ds Max, AutoCAD,
Photoshop
Juan Altieri, A2T,
URUGUAY *[above]*

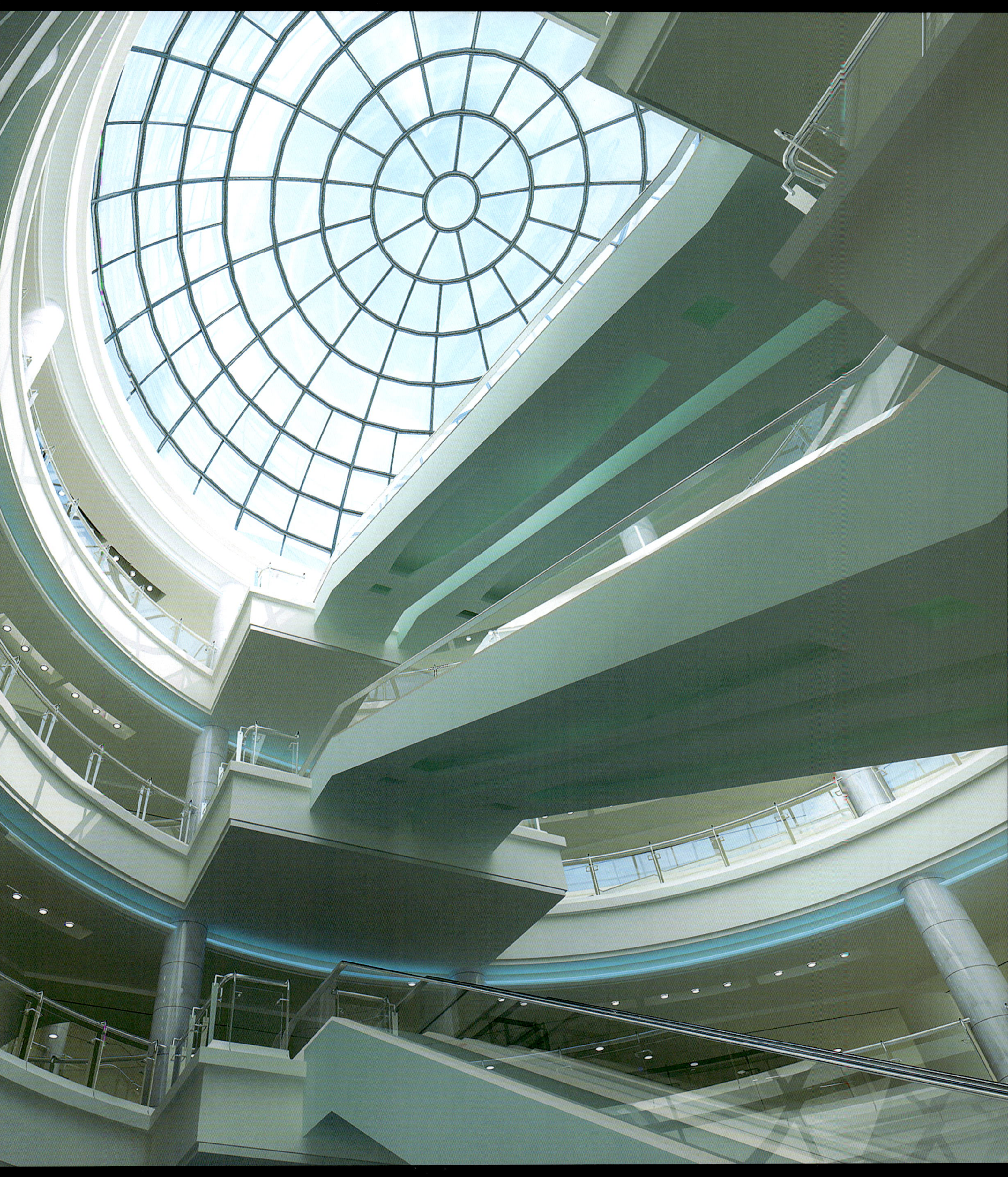

Looby
VIZ
Chen Qingfeng,
Chen3D.com, CHINA

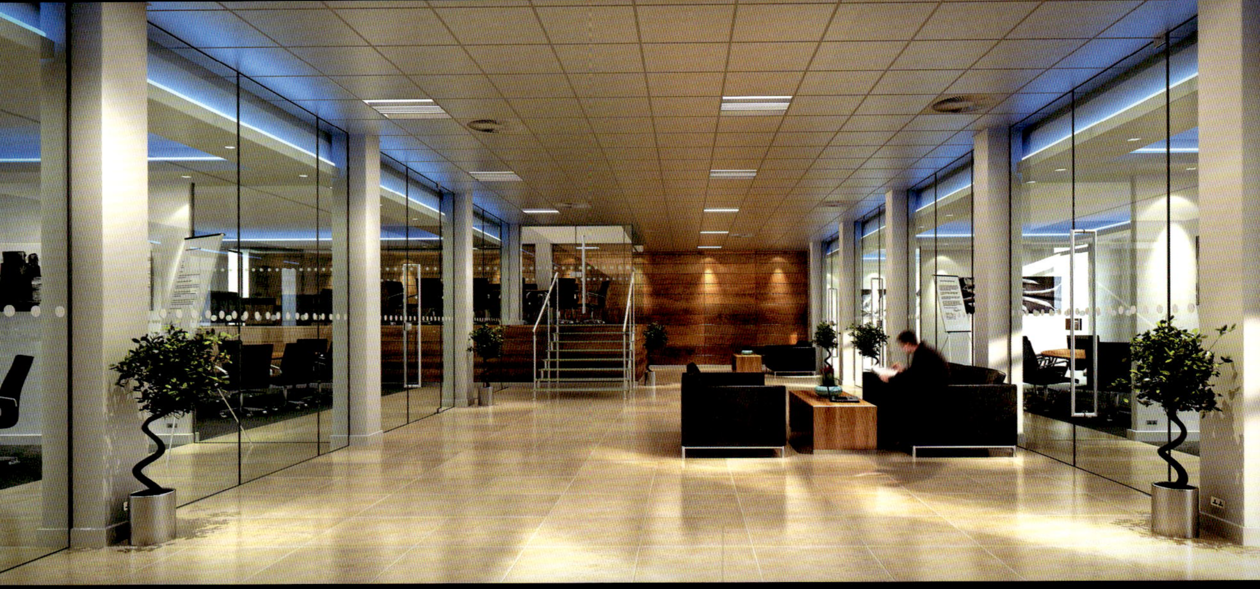

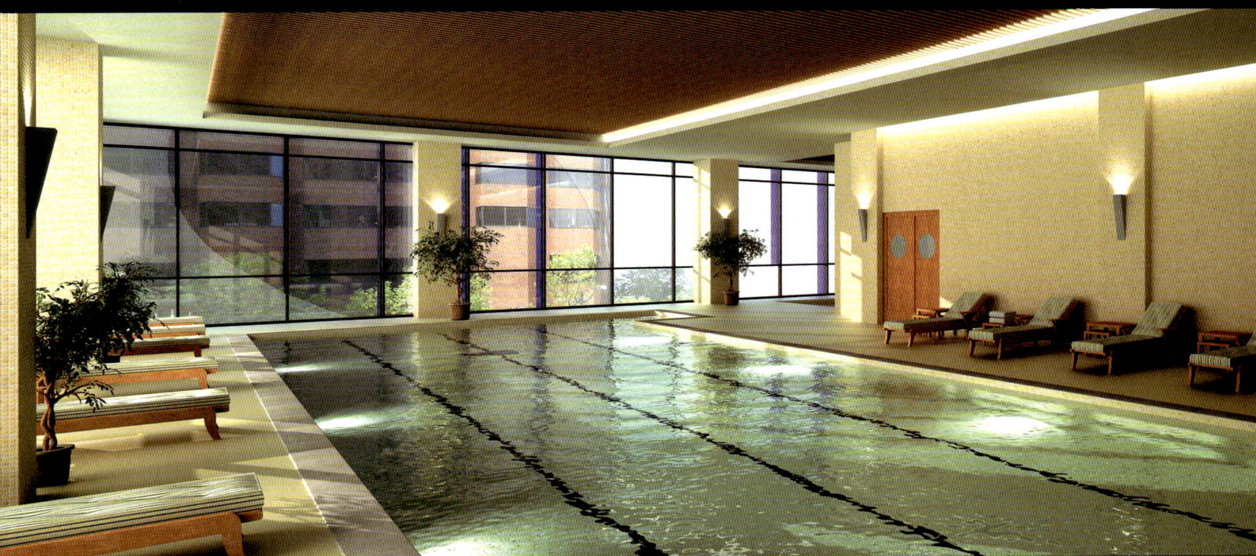

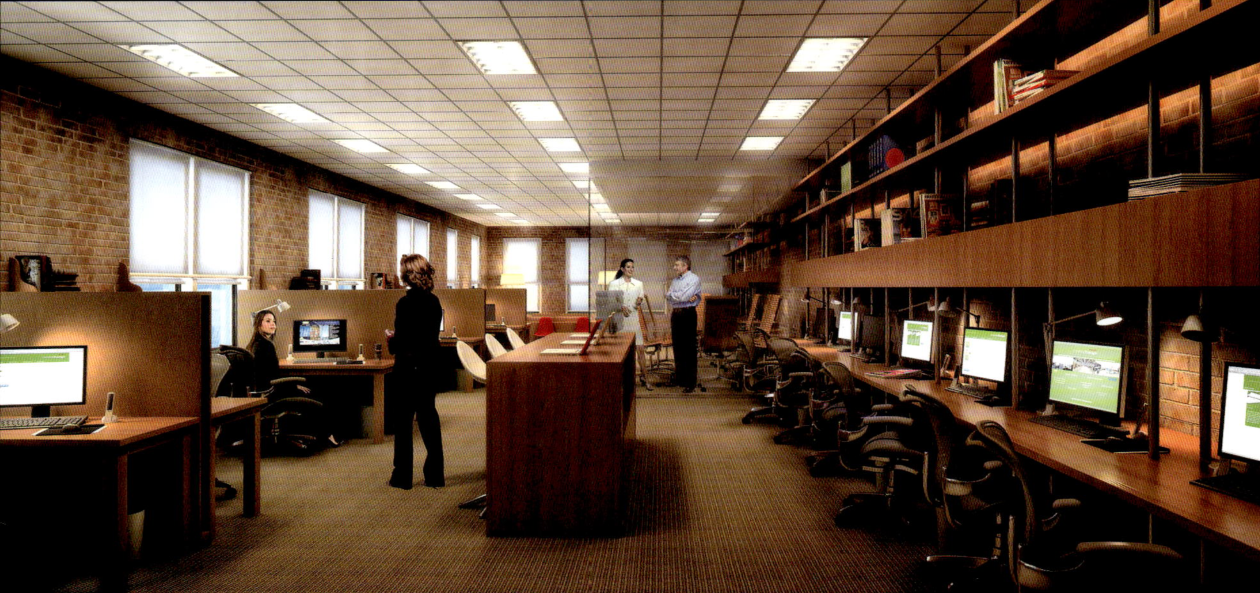

57 Mosley Street Office Internal
3ds Max, V-Ray, Photoshop
Phil Greaves, AHD-Imaging,
GREAT BRITAIN
[top]

Olive8 Pool
3ds Max, V-Ray, Photoshop
Client: RC Hedreen
Steve Johnson, Josh Jones and **Naomi Seto,**
Parsons Brinckerhoff Project Visualization, USA *[center]*

Columbia Light Pro
3ds Max, Photoshop
Client: Columbia Lighting
Spine3D, USA
[above]

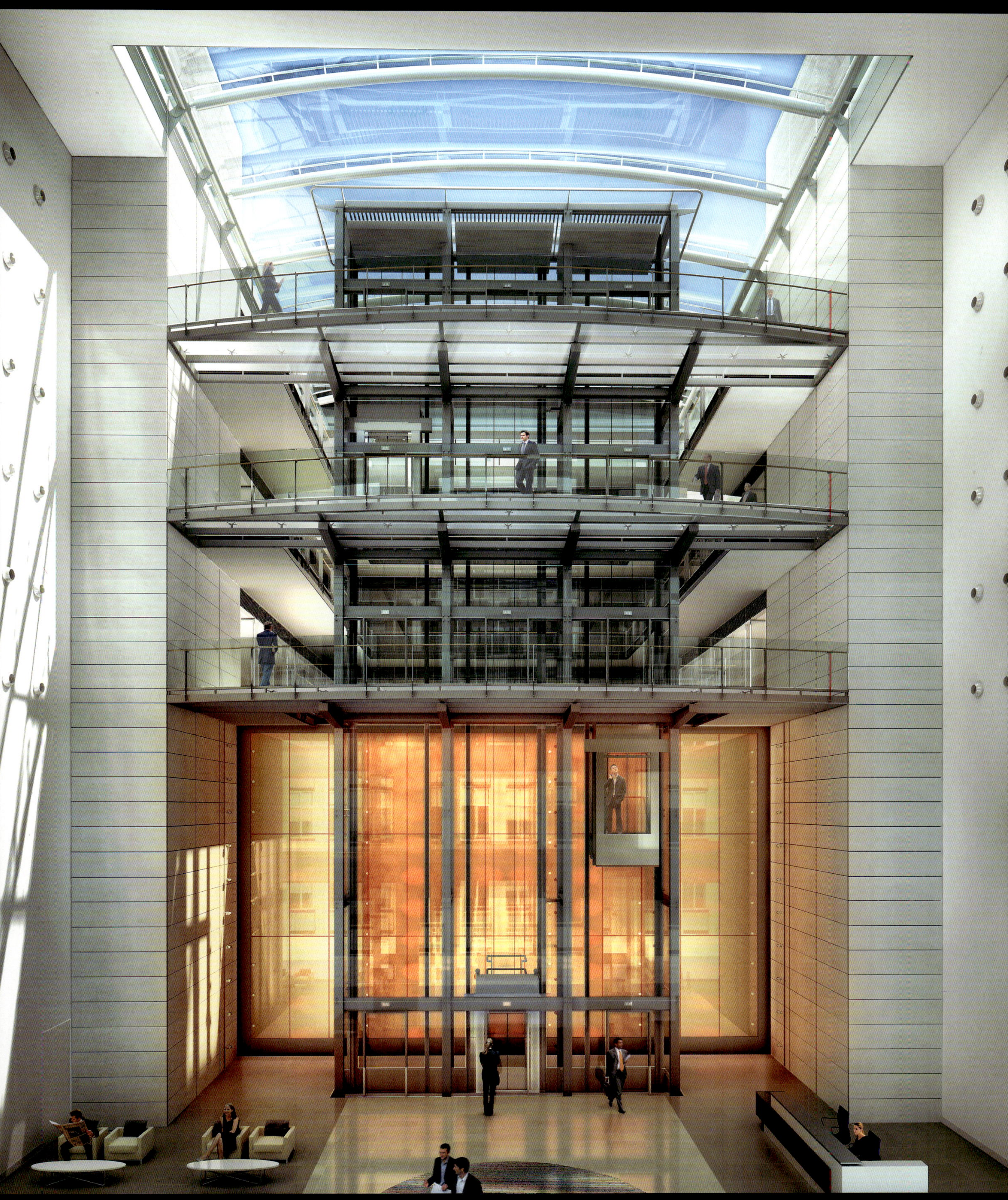

Regent Street Reception
3ds Max, V-Ray, Photoshop
Architect: Rolfe Judd
GMJ Visualisation,
GREAT BRITAIN

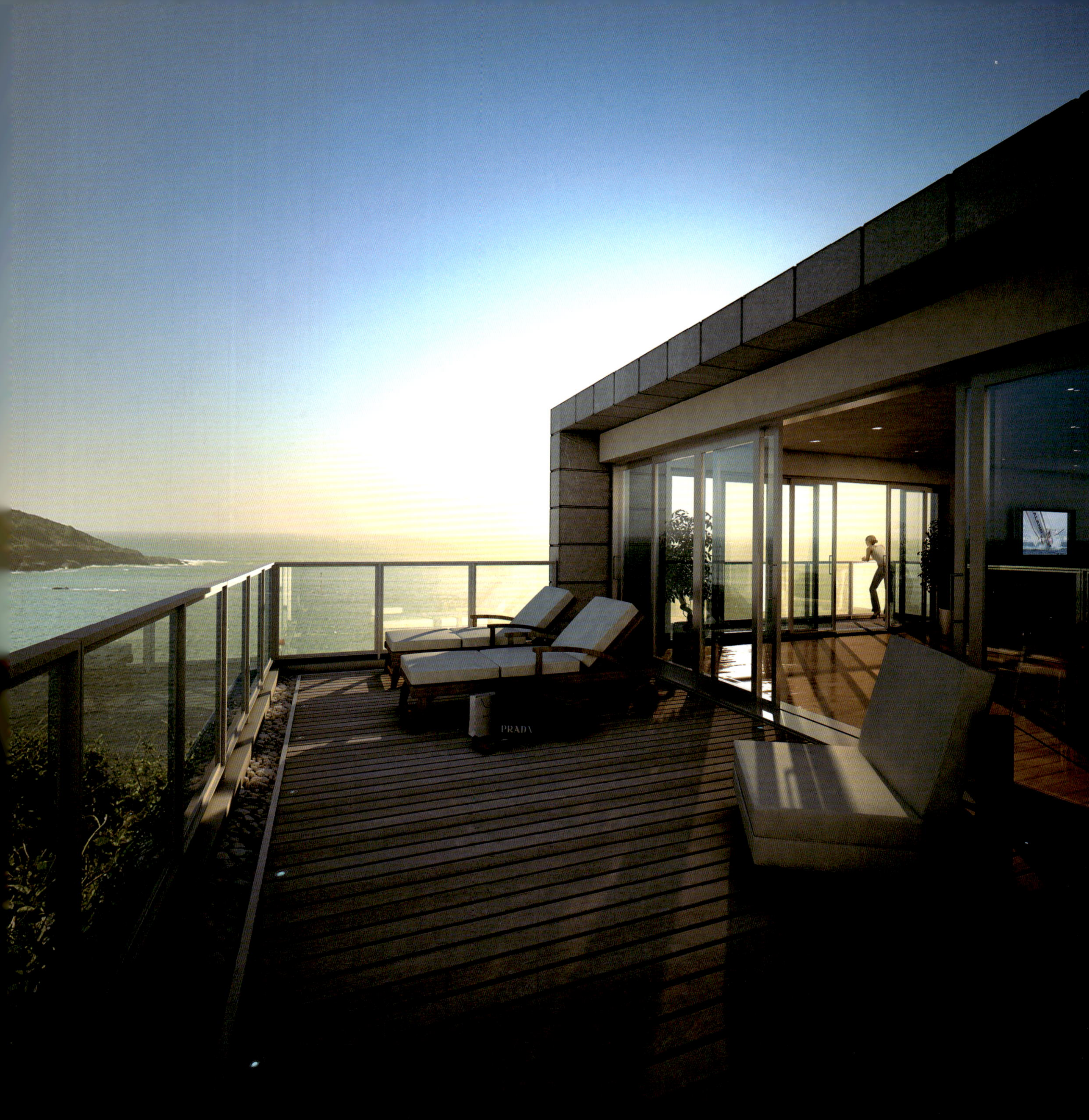

Master

Architecture Exterior (Residential)

Sea View
3ds Max, Photoshop, V-Ray
John Crighton, Visualisation One Ltd,
GREAT BRITAIN

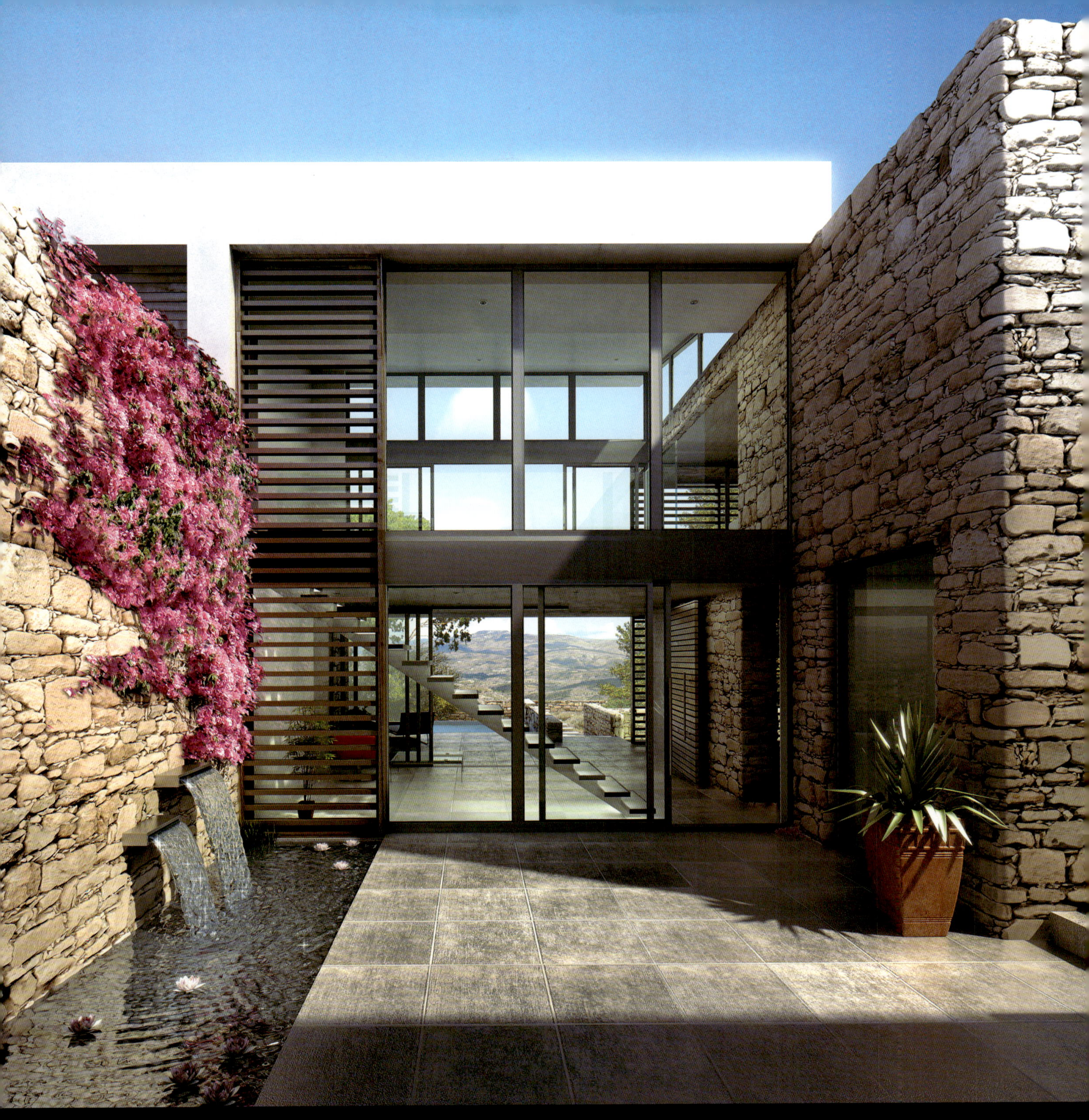

Villa Courtyard
3ds Max, V-Ray, Photoshop
Gareth Thatcher, AHD-Imaging,
GREAT BRITAIN

Excellence

Architecture Exterior (Residential)

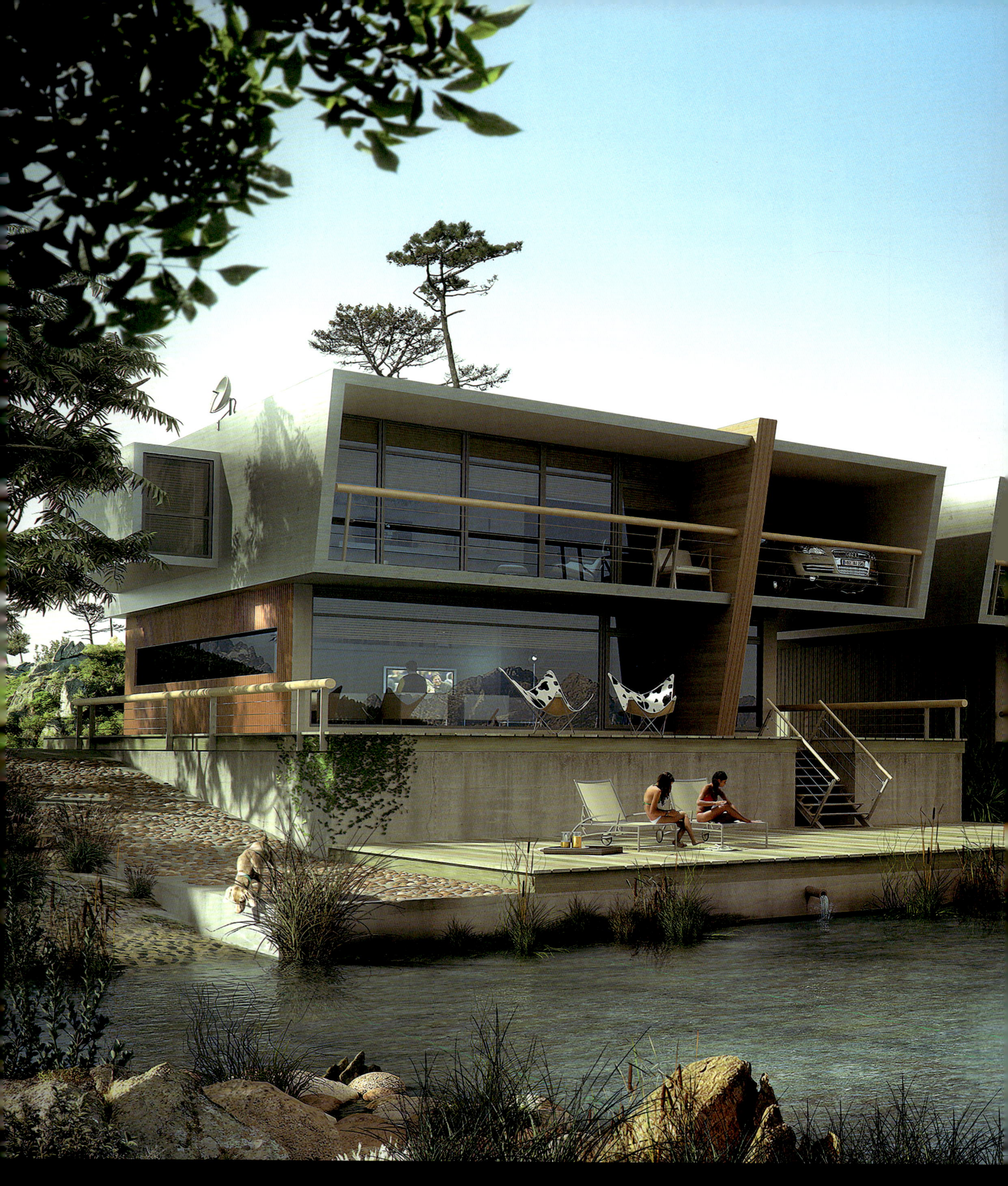

Excellence

Architecture Exterior (Residential)

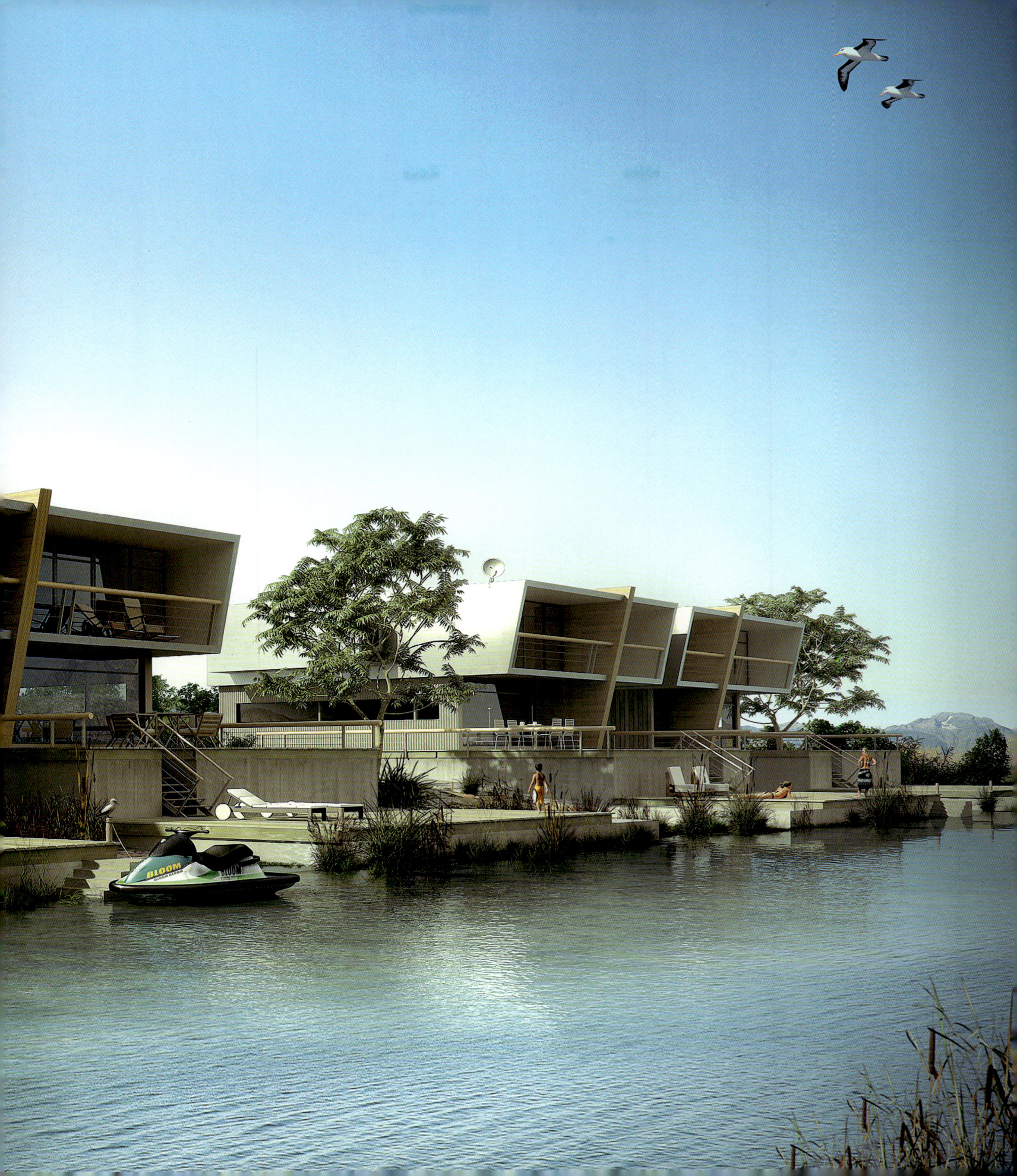
BLOOM
BLOOM

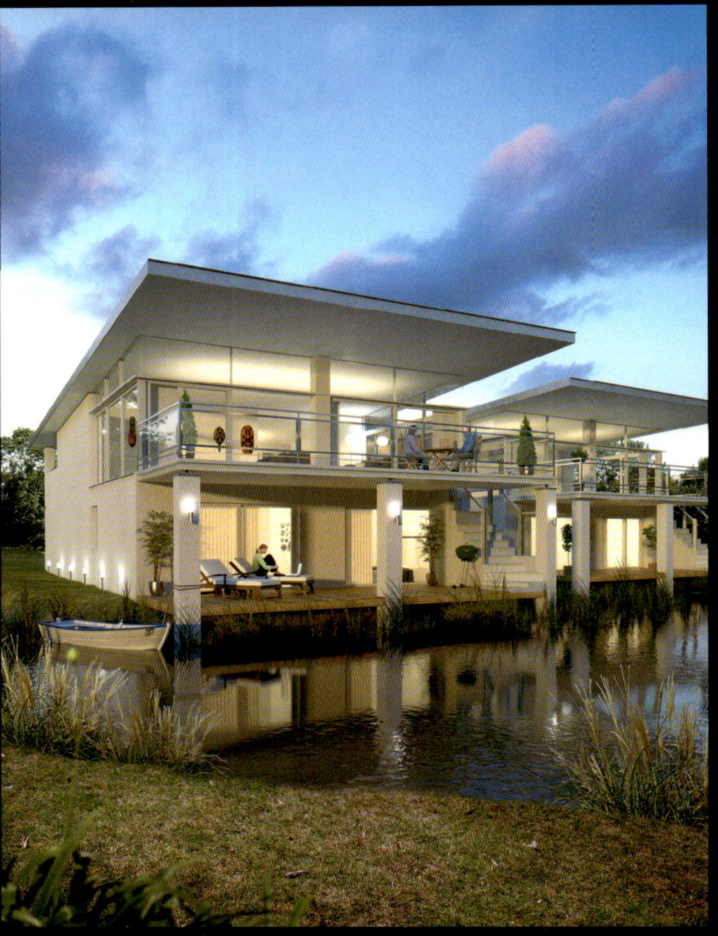

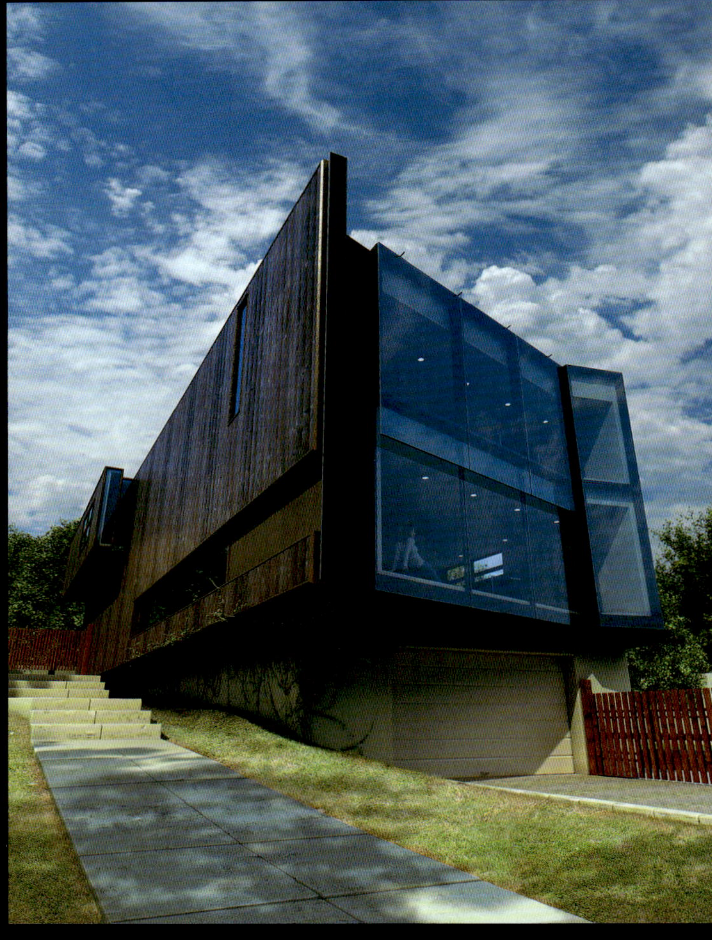

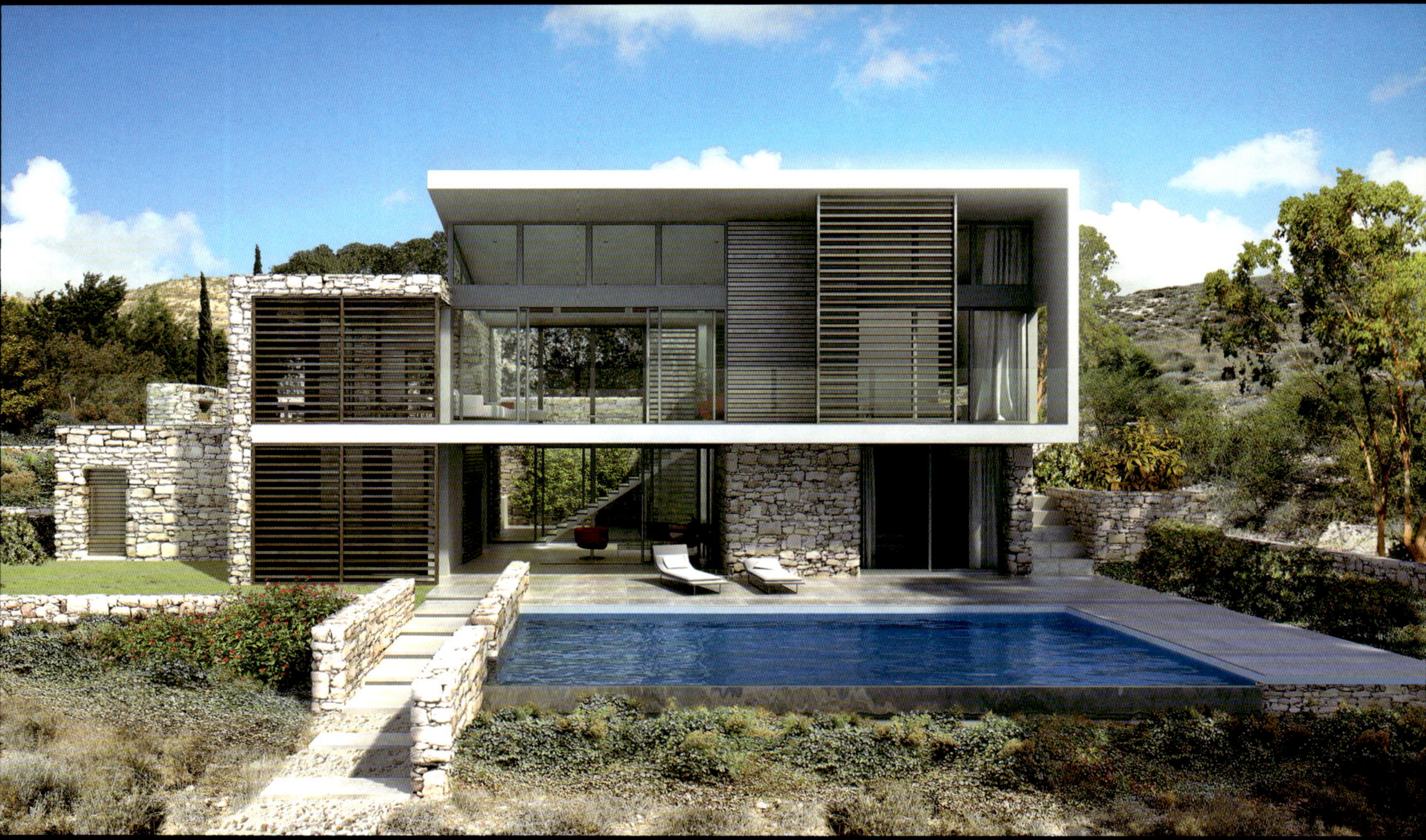

Valerian House on Nightingale Walk
3ds Max, V-Ray, Photoshop
Client: Lower Mill Estate
Architect: Richard Reid and Associates
Martin Drake, Preconstruct, GREAT BRITAIN *[top]*

Minthis Hills
3ds Max, Photoshop, V-Ray
Gareth Thatcher, AHD-Imaging,
GREAT BRITAIN
[above]

City Hill House
3ds Max, Photoshop, V-Ray
Design: John Wardle Architects
Ian Brink, thebrinc, SOUTH AFRICA
[top]

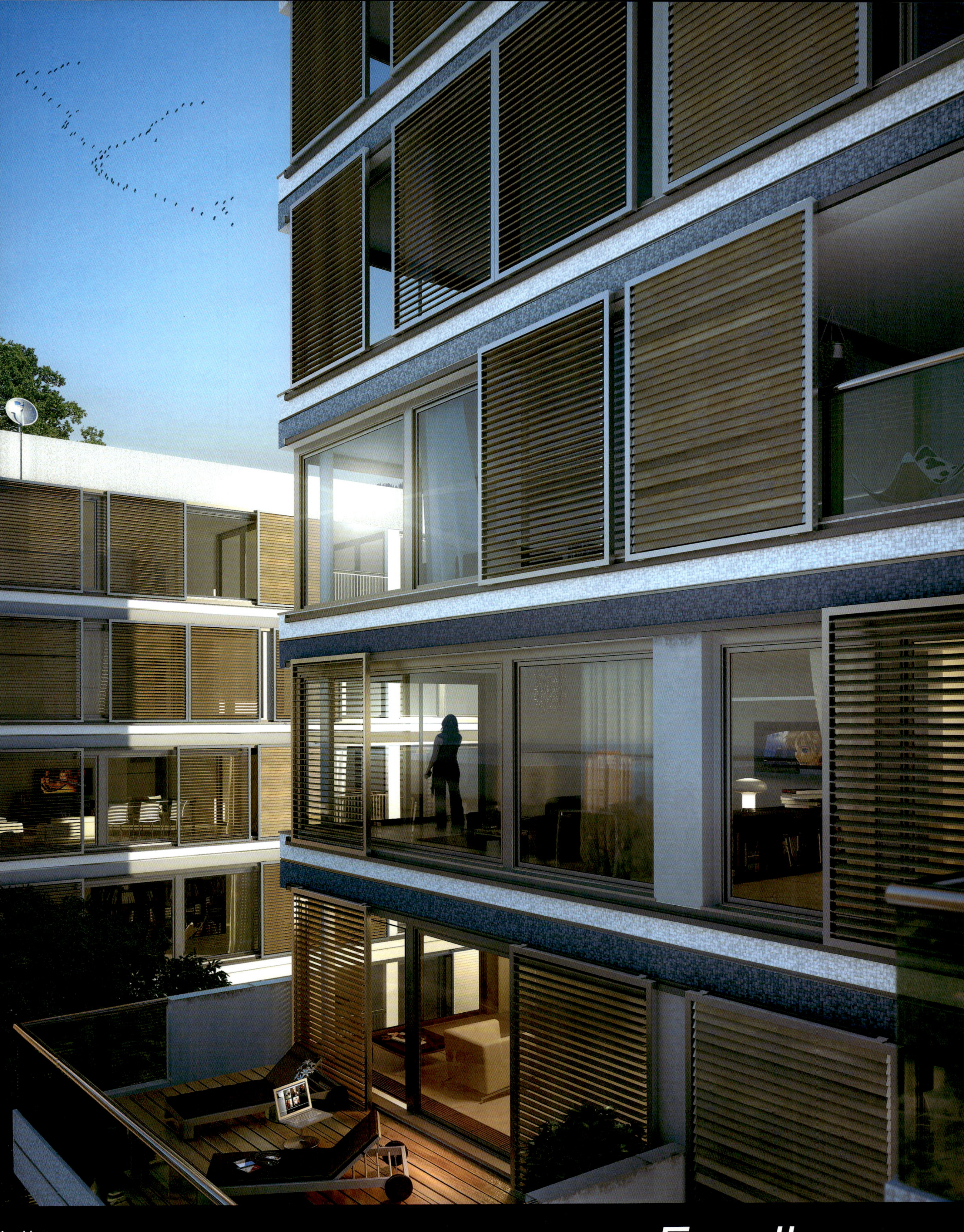

Looking
AutoCAD, 3ds Max, Photoshop
Juan Altieri, A2T, URUGUAY

Excellence

Architecture Exterior (Residential)

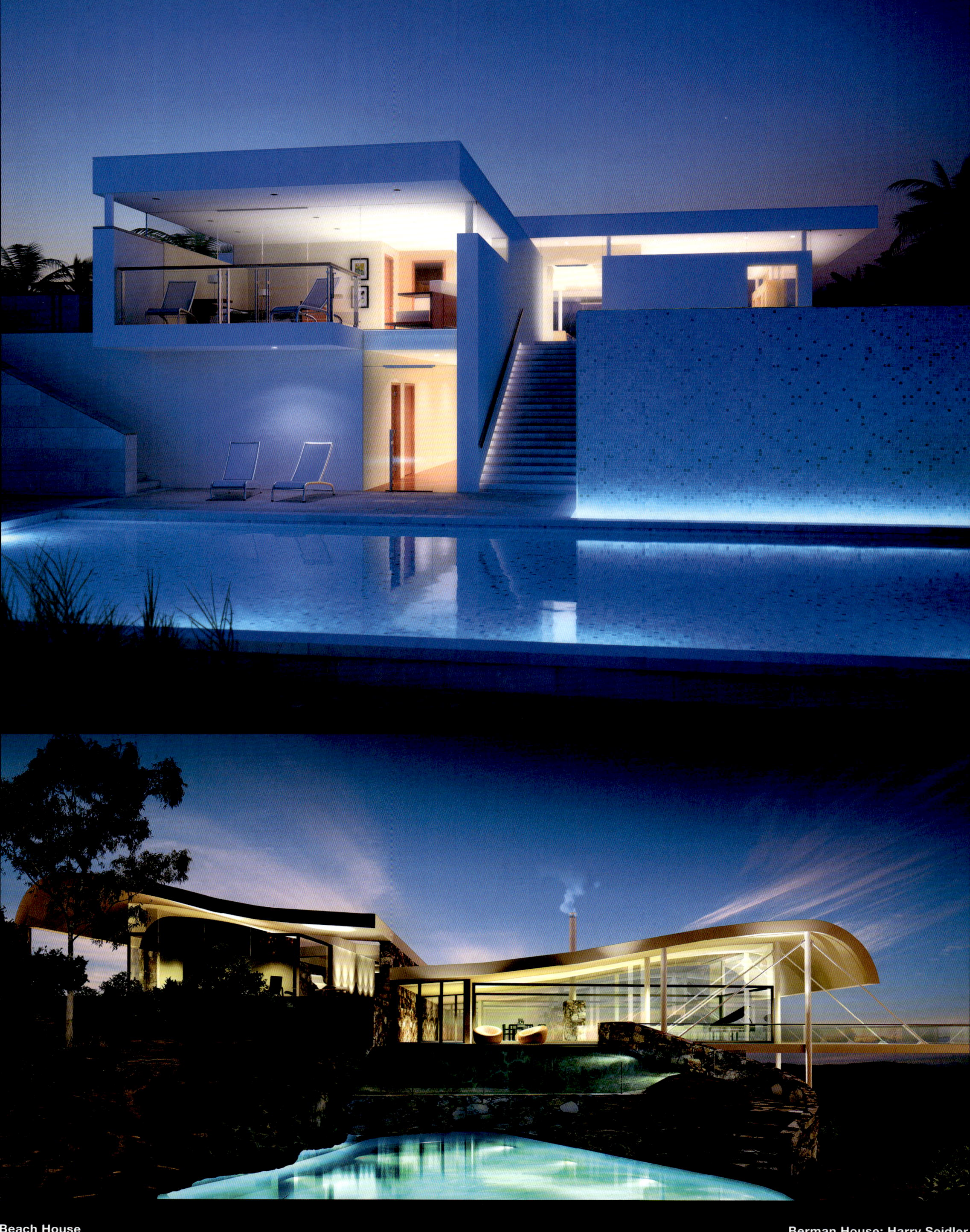

Beach House
3ds Max, V-Ray, Photoshop, SketchUp
Aaron Coon, Conceptual Design Studio, USA
[top]

Berman House: Harry Seidler
3ds Max, V-Ray, Photoshop
Quisinh Tran,
Vivid Consultants Dubai, UAE
[above]

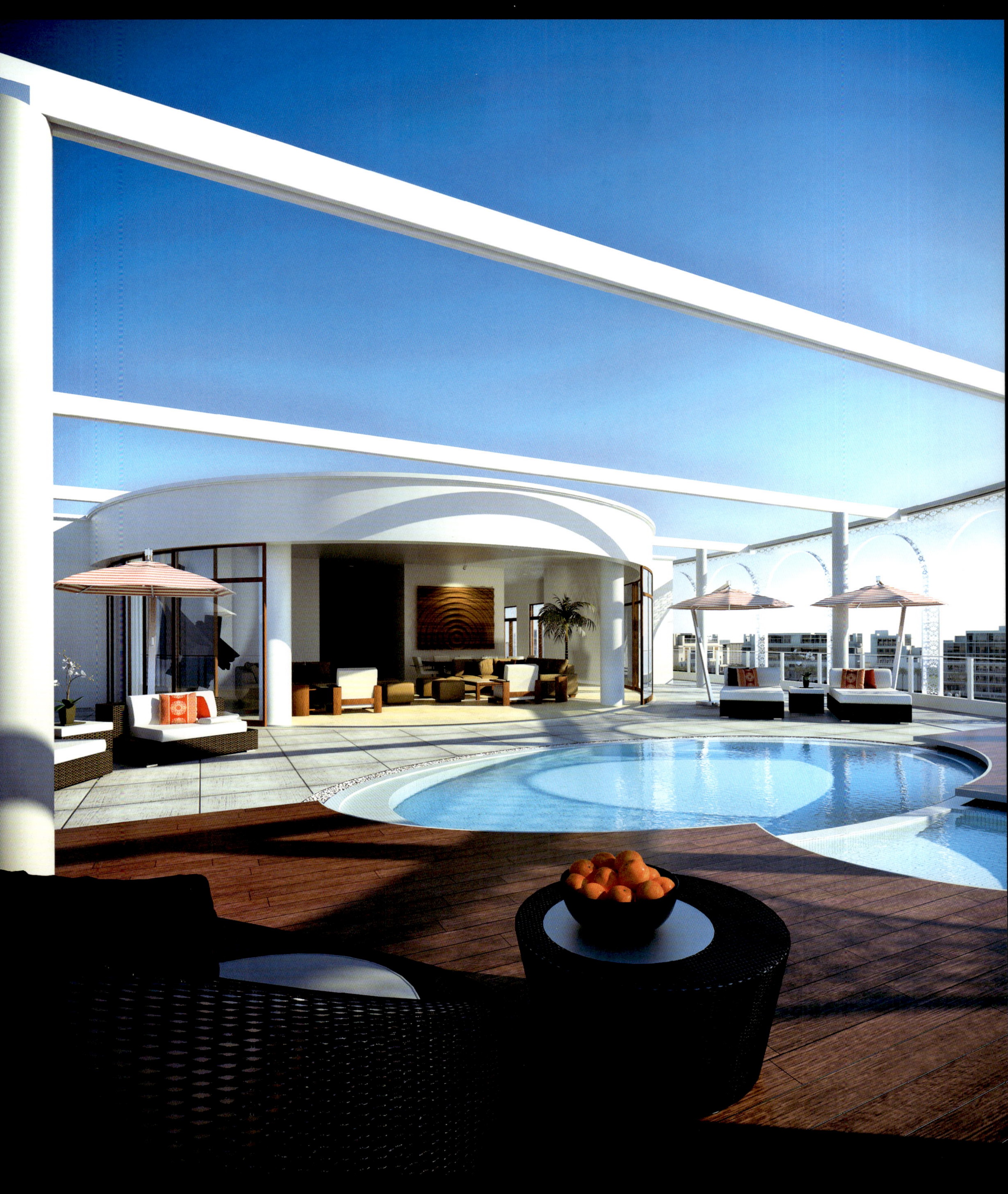

Penthouse Terrace
3ds Max, V-Ray, Photoshop
Rodrigo Lopez, Neoscape, Inc., USA

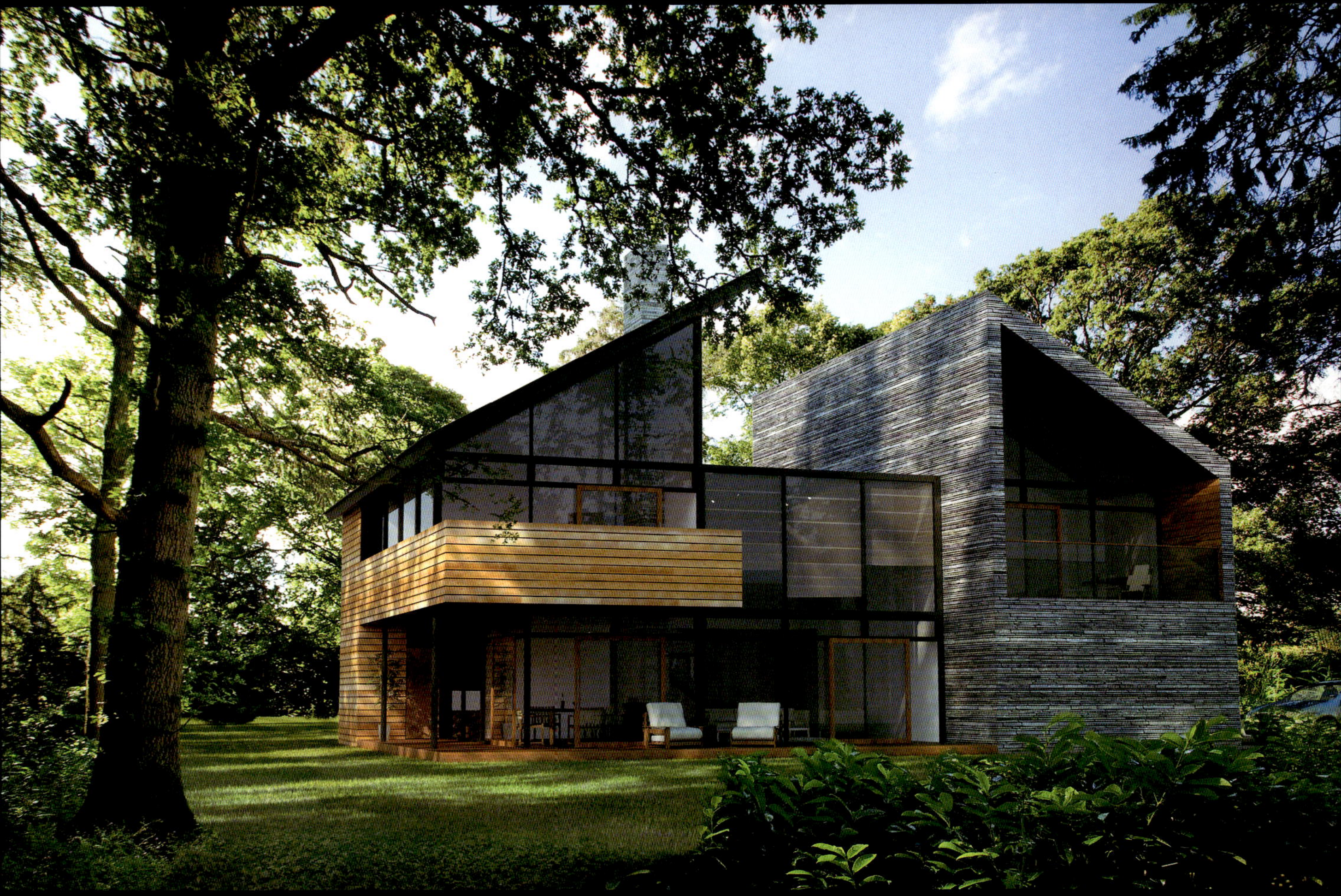

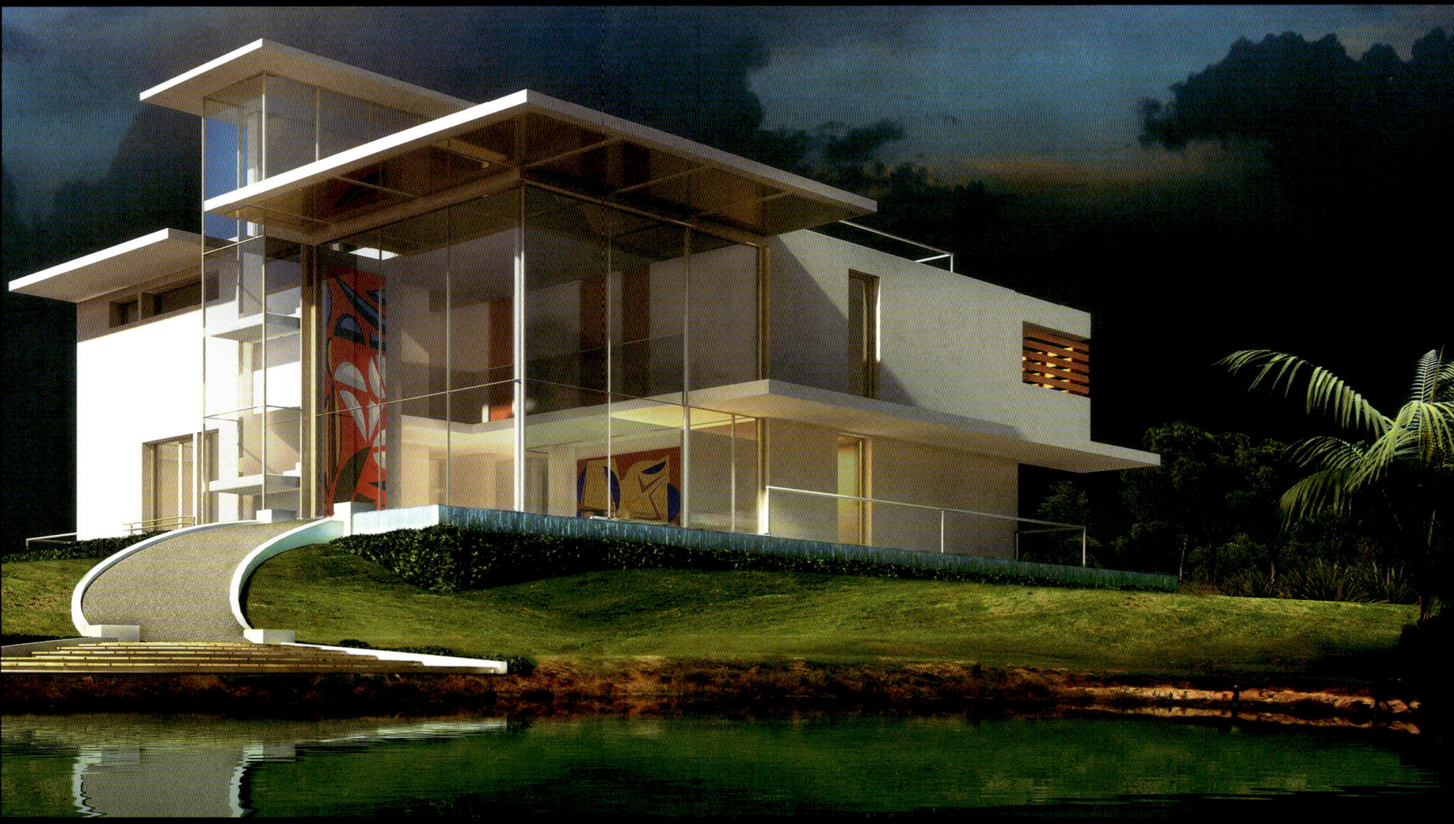

Woodland Villa External
3ds Max, V-Ray, Photoshop
Client: Zebrano Design
Peter Guthrie, GREAT BRITAIN
[top]

Quinta do Lago view 3
3ds Max, V-Ray, Photoshop
Client: E3 Property
Ximo Peris, Smoothe Ltd., GREAT BRITAIN
[above]

Fairway View Villa: End Elevation
3ds Max, V-Ray, Photoshop
Client: Zebrano Design
Peter Guthrie, GREAT BRITAIN
[right]

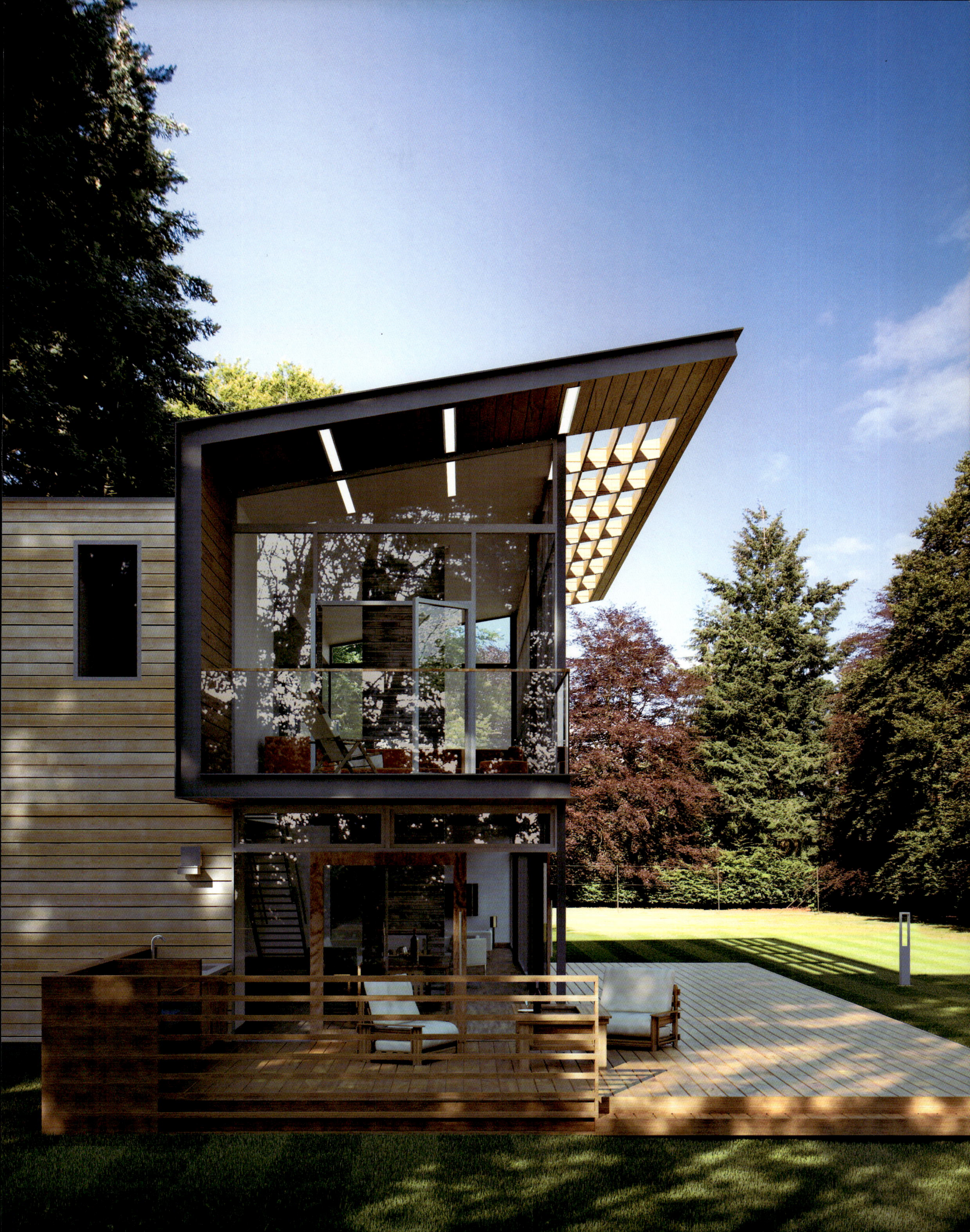

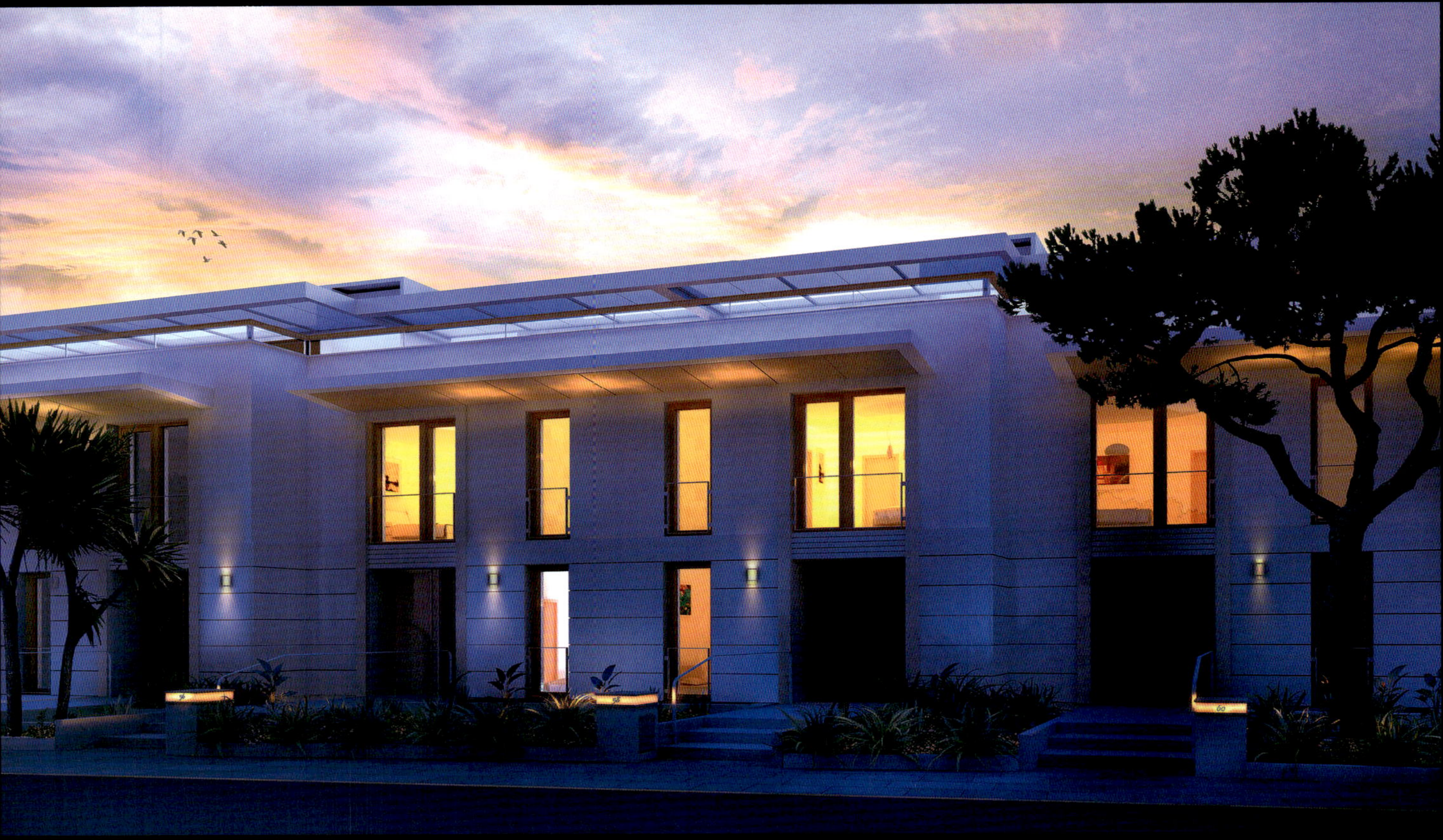

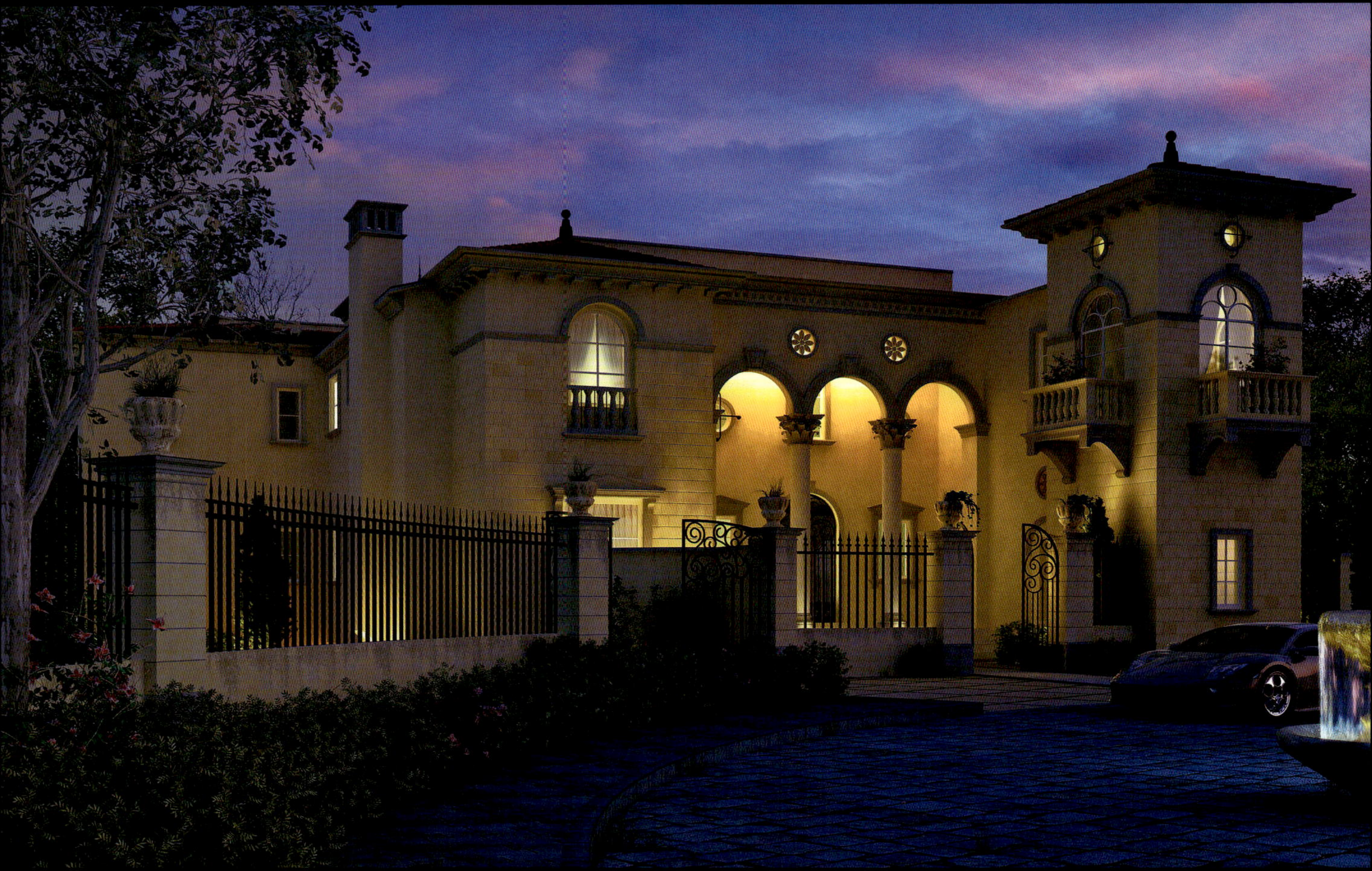

Quinta do Lago view 2
3ds Max, V-Ray, Photoshop
Client: E3 Property
Carlos Carbonar and **Ximo Peris**,
Smoothe Ltd., GREAT BRITAIN
[top]

House Tizzano
3ds Max, V-Ray, Photoshop
Client: Ashai Design
Karuna Karan and **Kumaresan**,
Khan Global, INDIA
[above]

An Evening in the Cotswolds
3ds Max, V-Ray, Photoshop
Client: Lower Mill Estate
Architects: Richard Reid and Associates
Martin Drake, Preconstruct, GREAT BRITAIN
[right]

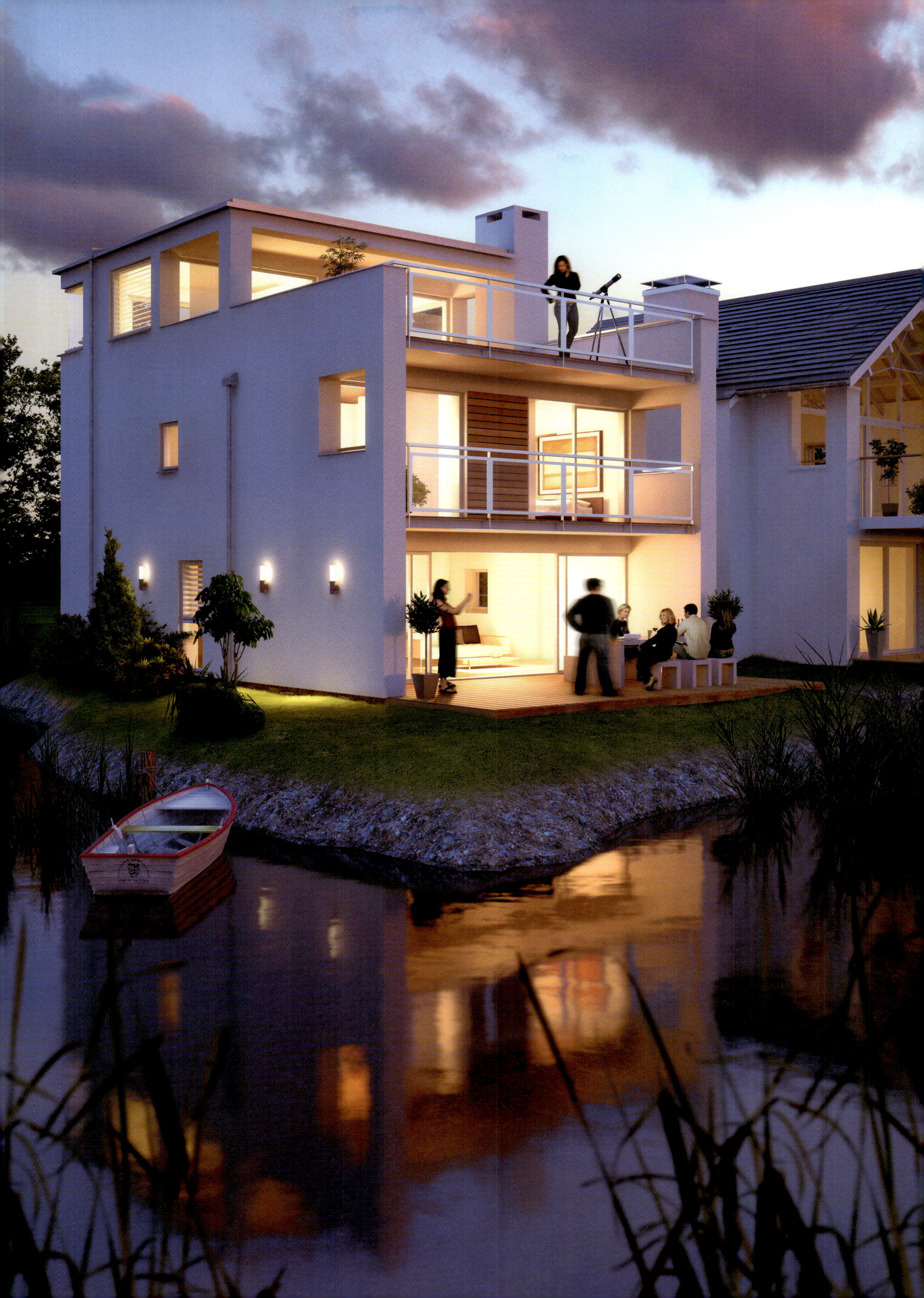

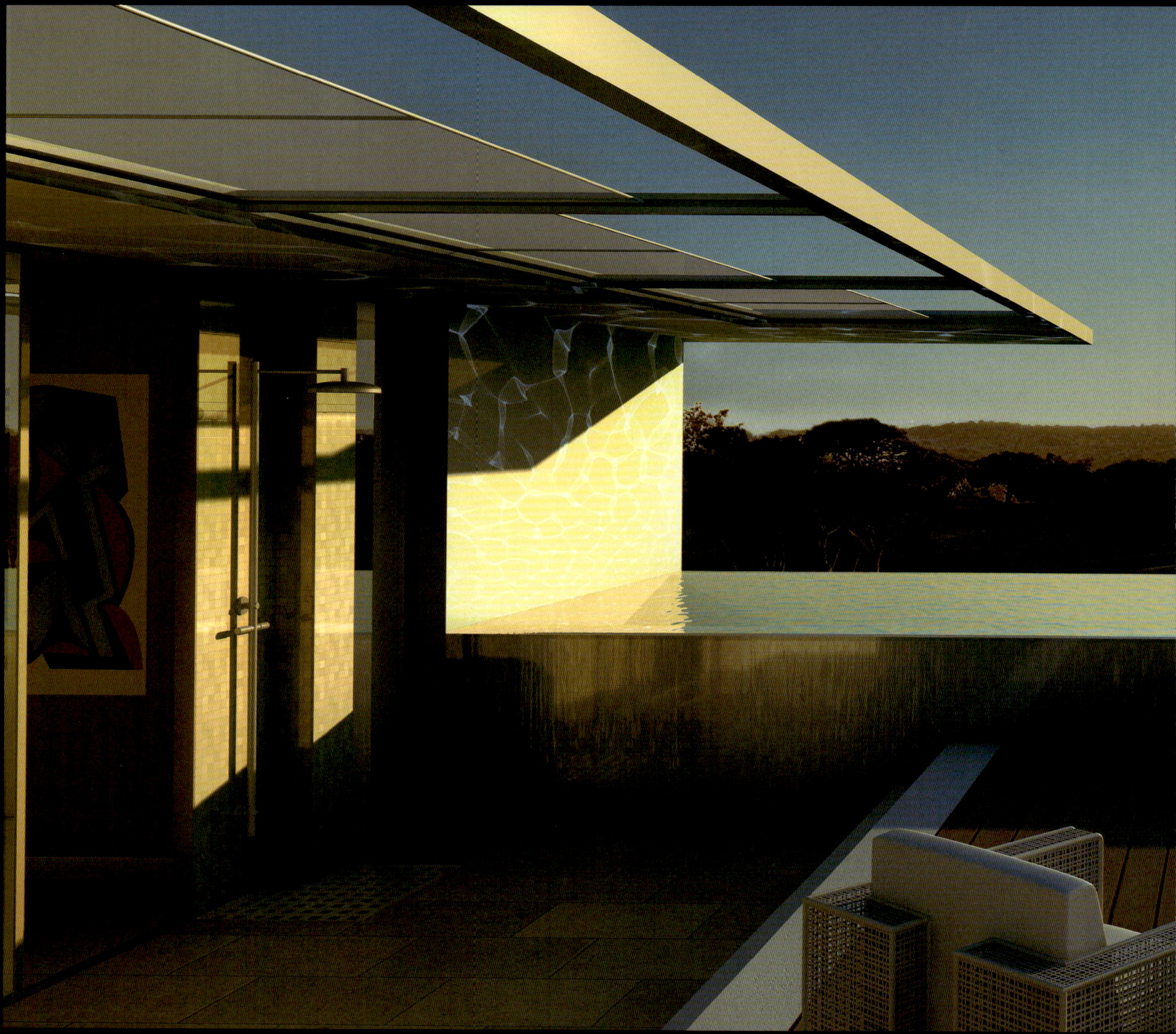

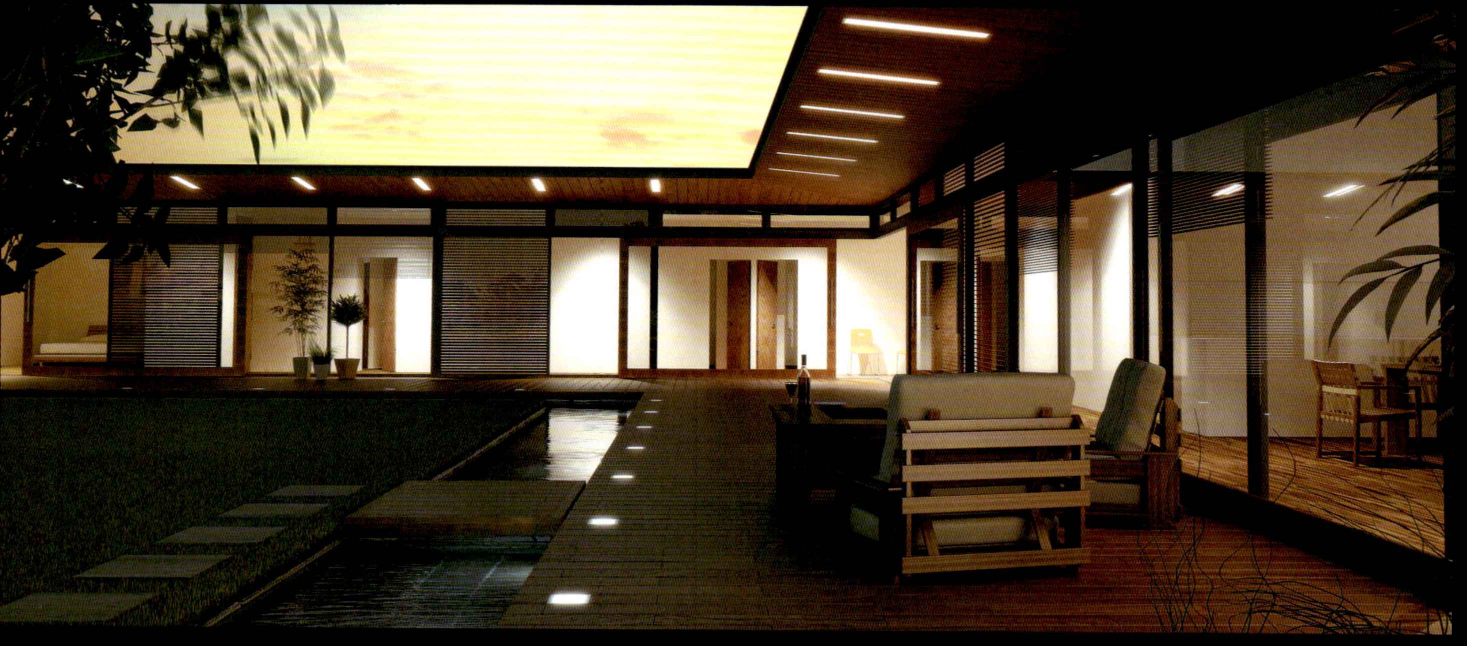

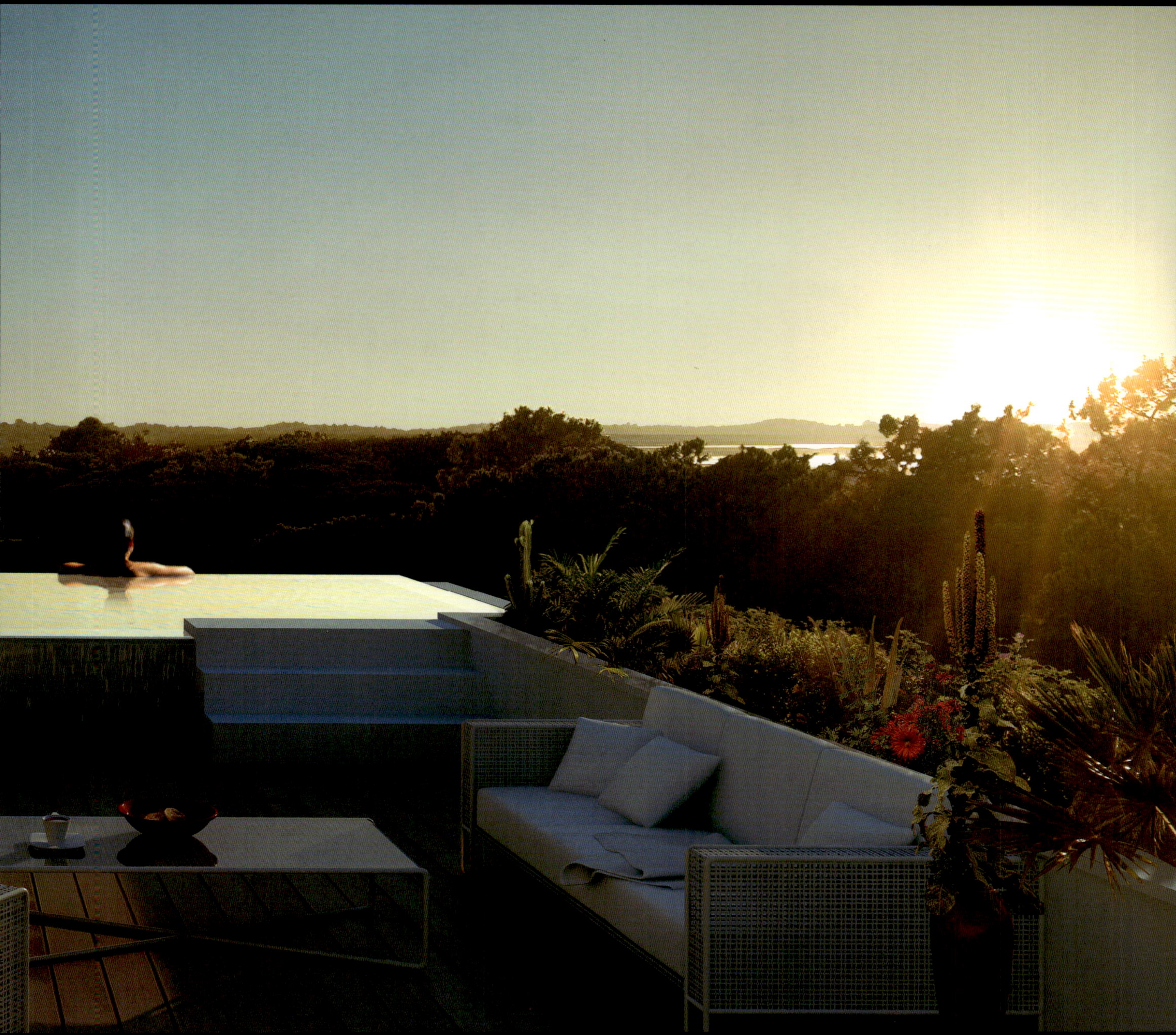

Quinta do Lago view 1
3ds Max, V-Ray, Photoshop
Client: E3 Property
Vanessa Forner and
Ximo Peris, Smoothe Ltd.,
GREAT BRITAIN
[above]

Walled Garden Villa Dusk
3ds Max, V-Ray, Photoshop
Client: Zebrano Design
Peter Guthrie,
GREAT BRITAIN
[left]

Escape to the Cotswolds
3ds Max, V-Ray, Photoshop
Client: Lower Mill Estate
Architect: Richard Reid
and Associates
Martin Drake, Preconstruct,
GREAT BRITAIN
[right]

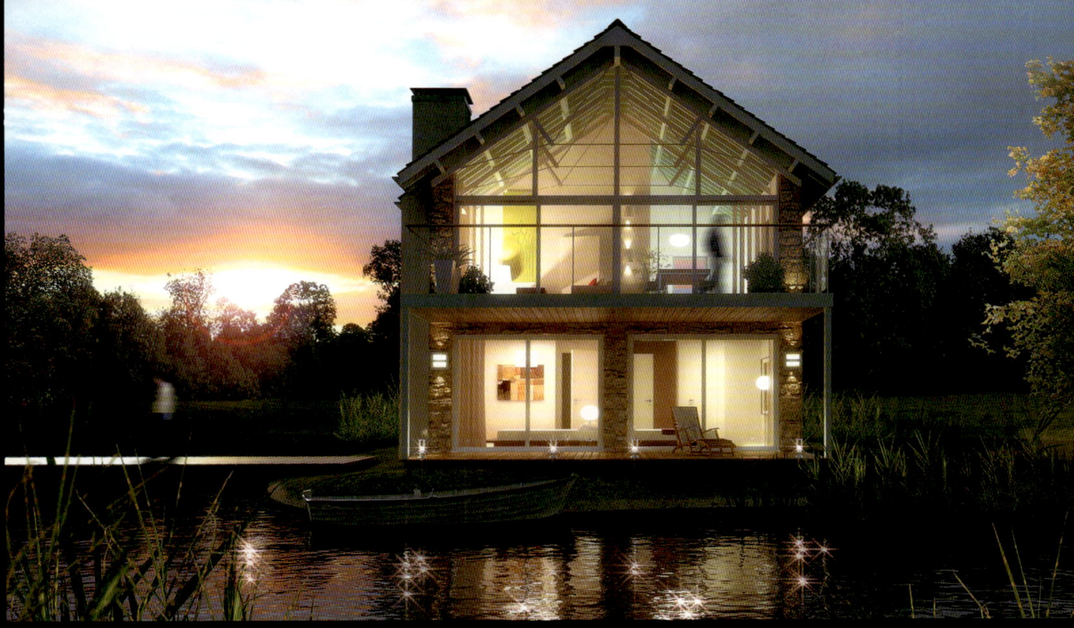

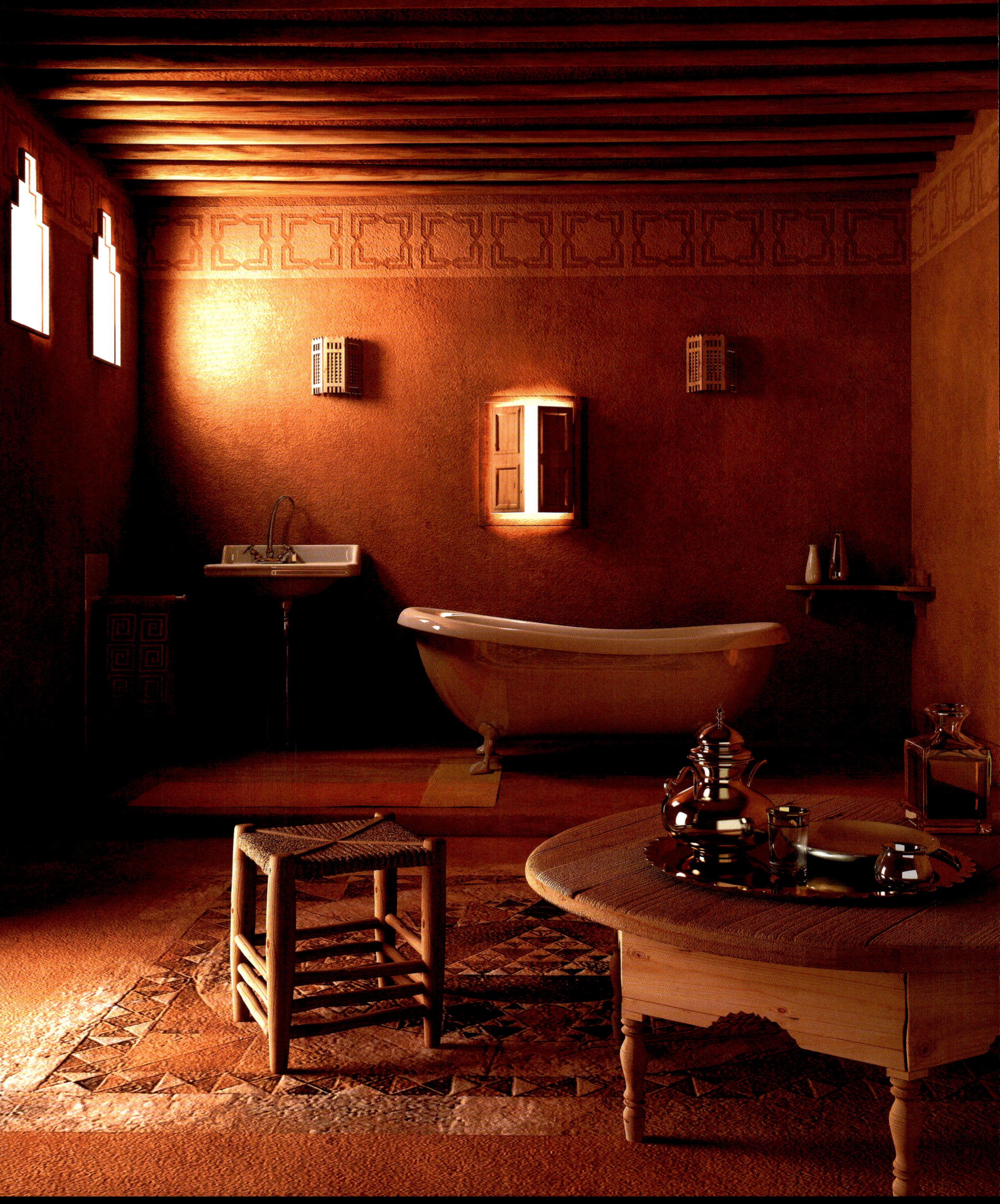

Master

Architecture Interior (Residential)

Arabic Bath
3ds Max
Alberto Luque, Gárgola Estudio,
SPAIN

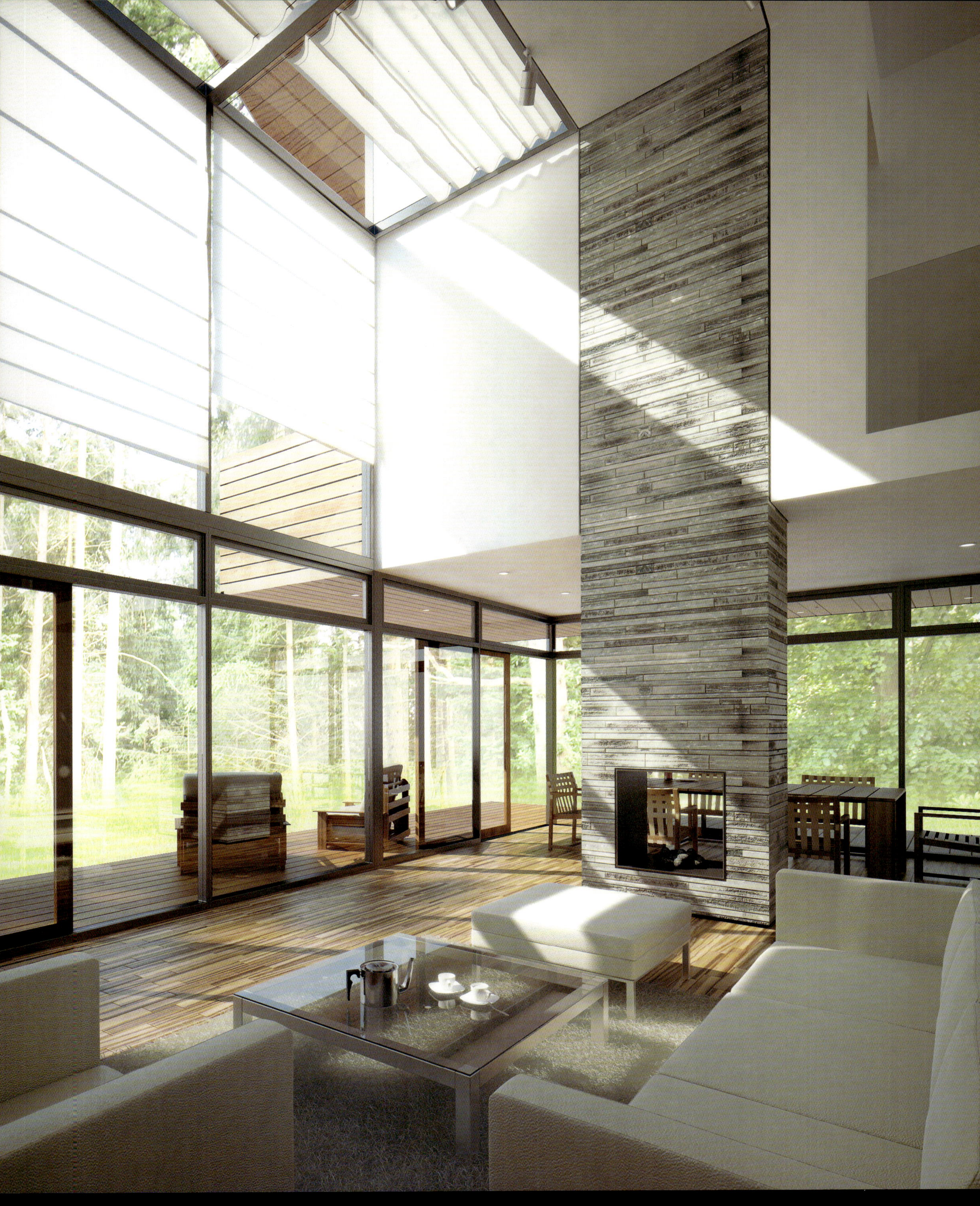

Woodland Villa Internal
3ds Max, V-Ray, Photoshop
Client: Zebrano Design
Peter Guthrie, GREAT BRITAIN

Excellence
Architecture Interior (Residential)

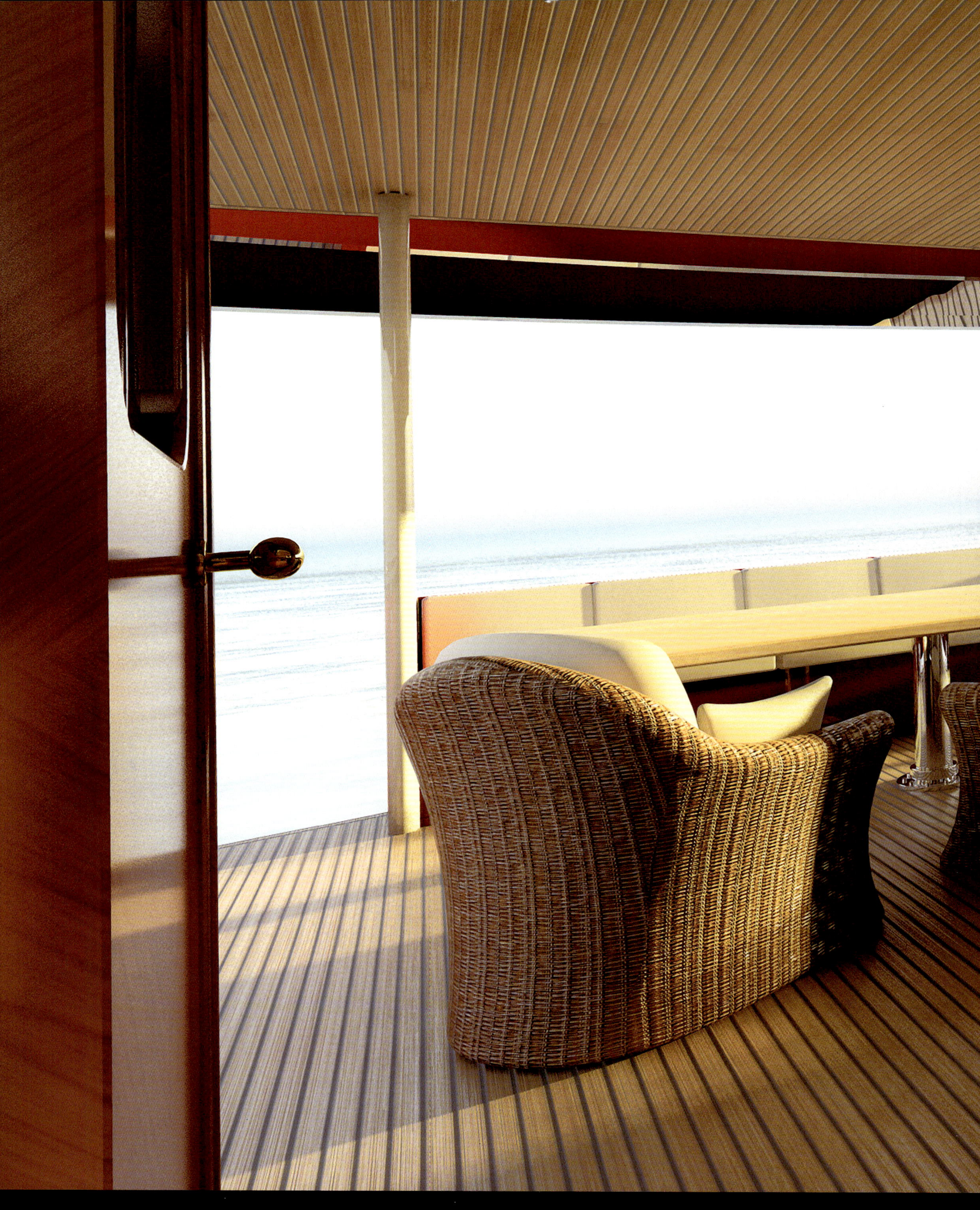

Excellence

Architecture Interior (Residential)

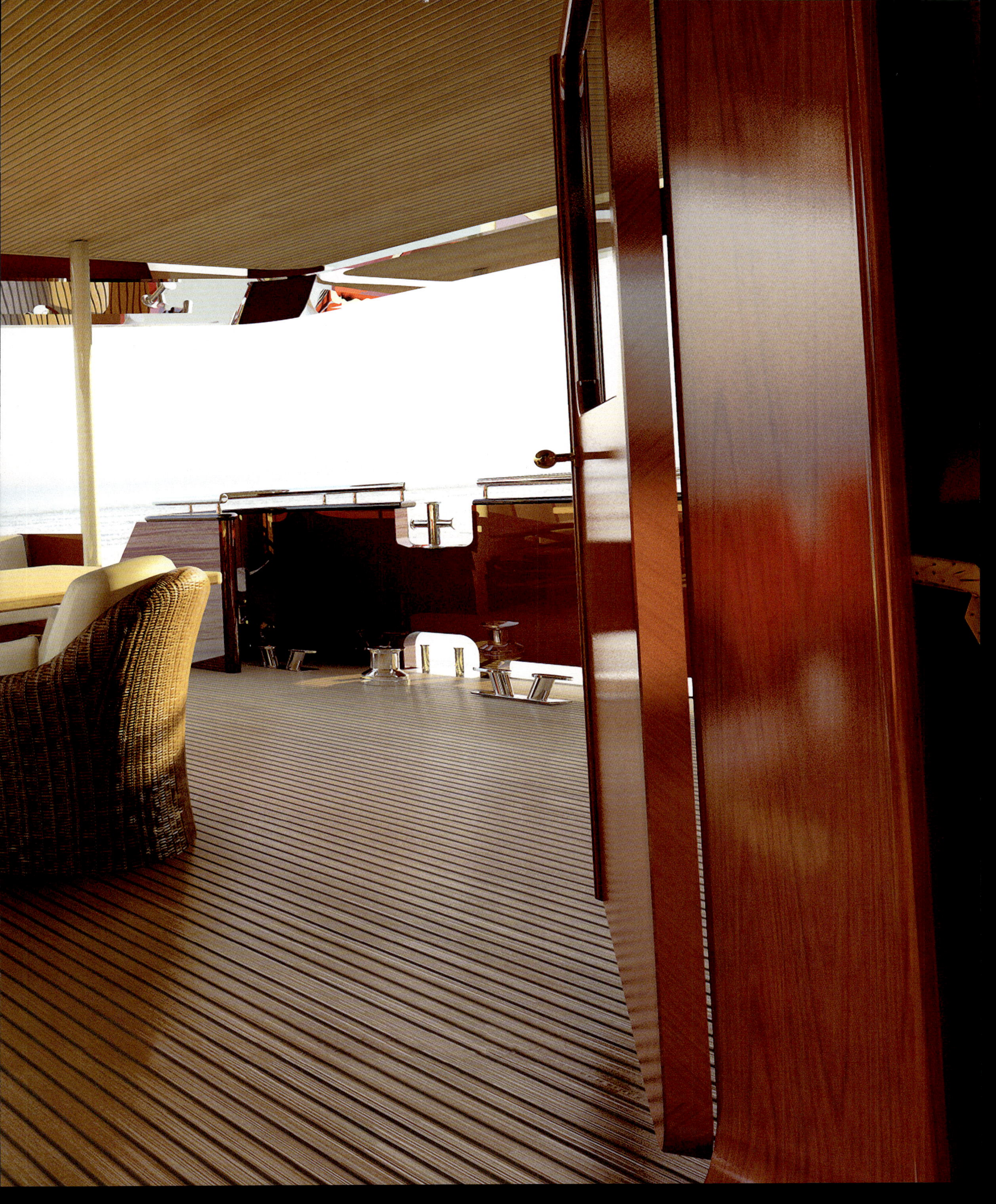

Yacht Interior
3ds Max, mental ray
Giorgio Vecchio, Absolute 2001,
ITALY

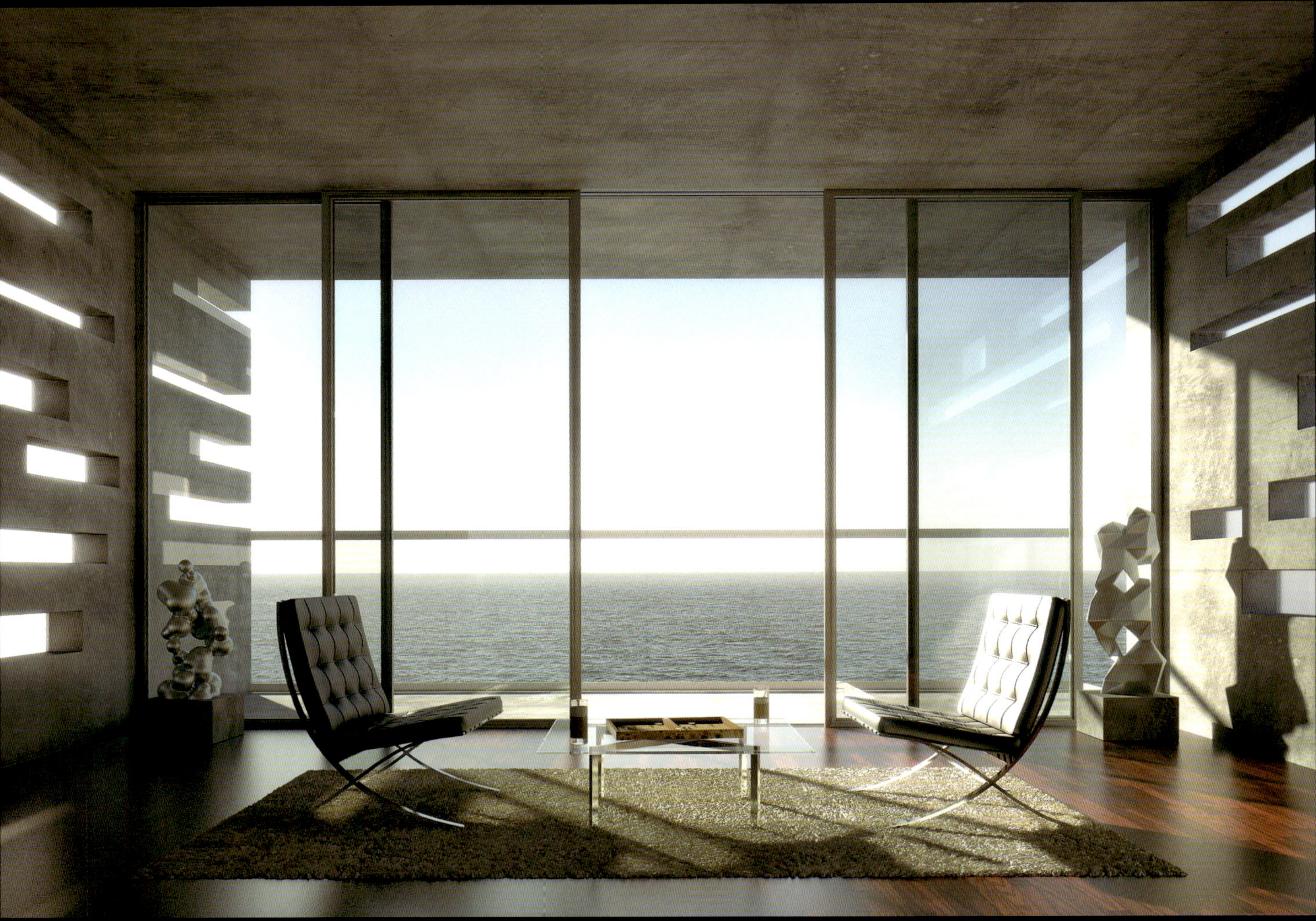

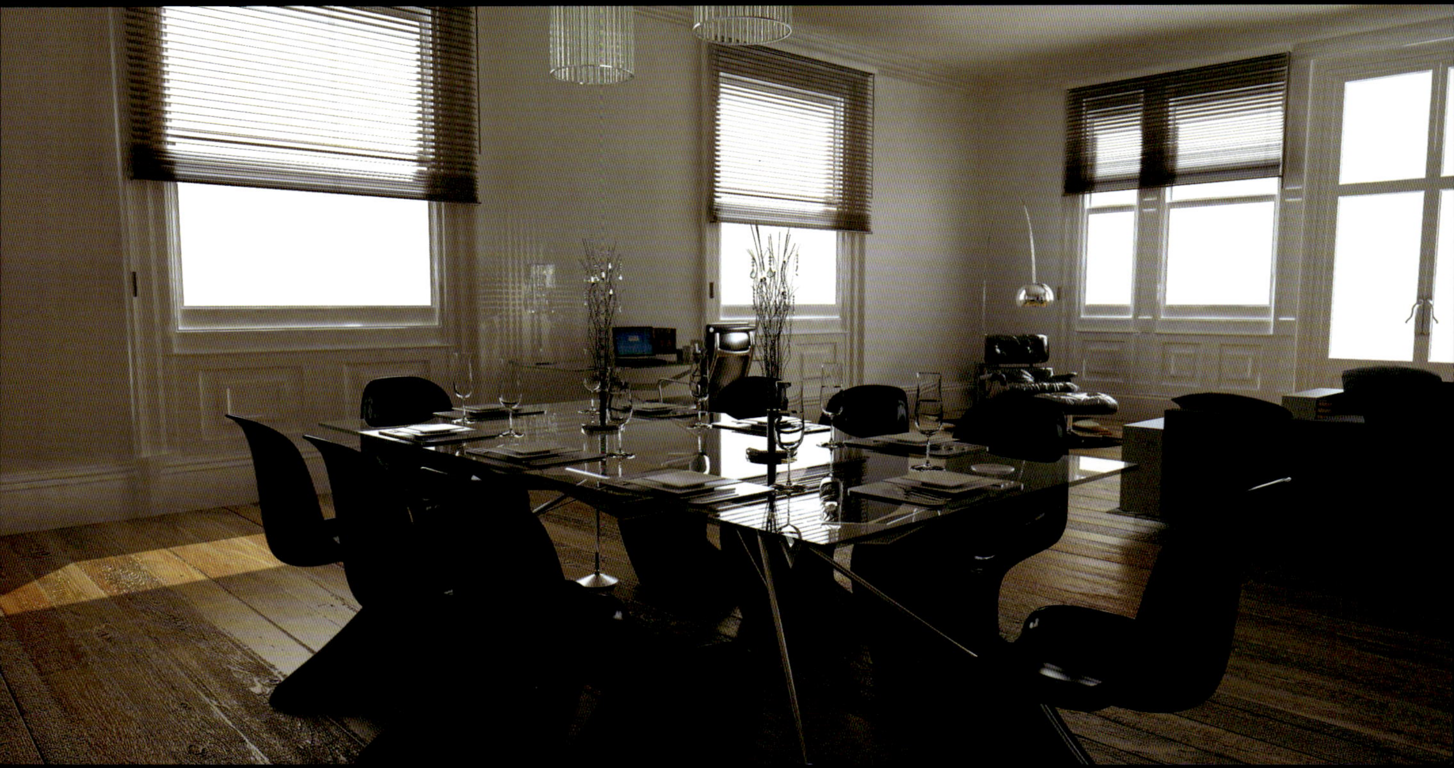

Frappe
3ds Max, V-Ray, Photoshop
Vladimir Mulhem, GREAT BRITAIN
[top]

Concept Room
3ds Max, V-Ray
Aedas Imaging, GREAT BRITAIN
[above]

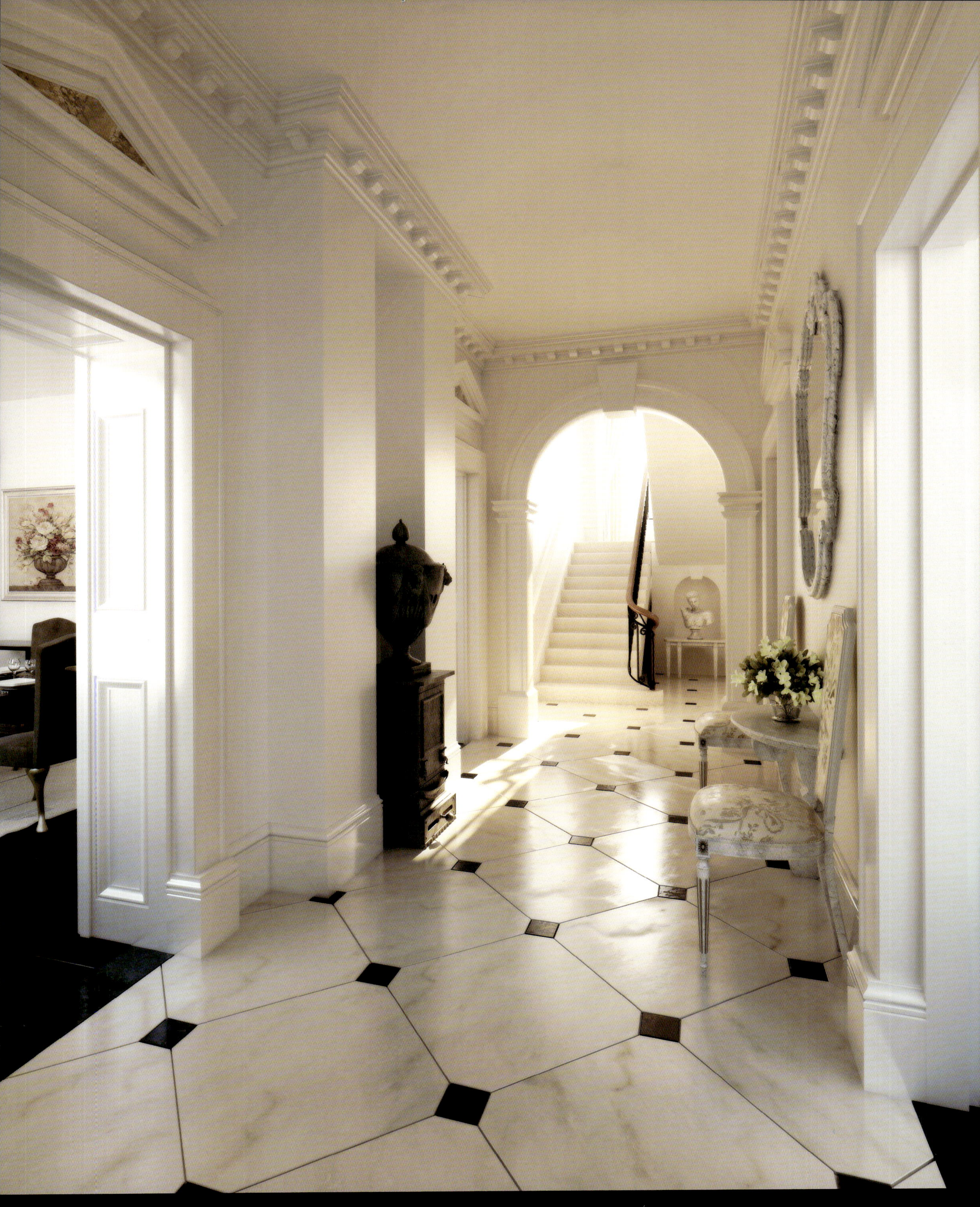

Hallway
3ds Max, V-Ray, Photoshop
Pat Corcoran, Visualisation One Ltd,
GREAT BRITAIN

Excellence
Architecture Interior (Residential)

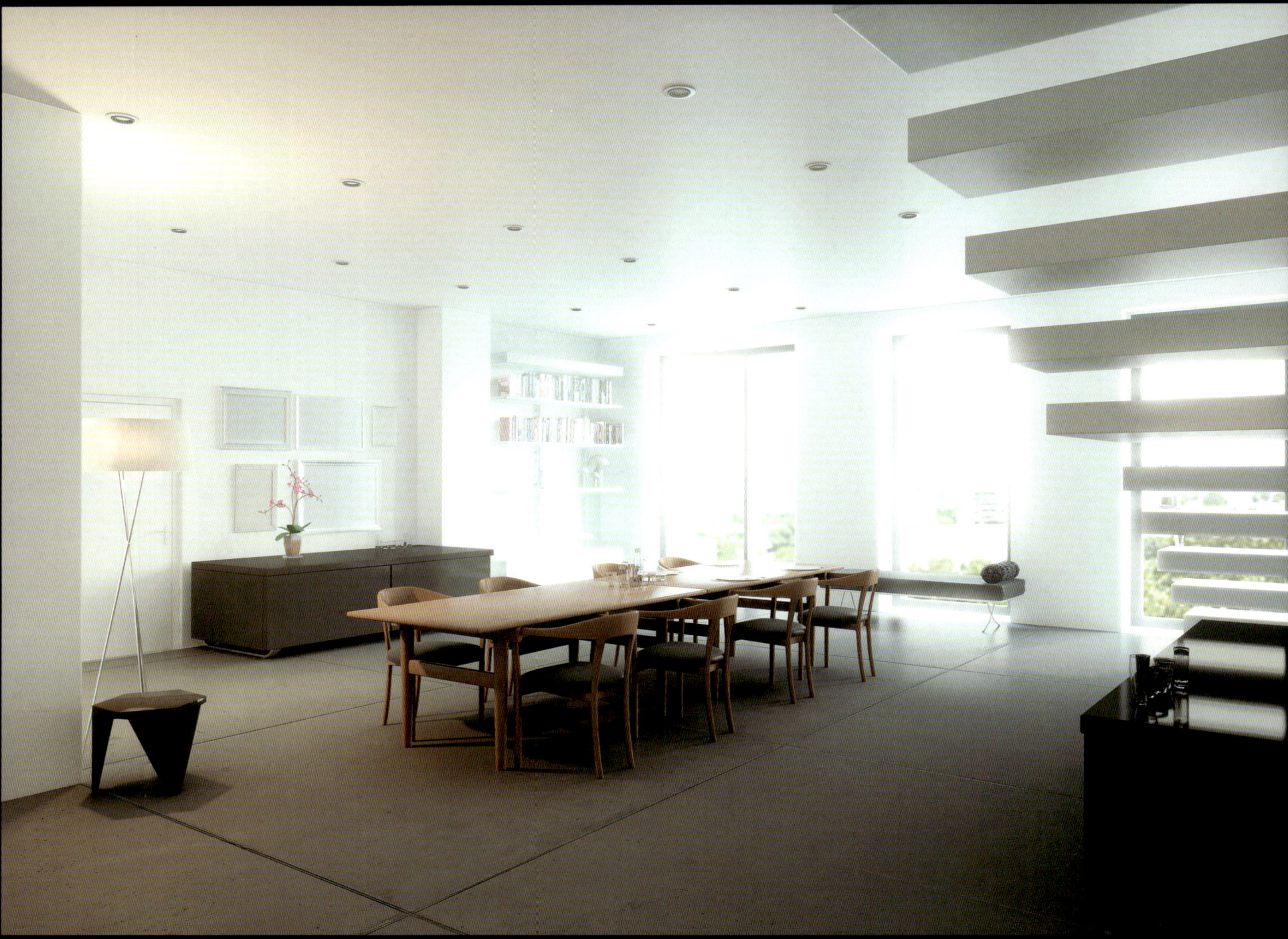

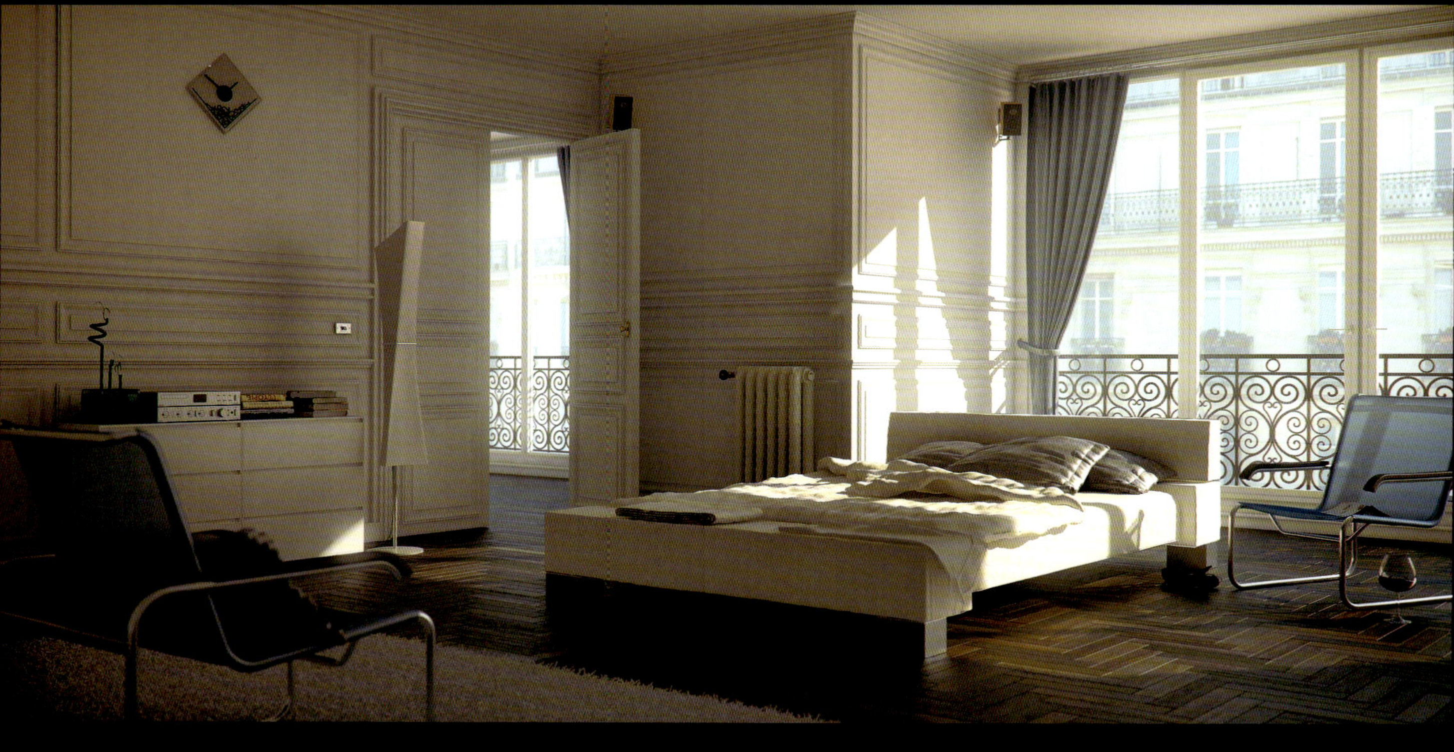

Stanislavsky Modern
3ds Max, mental ray, Photoshop
Peter Aylward, Smoothe Ltd.,
GREAT BRITAIN
[top]

Classic interior
3ds Max, Photoshop
Neil Griffiths,
GREAT BRITAIN
[above]

N-stack
VIZ, V-Ray, Photoshop
Geoffrey Packer,
GREAT BRITAIN
[right]

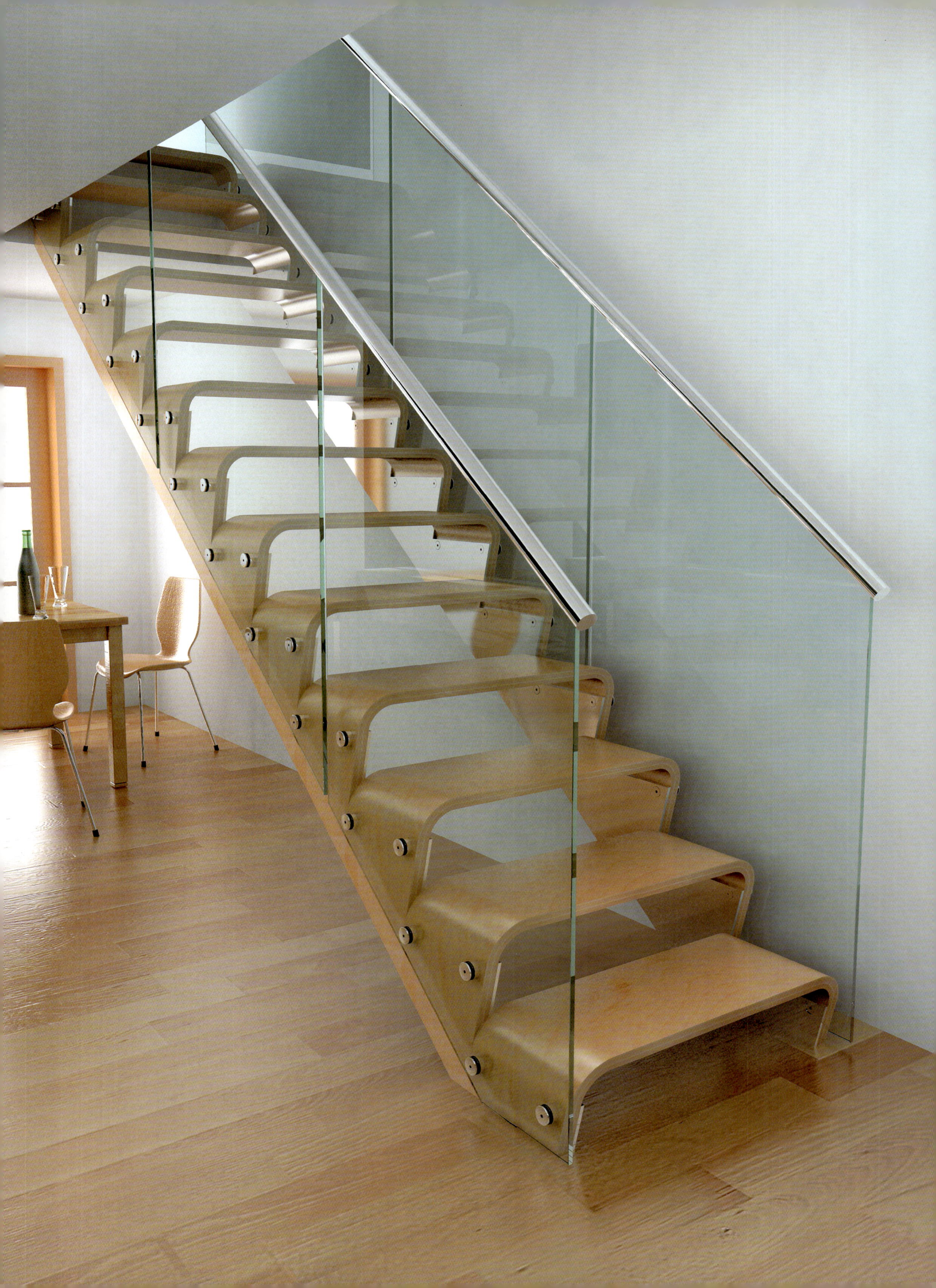

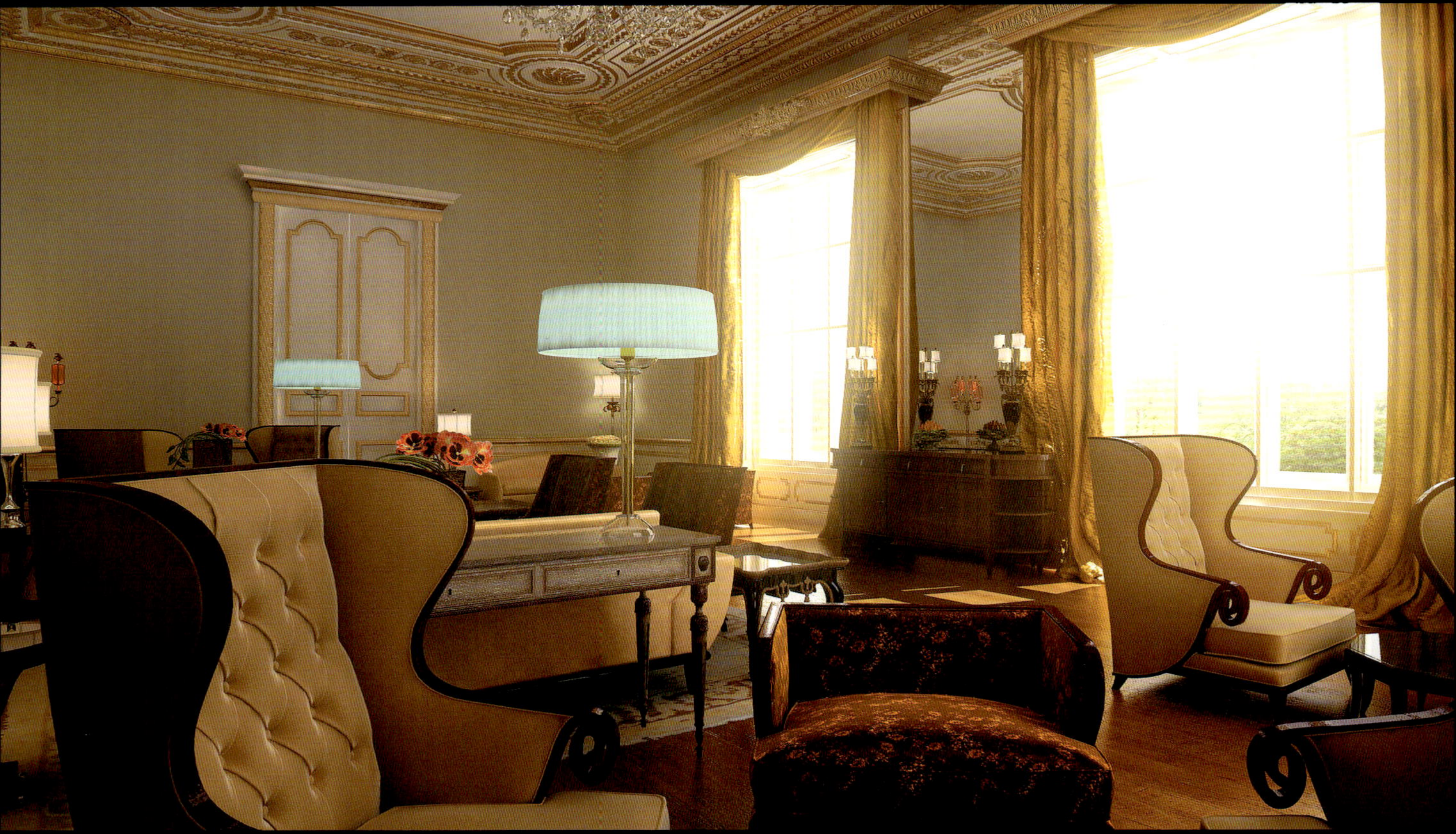

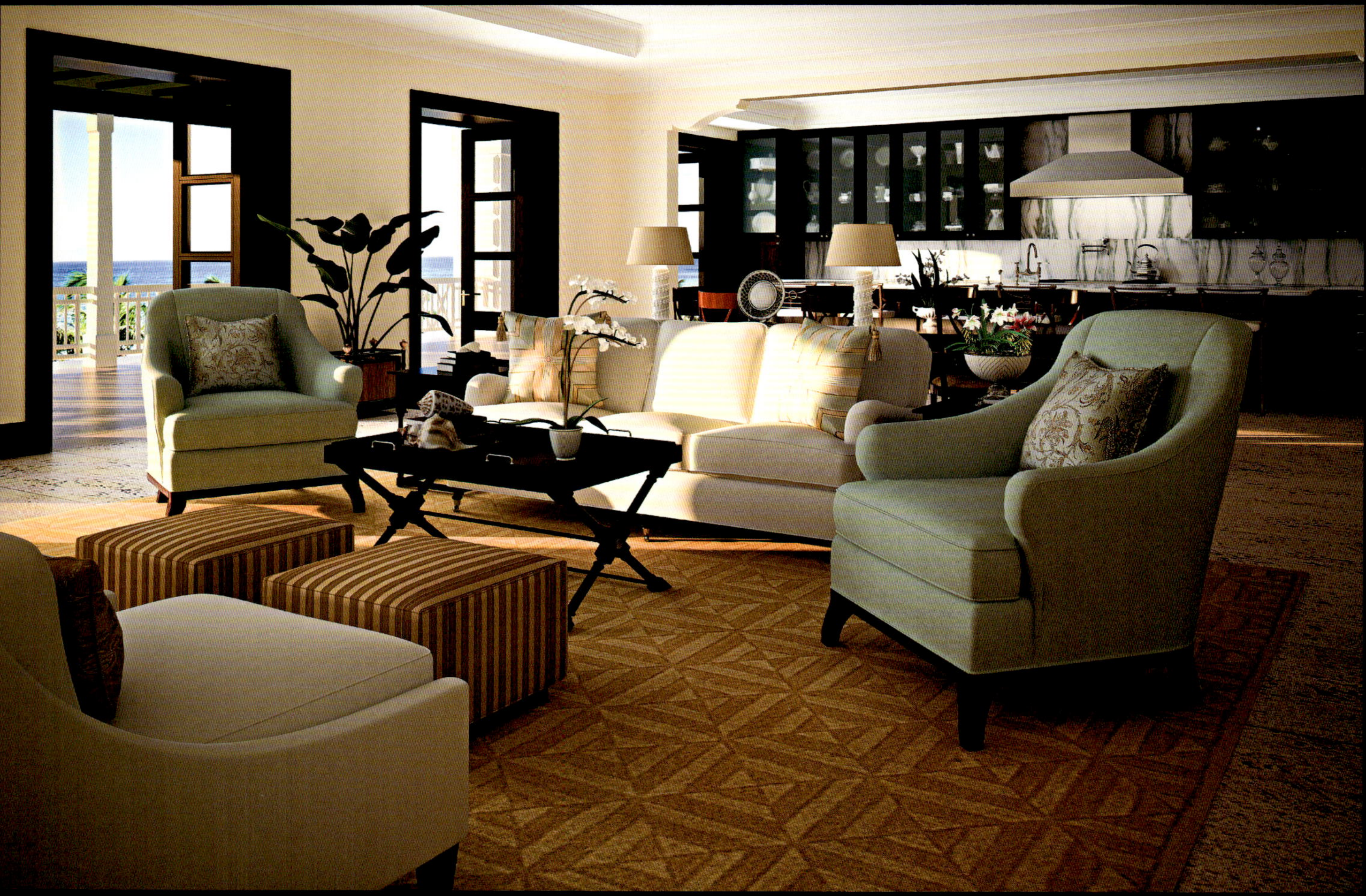

Gold room
3ds Max, V-Ray, Photoshop
SPLITT Ltd/3D Helps,
GREAT BRITAIN
[top]

Penthouse Living Room
3ds Max, V-Ray, Photoshop
Lon Grohs, Neoscape,
Inc., USA
[above]

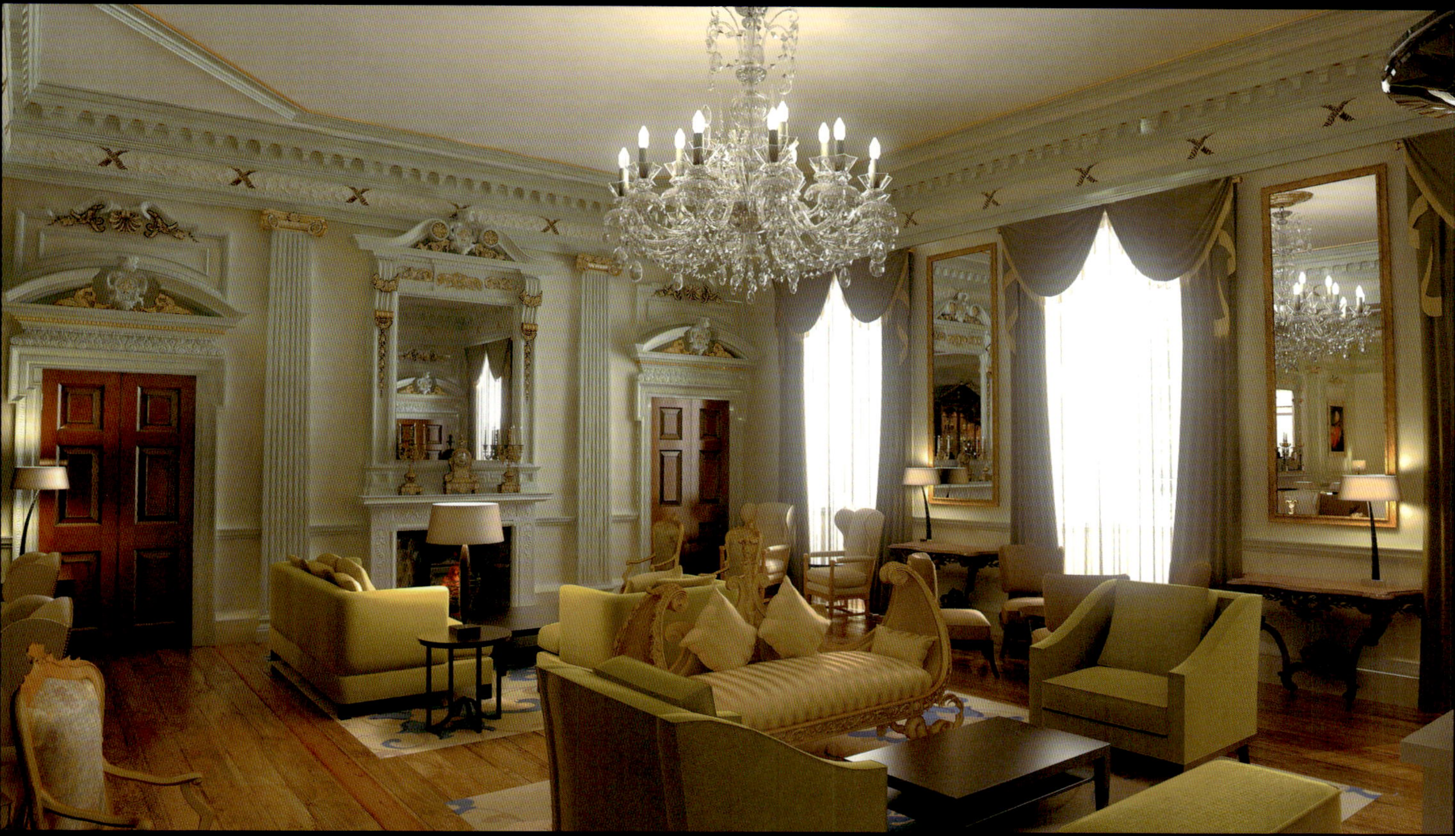

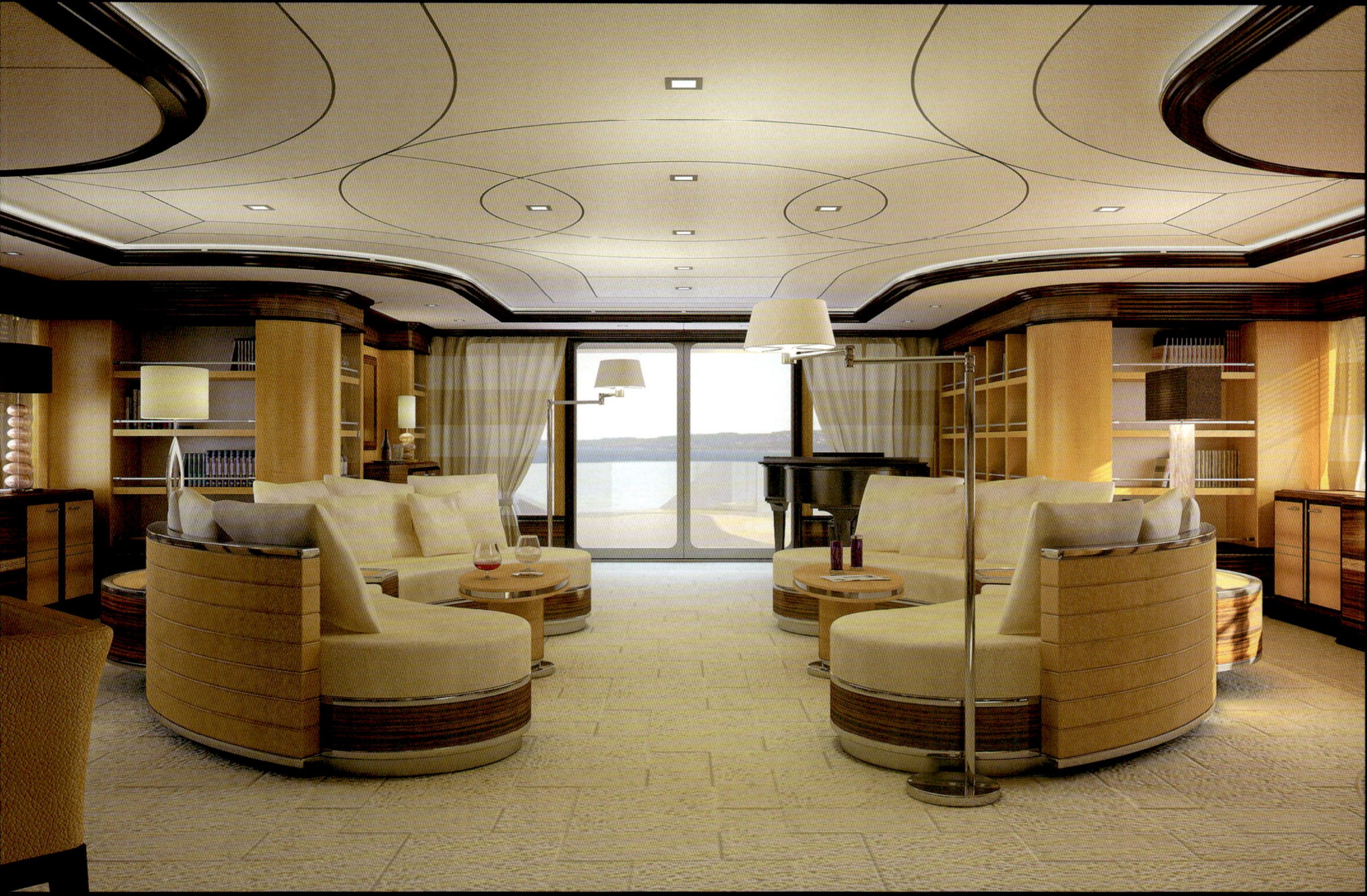

Drawing room
3ds Max, V-Ray, Photoshop
SPLITT Ltd/3D Helps,
GREAT BRITAIN
[top]

Yacht interior: Upper Deck Salon
3ds Max, V-Ray, Photoshop
Massimo Dughiero and **Andrea Dughiero**,
ITALY
[above]

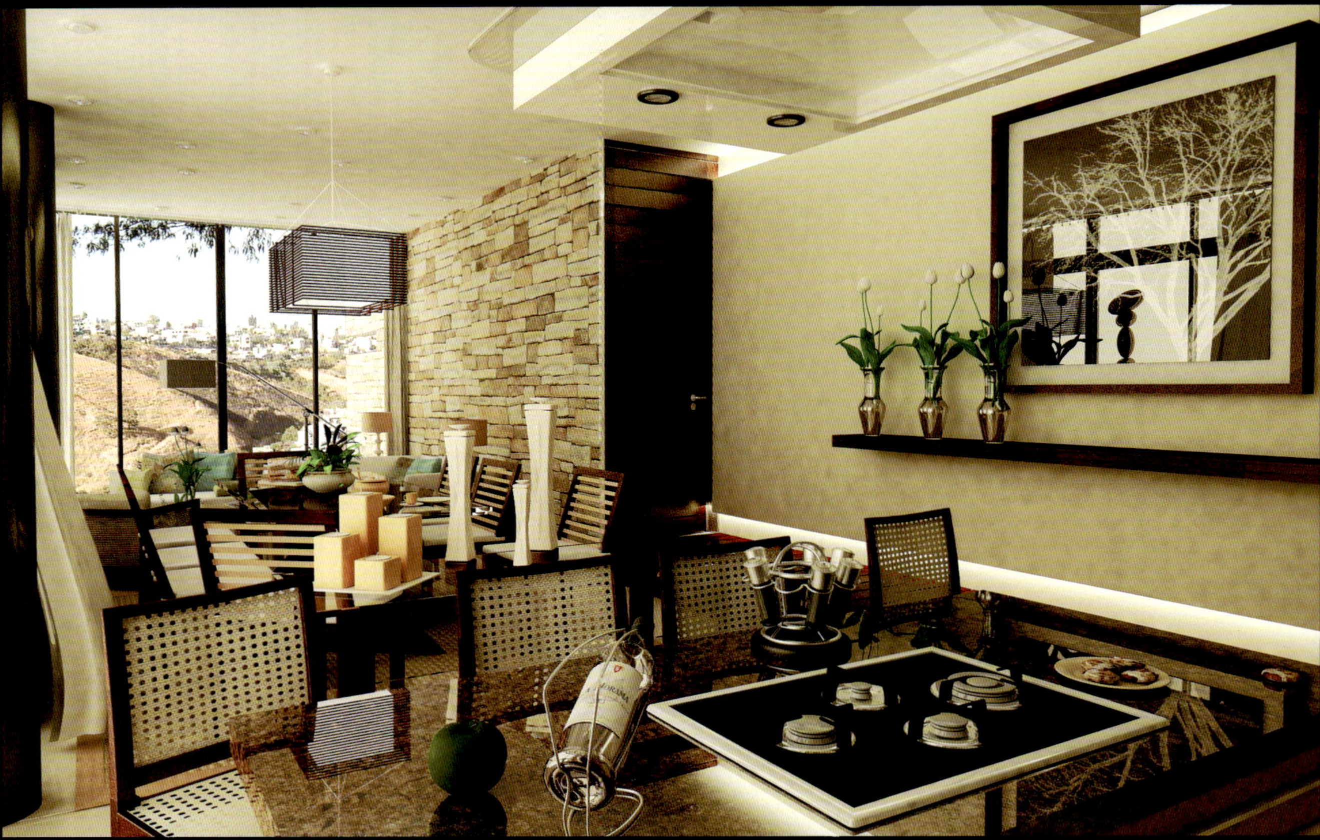

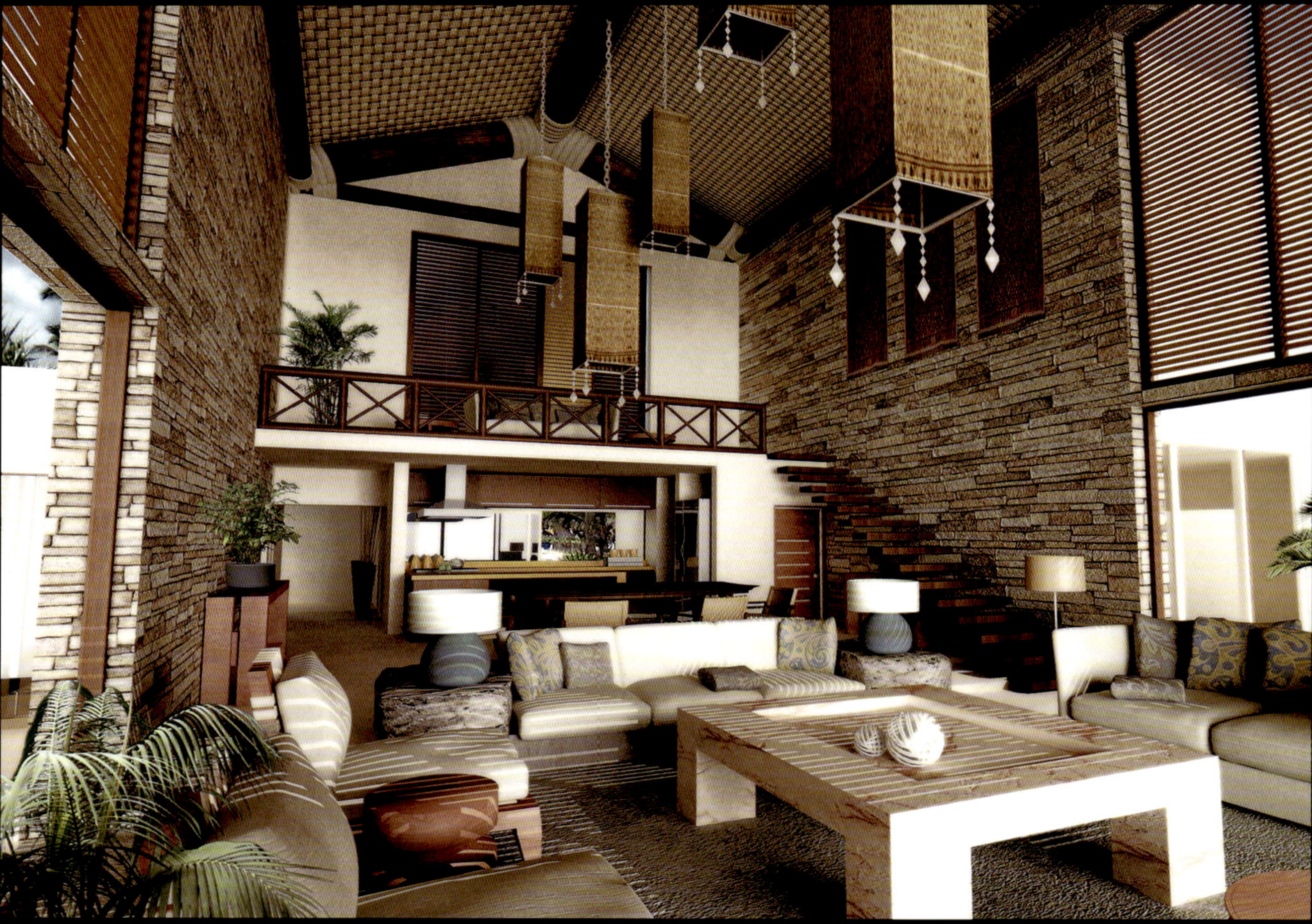

Kitchen
3ds Max, V-Ray, CorelDRAW, Photoshop
Client: Santoscoy Arquitectos
Roberto Carlos Jaramillo Saavedra,
Rendermotion, MEXICO
[top]

The Beach
3ds Max, V-Ray, CorelDRAW, Photoshop
Client: Santoscoy Arquitectos
Roberto Carlos Jaramillo Saavedra,
Rendermotion, MEXICO
[above]

To read in silence
Maya, mental ray, Photoshop
José Pedro Costa, PORTUGAL
[right]

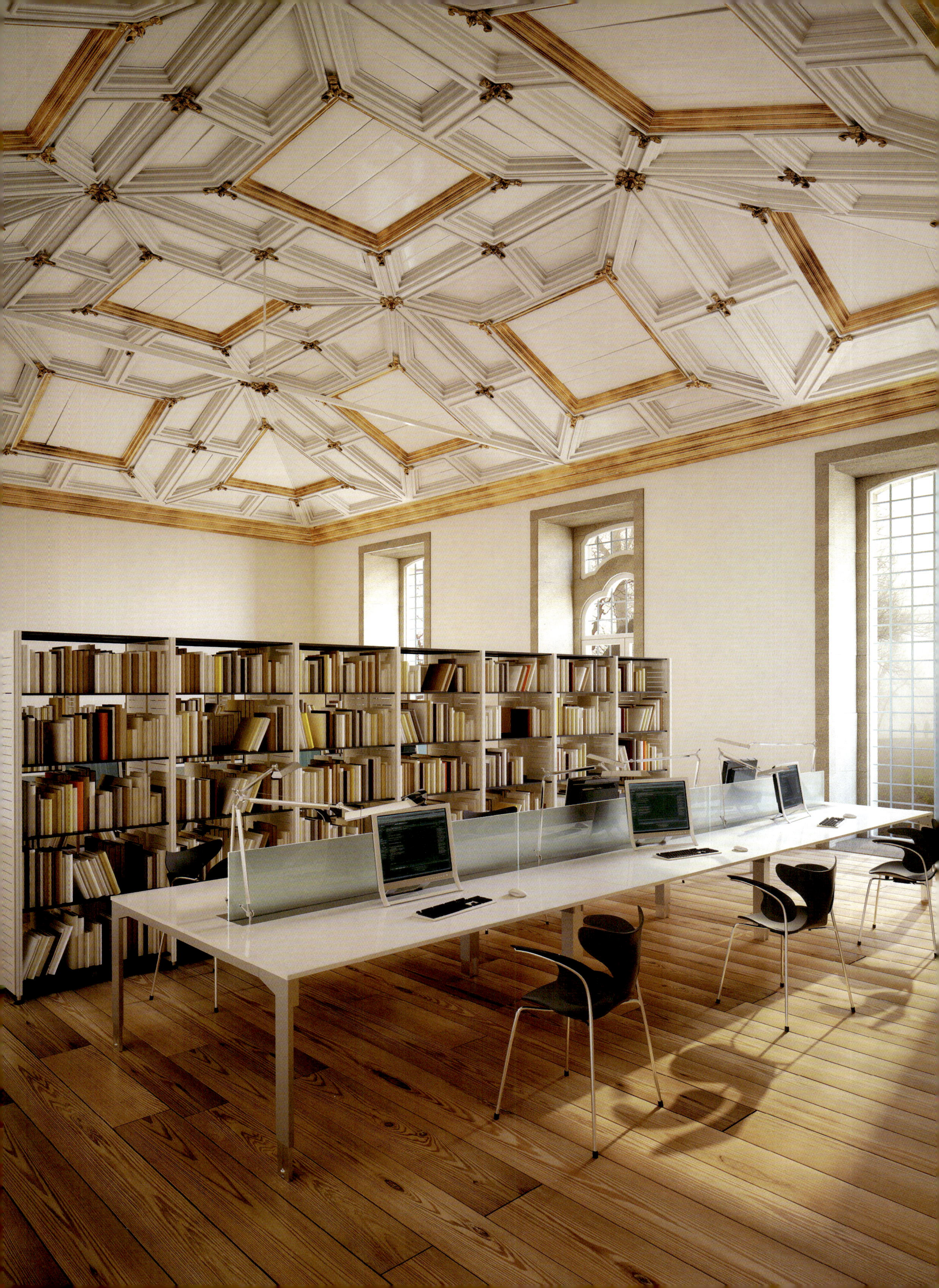

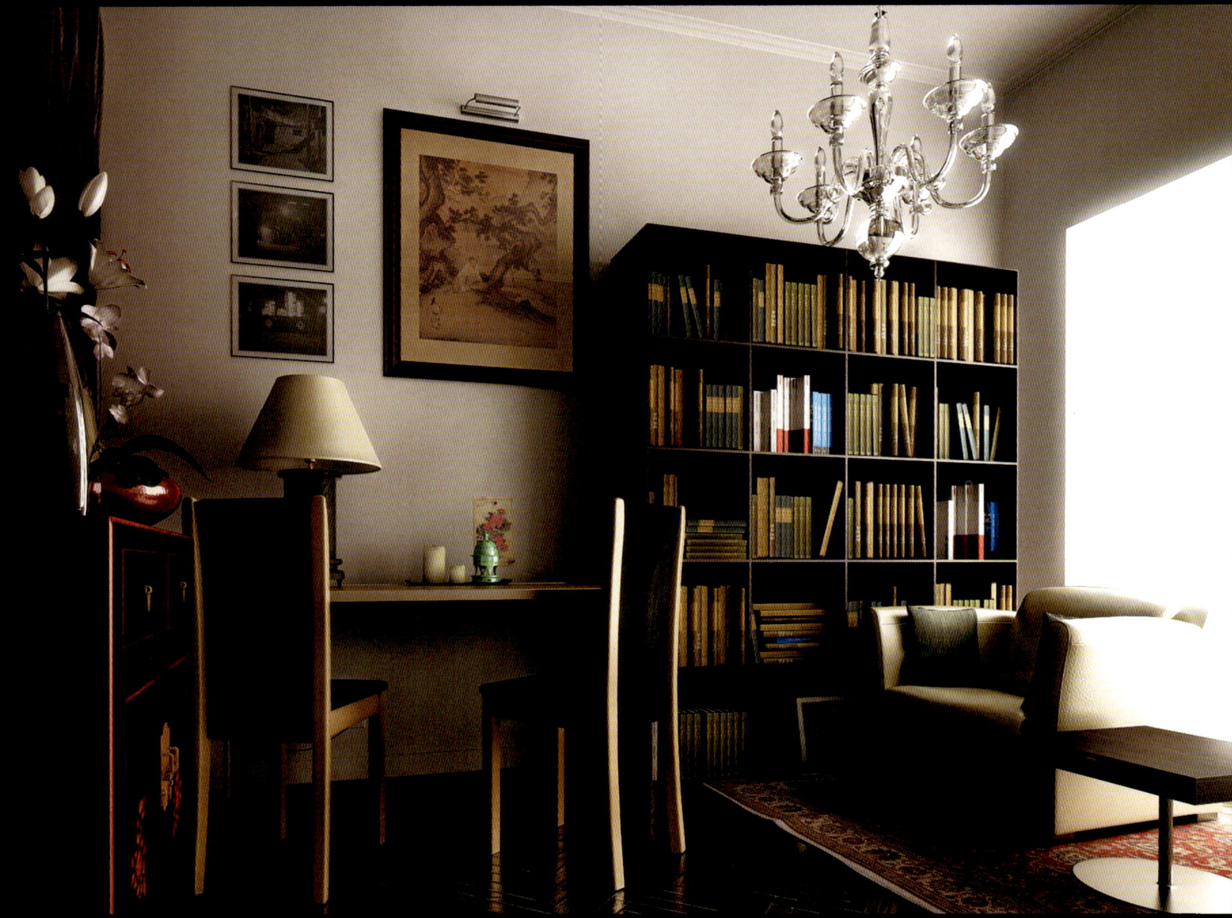

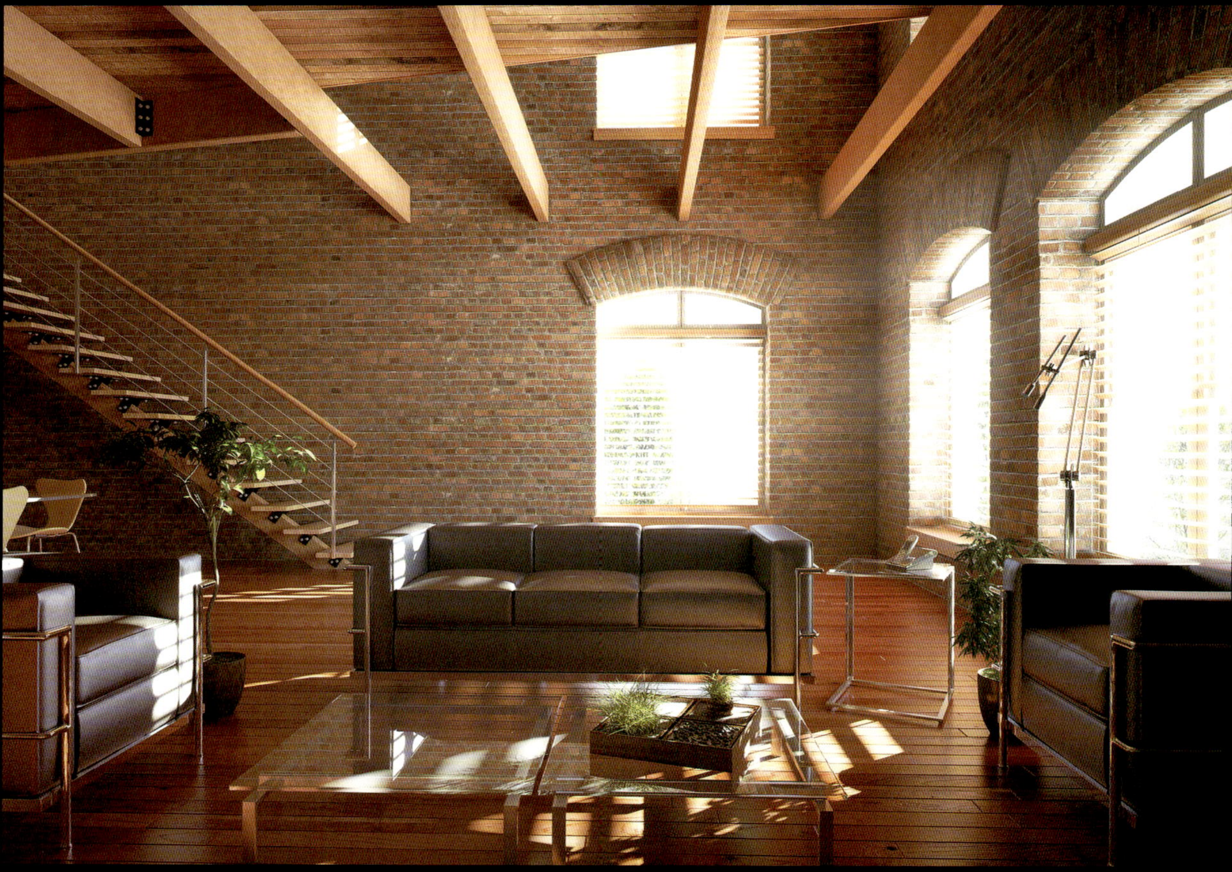

Home interior 2
3ds Max, V-Ray, Photoshop
Charley Cloris, FRANCE
[top]

The Loft
3ds Max, V-Ray, Photoshop, SketchUp
Aaron Coon, Conceptual Design Studio, USA
[above]

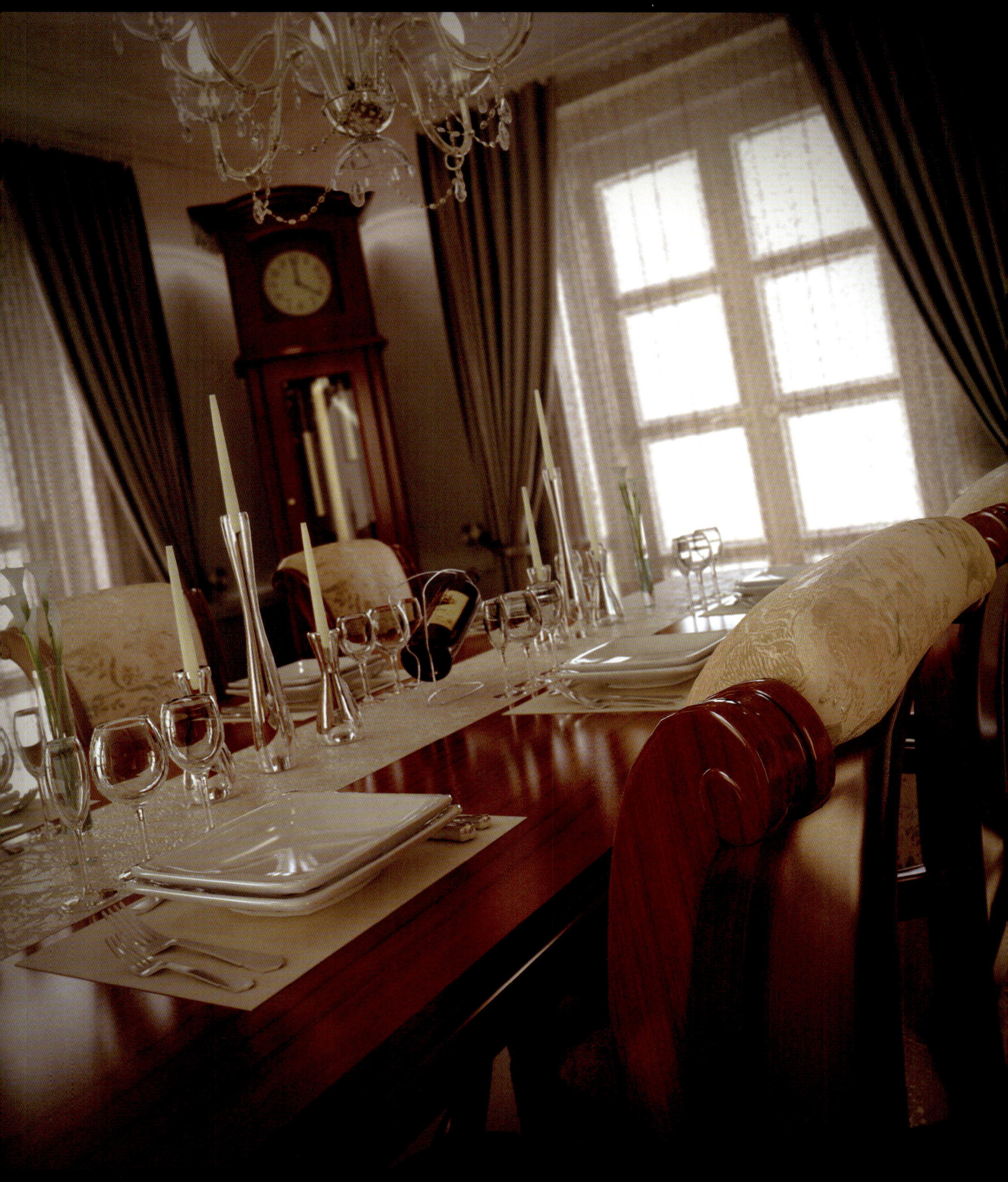

Dining
3ds Max
James Orchard,
Visualisation One Ltd,
GREAT BRITAIN

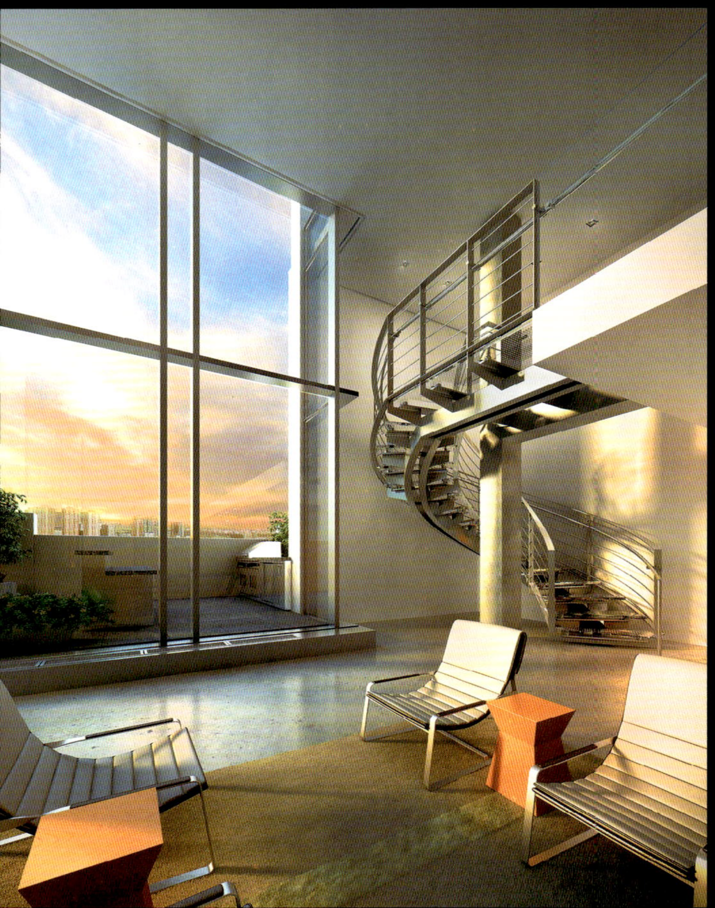

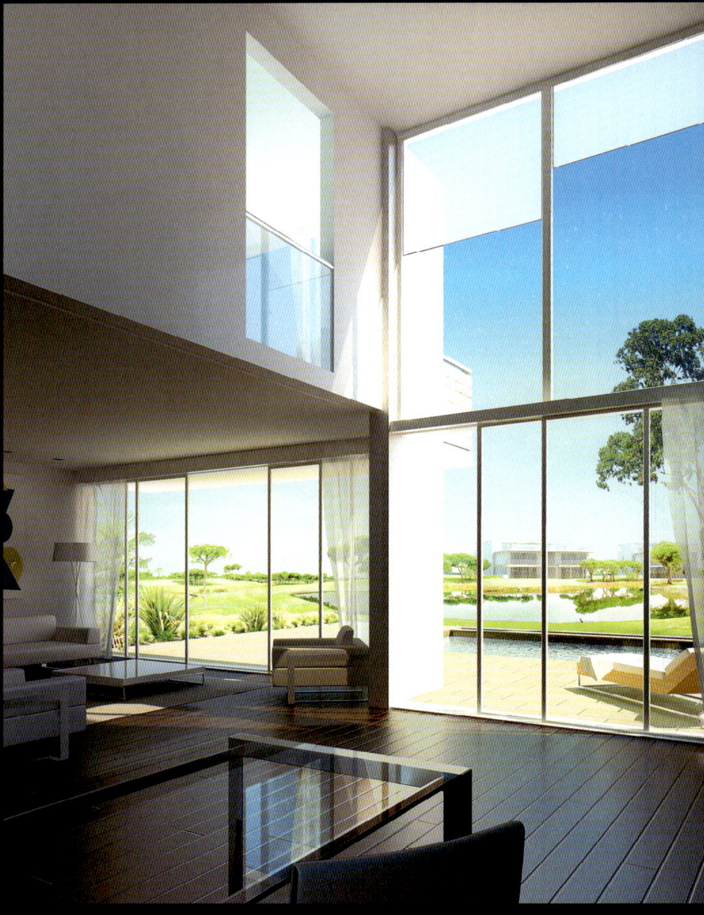

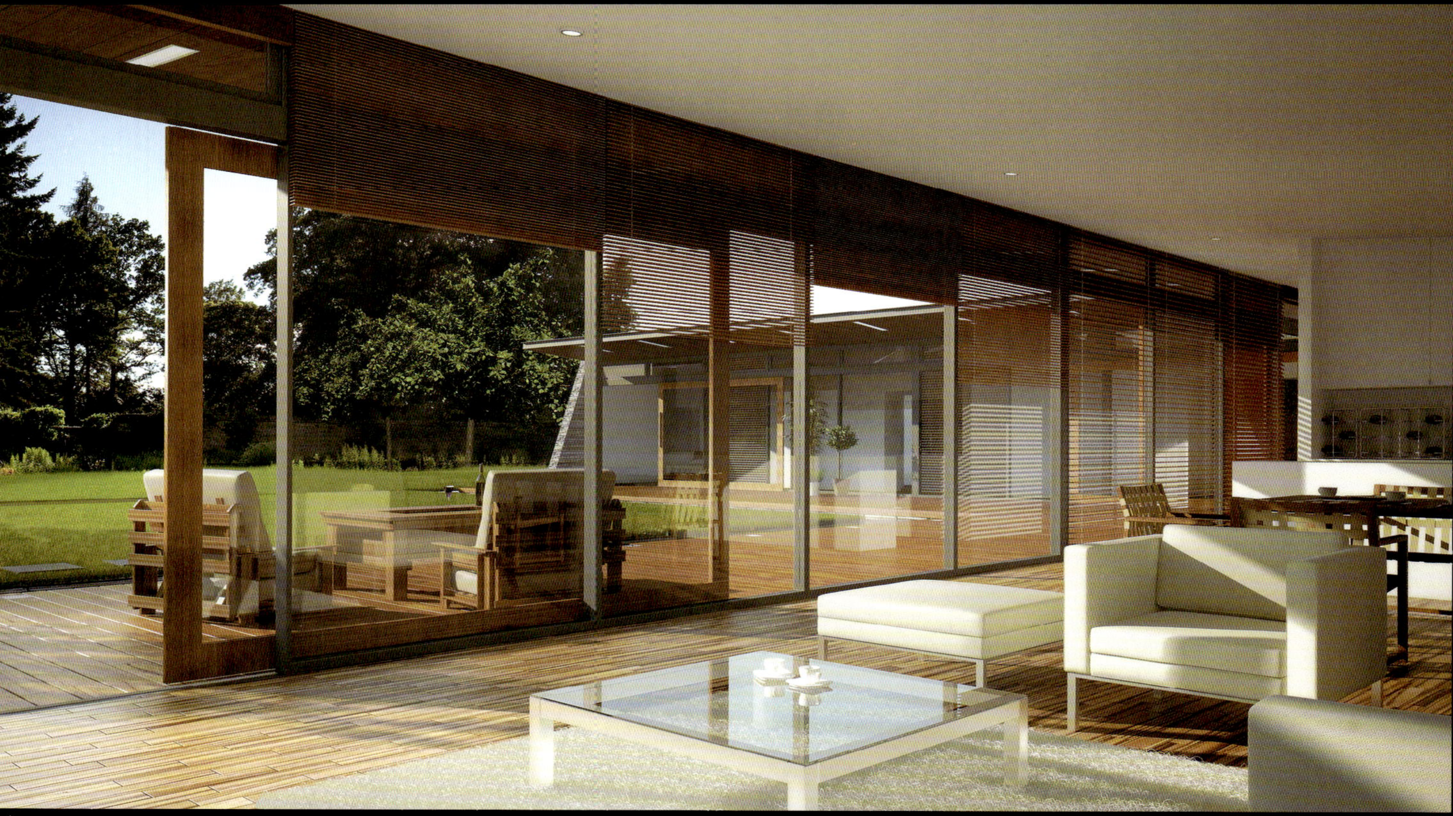

Skylofts Stairway
3ds Max, V-Ray, Photoshop
Client: 145 Hudson Street

Walled Garden Internal
3ds Max, V-Ray, Photoshop
Client: Zebrano Design

Quinta do Lago
3ds Max, V-Ray, Photoshop
Client: E3 Property

Box Stack Stair
VIZ, V-Ray, Photoshop
Geoffrey Packer

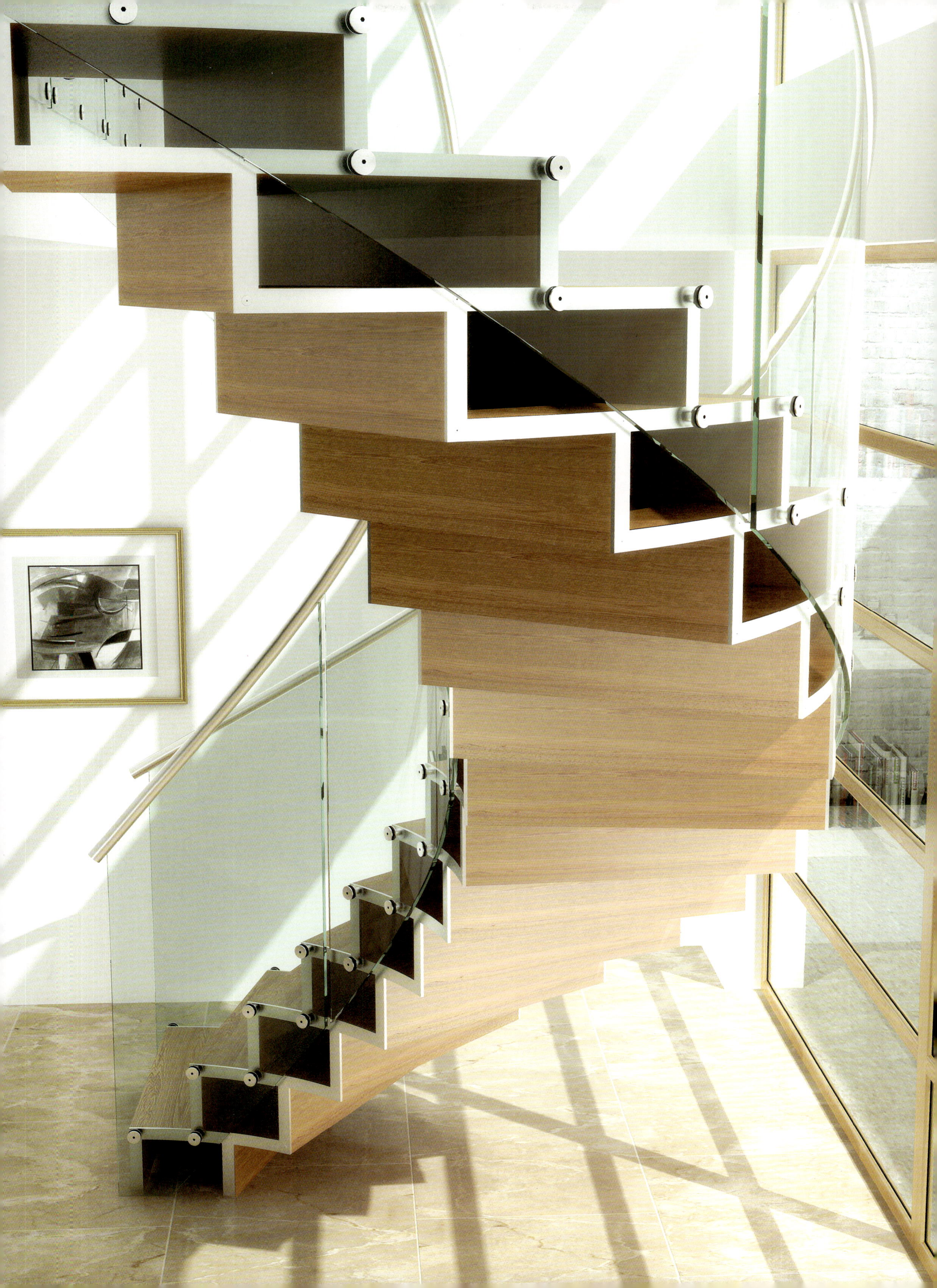

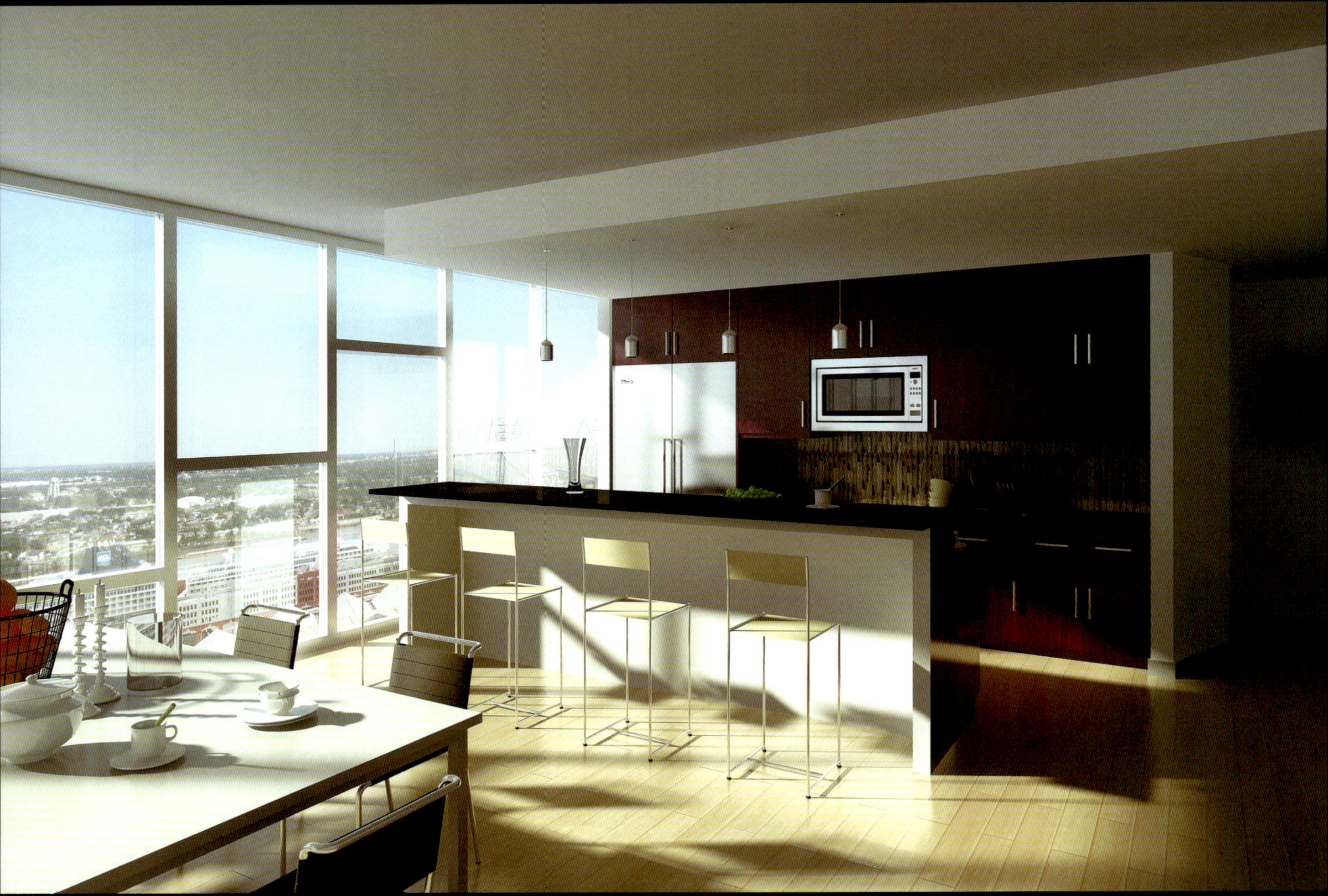

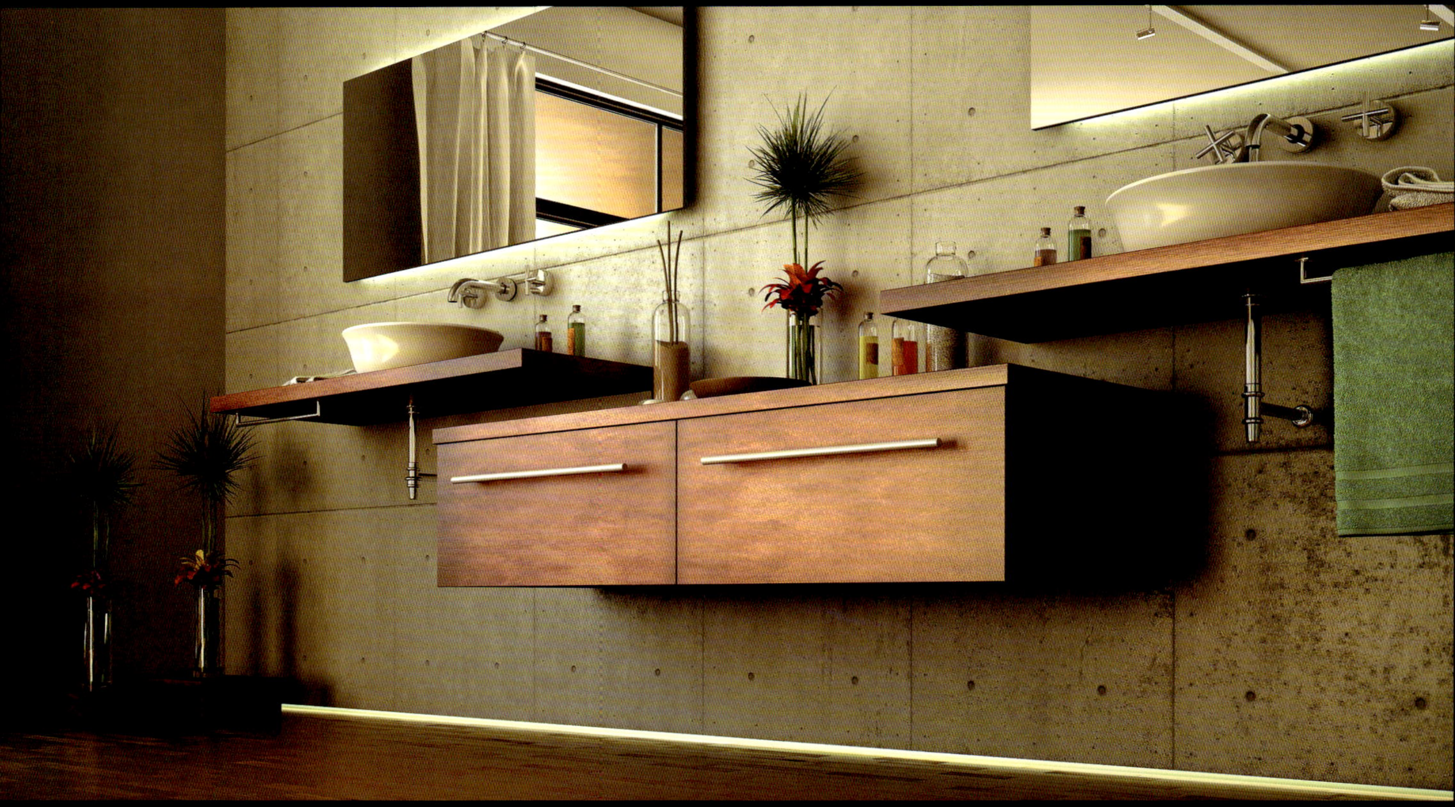

Kitchen
VIZ
Chen Qingfeng, Chen3d.com,
CHINA
[top]

Bathroom at dusk
3ds Max, V-Ray, Photoshcp
Christophe Landrain,
BELGIUM
[above]

Ensuite
3ds Max, V-Ray, Photoshop
Pat Corcoran, Visualisation One Ltd,
GREAT BRITAIN
[right]

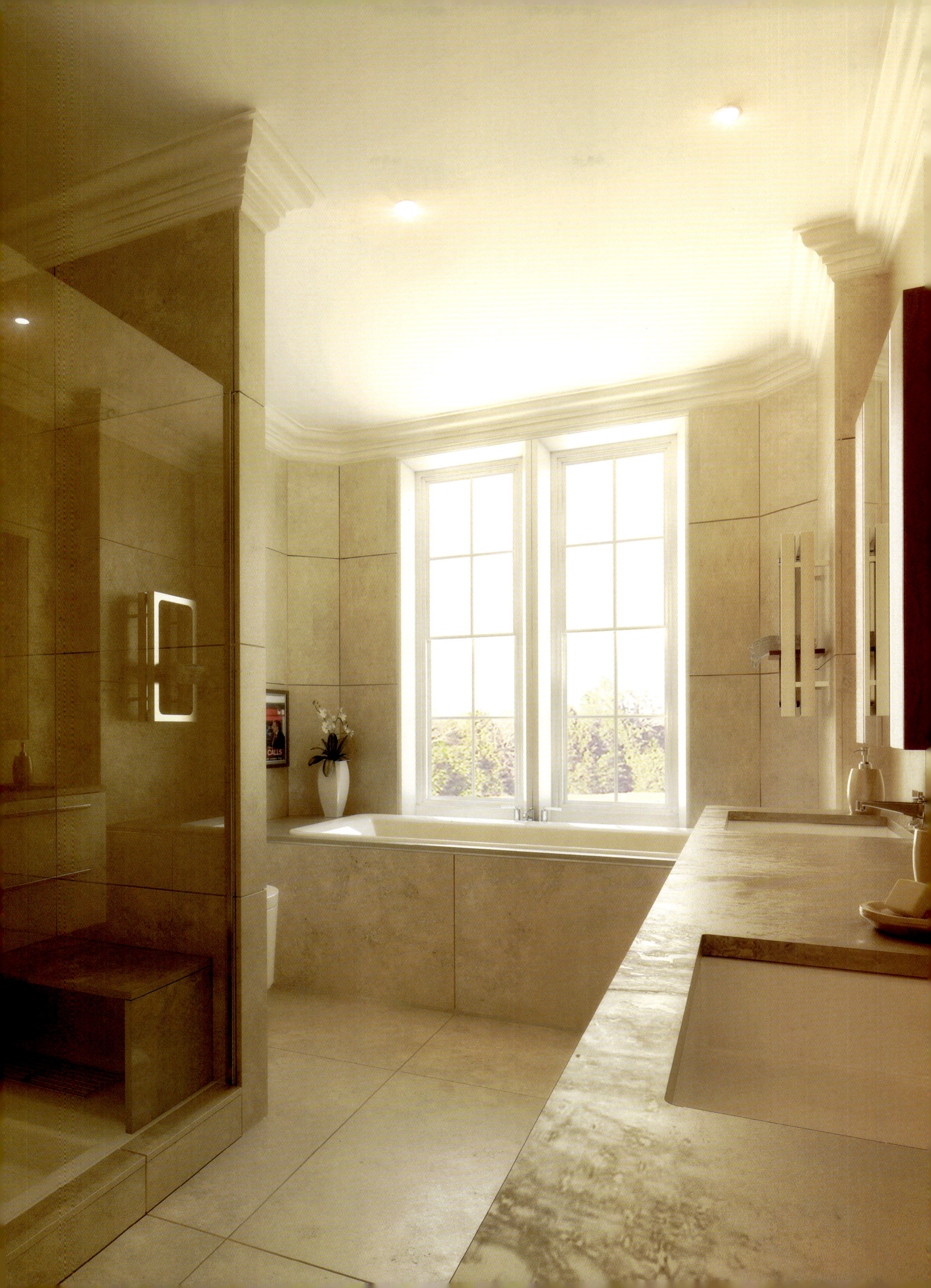

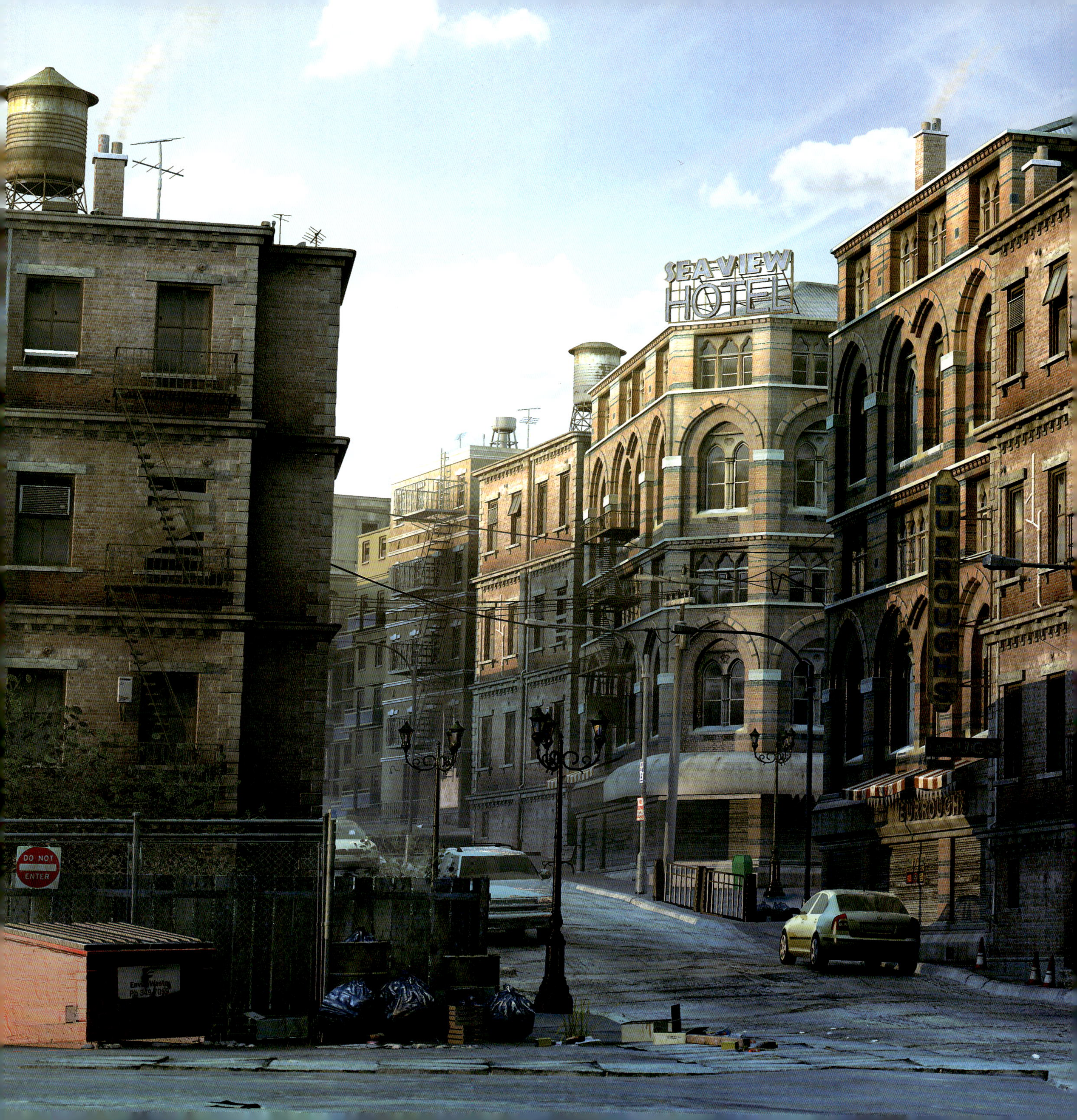
SEA VIEW
HOTEL
BURROUGHS
DO NOT
ENTER
BURROUGHS

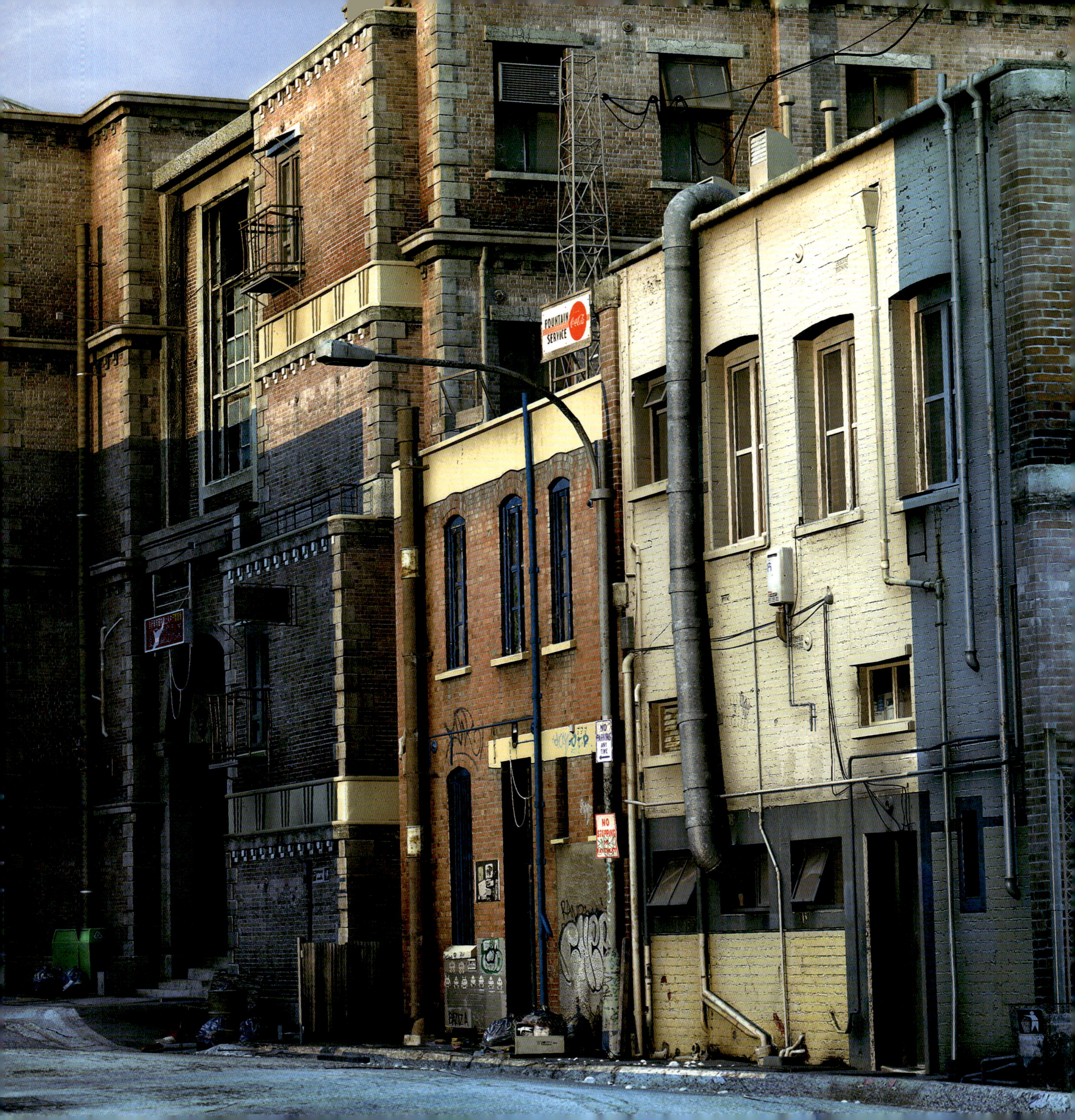
FOUNTAIN SERVICE
NO PARKING ANY TIME
NO STOPPING

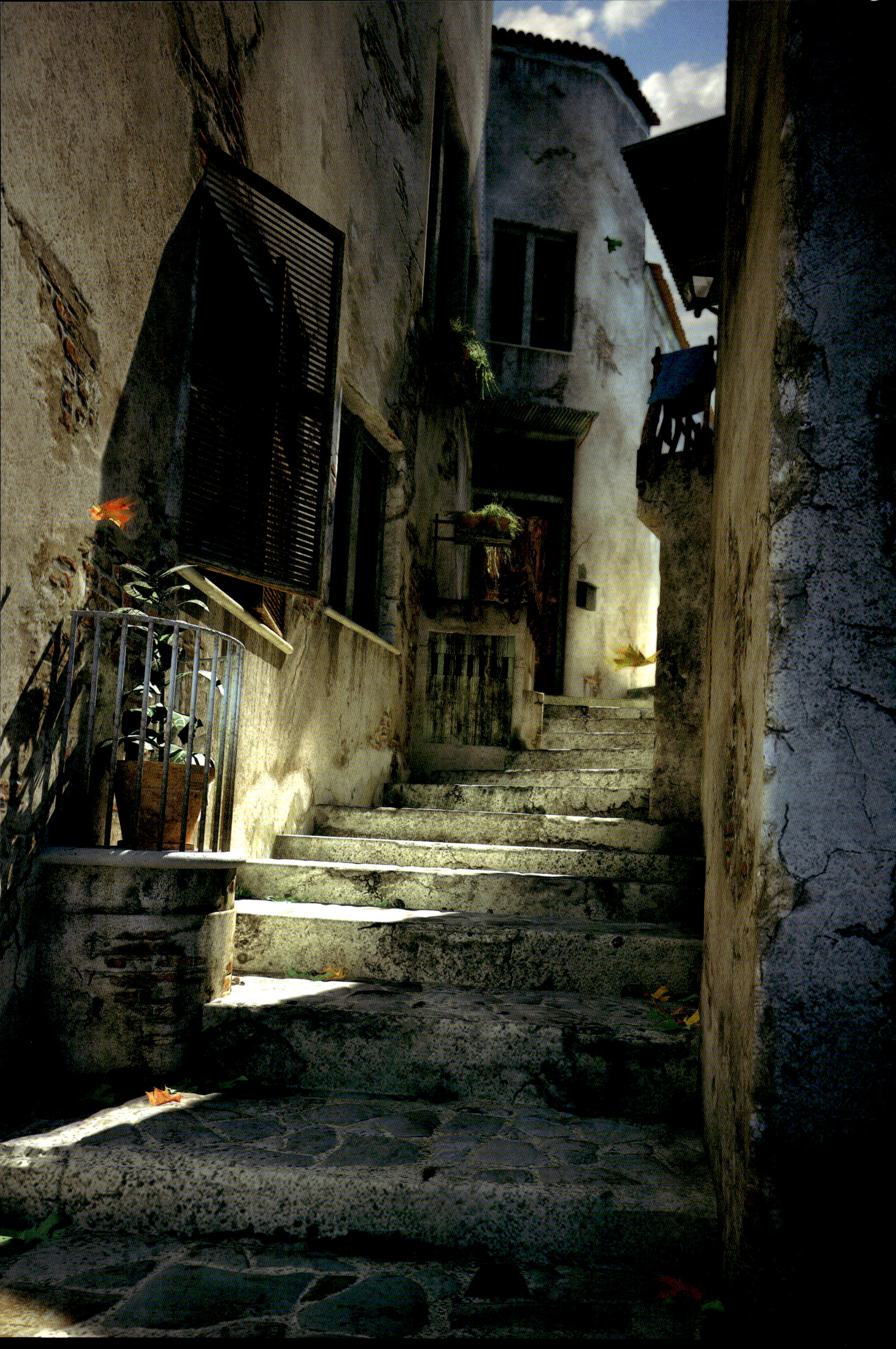

Excellence

Architecture Reconstruction

Tuscan Alley
3ds Max, V-Ray,
Photoshop, Combustion
Gavyn Thompson, GTVFX
USA

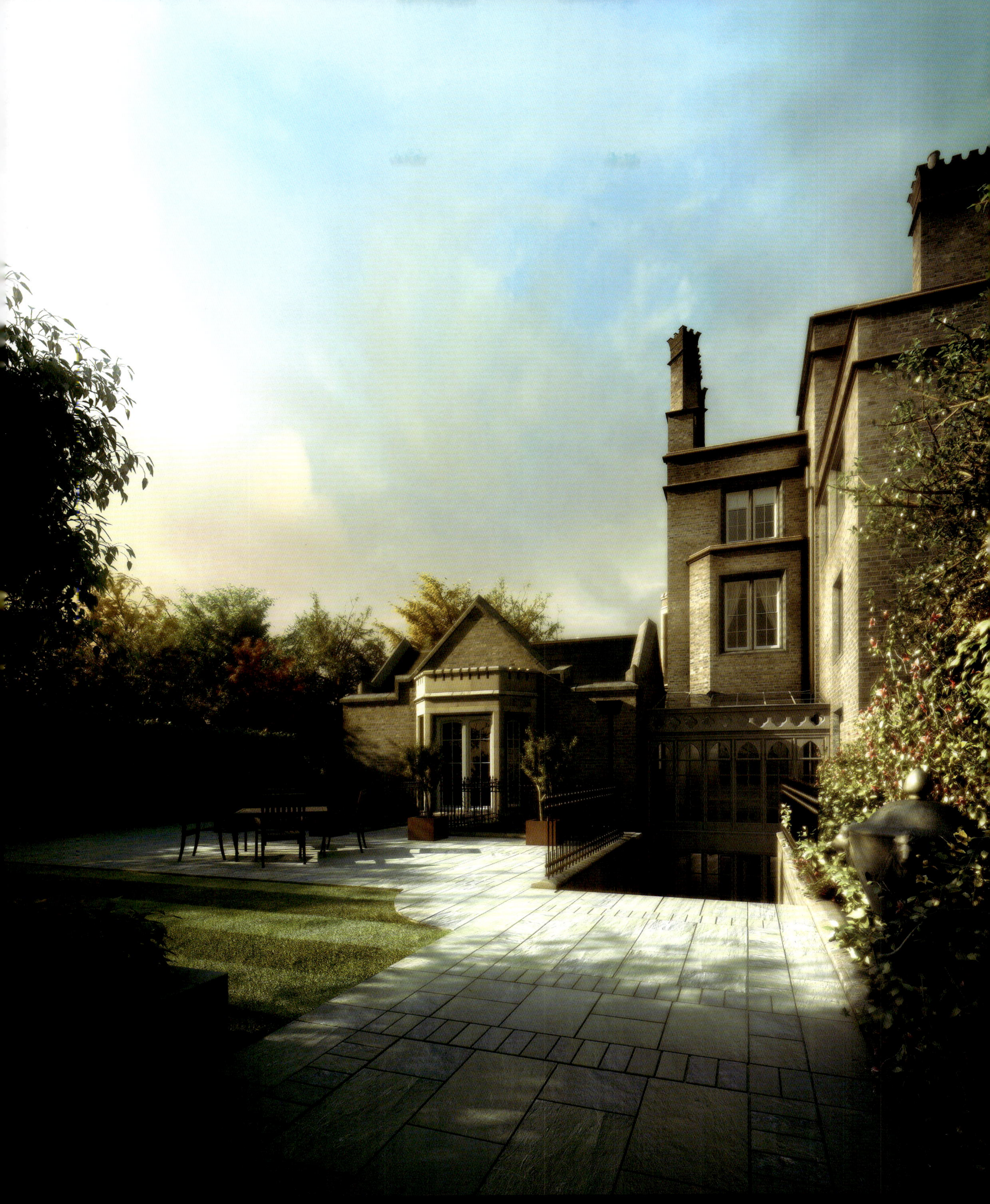

St. Katherine's
3ds Max, V-Ray, Photoshop
Pat Corcoran, Visualisation One Ltd,
GREAT BRITAIN

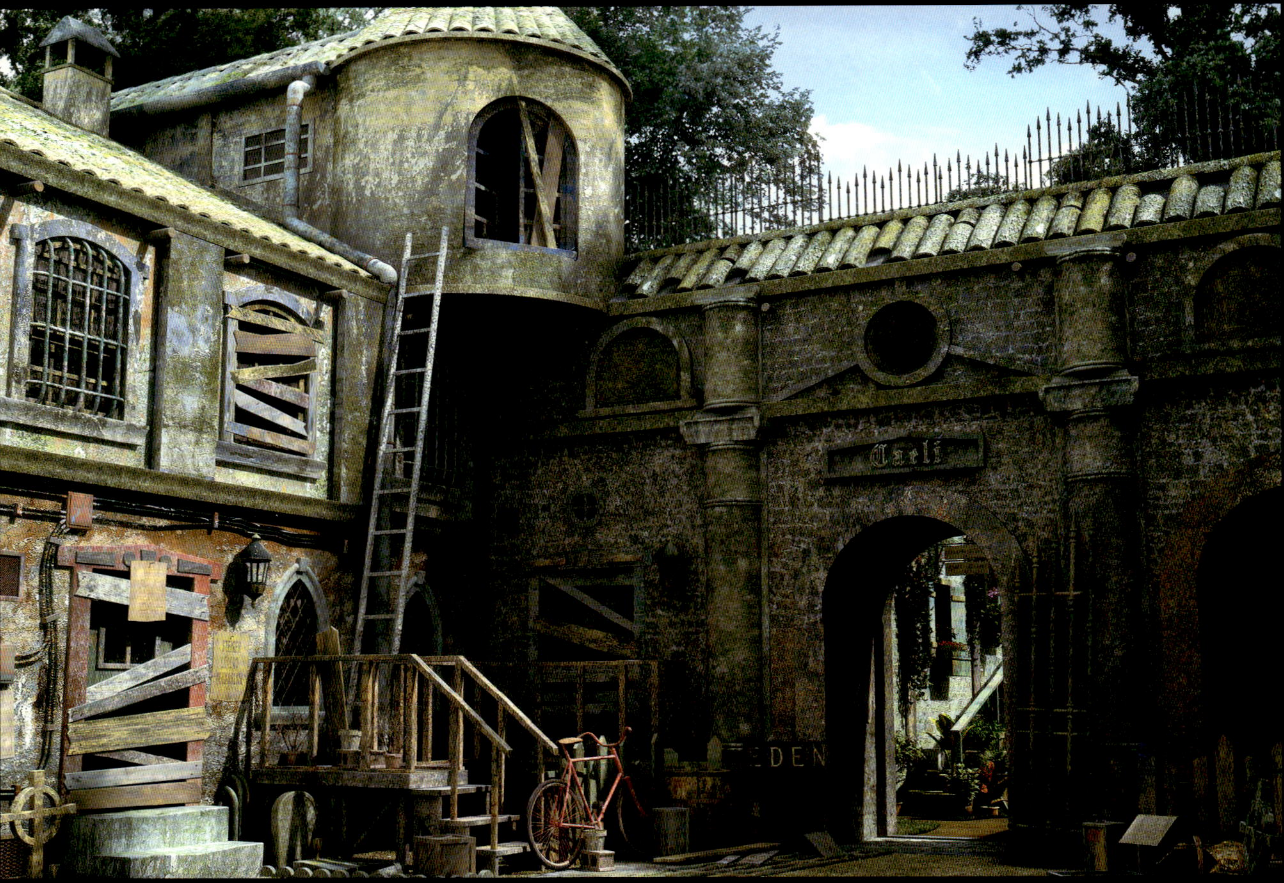

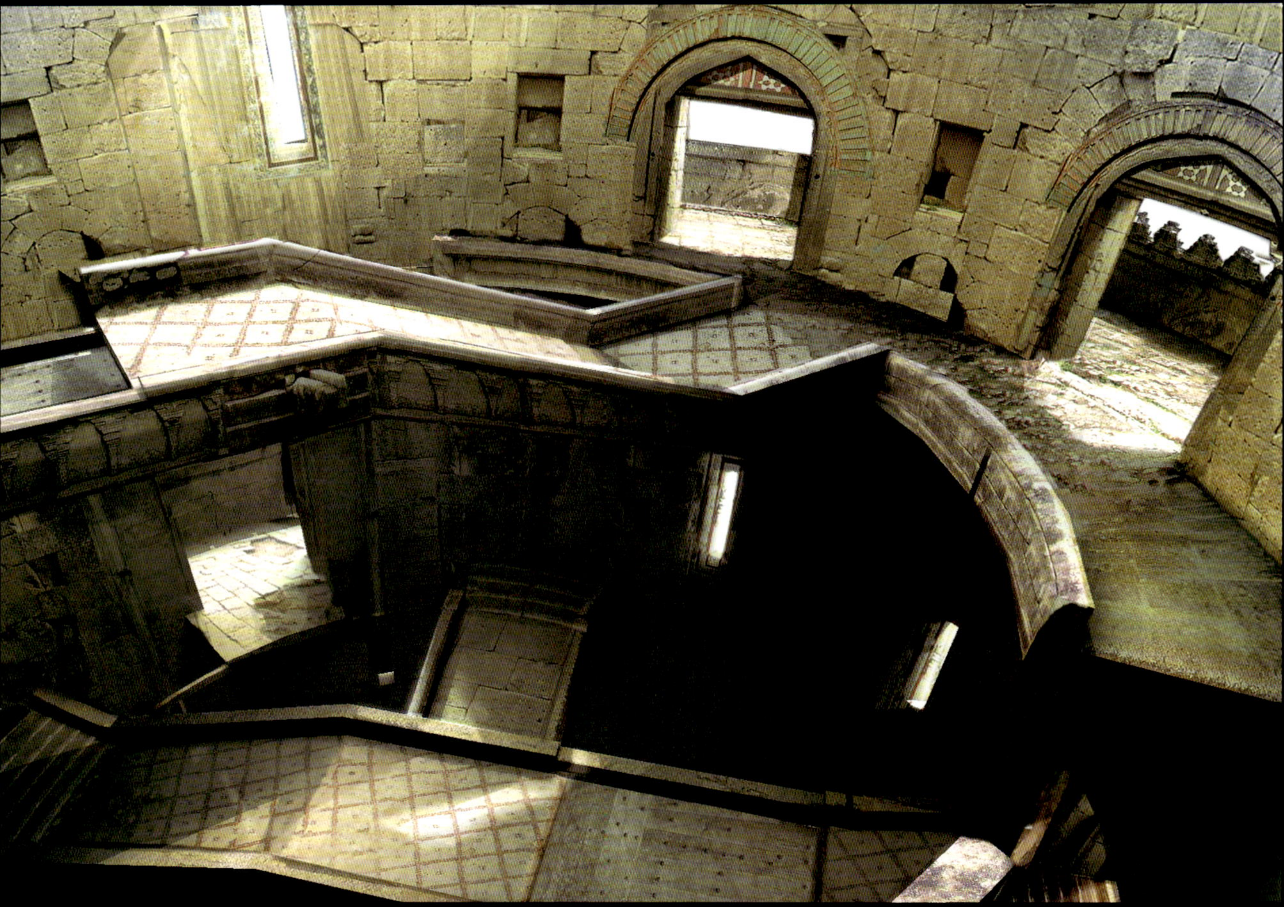

Exodus
3ds Max, V-Ray, Photoshop
Jason Godbey, Bottlerocket Entertainment, USA
[top]

Gondi Tower
Maya, Photoshop
Stephen Cooper, GREAT BRITAIN
[above]

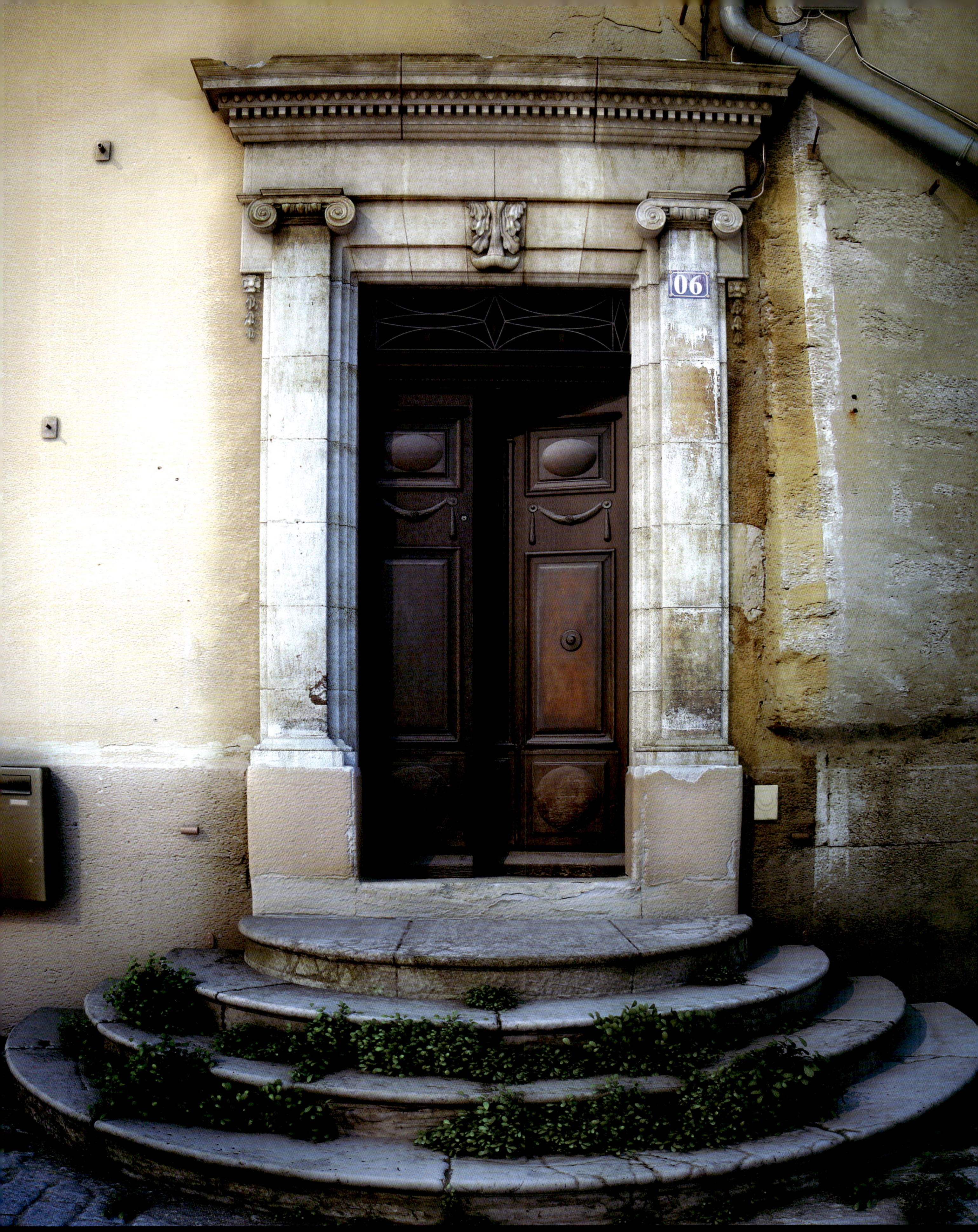

The Door To...
3ds Max, V-Ray, Photoshop
Aleksander Marcello Braz,
TSI Animation, BRAZIL

Excellence
Architecture Reconstruction

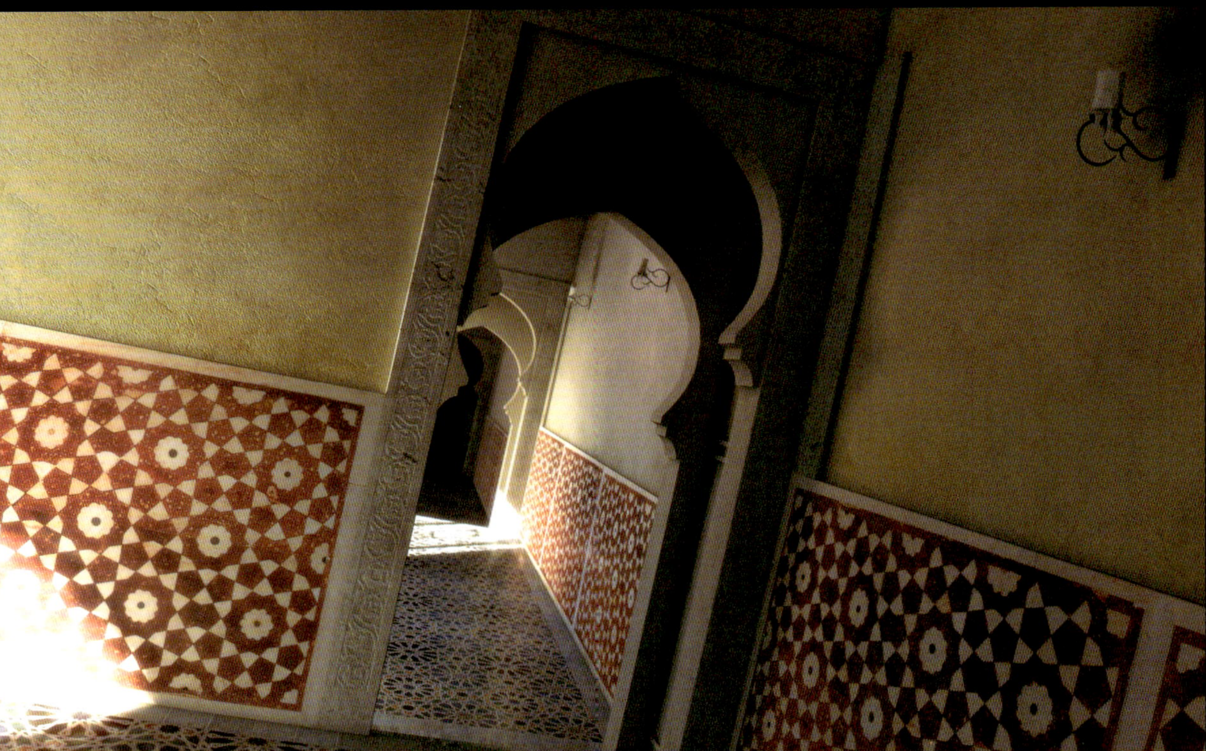

In a dream
3ds Max, finalRender, Photoshop
Marco Lazzarini, ITALY
[left]

Vaulted Street
3ds Max, Photoshop, mental ray
Çetin Tüker, TURKEY
[right]

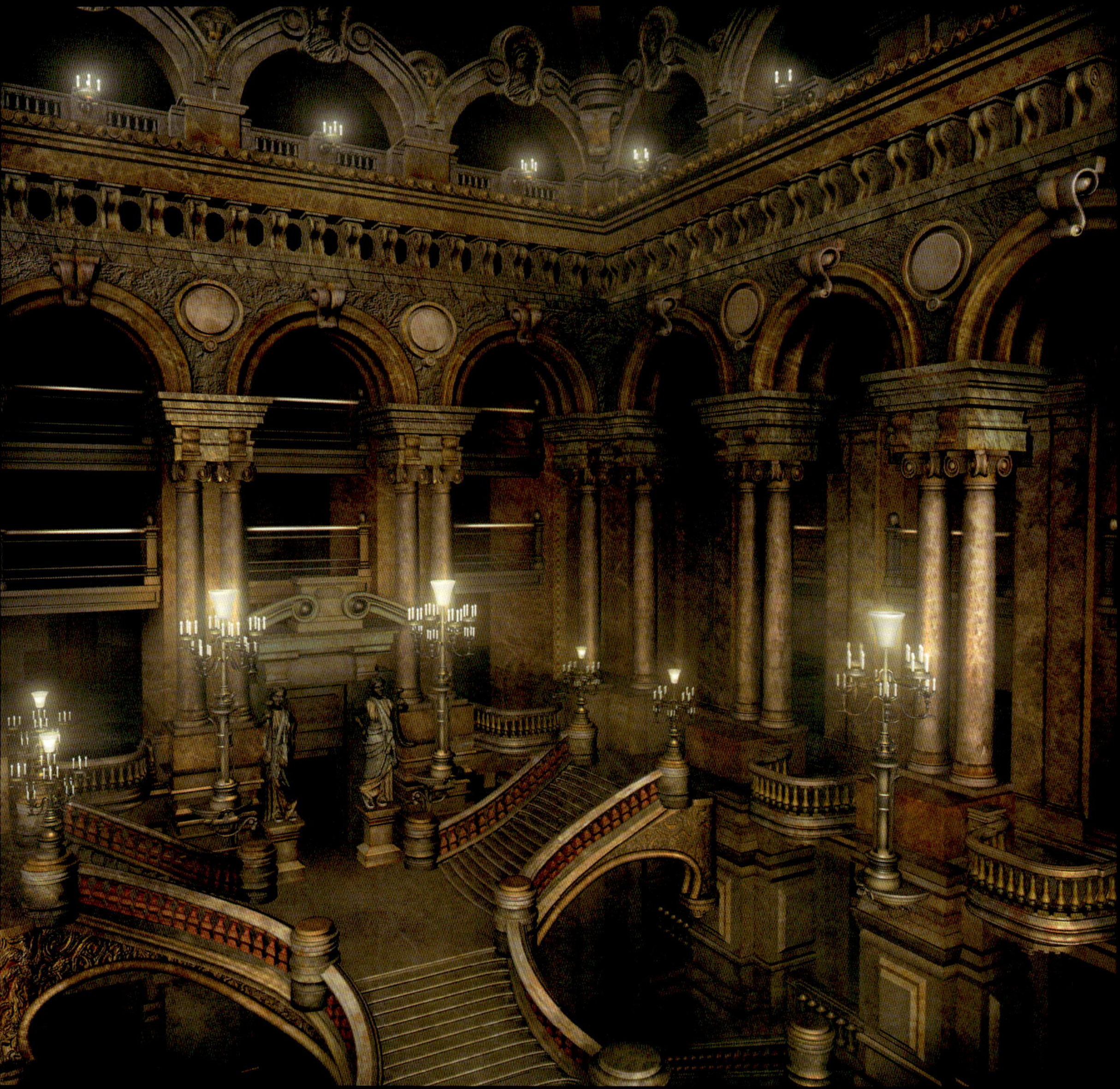

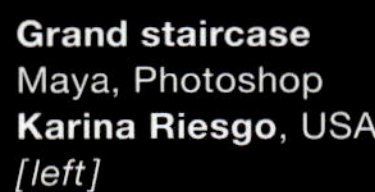

Grand staircase
Maya, Photoshop
Karina Riesgo, USA
[left]

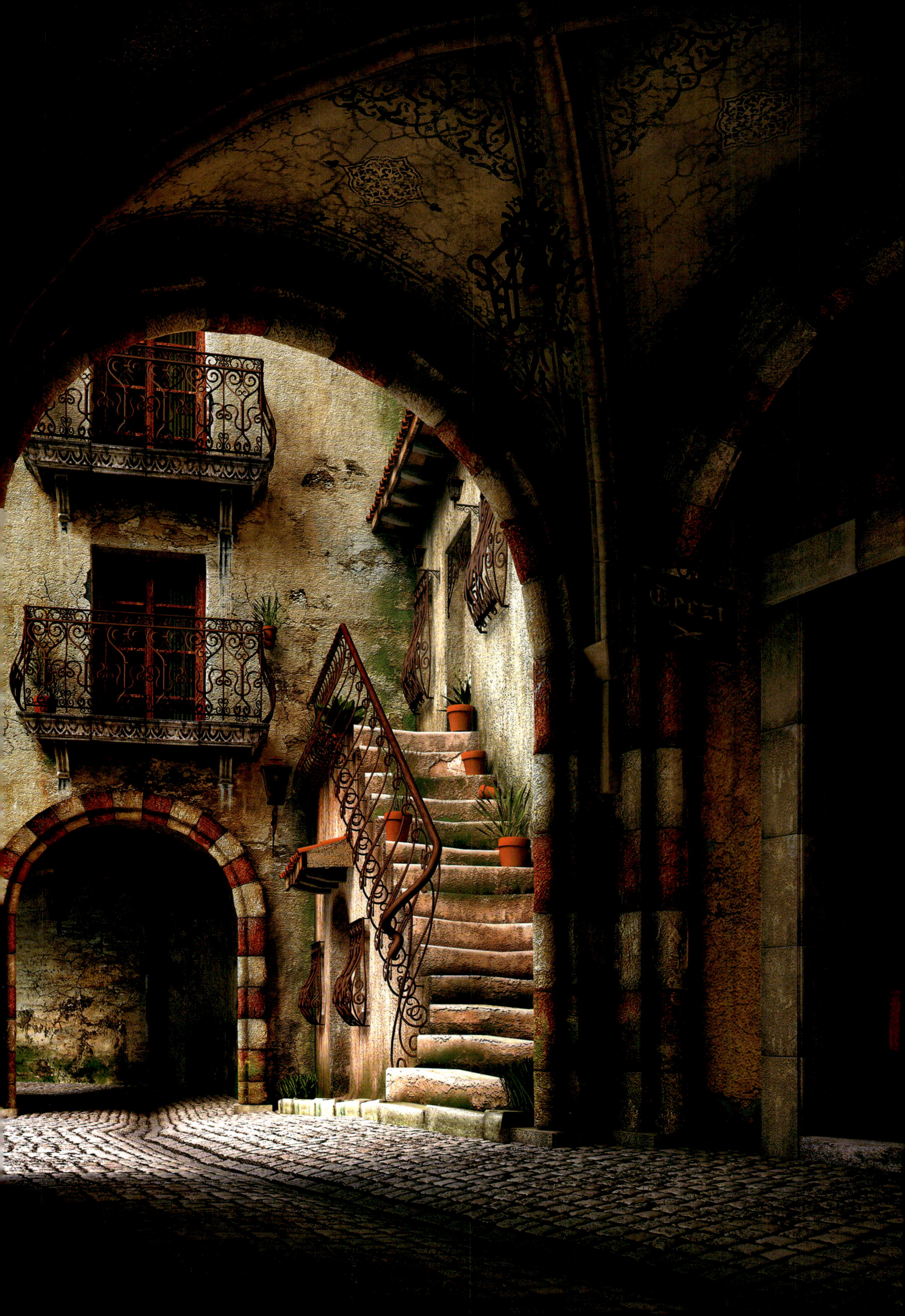

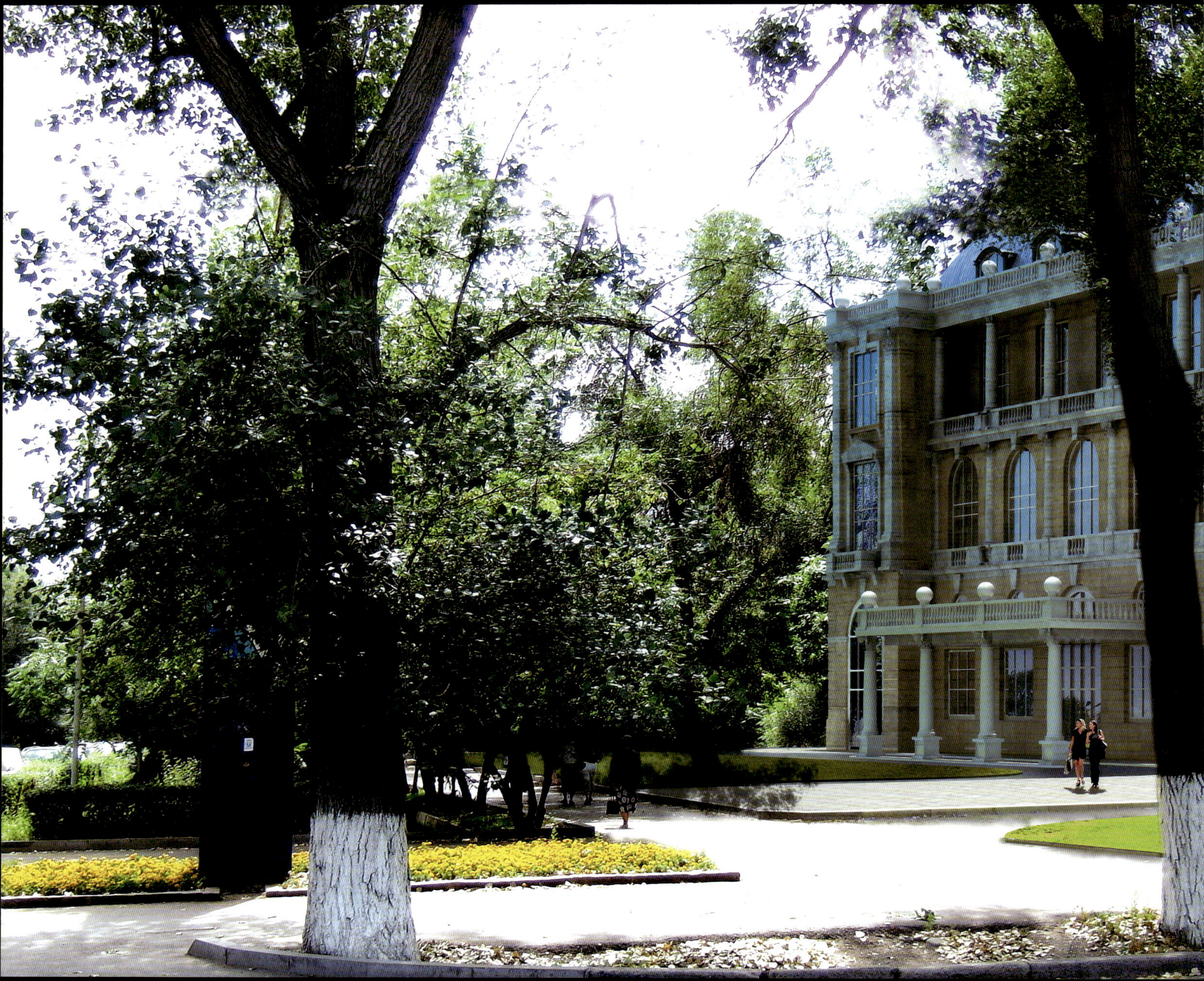

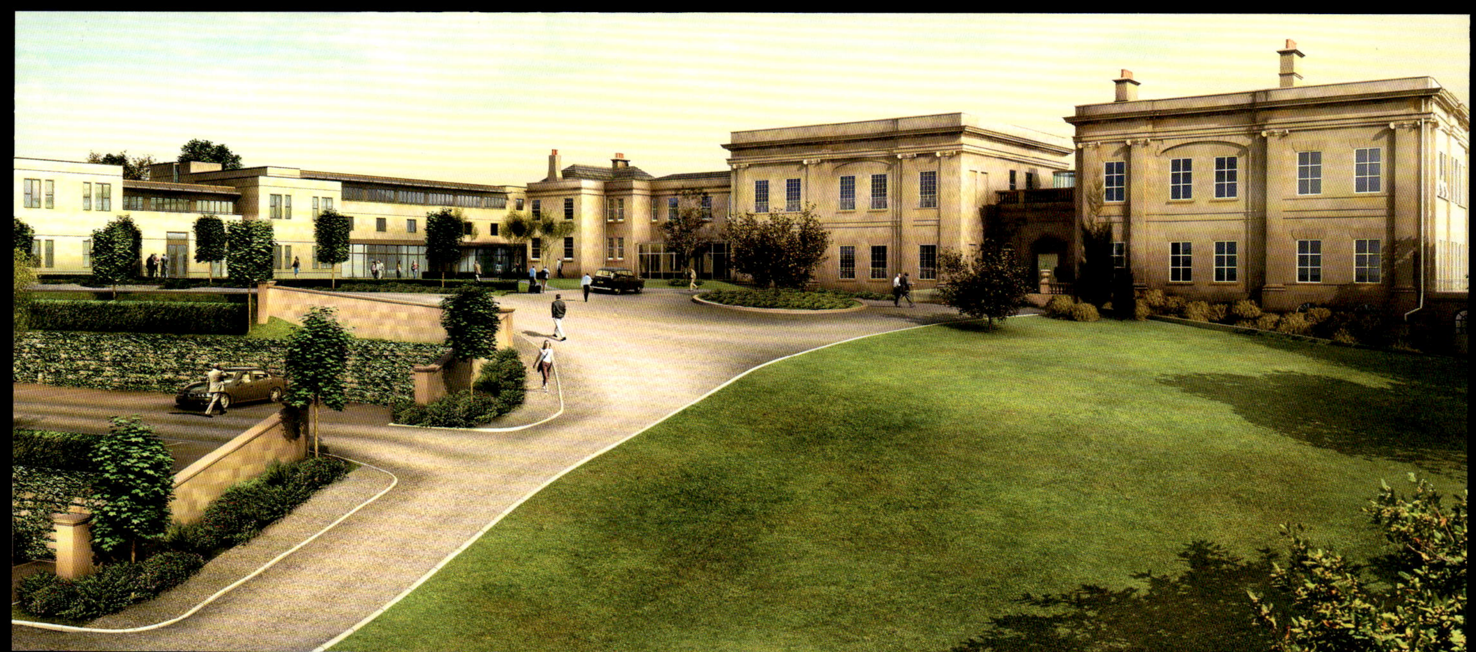

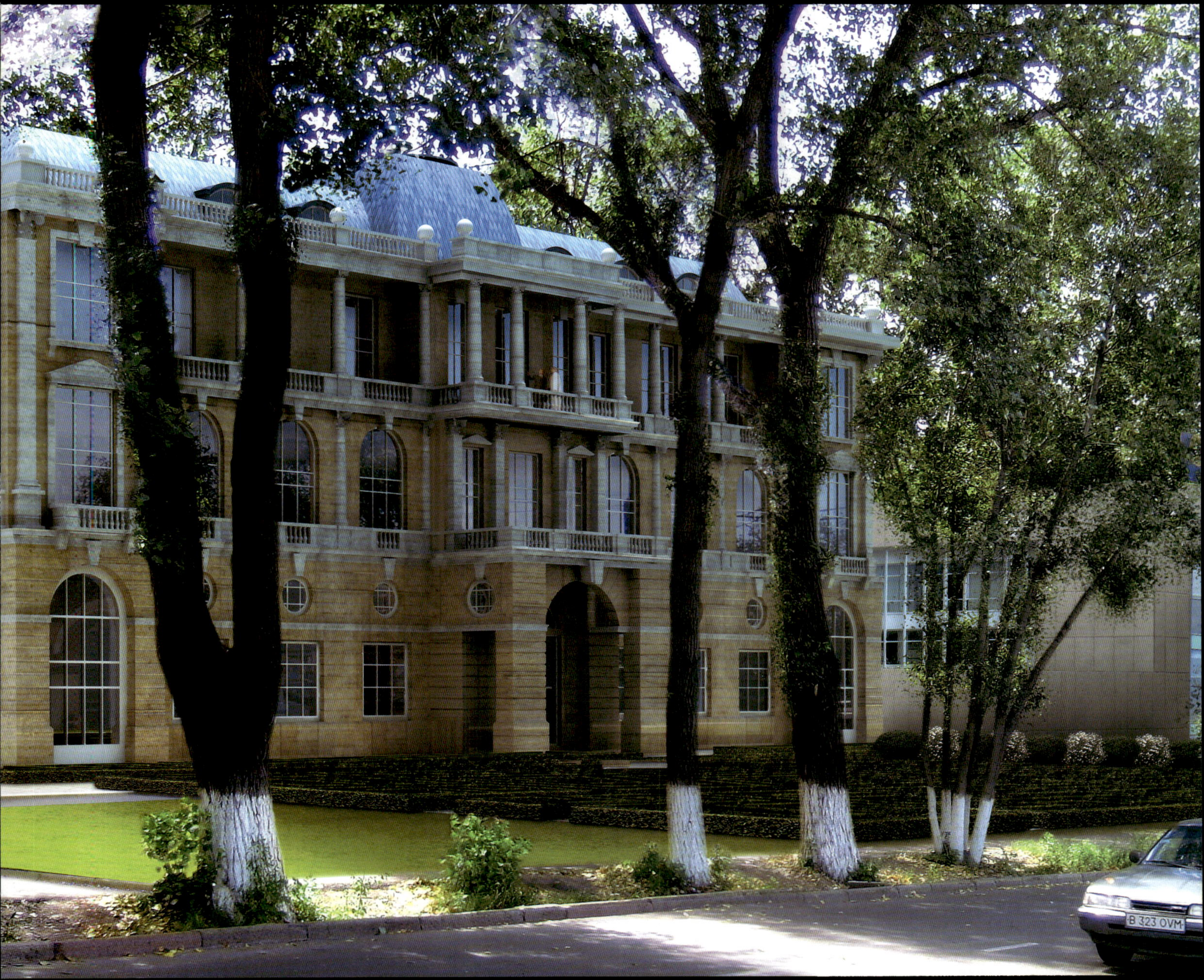

Abaya Bookshop
3ds Max, V-Ray, Photoshop
Aedas Imaging,
GREAT BRITAIN
[above]

Bailbrook House
3ds Max, V-Ray, Photoshop
John Crawshaw,
AHD-Imaging, GREAT BRITAIN
[left]

El callejon
3ds Max
Sergey Aleynikov, n3 design,
RUSSIA
[right]

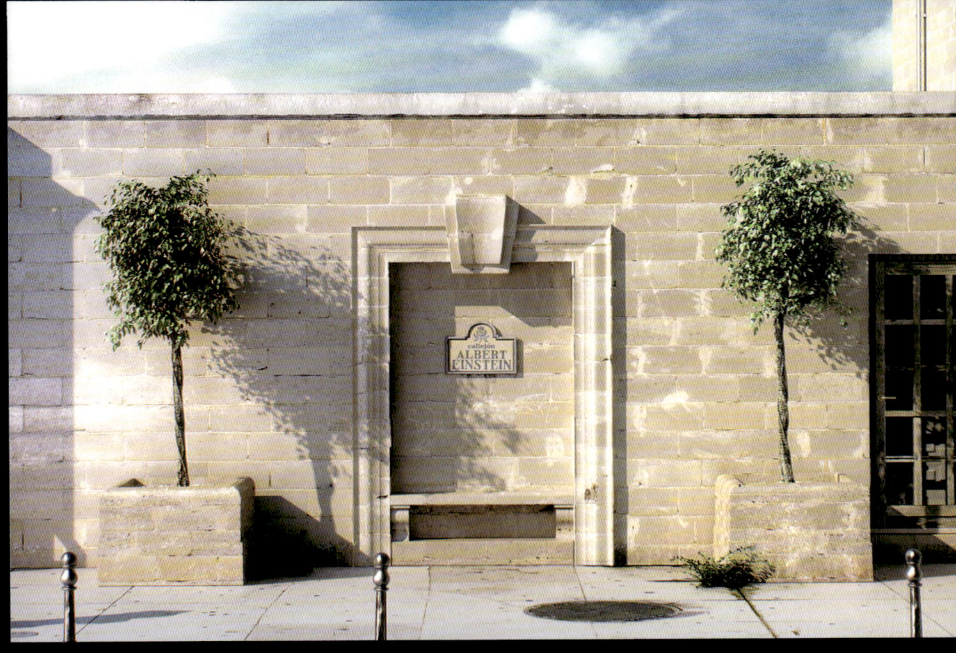

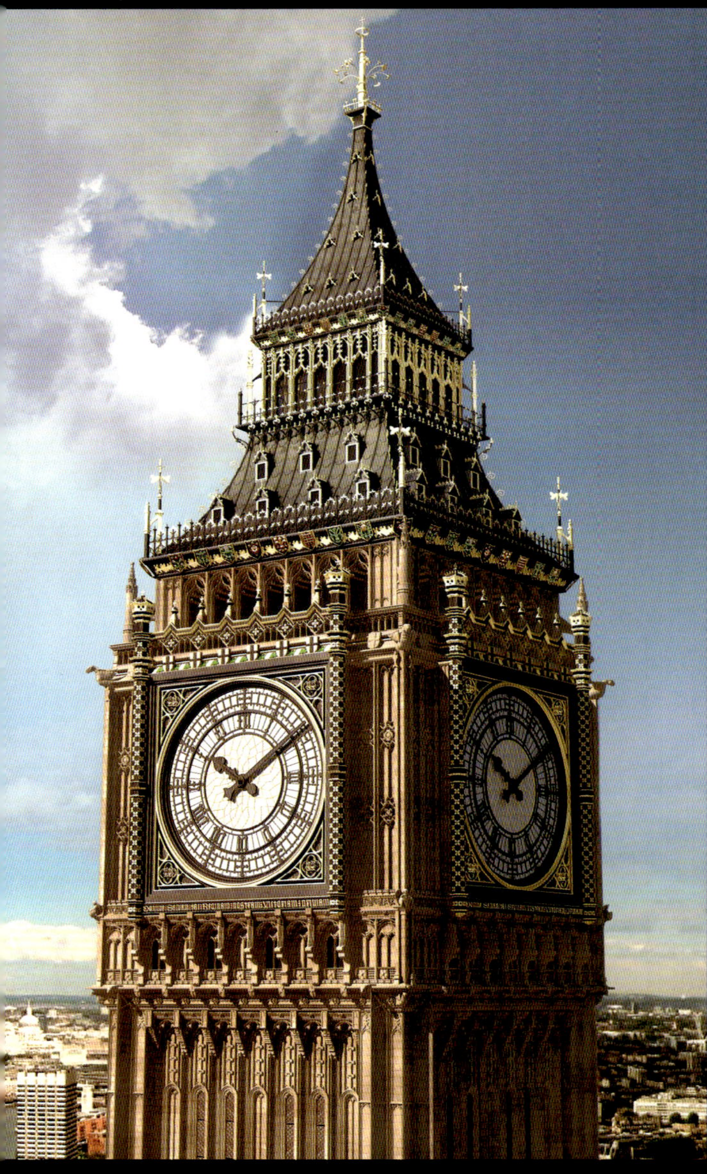

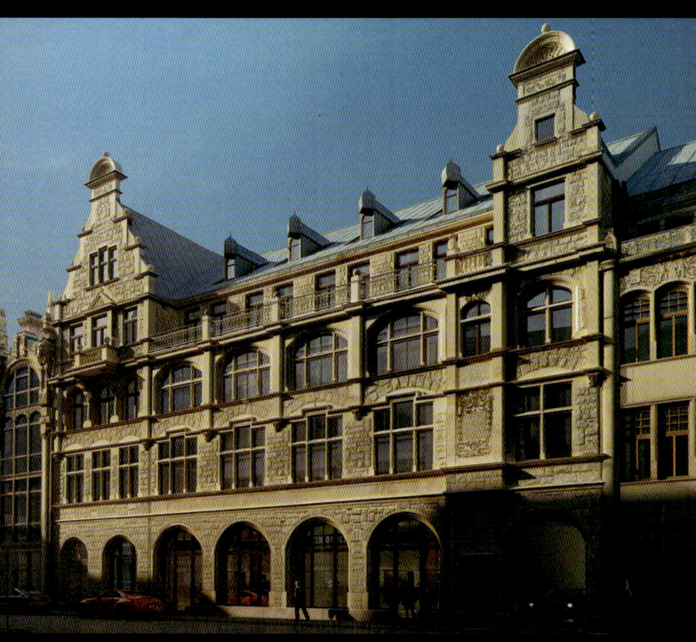

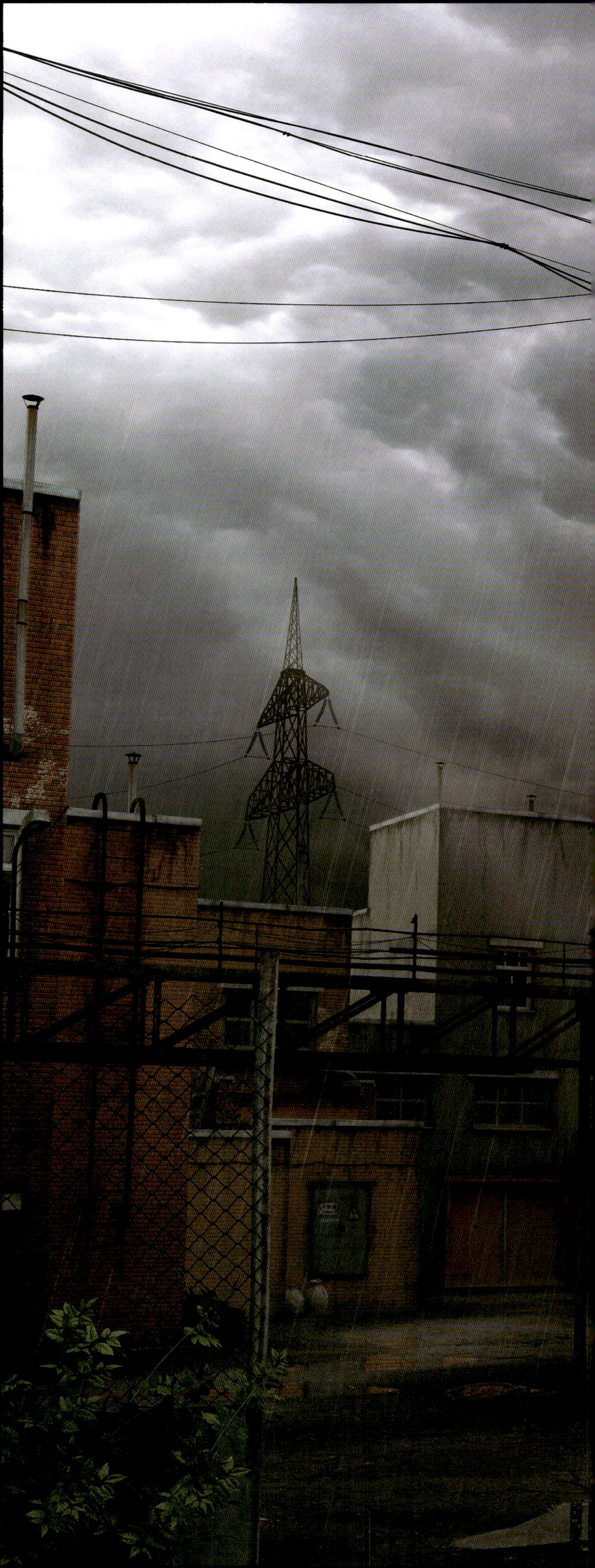

Big Ben
3ds Max, Photoshop
Luciano Neves,
INFINITE CG, BRAZIL
[top]

Heritage Gates
3ds Max, V-Ray, Photoshop
Lukasz Truchalski,
POLAND
[above]

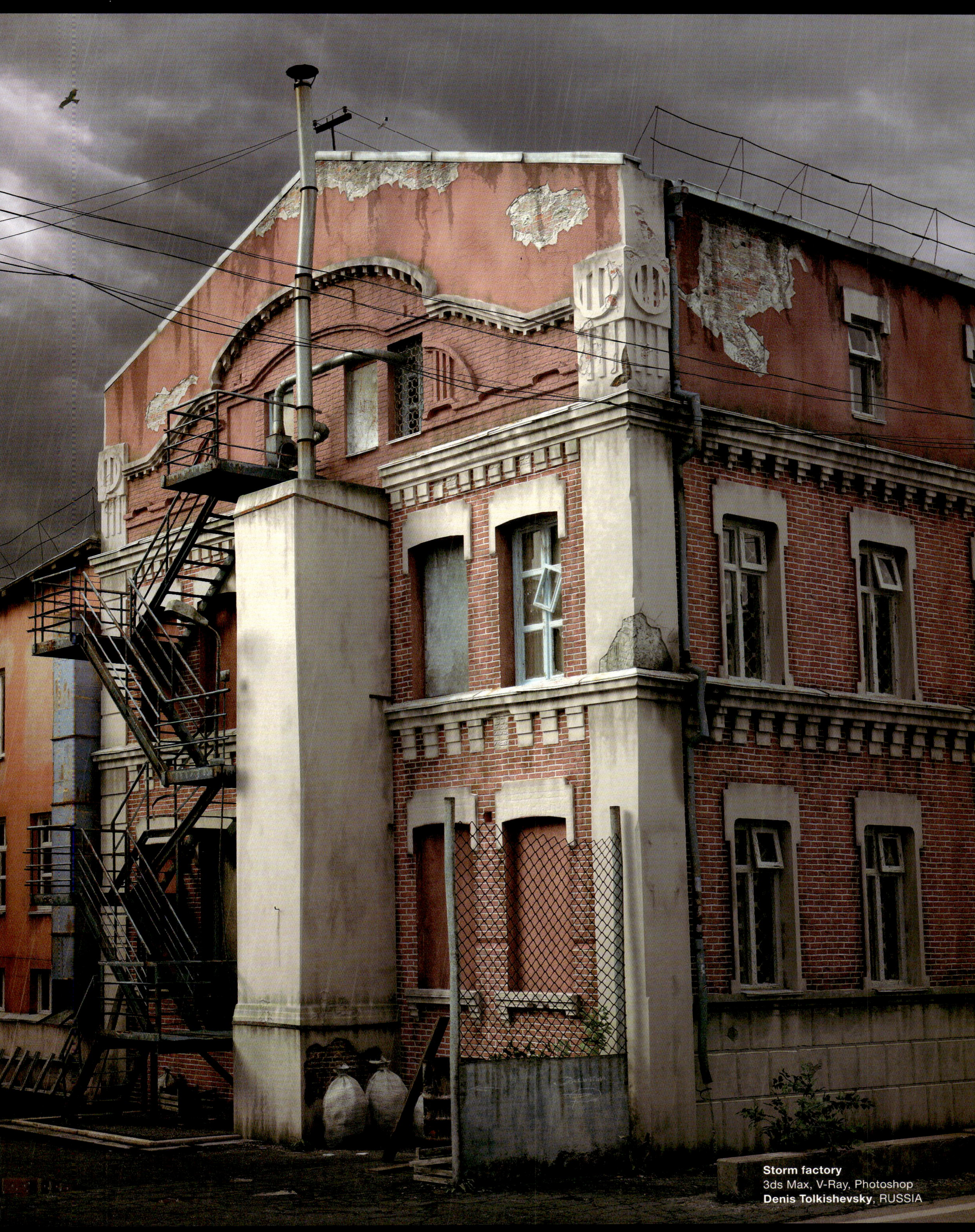

Storm factory
3ds Max, V-Ray, Photoshop
Denis Tolkishevsky, RUSSIA

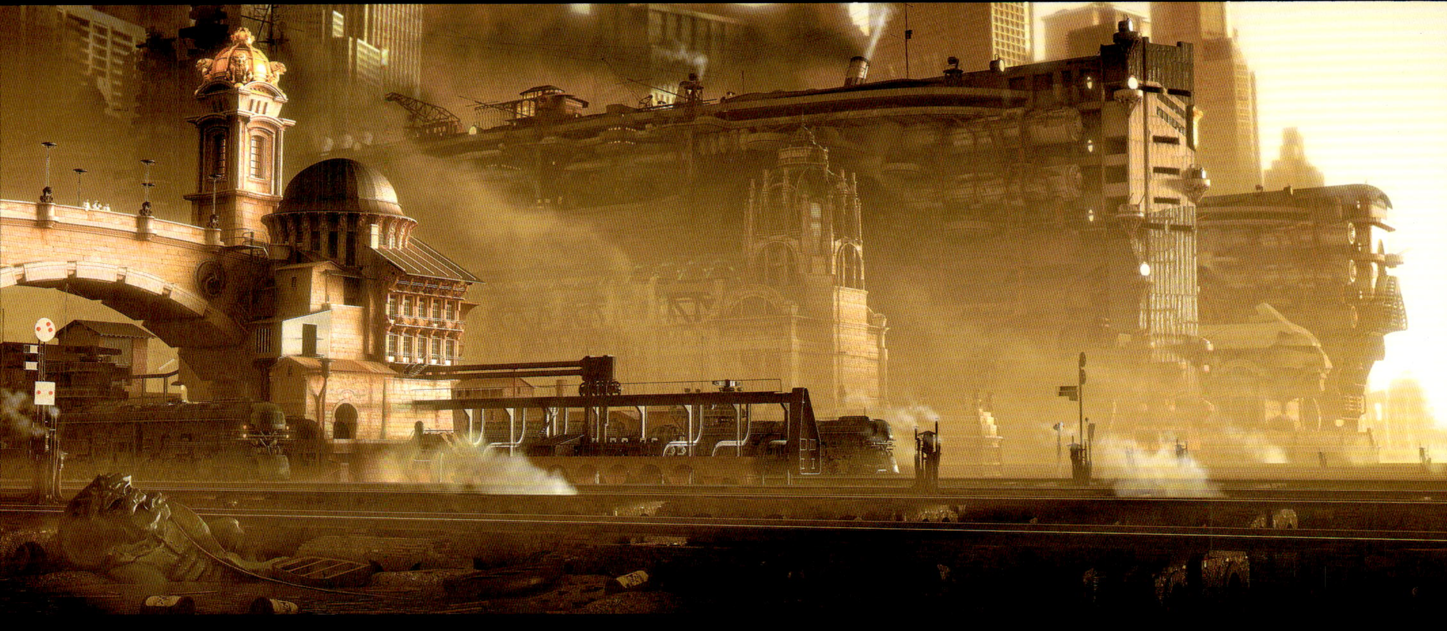

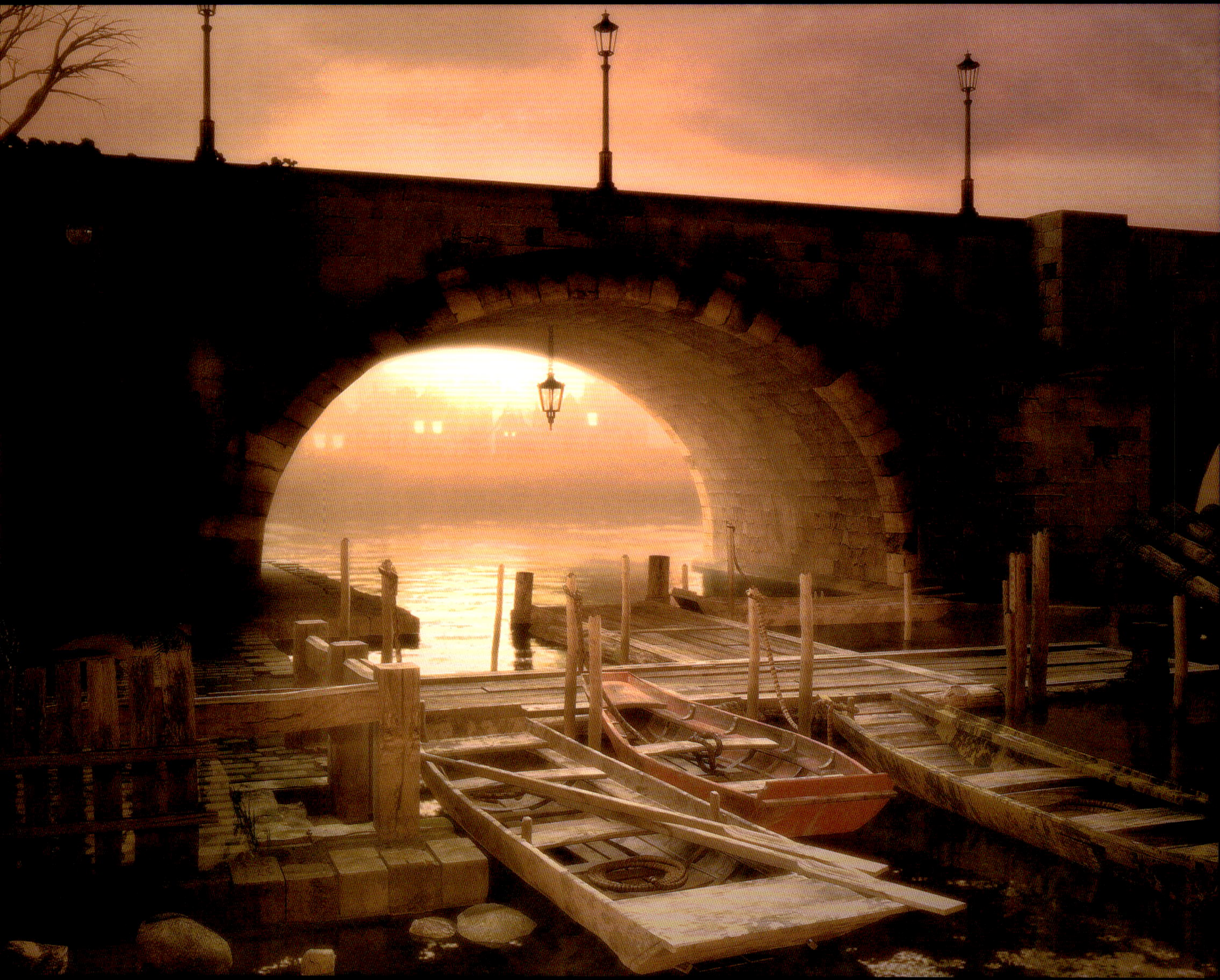

Rail haven
3ds Max, V-Ray
Marco Edel Rolandi, ITALY
[top]

When day is done
3ds Max
Mathieu Aerni, CANADA
[above]

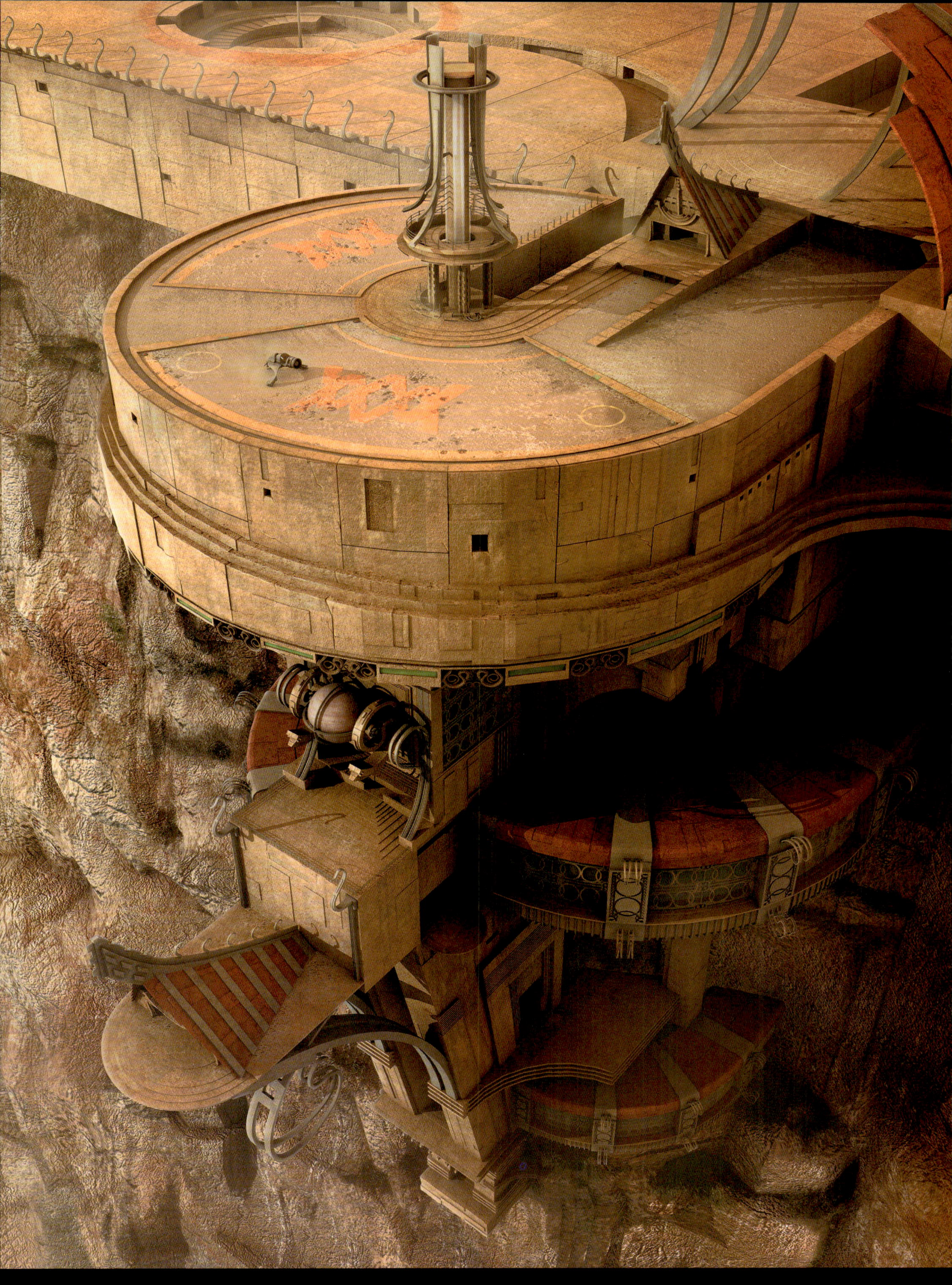

2200: City without a name
Maya, mental ray, Photoshop
Tiong-seah Yap, MALAYSIA

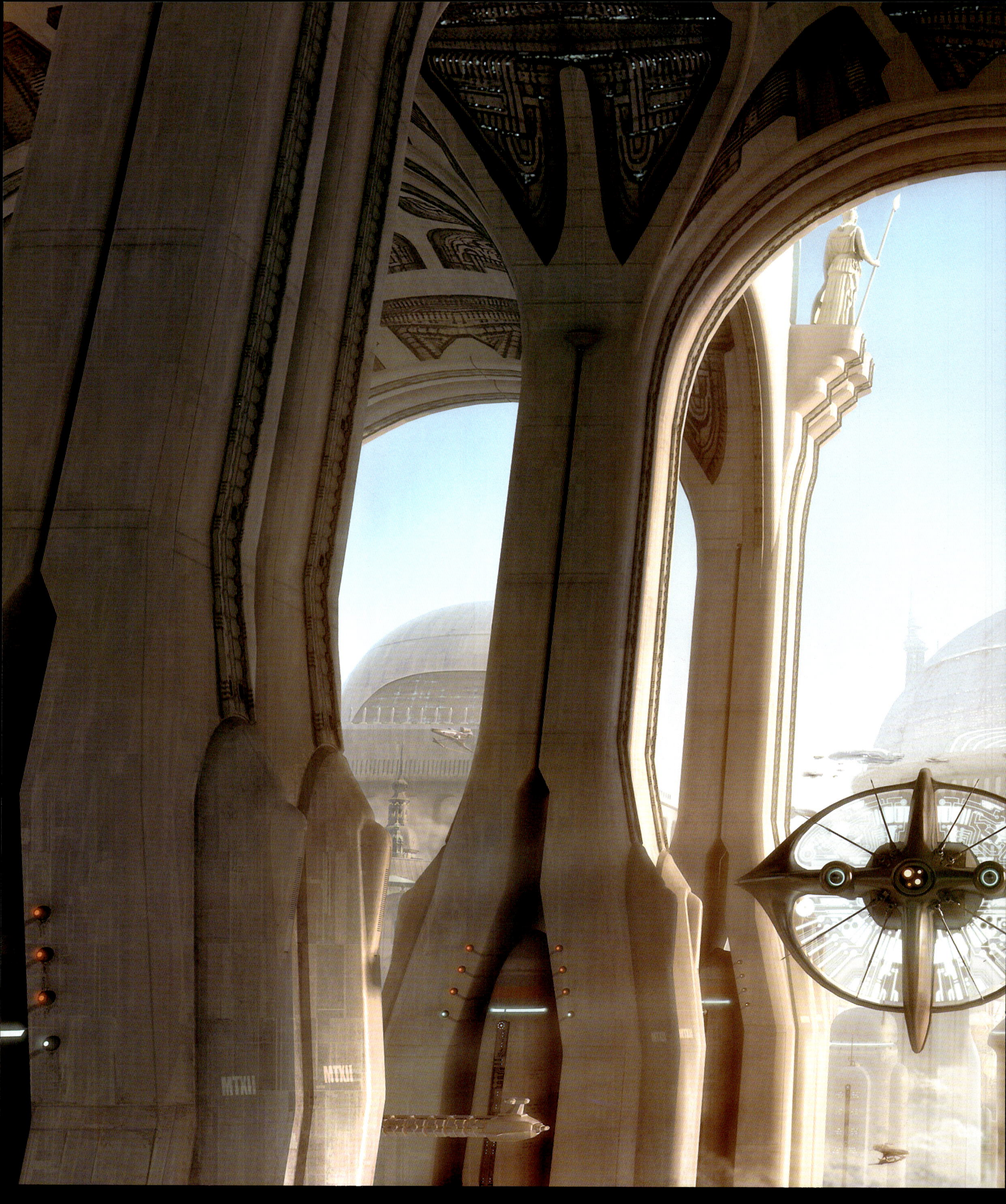

Excellence

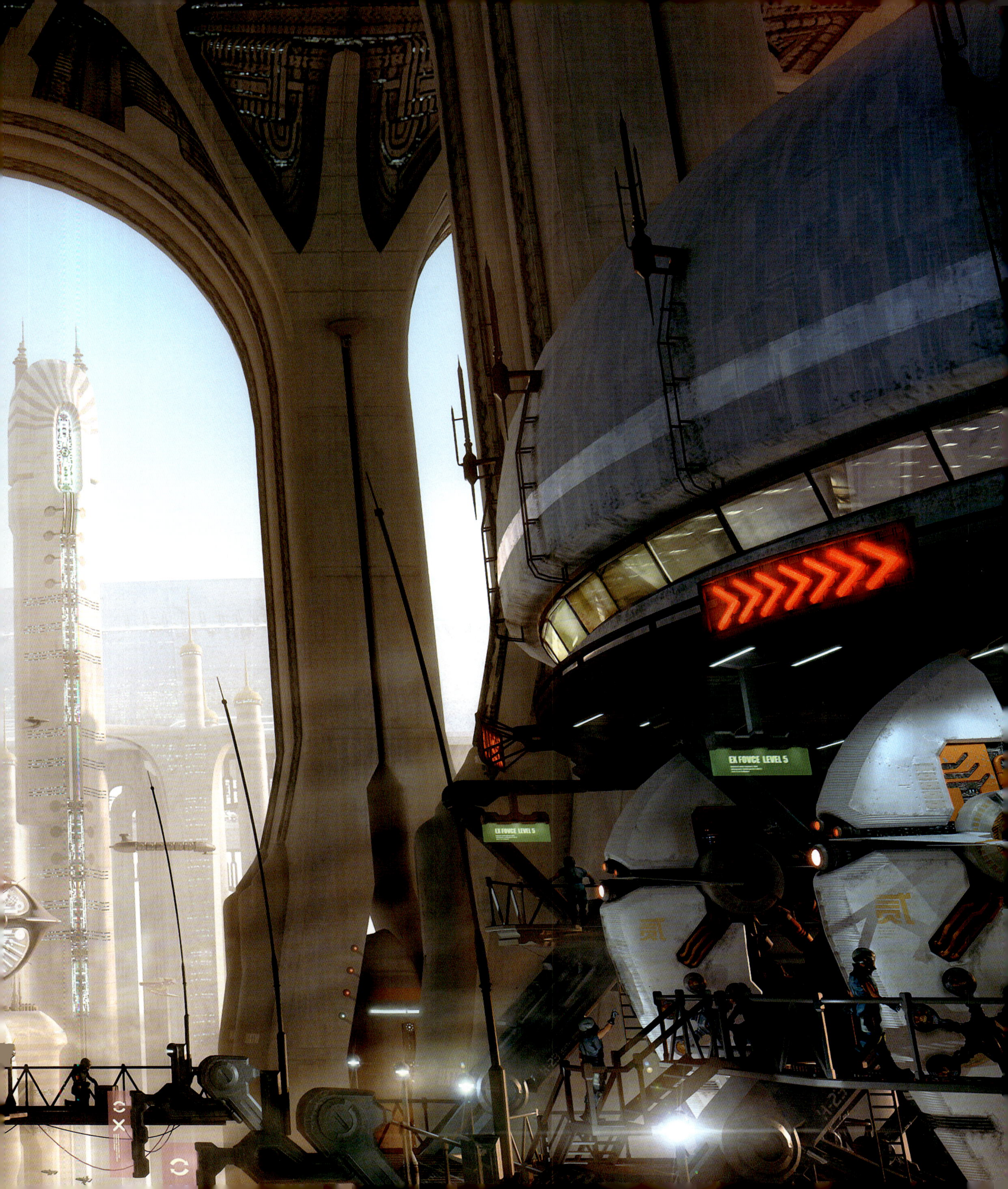
EX FOVCE LEVEL 5
EX FOVCE LEVEL 5

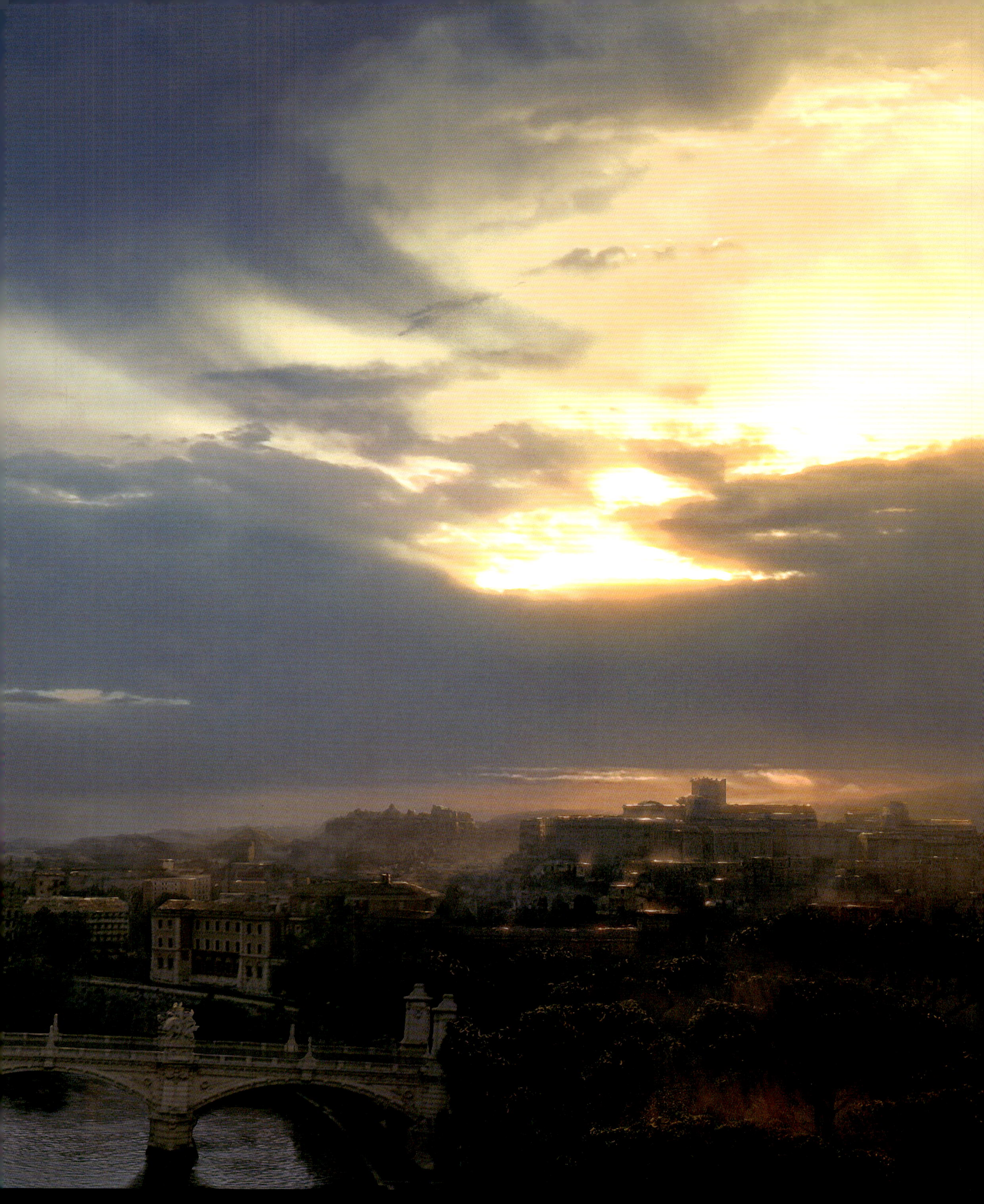

Excellence

Environment

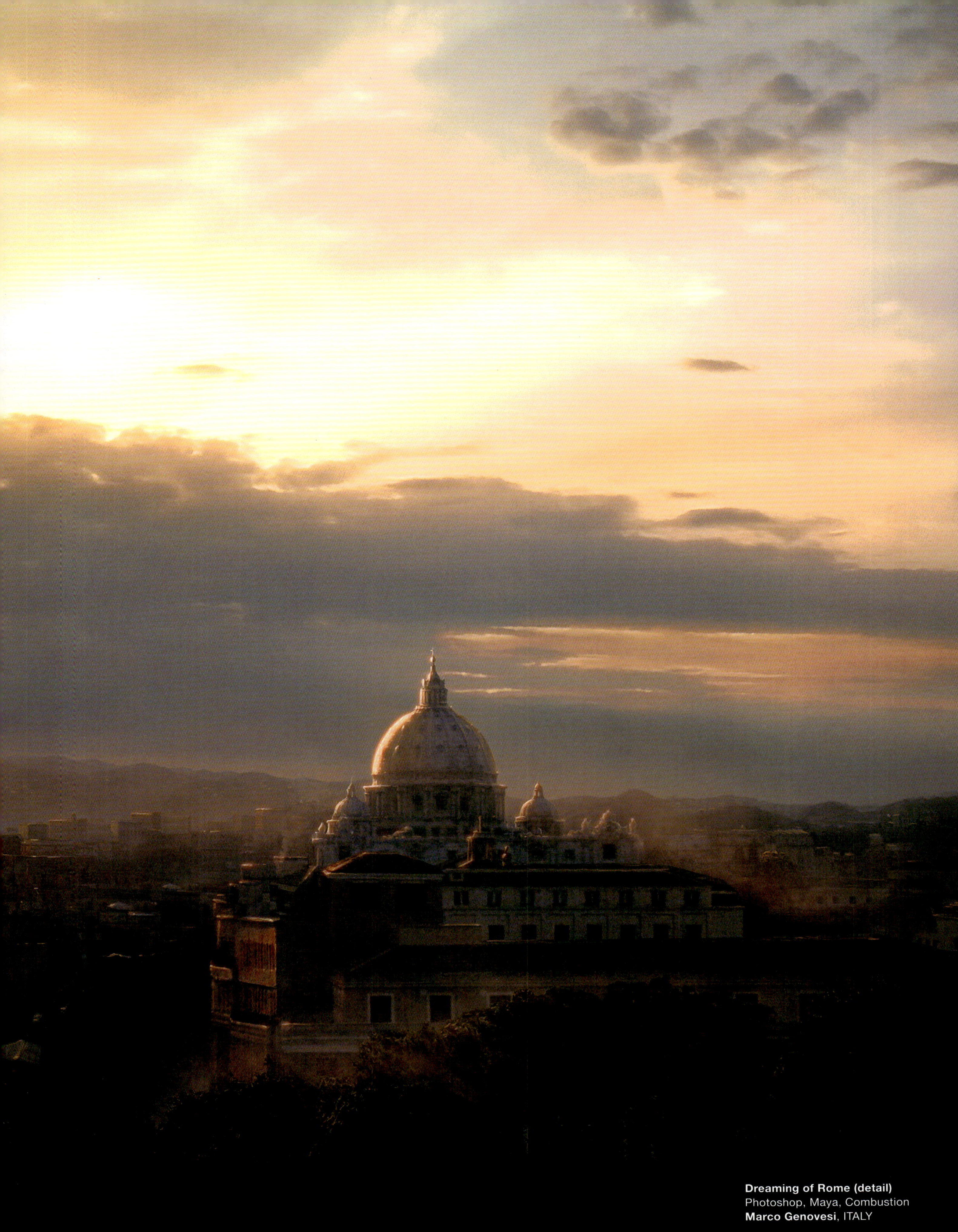

Dreaming of Rome (detail)
Photoshop, Maya, Combustion
Marco Genovesi, ITALY

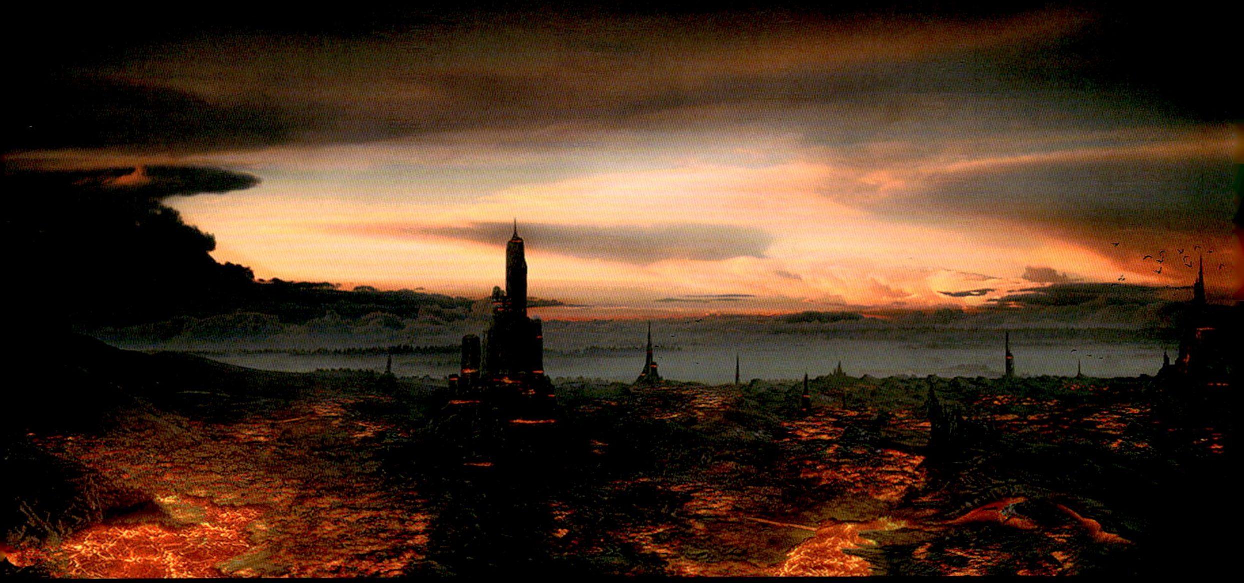

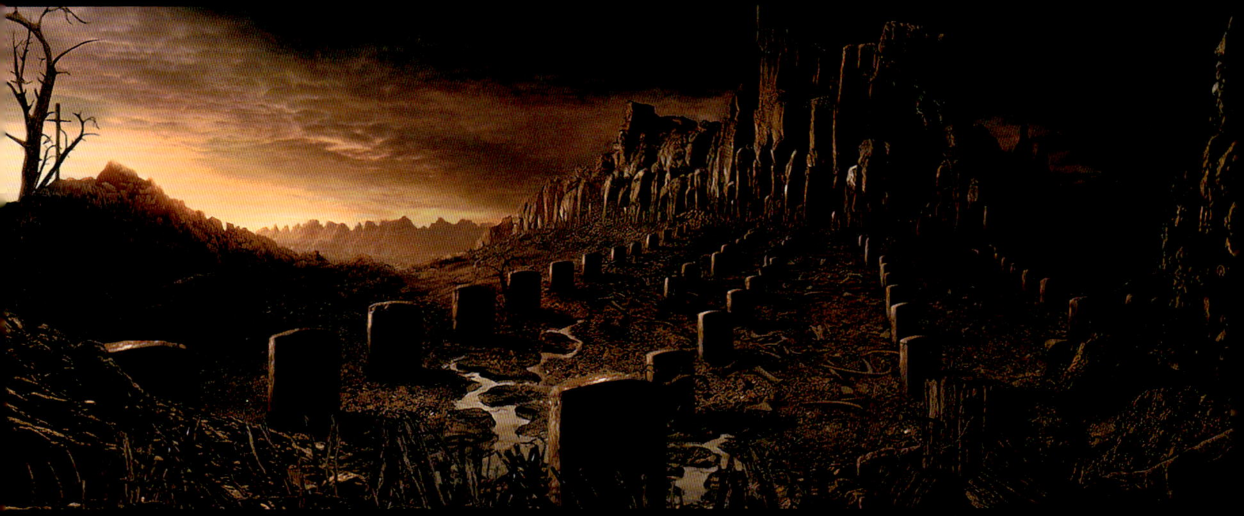

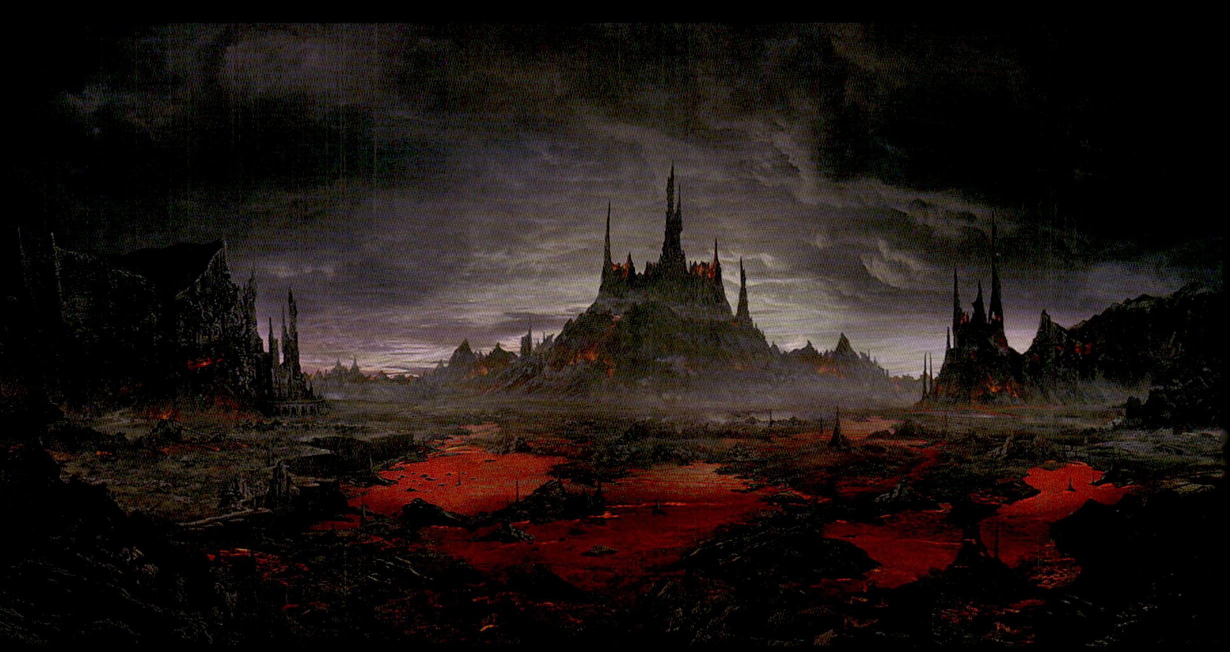

Lava city
3ds Max, ZBrush, Photoshop
Lubos dE Gerardo Surzin,
dE Gerard-Studio, GREAT BRITAIN
[top]

Cemetery
3ds Max, ZBrush, Photoshop
Lubos dE Gerardo Surzin,
dE Gerard-Studio, GREAT BRITAIN
[center]

Lava Environment 2
3ds Max, Photoshop
Lubos dE Gerardo Surzin,
dE Gerard-Studio, GREAT BRITAIN
[above]

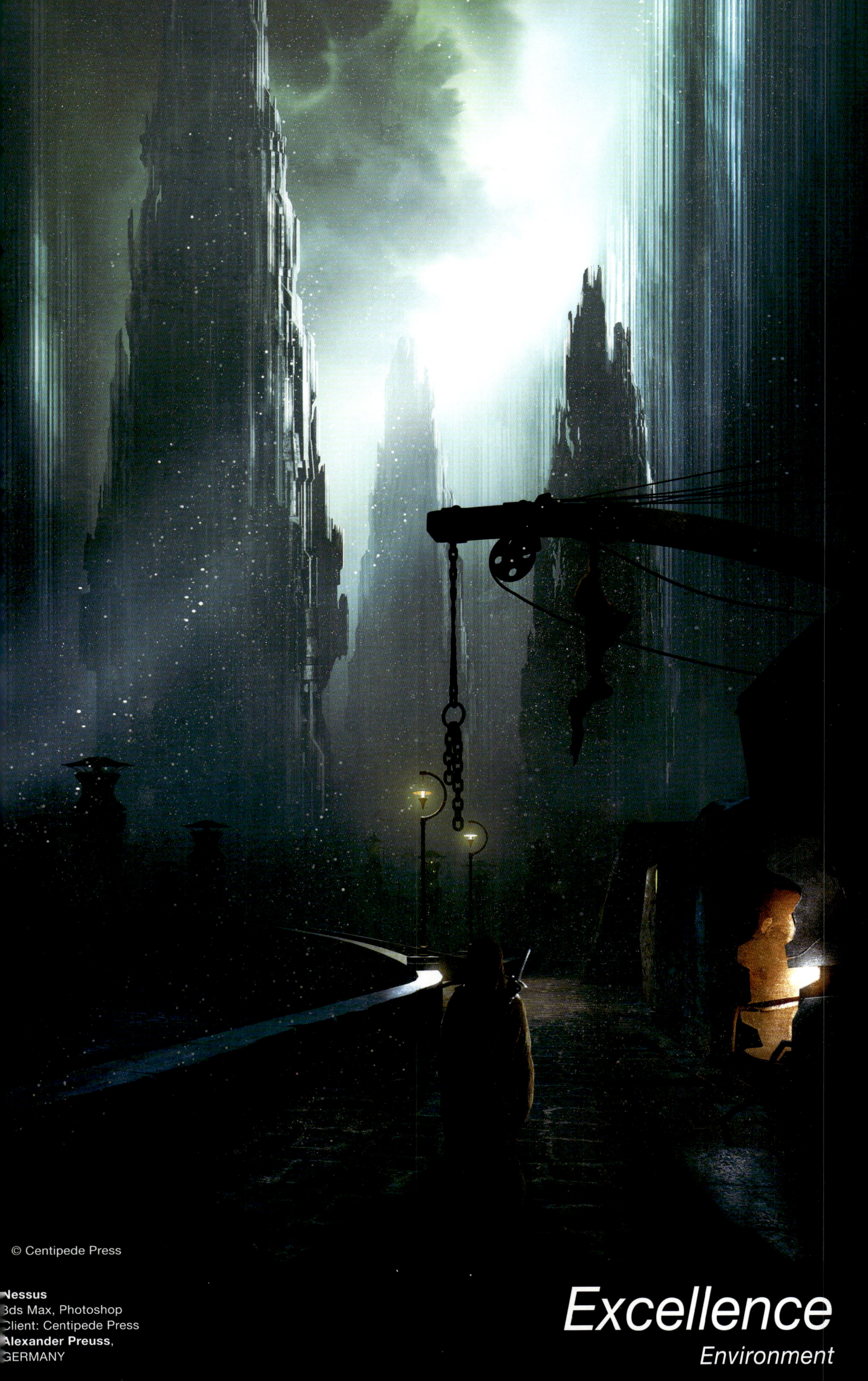

© Centipede Press

Nessus
3ds Max, Photoshop
Client: Centipede Press
Alexander Preuss,
GERMANY

Excellence
Environment

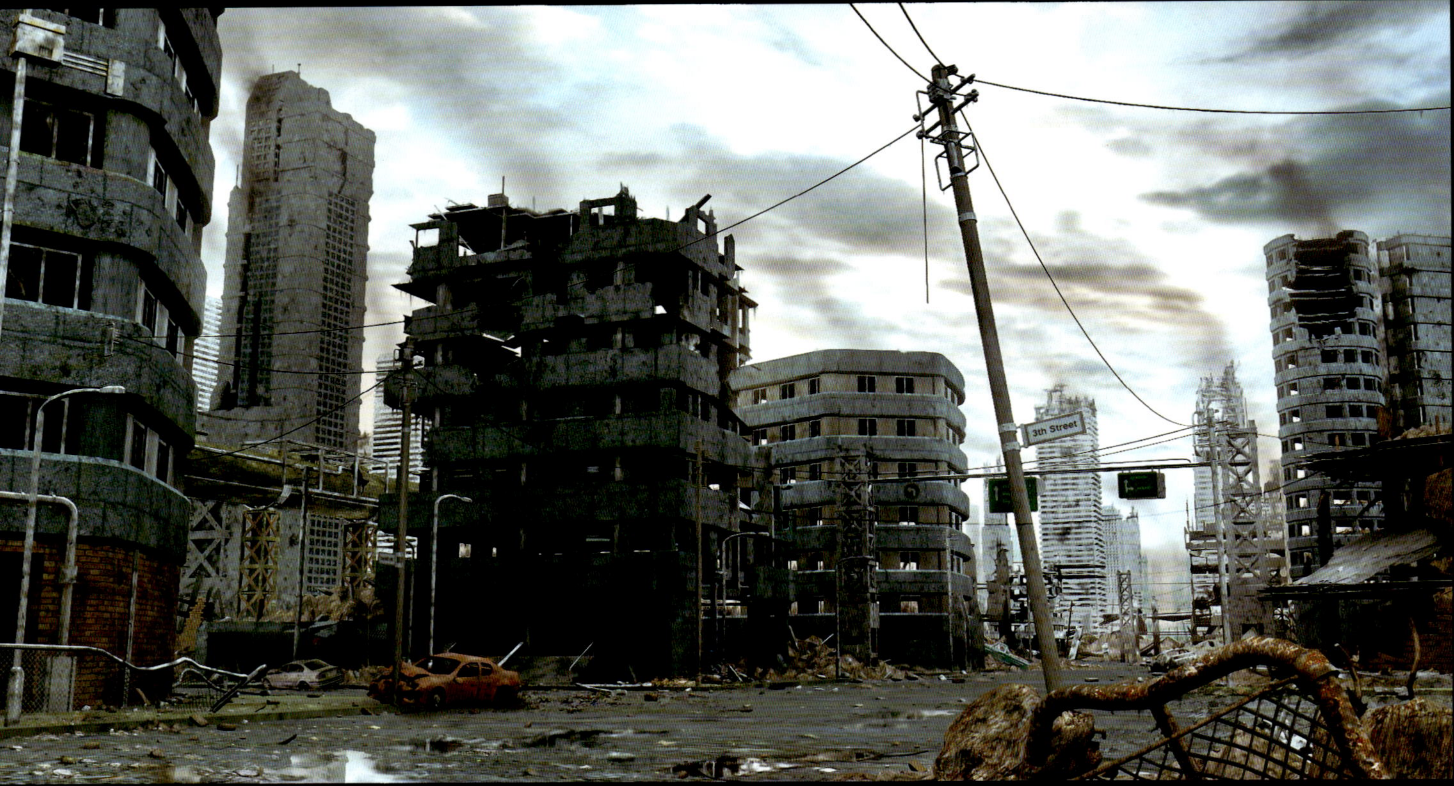

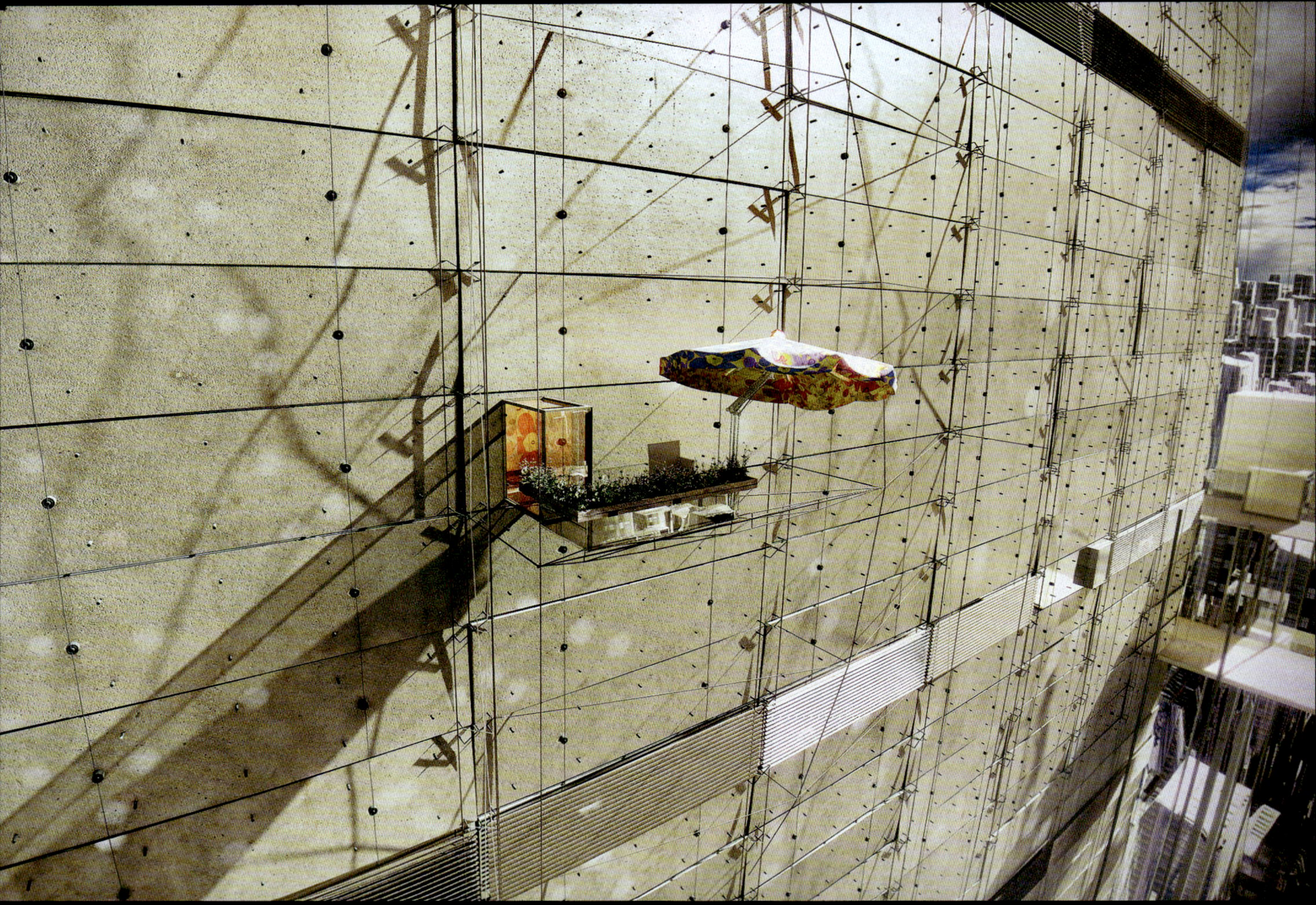

Downtown
3ds Max, Photoshop
Tero Mäkelä, FINLAND
[top]

Loneliness
3ds Max, V-Ray, Photoshop
Lukasz Truchalski, POLAND
[above]

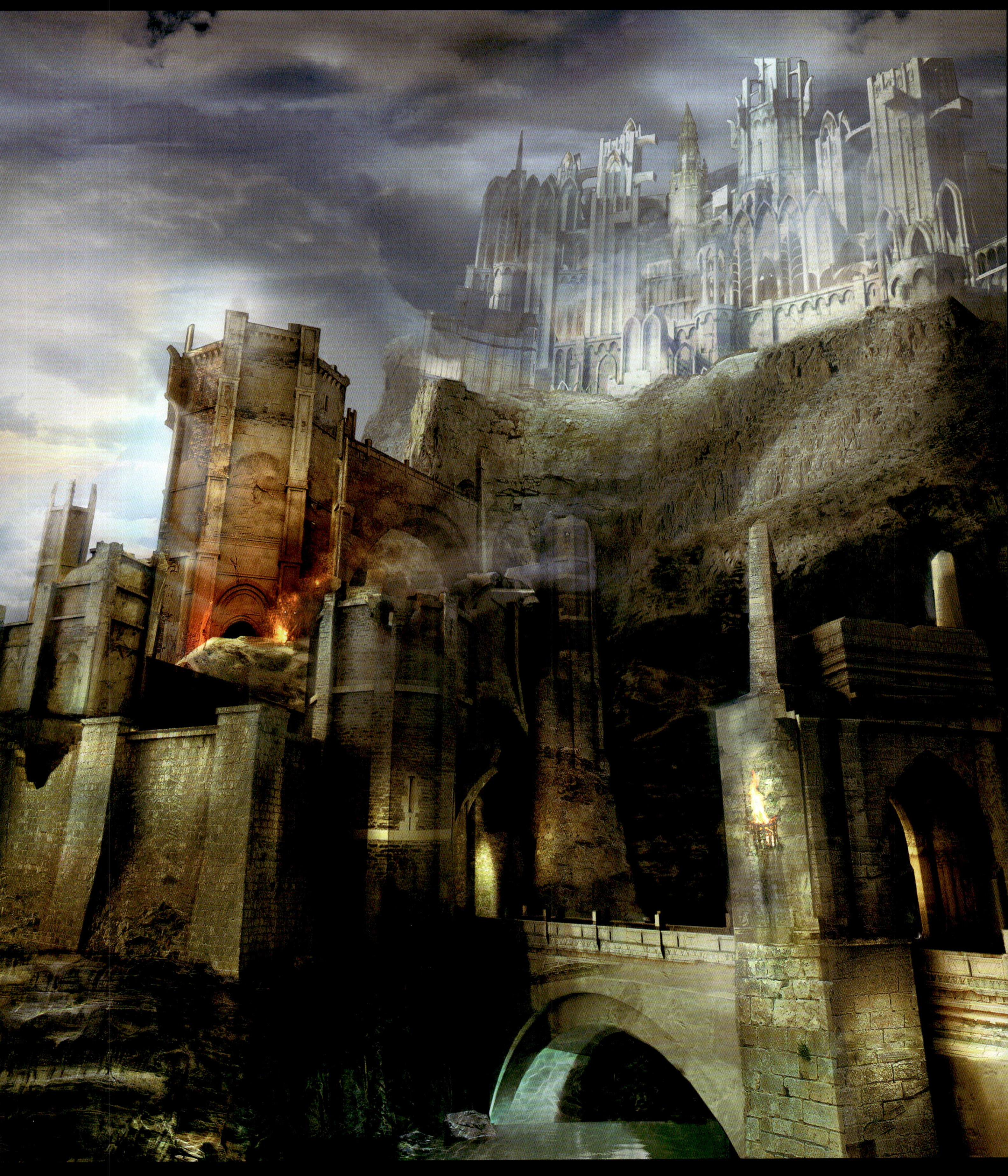

Serenisima
Maya, Photoshop
Stephen Cooper, GREAT BRITAIN

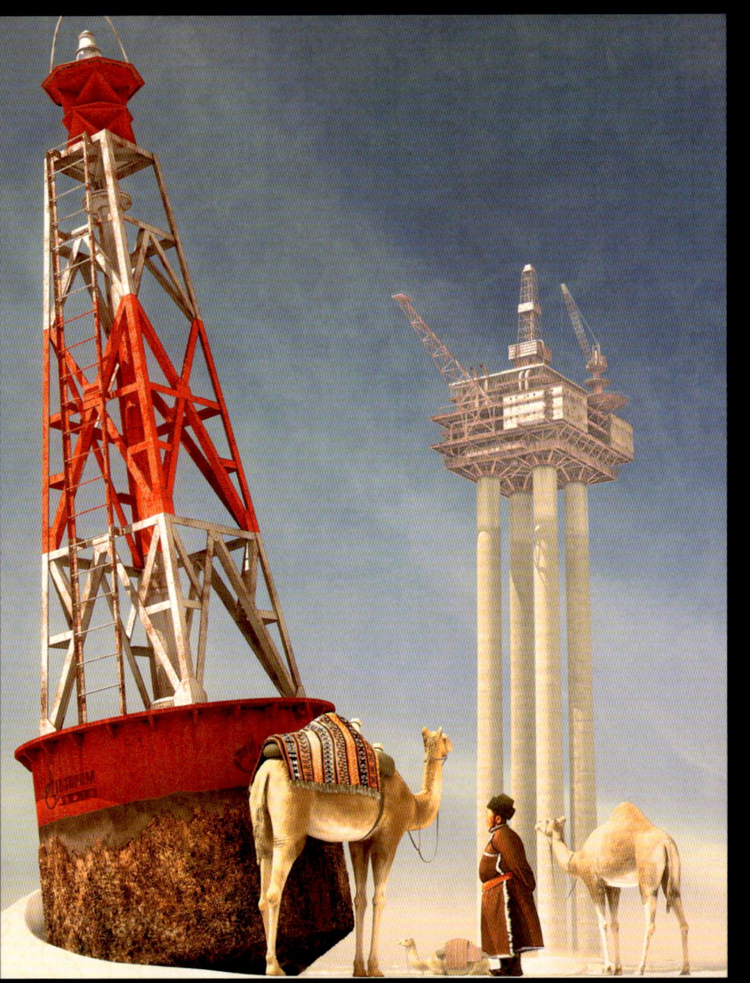

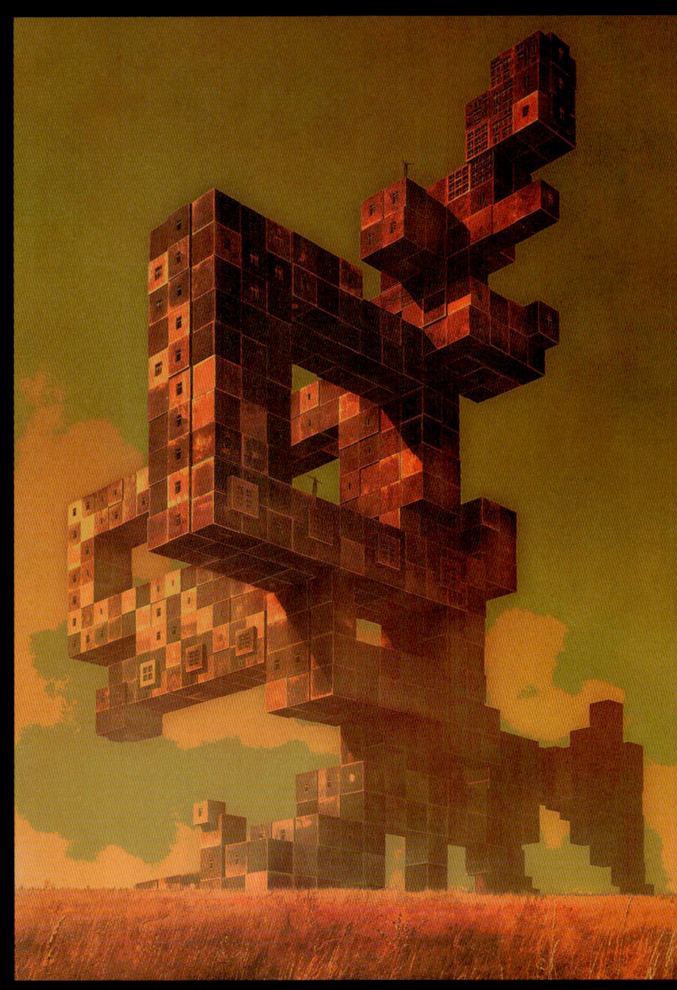

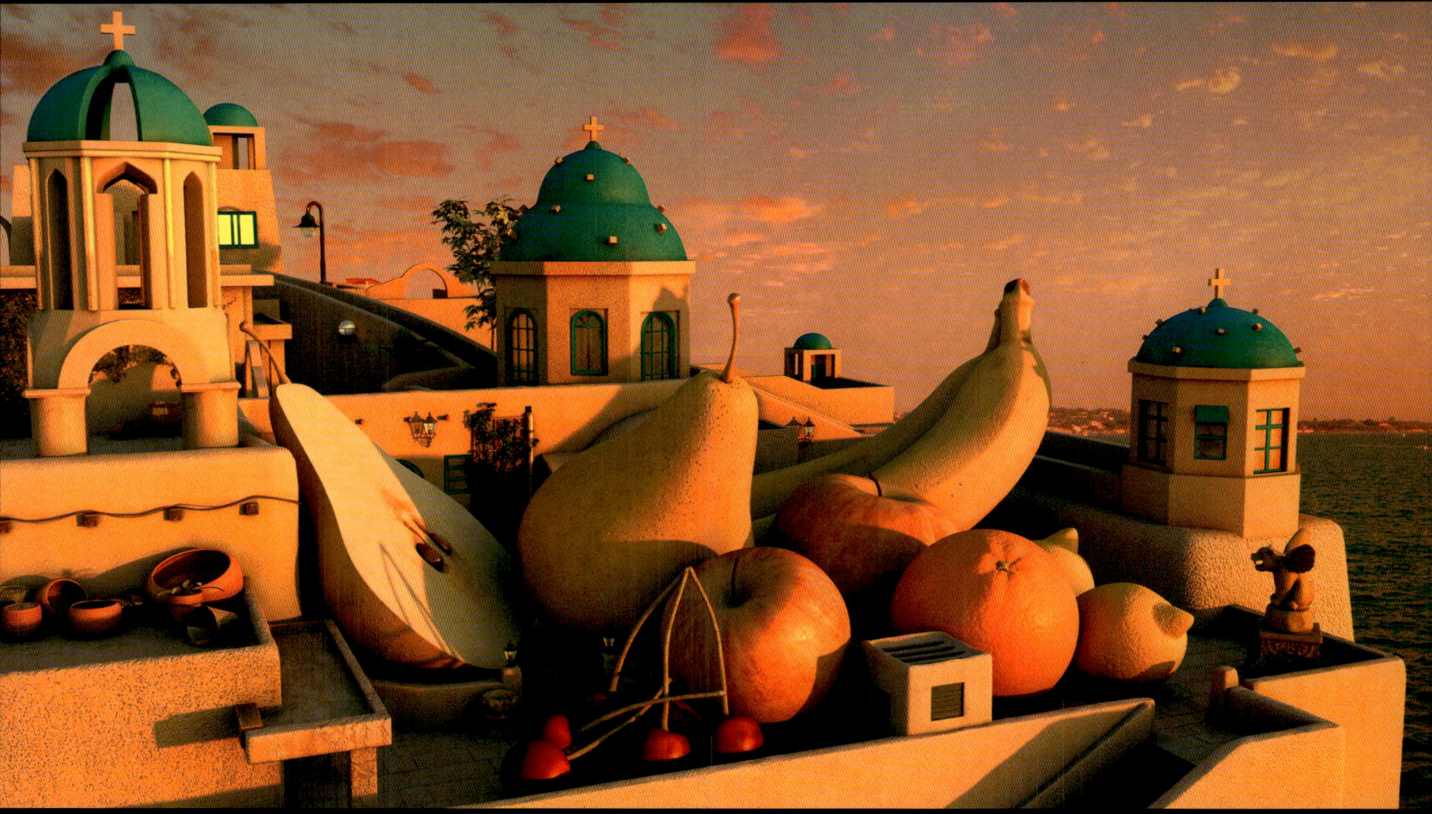

$996 per barrel
3ds Max, V-Ray, Photoshop
Petr Vlasenko,
UKRAINE
[top]

Fruits on Vacation
Maya, Photoshop
Rui Xu,
USA
[above]

Construction Set House
3ds Max, Photoshop
Sergey Skachkov,
RUSSIA
[top]

Nowhere land
Photoshop, Maya, Painter
Pablo Muñoz, Universidad Veritas,
COSTA RICA
[right]

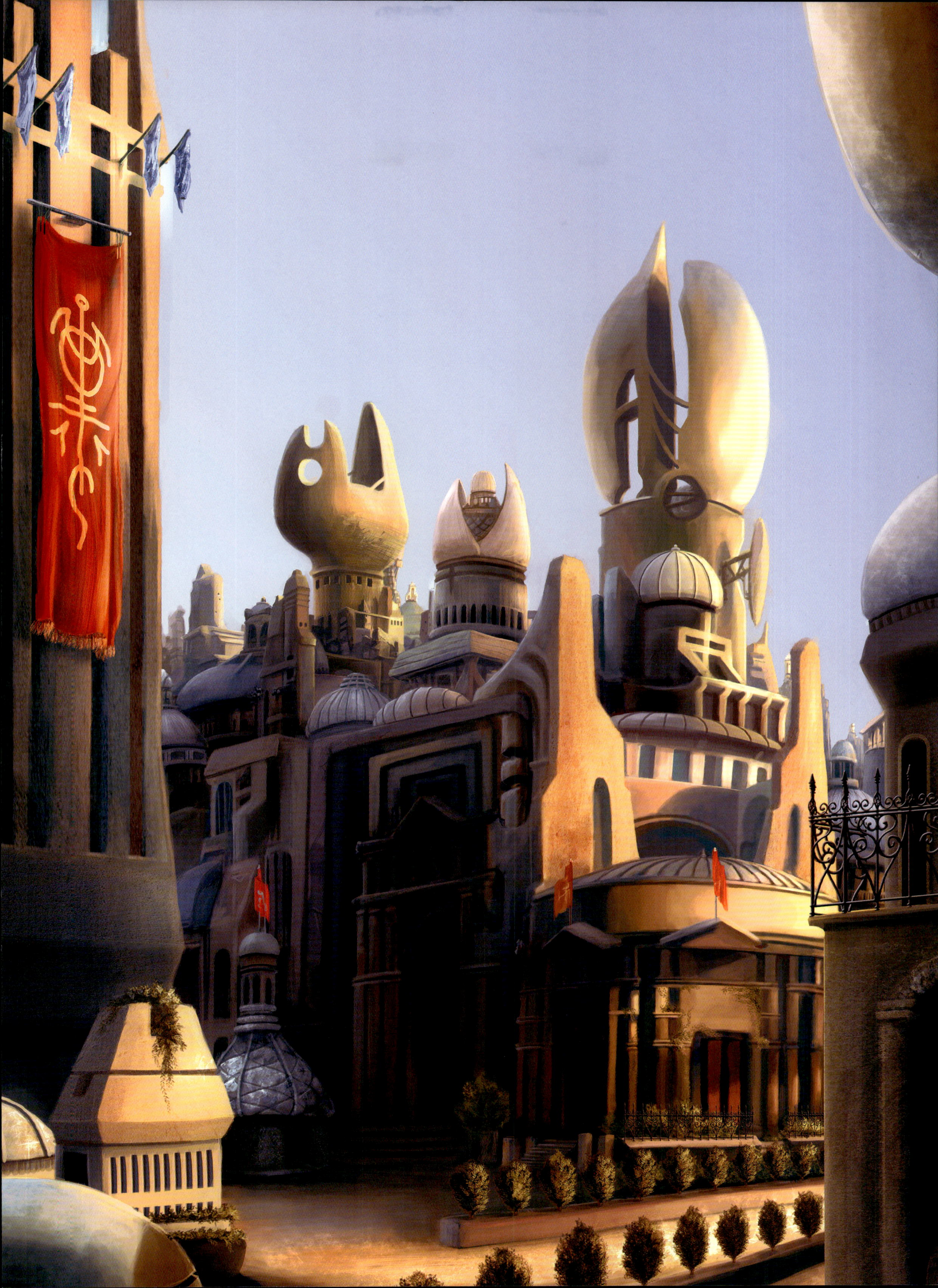

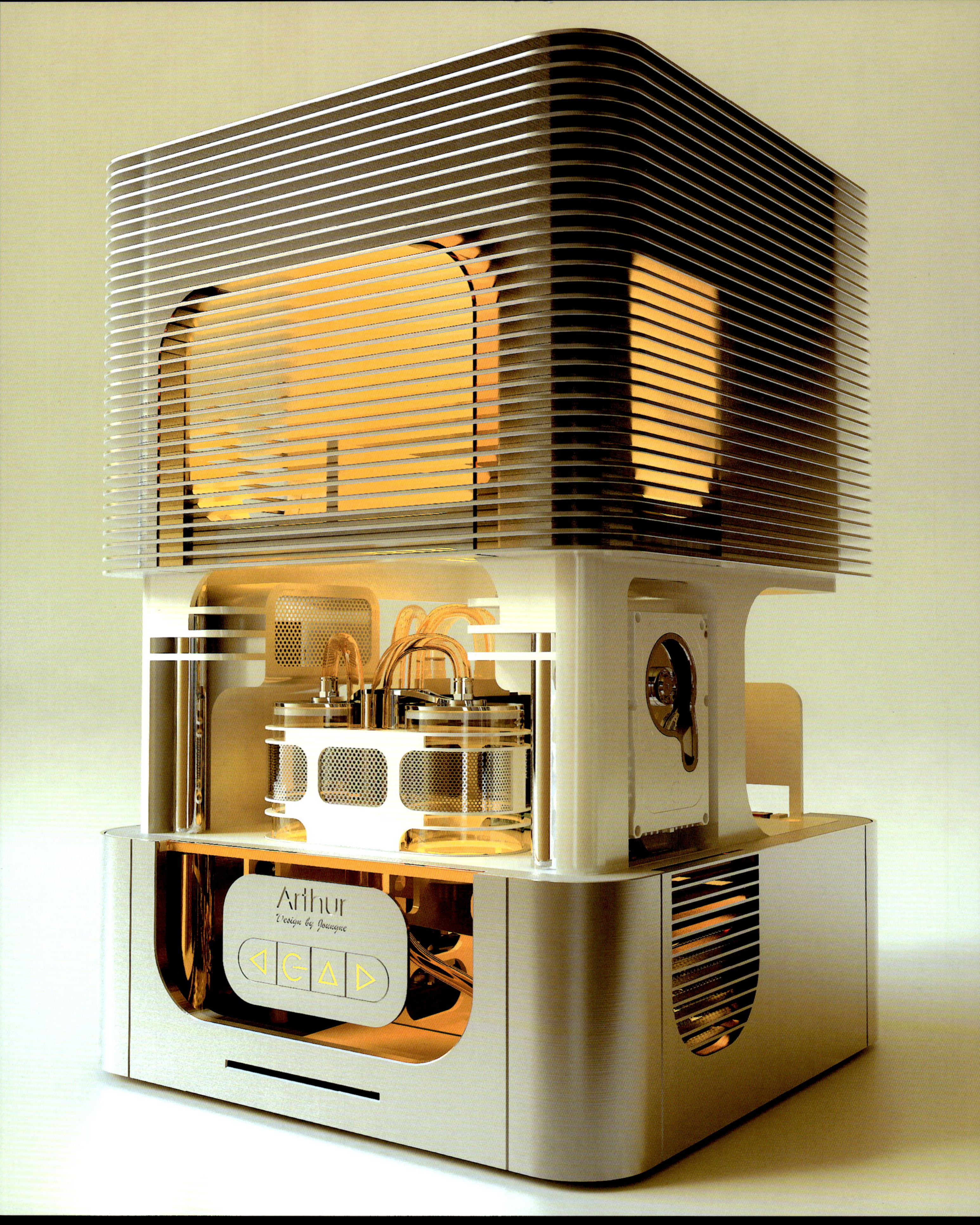

Master
Product Design

Arthur
3ds Max, V-Ray, Photoshop
Gert Swolfs, G2 BVBA,
BELGIUM

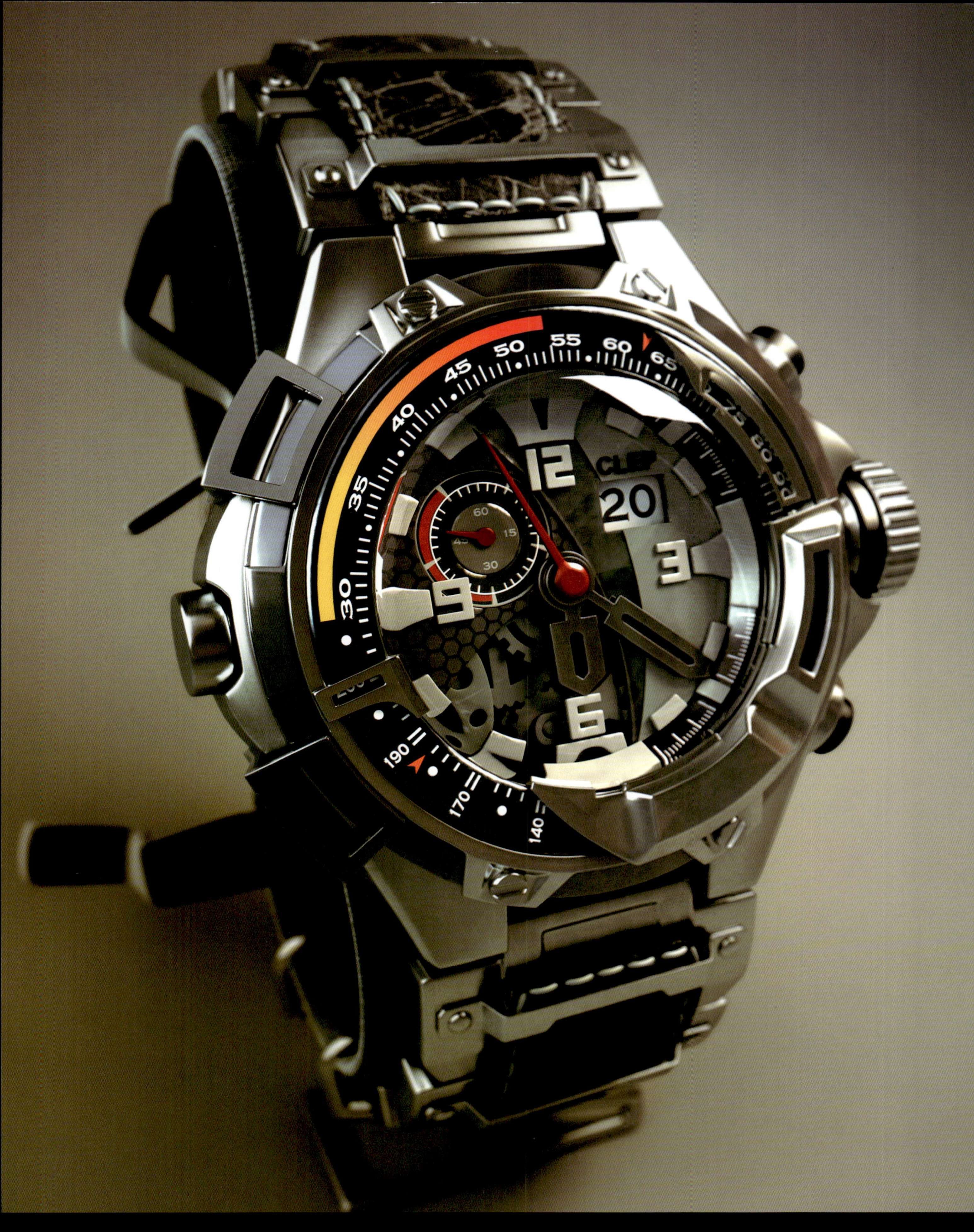

Clep
3ds Max, V-Ray, Photoshop
Felix Rodriguez Joleanes,
Immersion Games, COLOMBIA

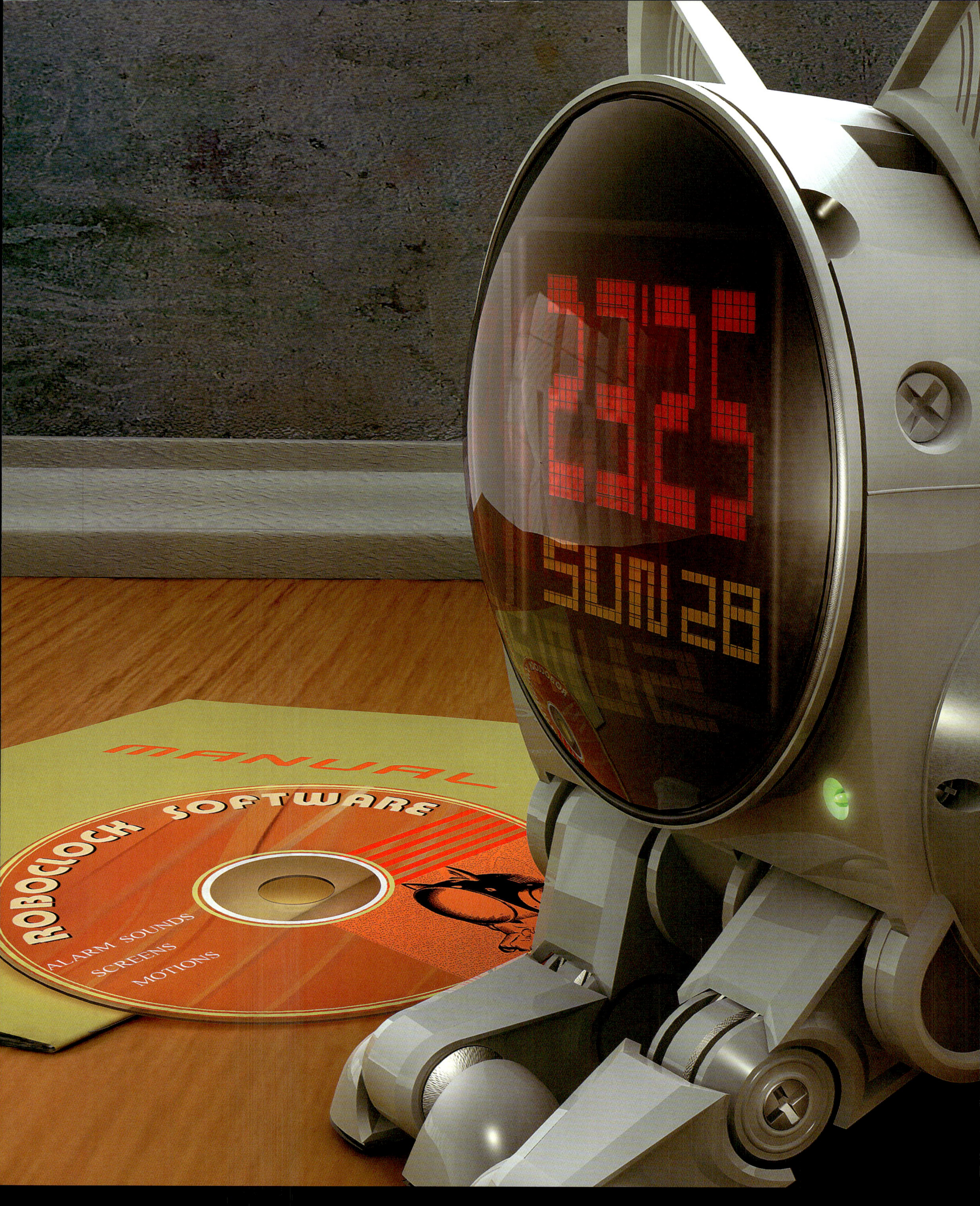

Excellence

Product Design

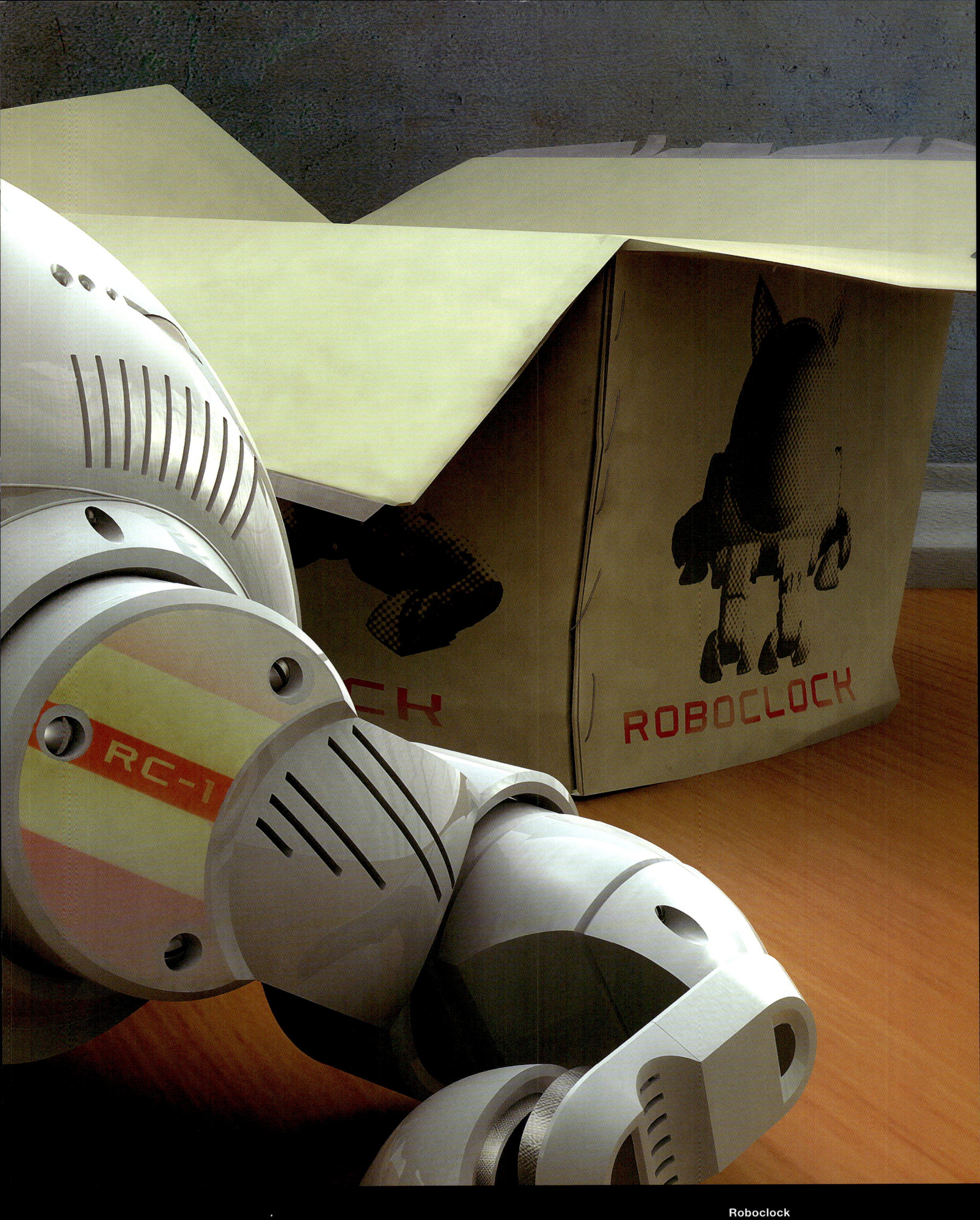

Roboclock
3ds Max, V-Ray
Juliy Trub, International Art Found.,
RUSSIA

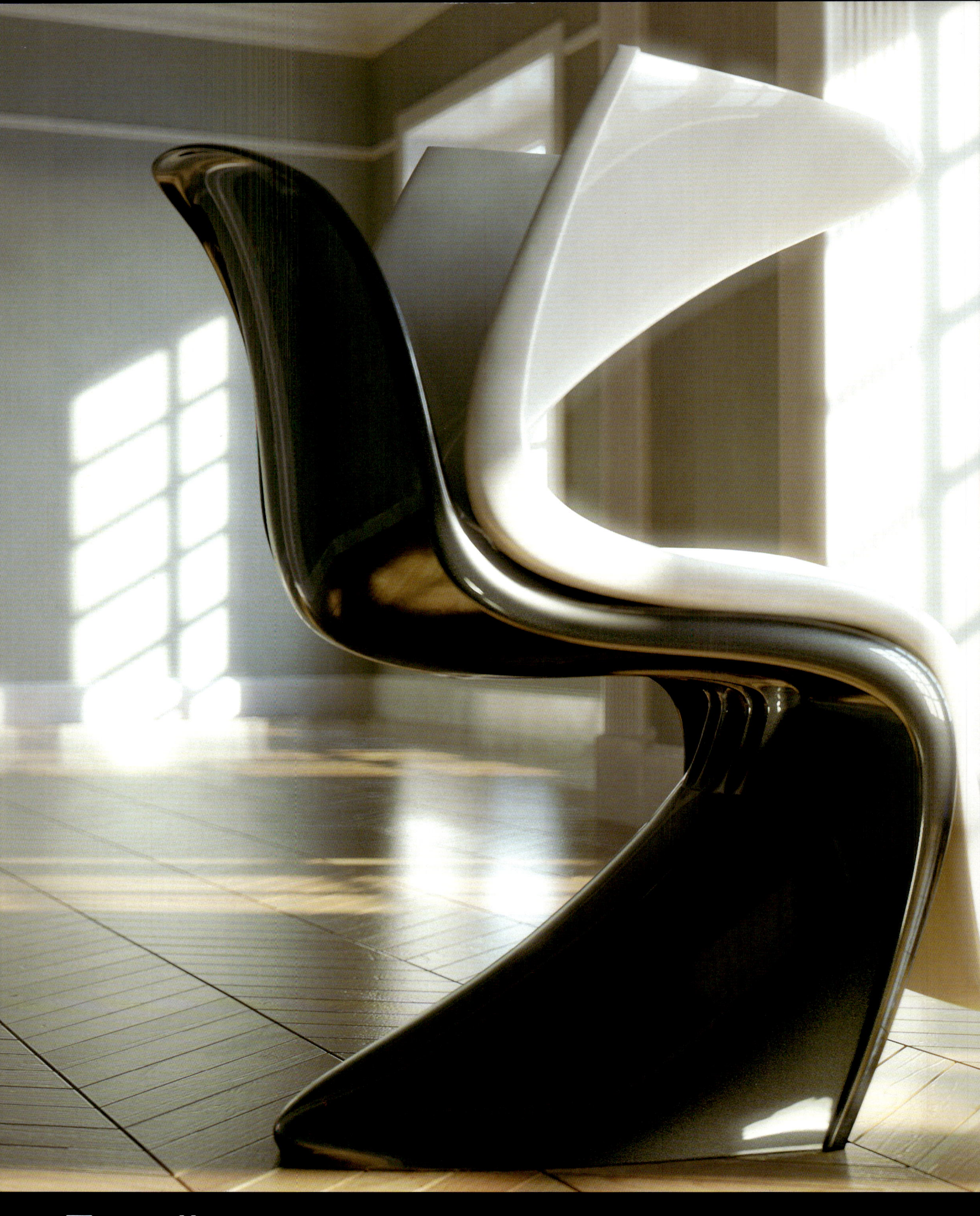

Excellence
Product Design

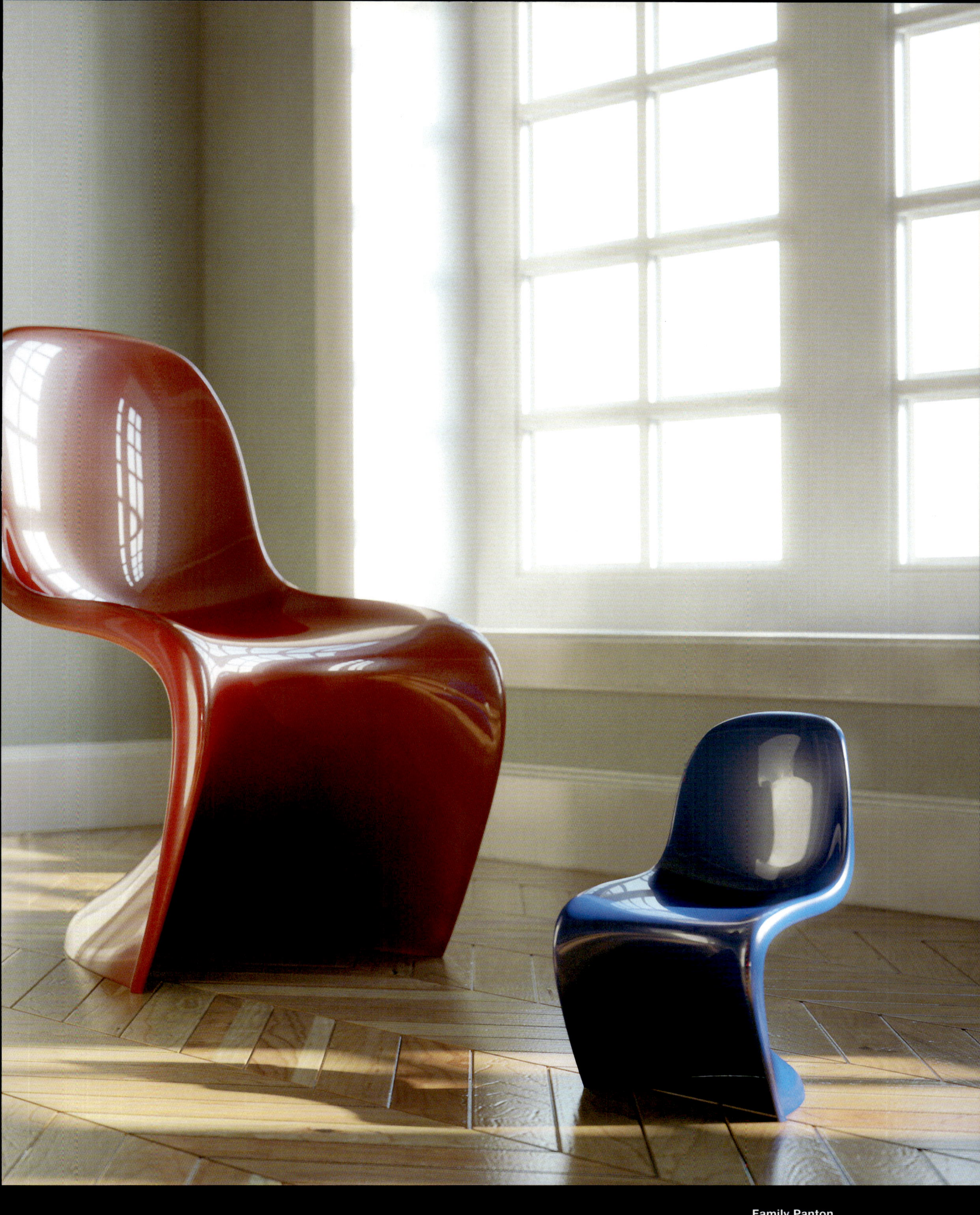

Family Panton
3ds Max, V-Ray
Peter Guthrie, GREAT BRITAIN

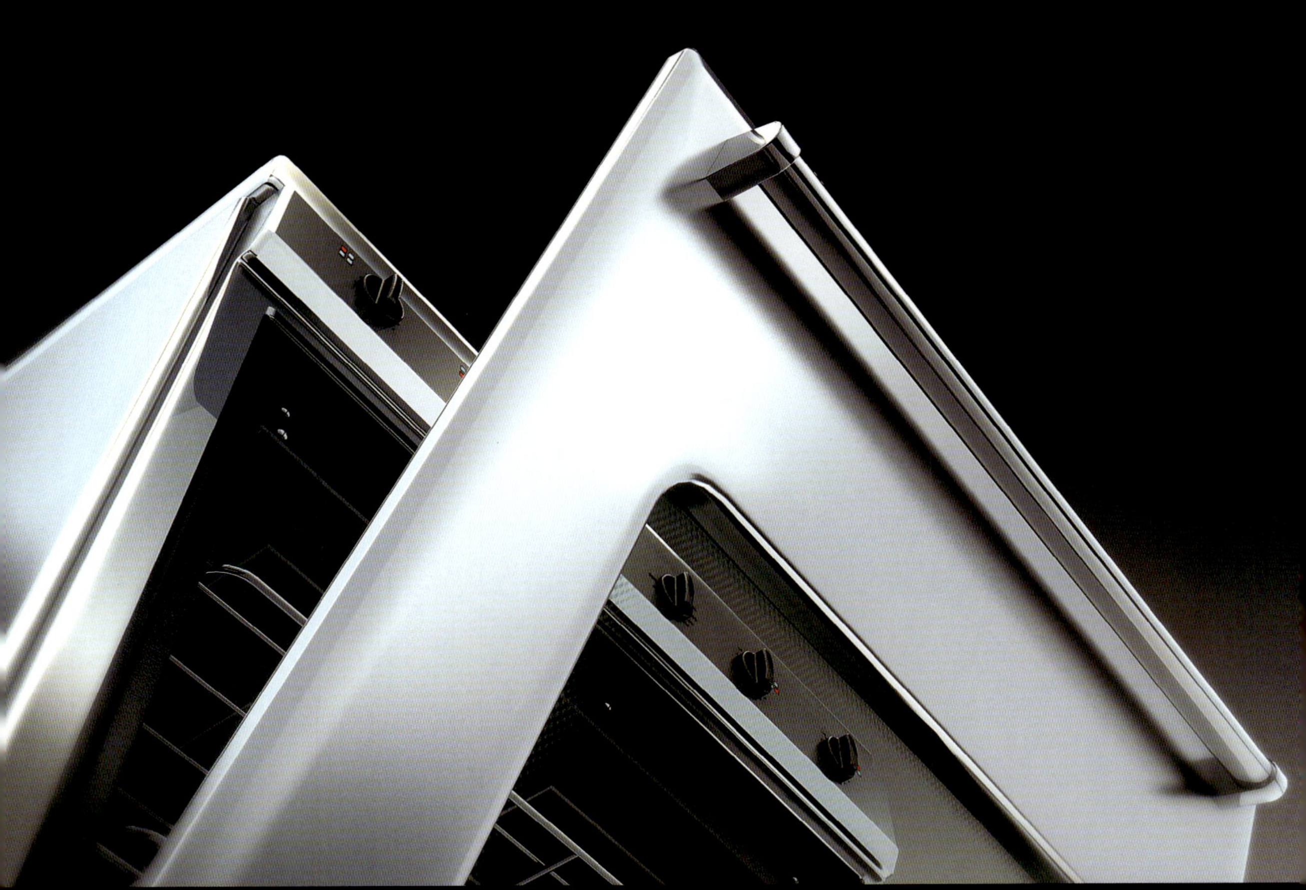

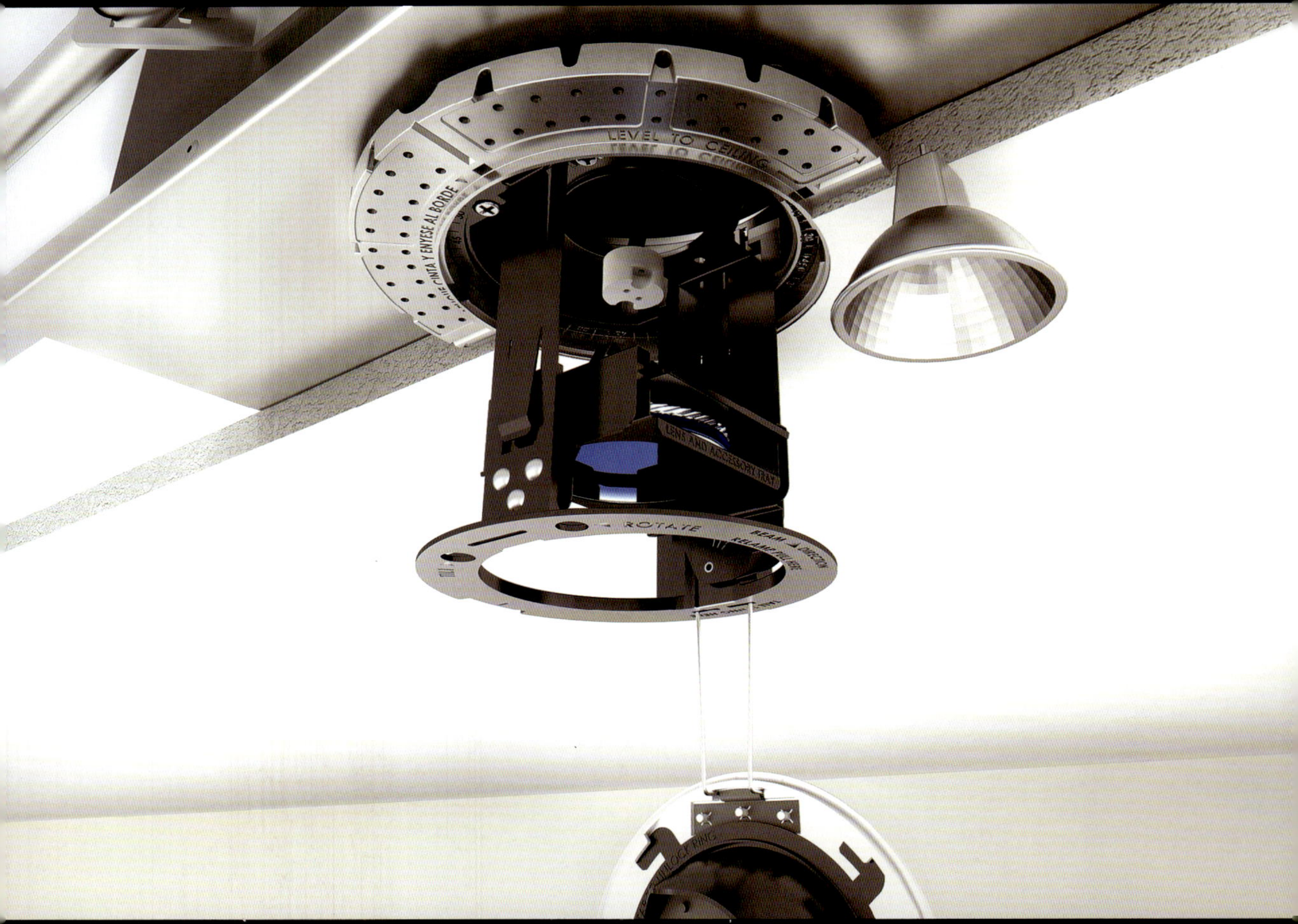

Range Against the Machine
3ds Max, Photoshop
Spine3D, USA
[top]

ID
3ds Max, Photoshop
Client: Focal Point
Spine3D, USA
[above]

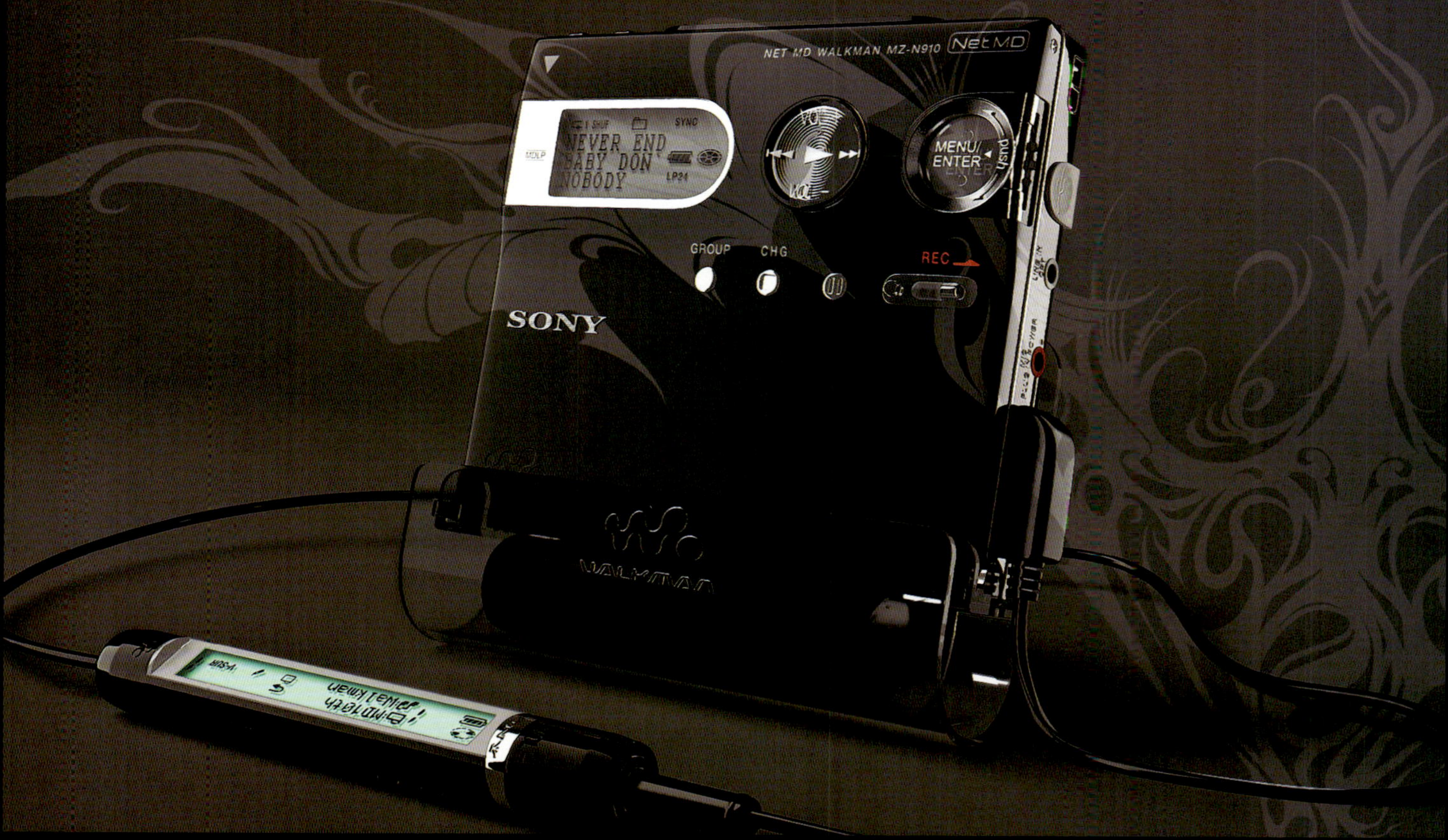

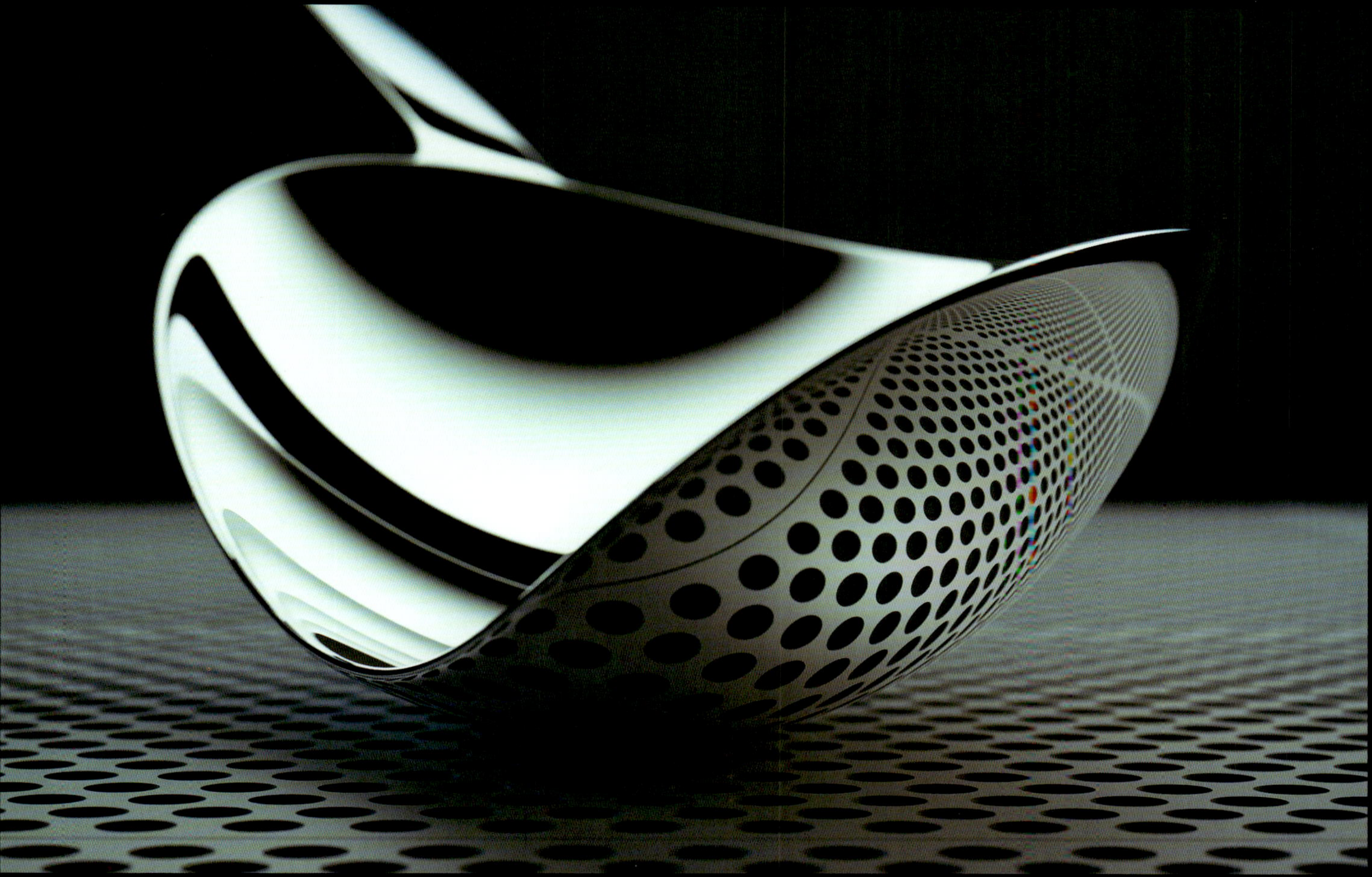

MZ-N910
3ds Max, mental ray, modo, Photoshop
Boyang Zhu, CHINA
[top]

No Spoon
3ds Max
Sergey Aleynikov, n3 design, RUSSIA
[above]

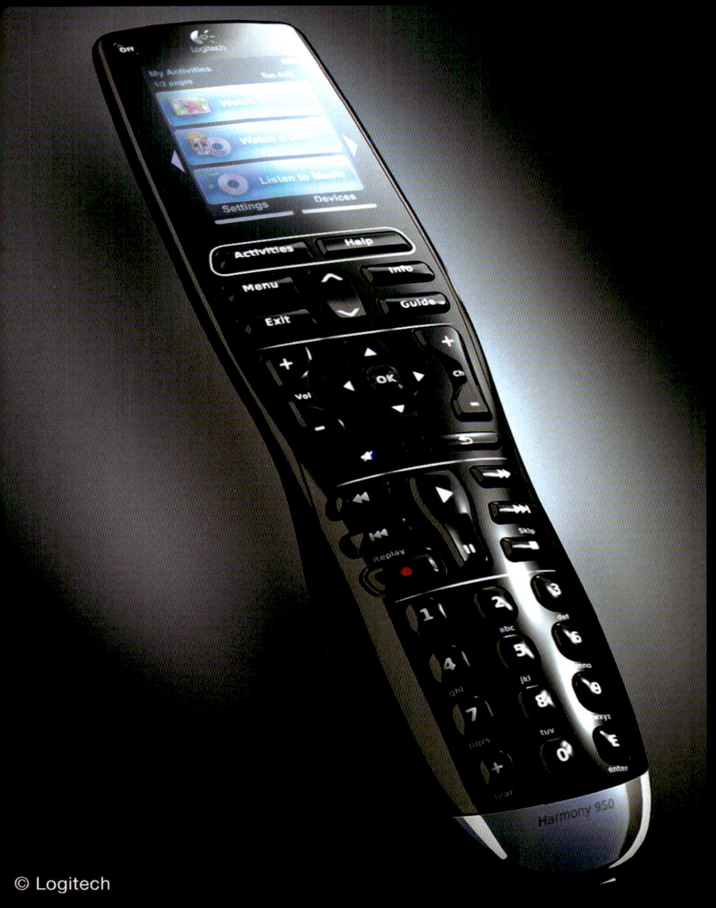

© Logitech

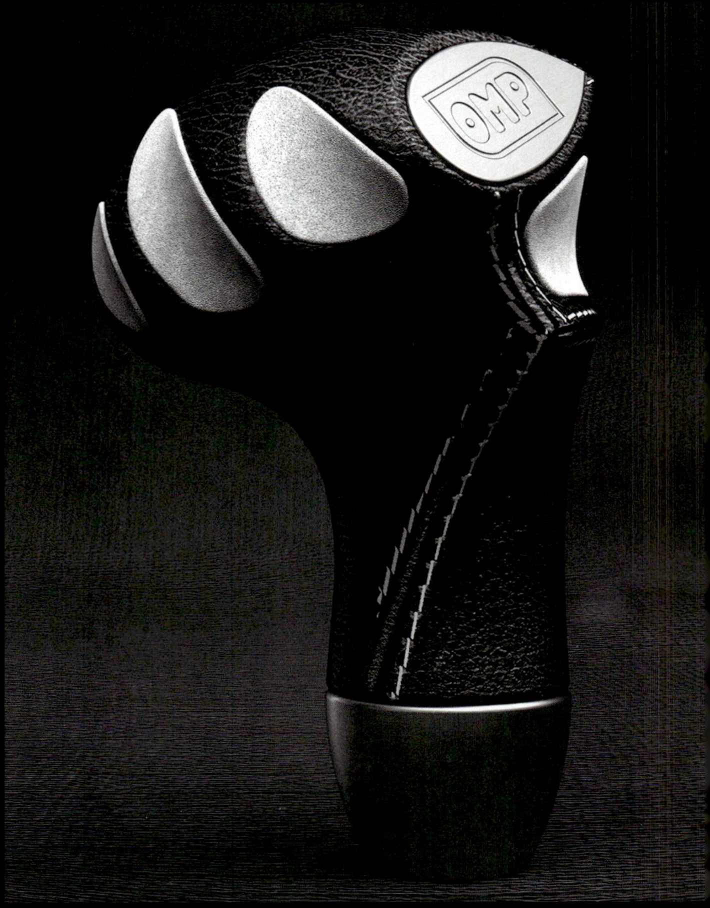

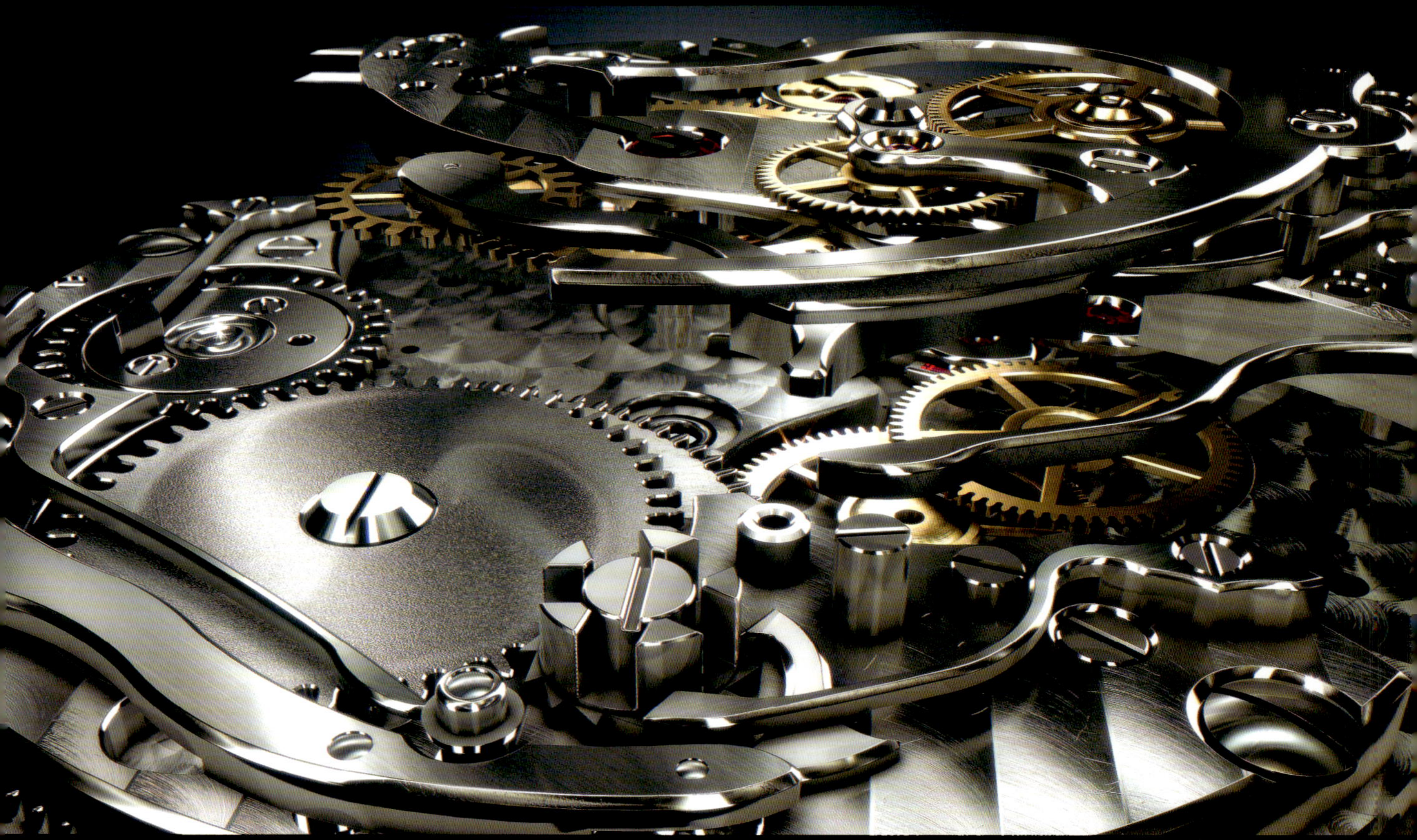

Logitech Harmony One Remote
Maya, Photoshop, Pro/ENGINEER
Client: Logitech
Ian Lennon, Design Partners, IRELAND
[top]

Minerva watch
Maya, Photoshop, Nuke
Client: Mont Blanc
Marco Bauriedel, abc Colorstudio, GERMANY
[above]

Gear Knob
SolidWorks, 3ds Max, mental ray
Giorgio Vecchio, Absolute 2001, ITALY
[top]

Blancpain Wrist Watch
3ds Max, Photoshop
Abdul Majid Movania, PAKISTAN
[right]

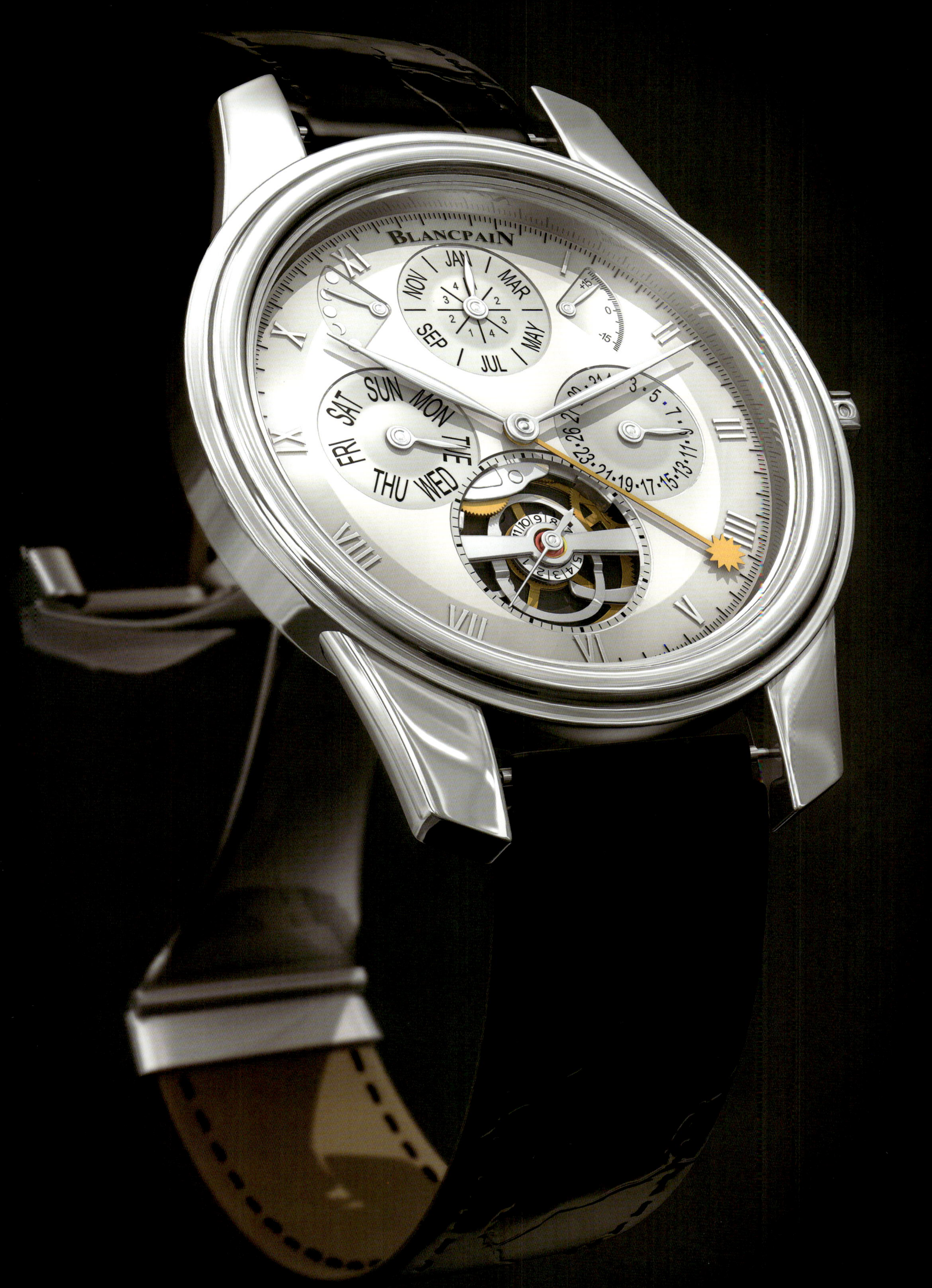
BLANCPAIN
JAN
MAR
MAY
JUL
SEP
NOV
SUN
MON
TUE
WED
THU
FRI
SAT
+15
0
-15

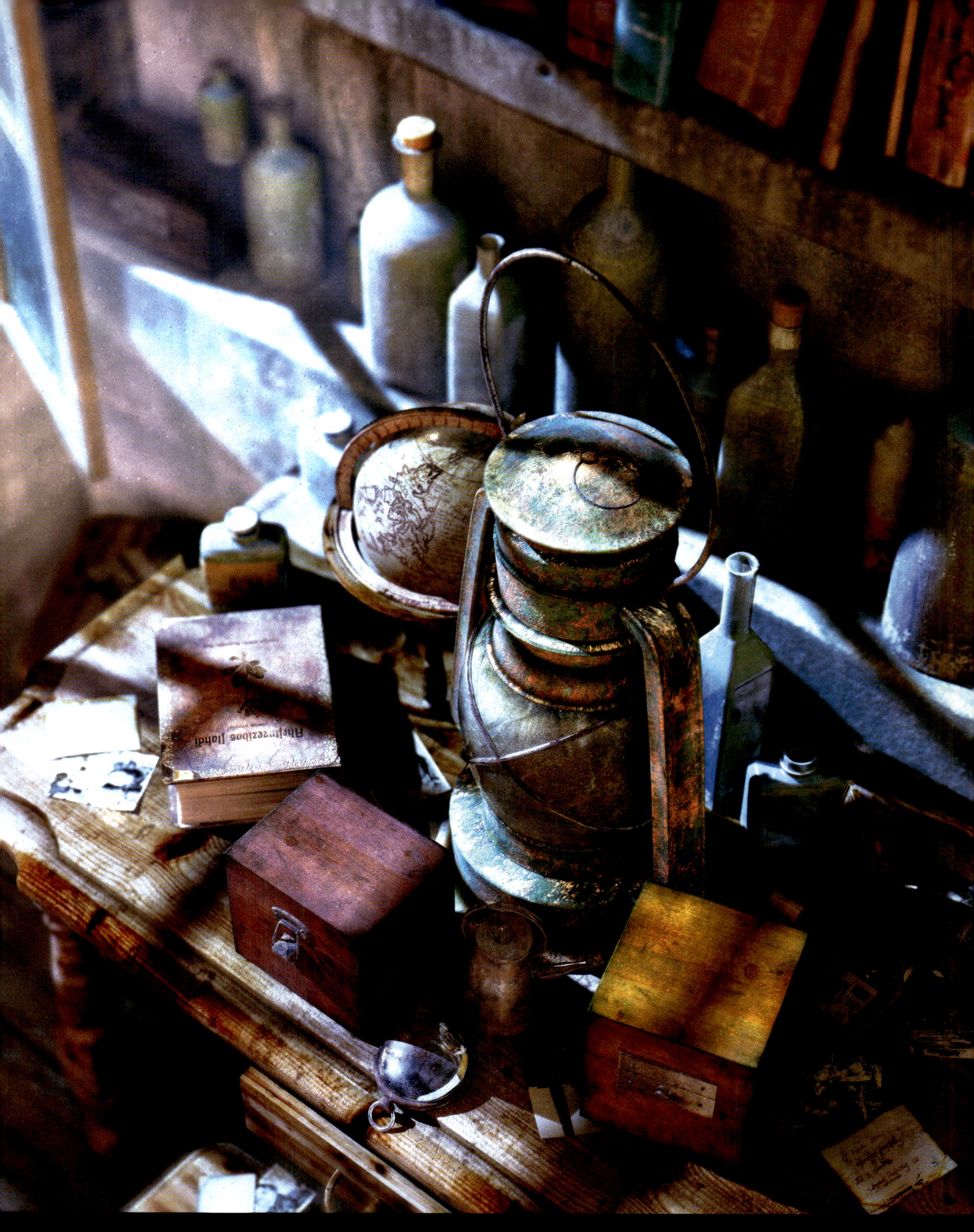

Master

Still Life

Long wait
3ds Max
Aiqiang Hao, CHINA

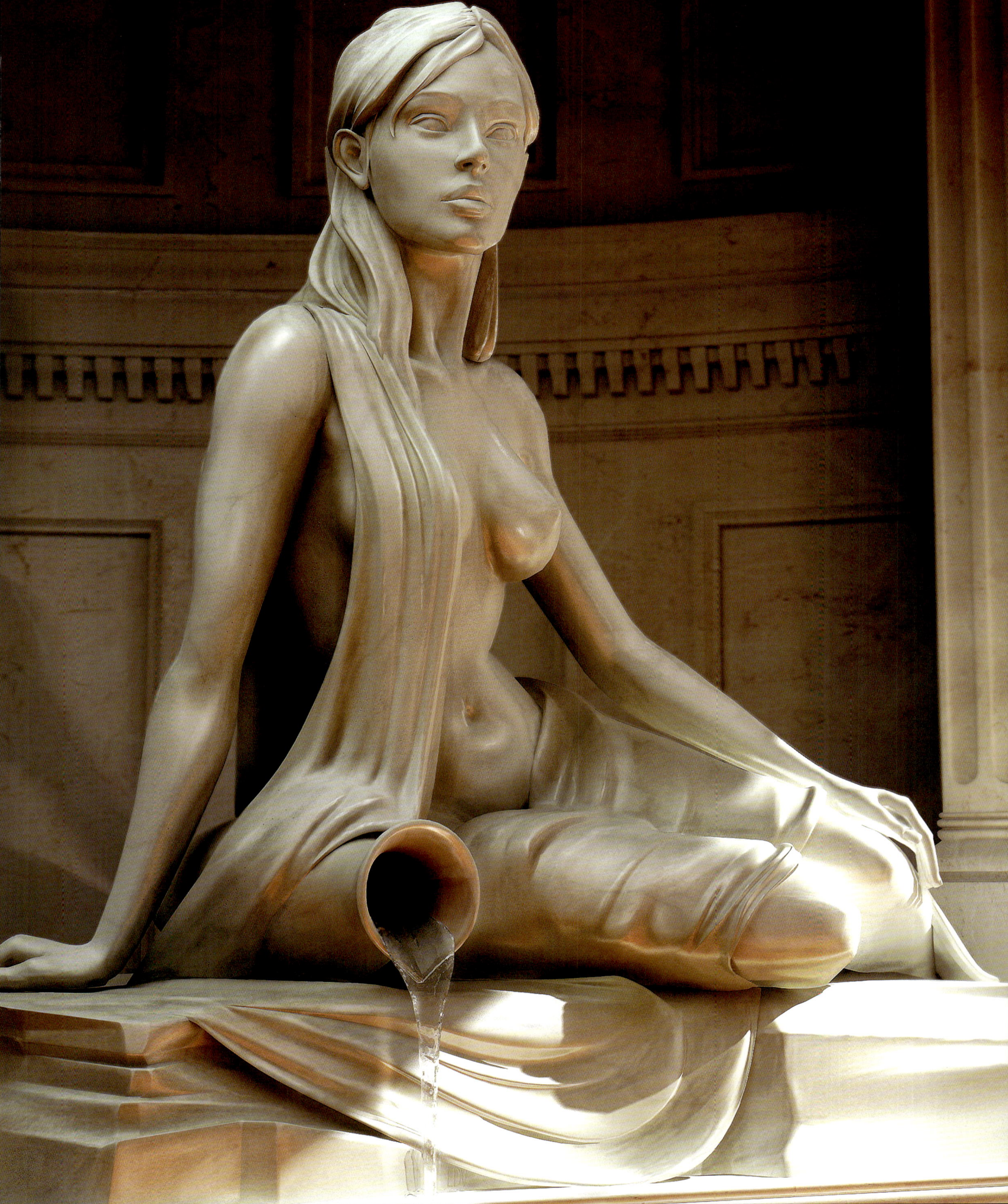

Statue
3ds Max, V-Ray, Photoshop
Dmitriy Egorov, KAZAKHSTAN

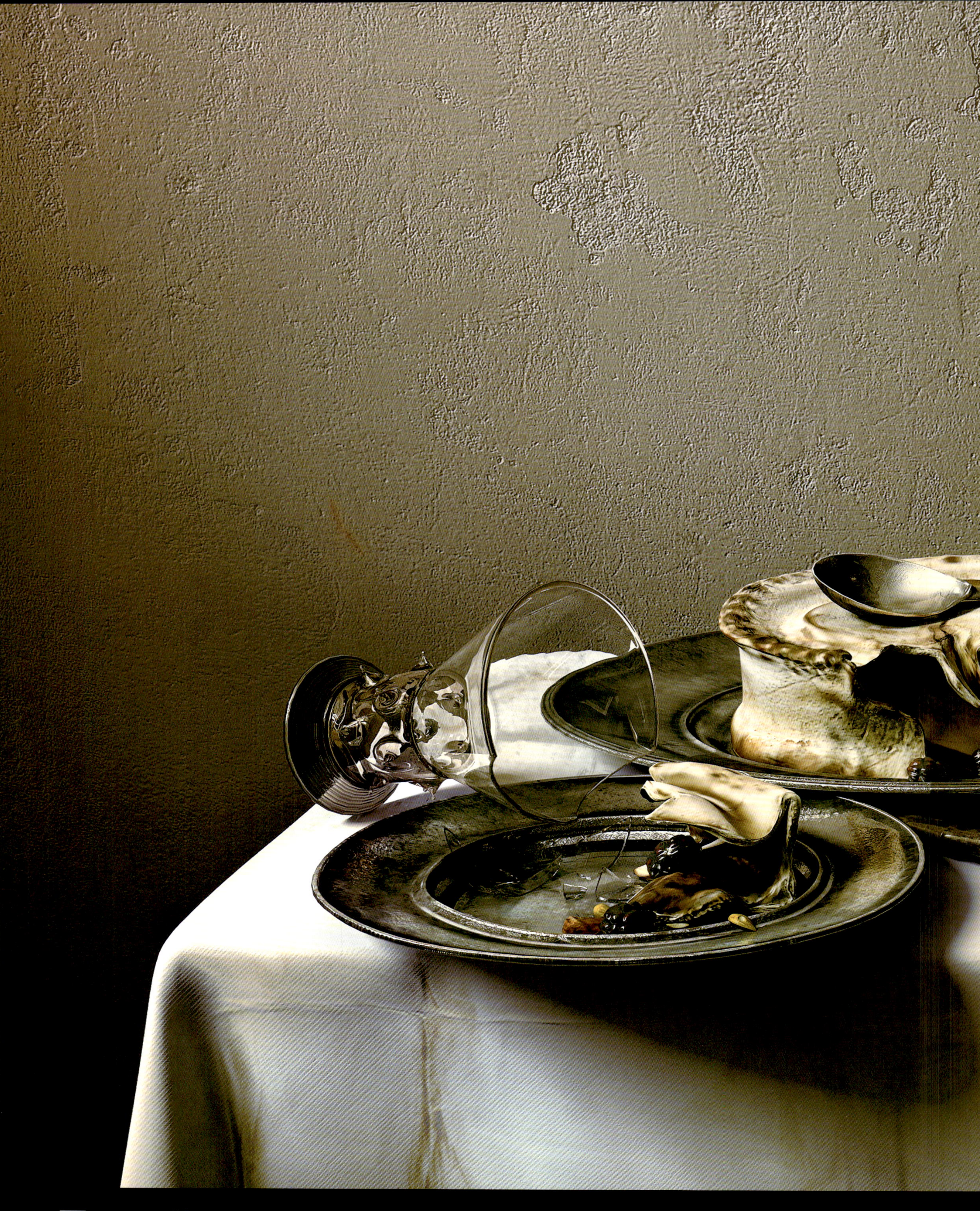

Excellence

Still Life

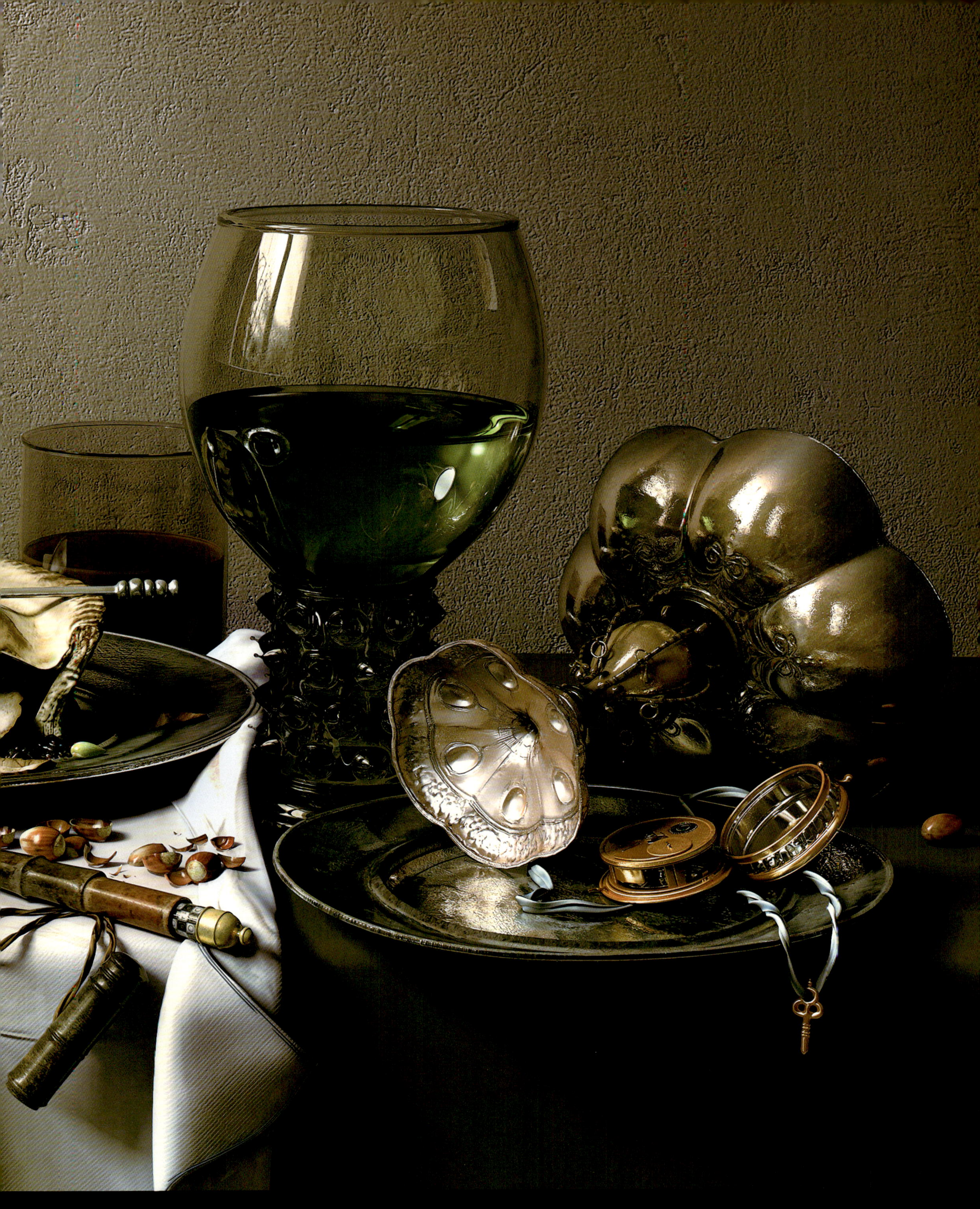

Stilleben
3ds Max, Photoshop
Aiqiang Hao, CHINA

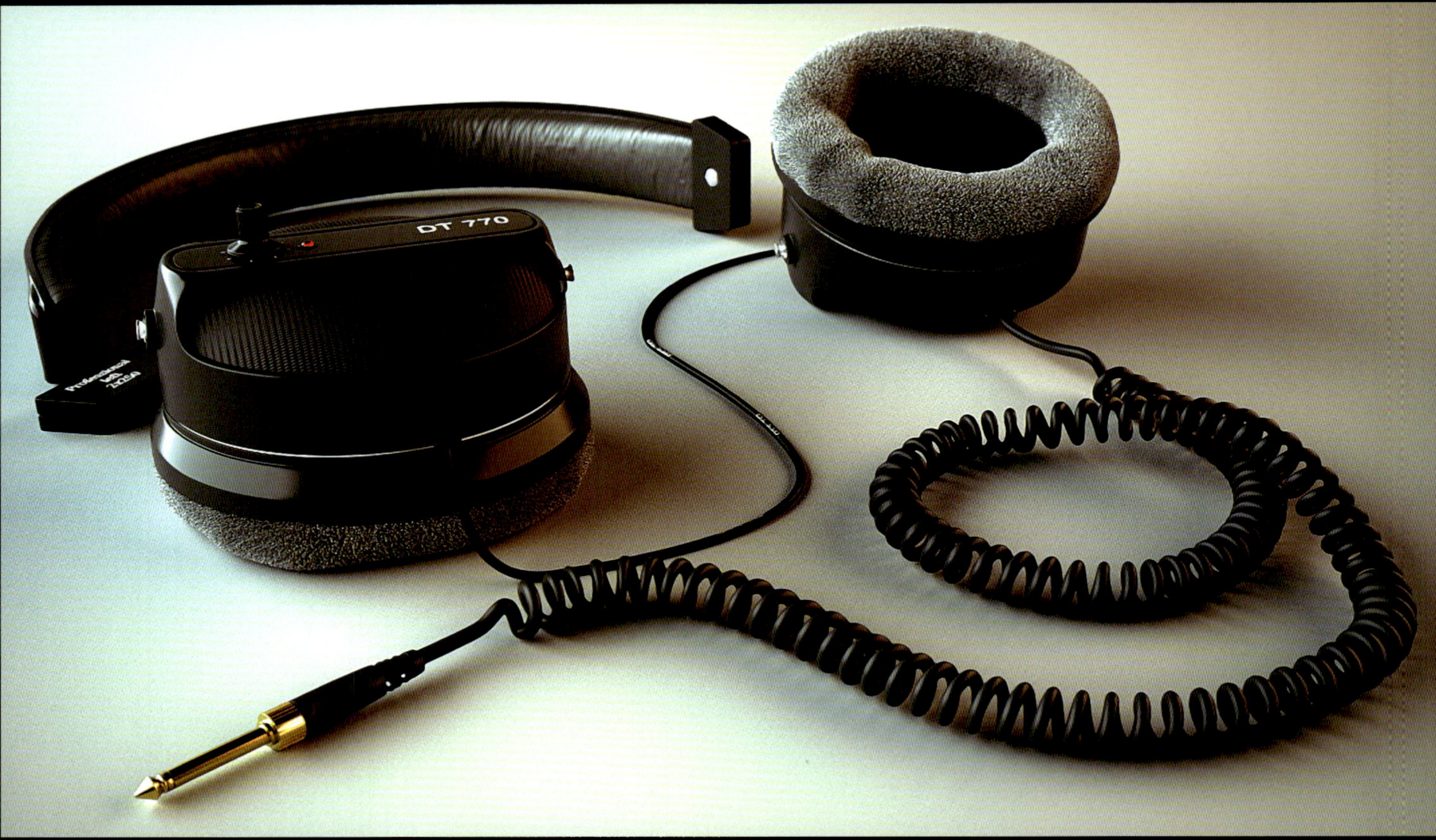

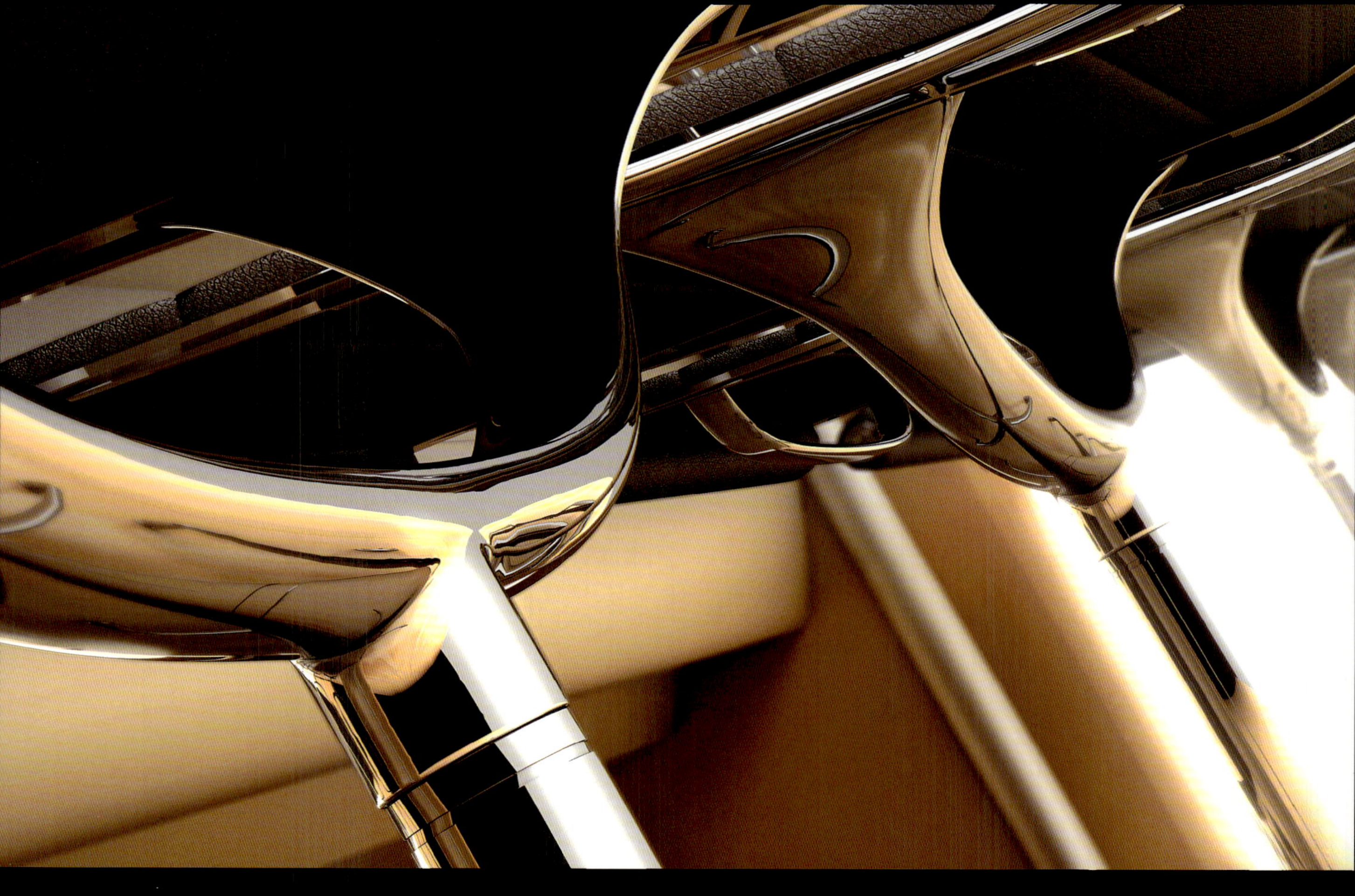

Ear-phone
3ds Max, V-Ray
Jonas Balzer, GERMANY
[top]

Bottoms Up
3ds Max, Photoshop
Spine3D, USA
[above]

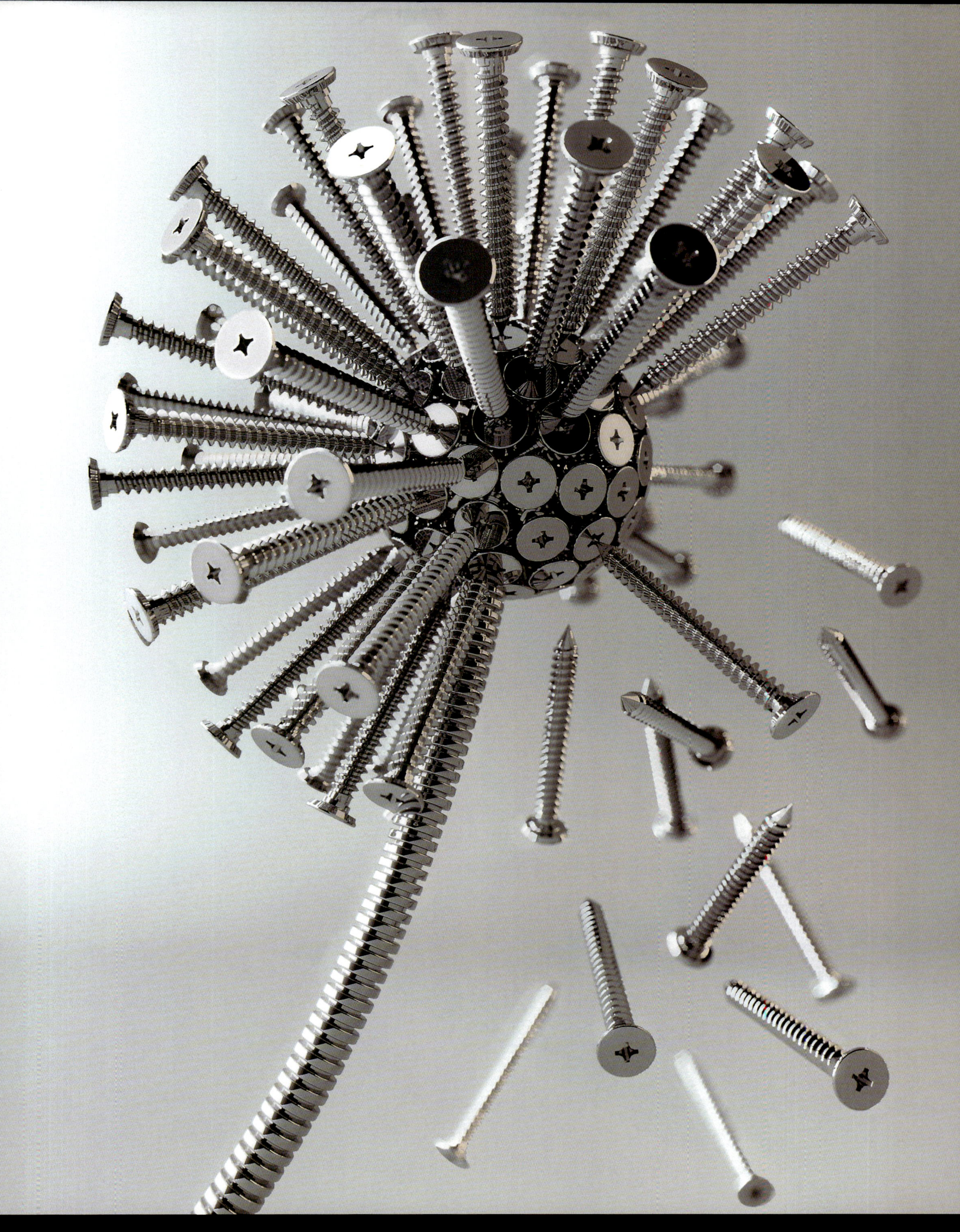

Dandelion of Screws
3ds Max mental ray, Photoshop
Andre Kutscherauer, GERMANY

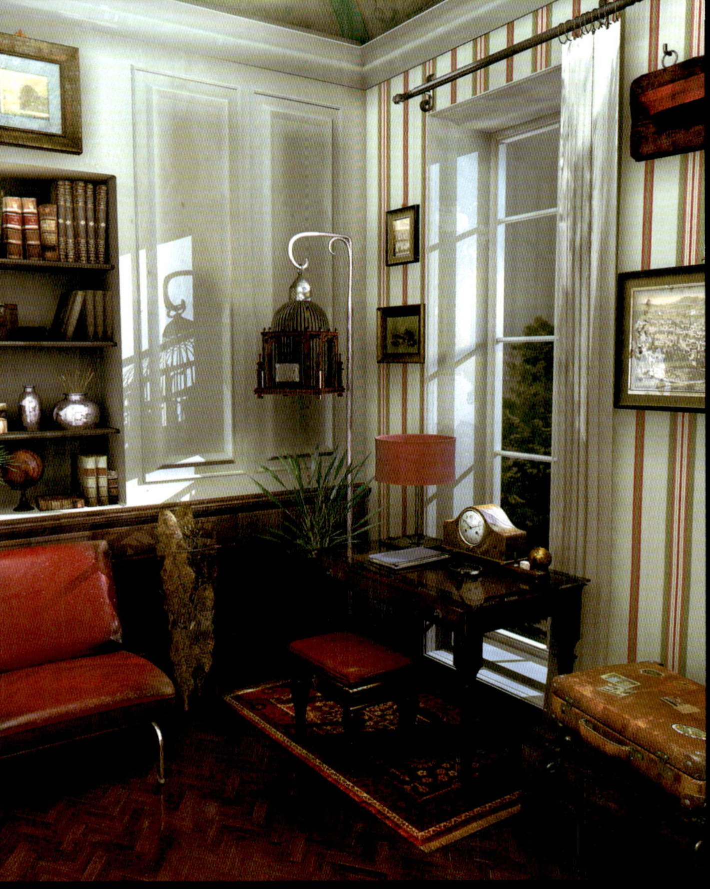

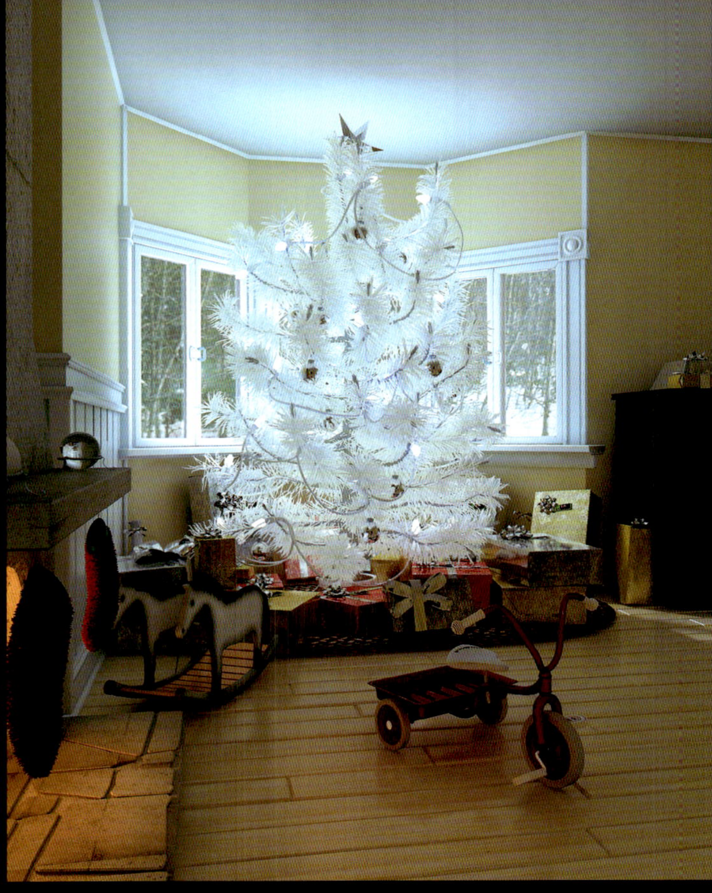

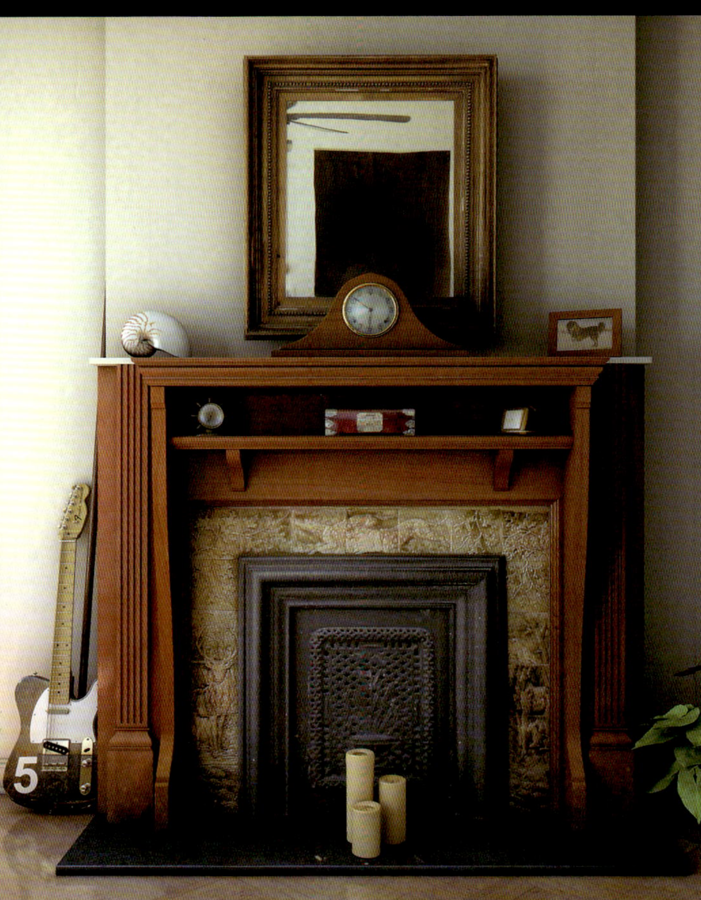

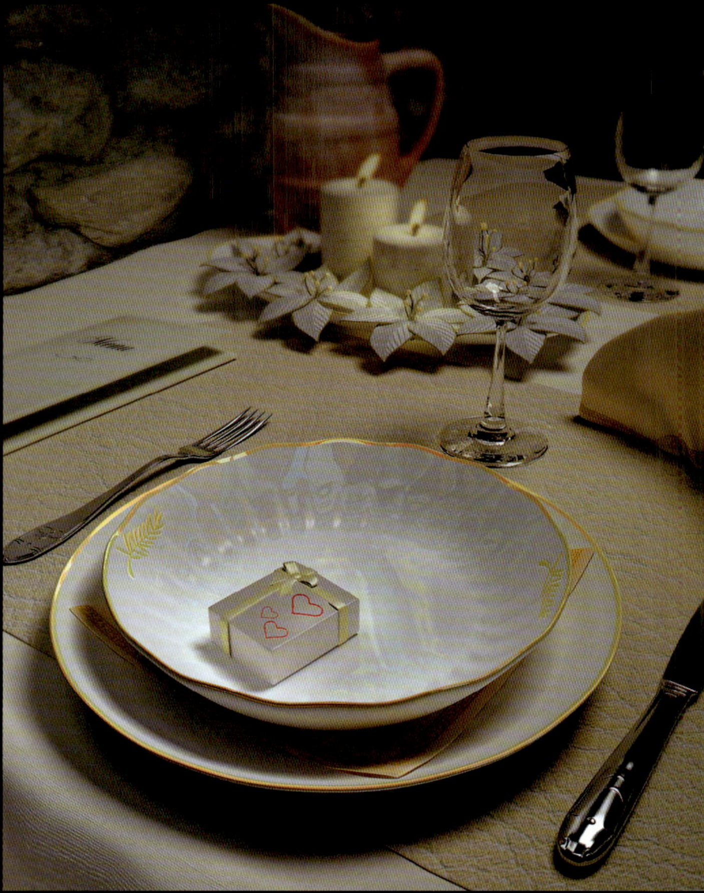

Love for details
3ds Max
Fabio Oscar Corica,
ITALY
[top]

Brooklyn Fireplace
3ds Max, mental ray, Photoshop
Robert Stava, Arup,
USA
[above]

White Christmas
3ds Max, finalRender, Photoshop
Modeling: Jeremy Birn
Vincent Jaramillo, Smithgroup, USA
[top]

For life
3ds Max, Photoshop, V-Ray
Aurelien Chapot,
FRANCE
[above]

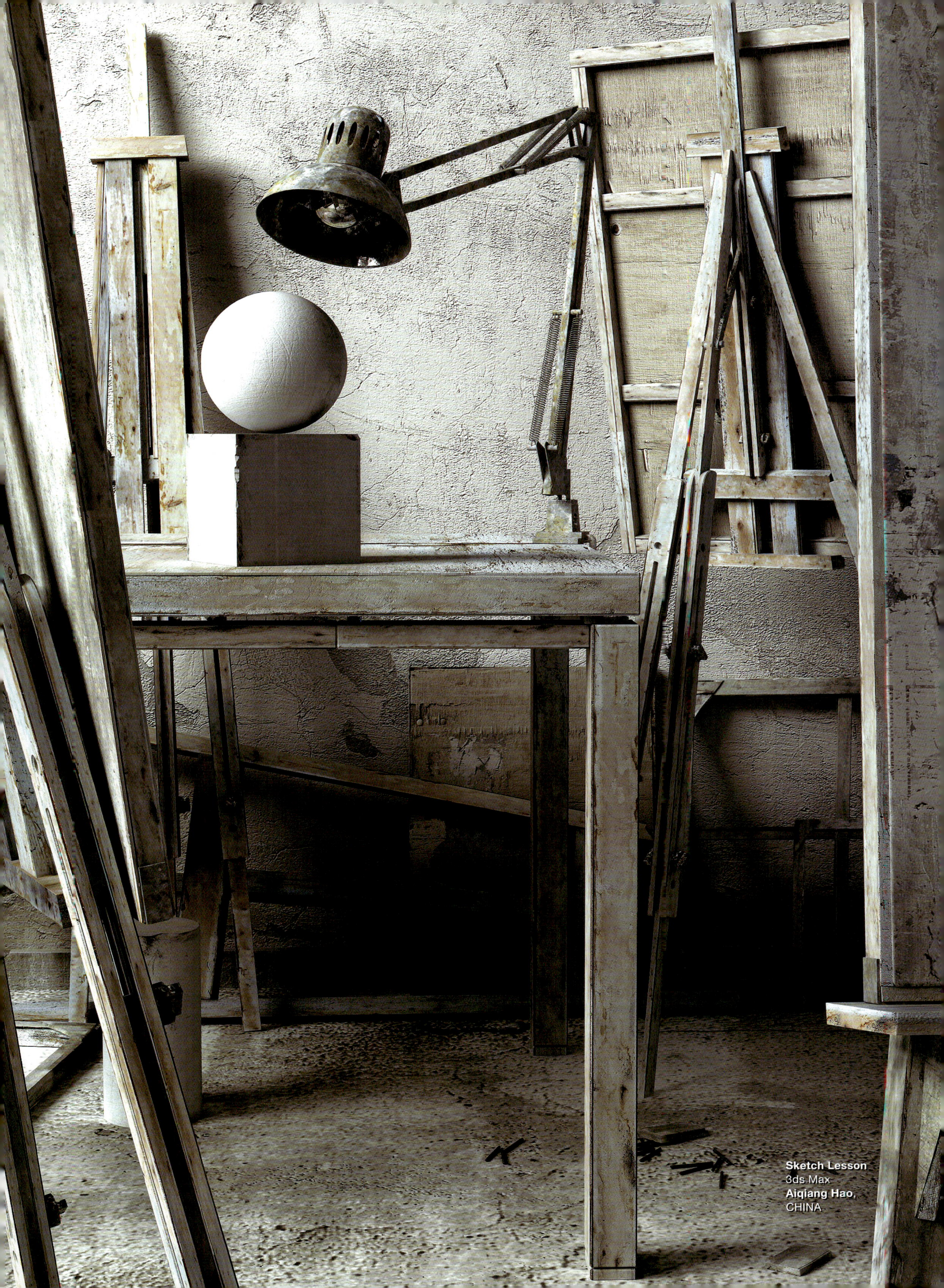

Sketch Lesson
3ds Max
Aiqiang Hao, CHINA

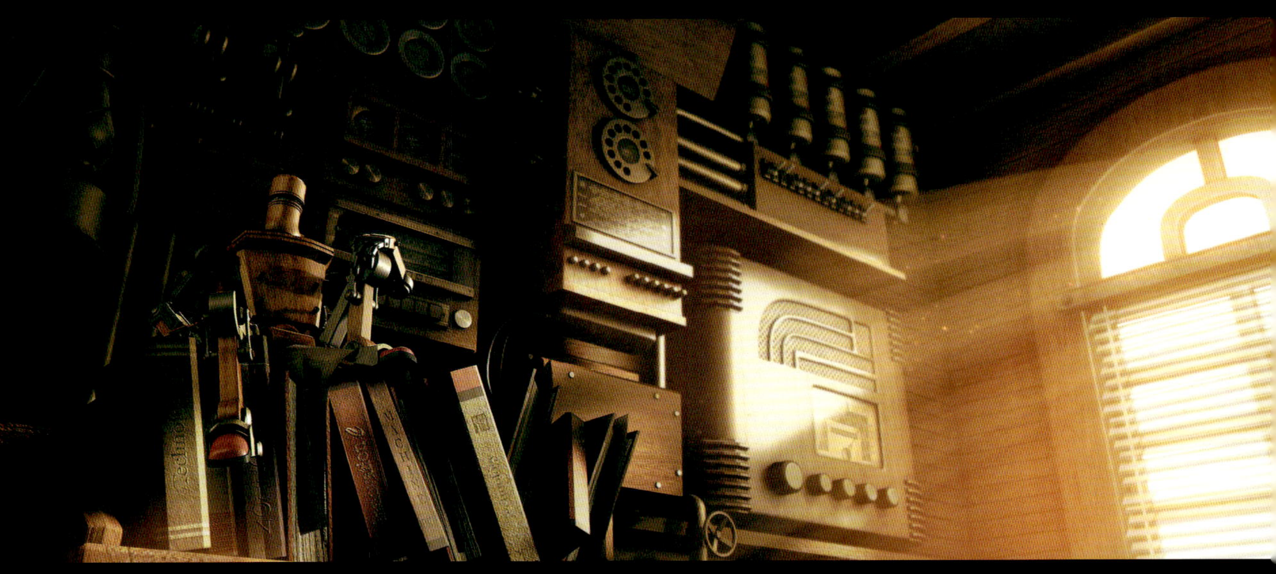

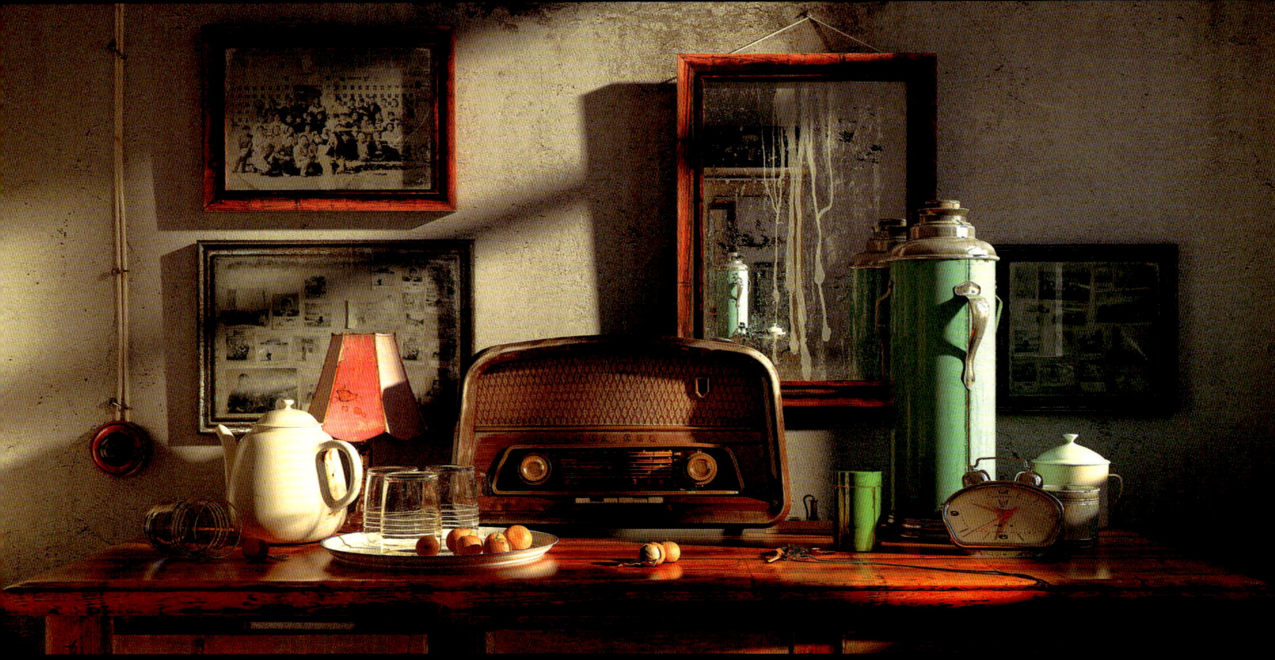

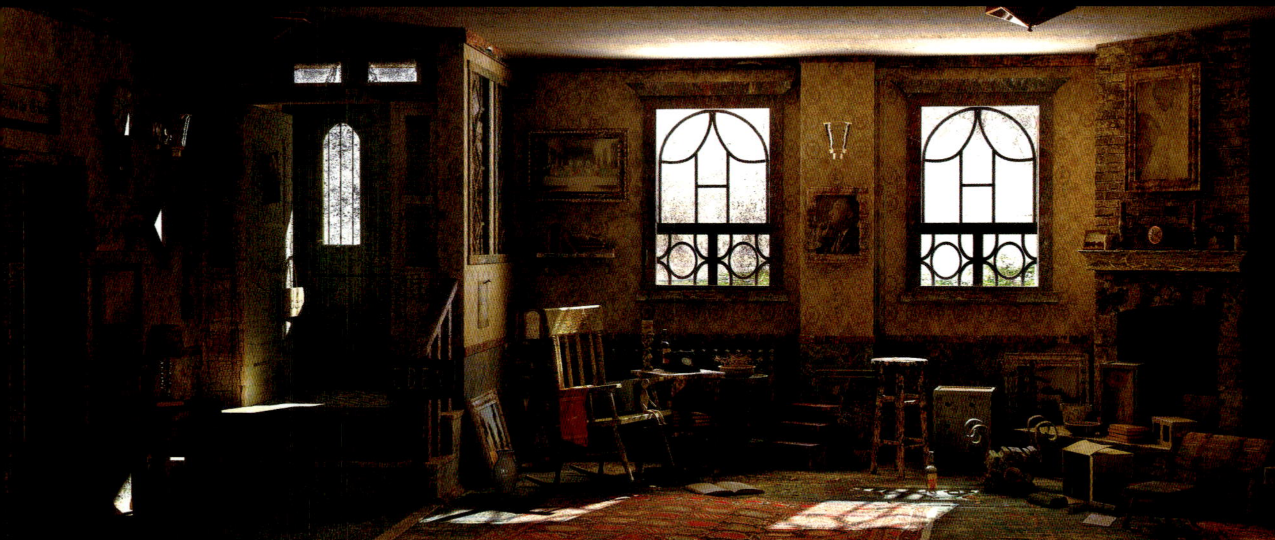

Philosopher
Maya, Shake, Photoshop
Tey ChengChan,
SINGAPORE
[top]

Story of time
3ds Max
Aiqiang Hao,
CHINA
[center]

Static
3ds Max, V-Ray, Photoshop
Jason Godbey,
Bottlerocket Entertainment, USA
[above]

DragONtFLY
3ds Max, V-Ray, Photoshop
Denis Tolkishevsky,
RUSSIA
[right]

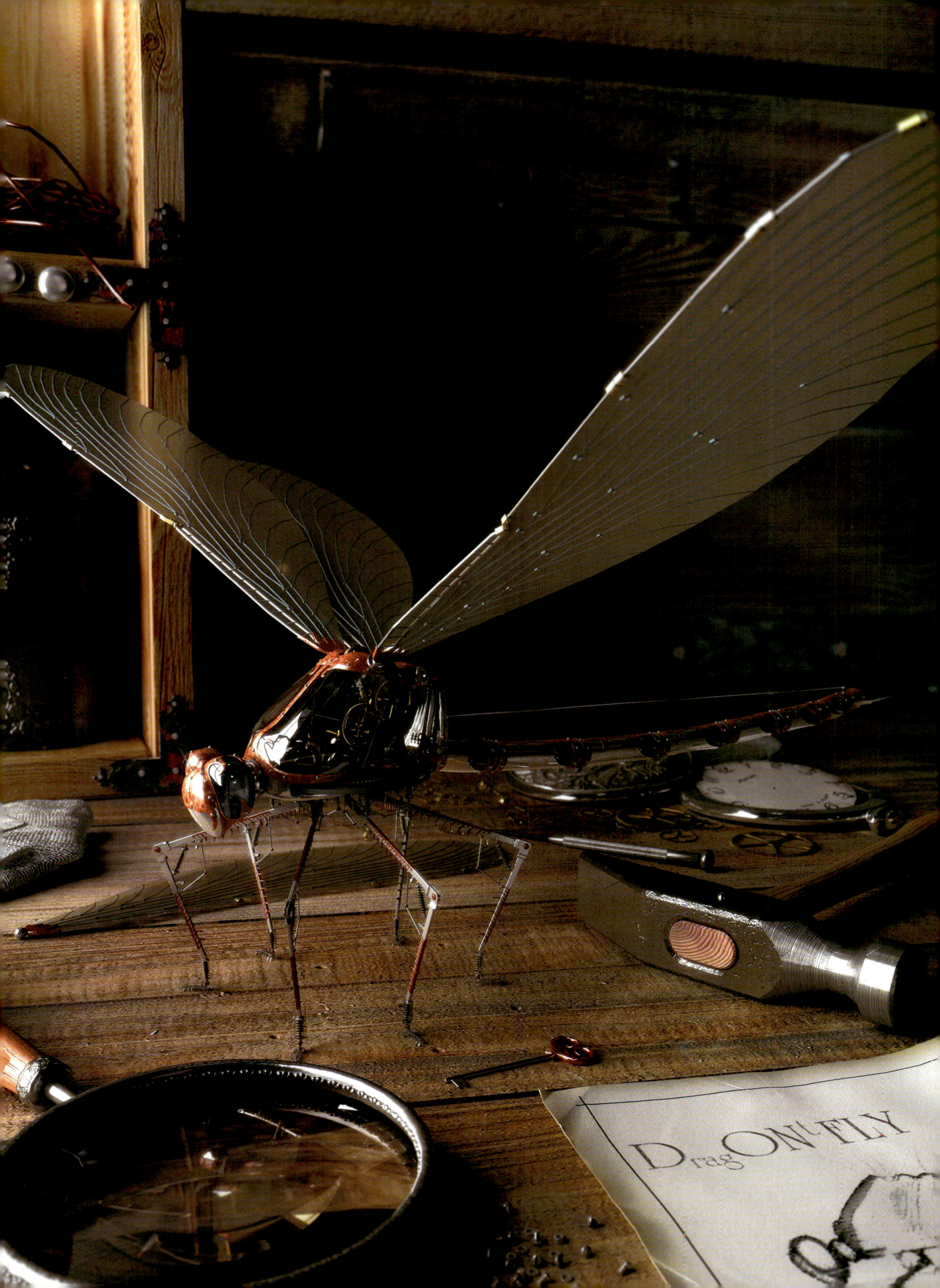
DragONtFLY

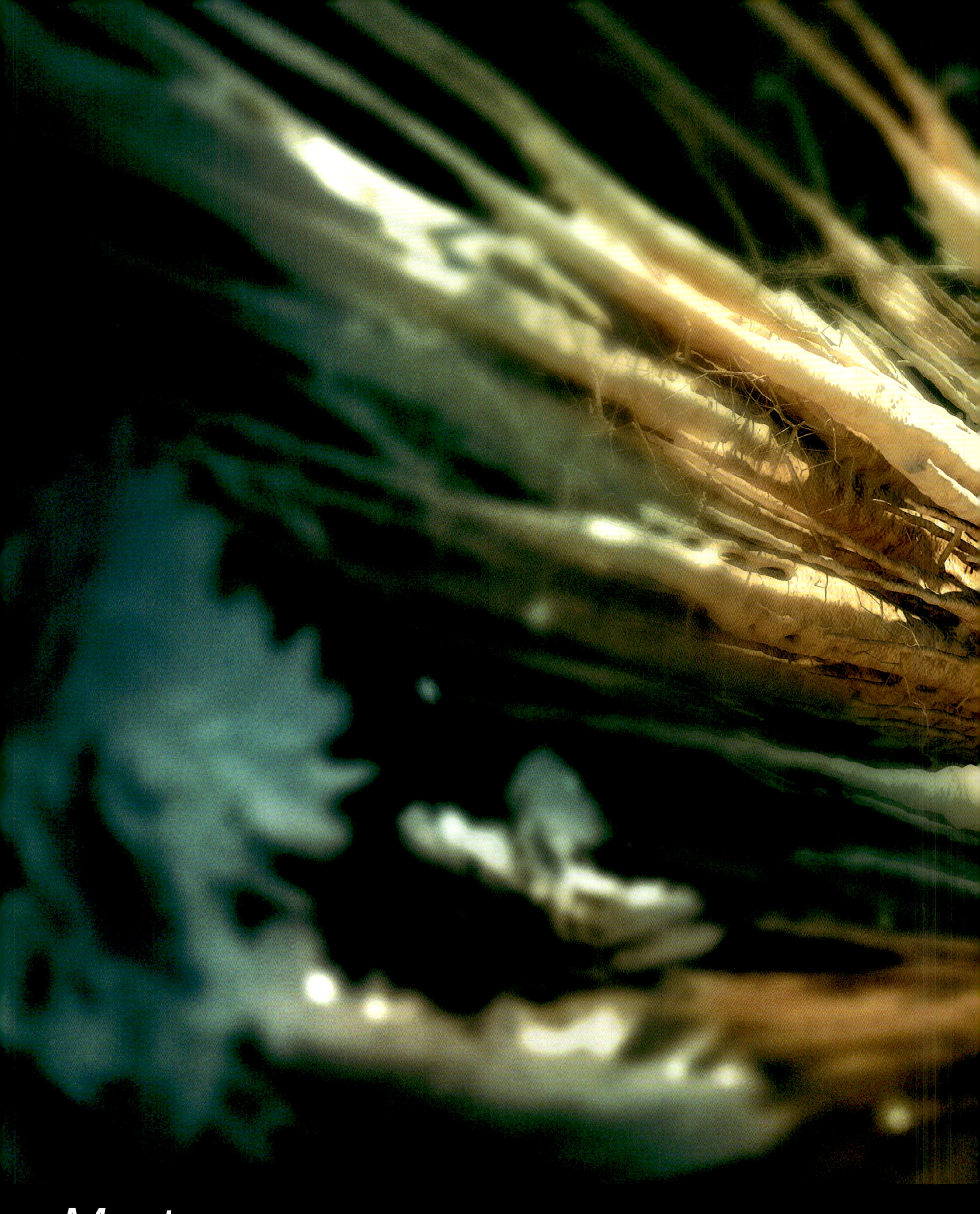

Master

Abstract

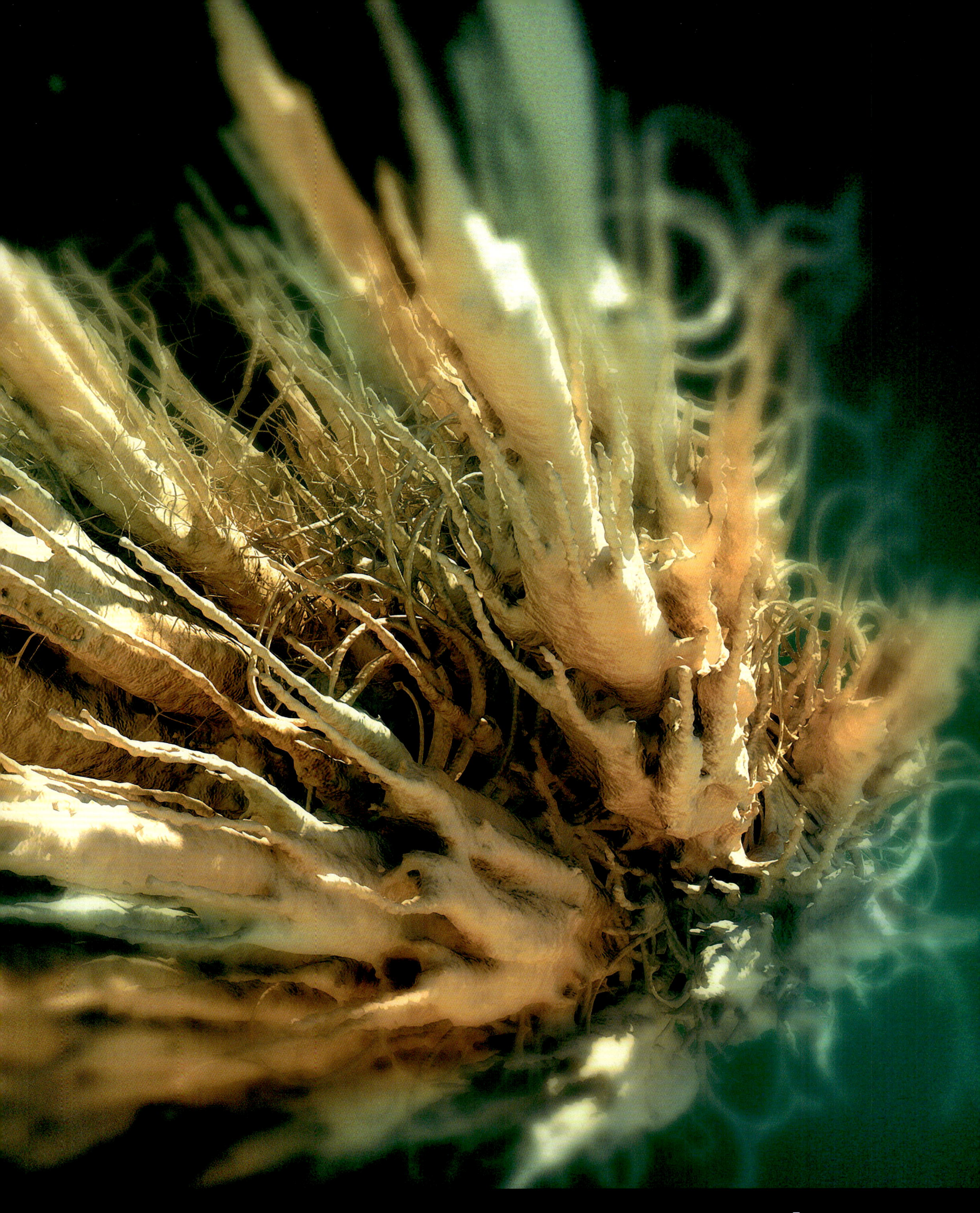

Torn
Maya, Photoshop
Monsit Jangariyawong, THAILAND

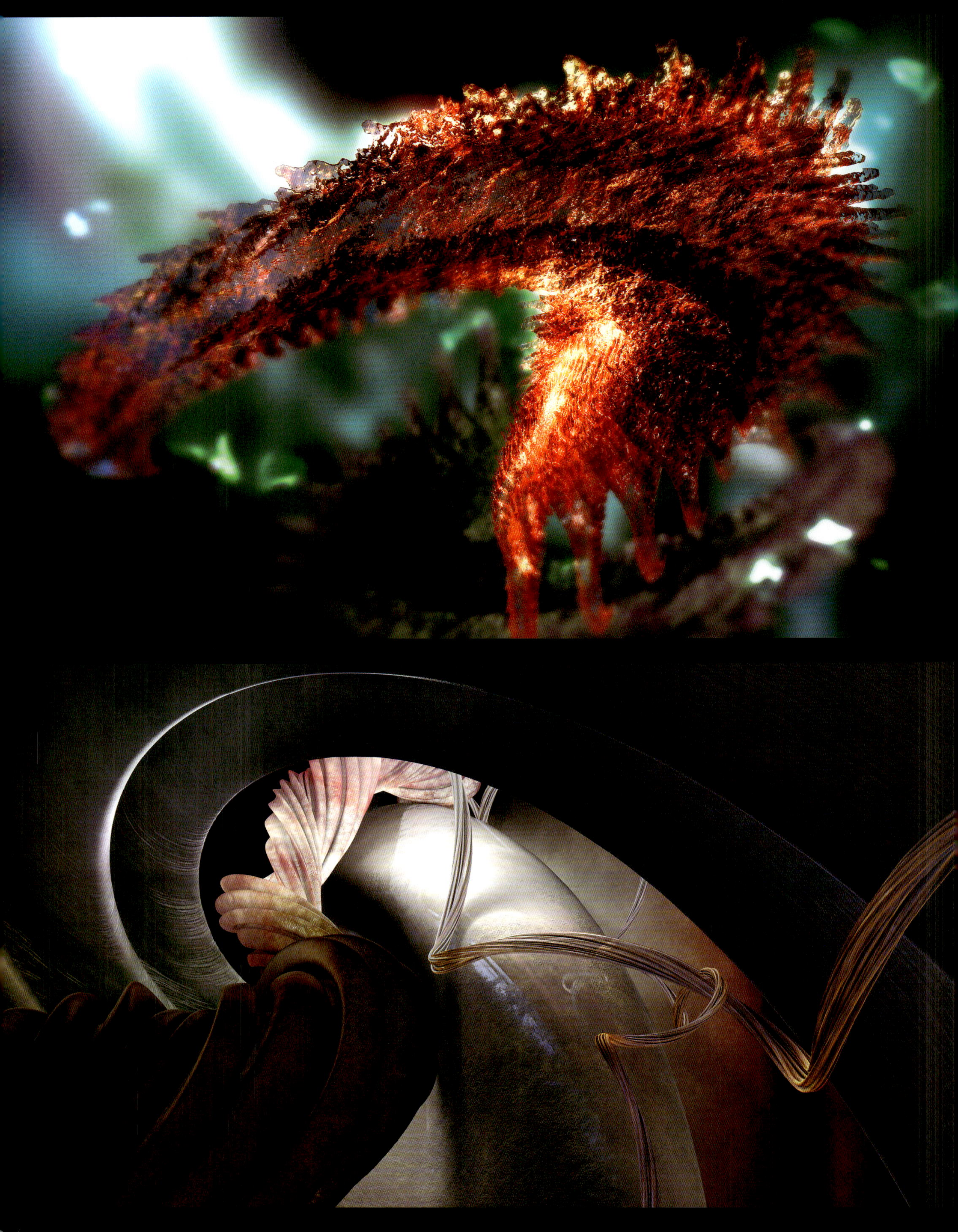

Tail
Maya, Photoshop
Monsit Jangariyawong,
THAILAND
[top]

Movement
Maya, mental ray, Photoshop
Jordan Rempel,
USA
[above]

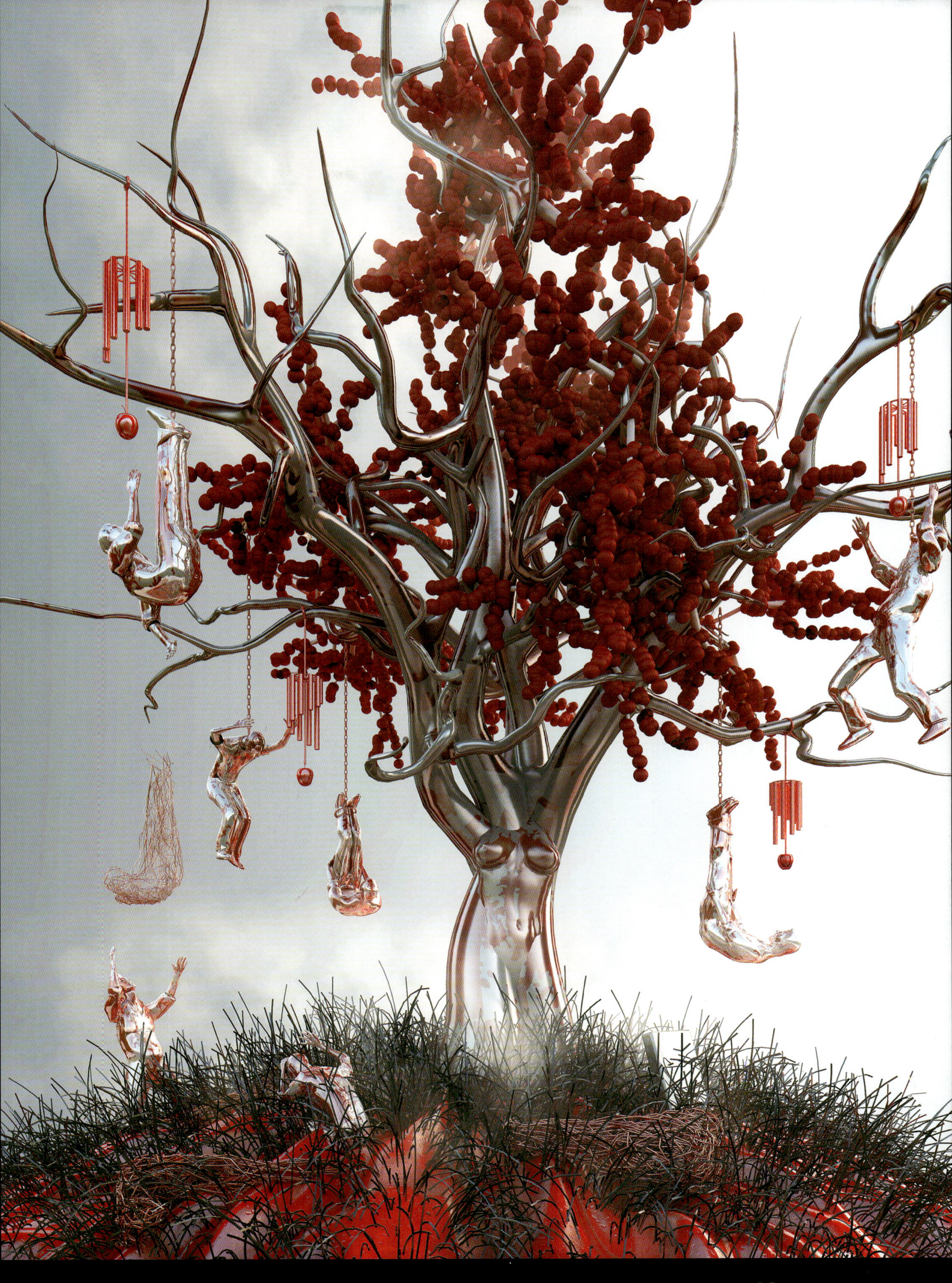

Wind Chime
3ds Max, Photoshop
Sam A. Nassar, SYRIA

Excellence
Abstract

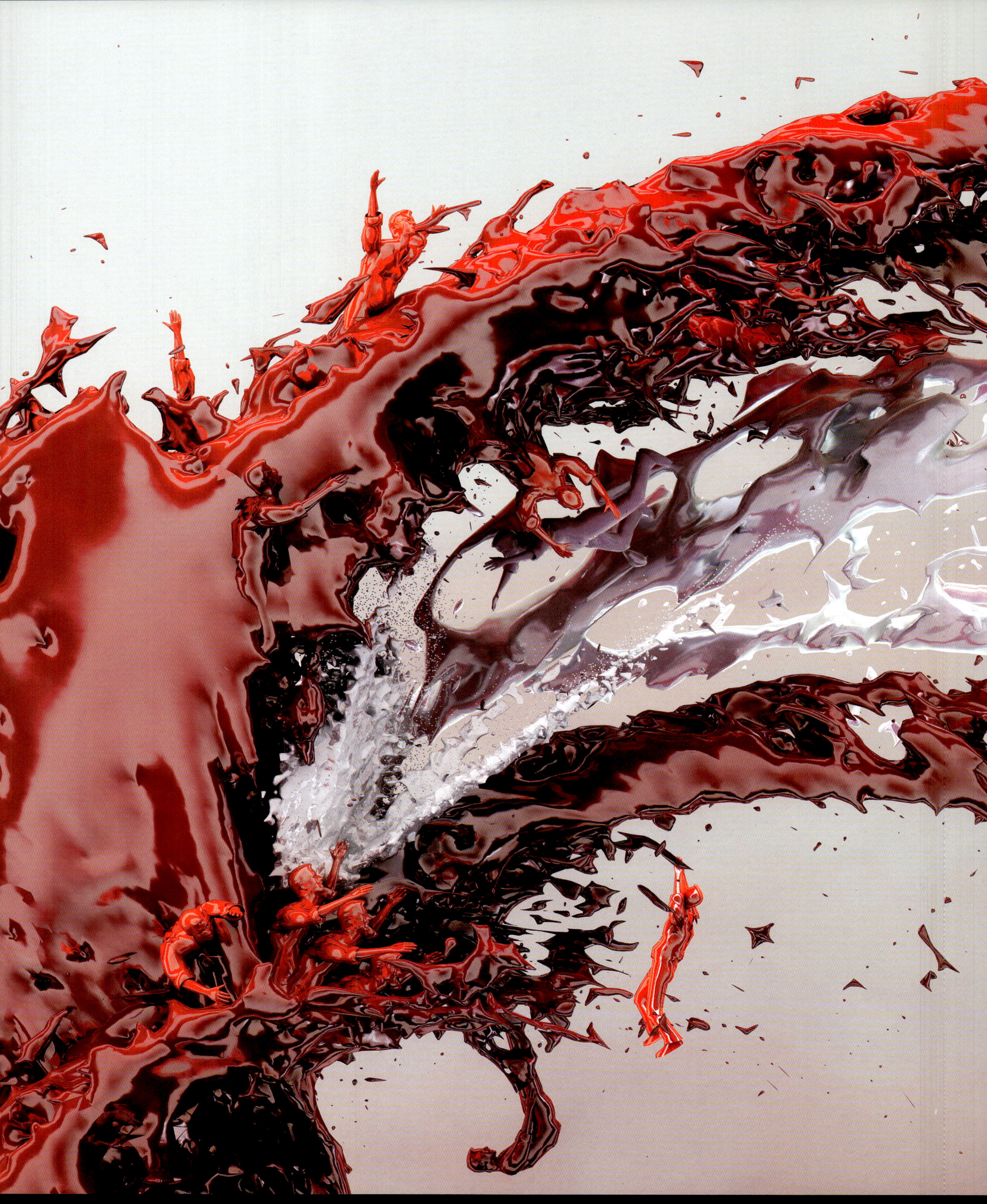

Excellence

Abstract

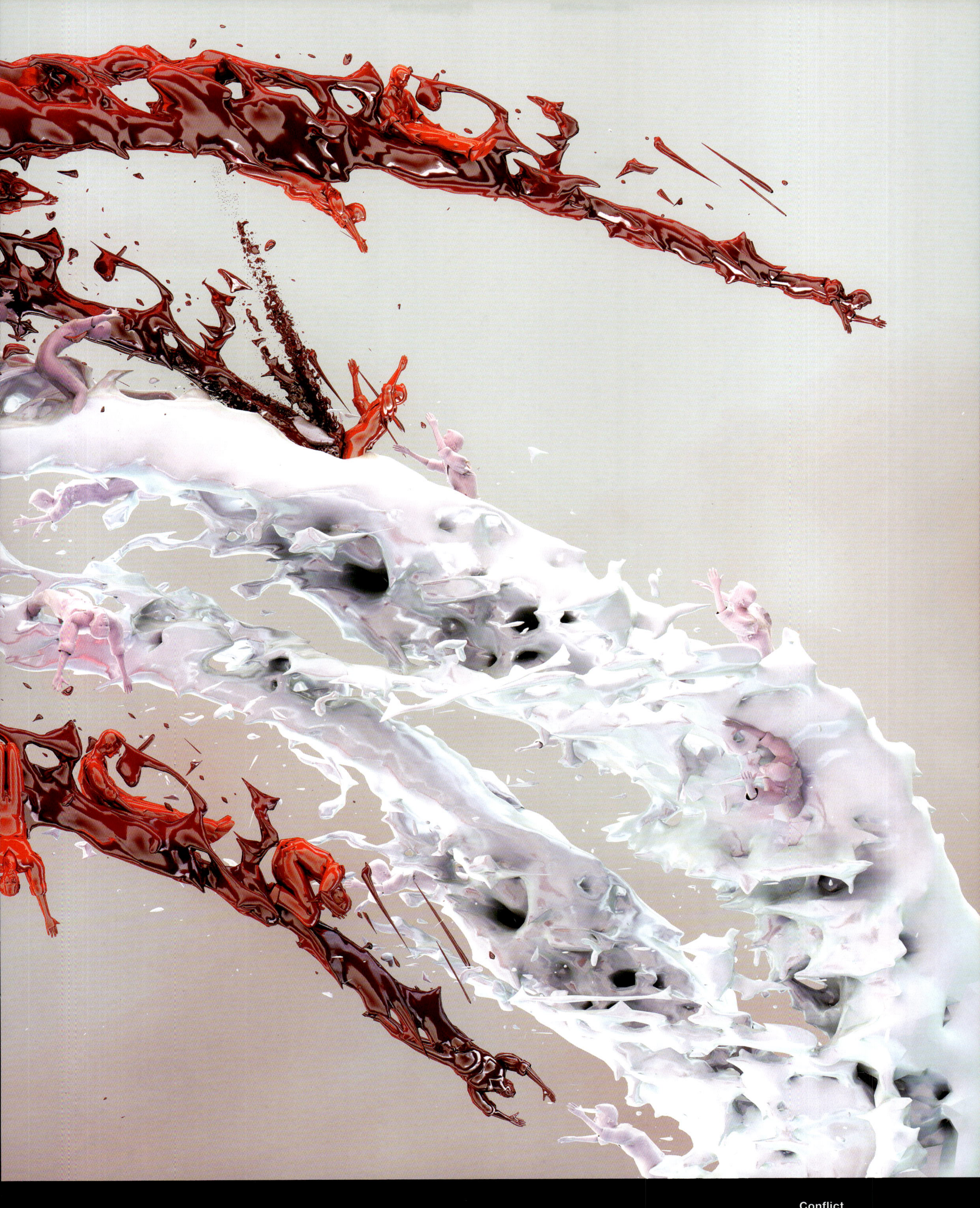

Conflict
3ds Max, Photoshop
Sam A. Nassar, SYRIA

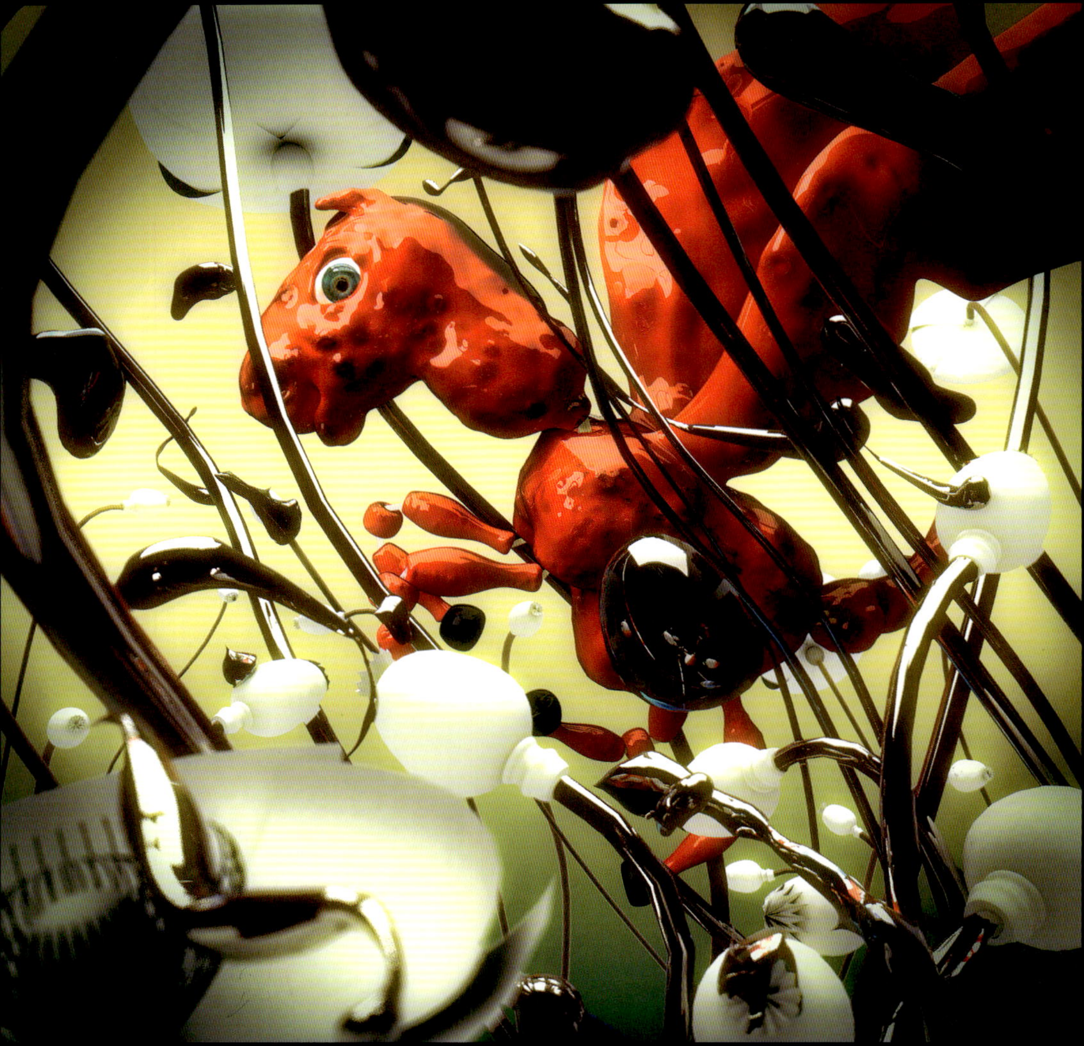

Toy horse
Maya, 3ds Max, Photoshop
Hou Jian, CHINA
[left]

Moment of panic
3ds Max, V-Ray, Photoshop
Lionel Verlinden, BELGIUM
[right]

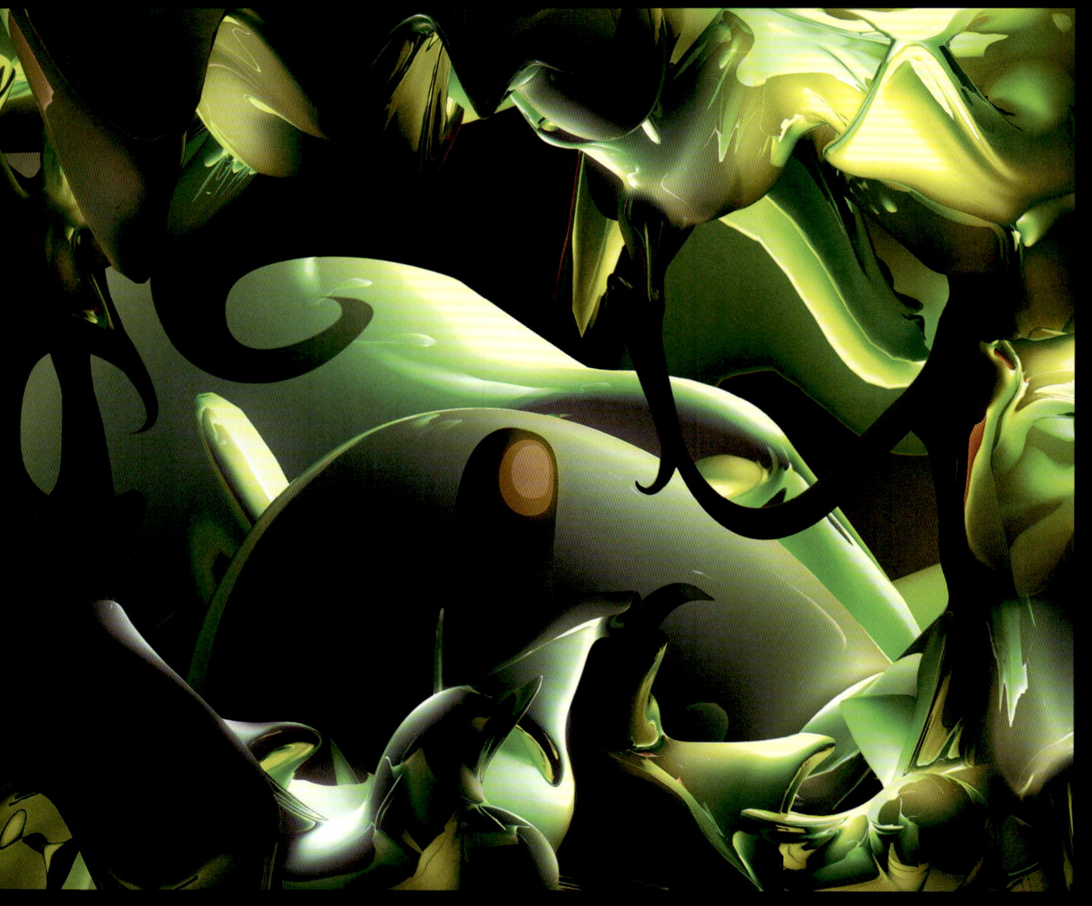

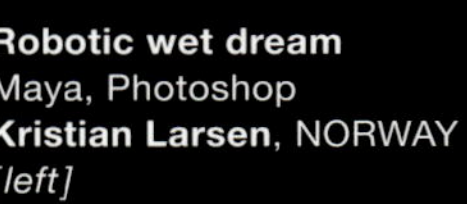

Robotic wet dream
Maya, Photoshop
Kristian Larsen, NORWAY
[left]

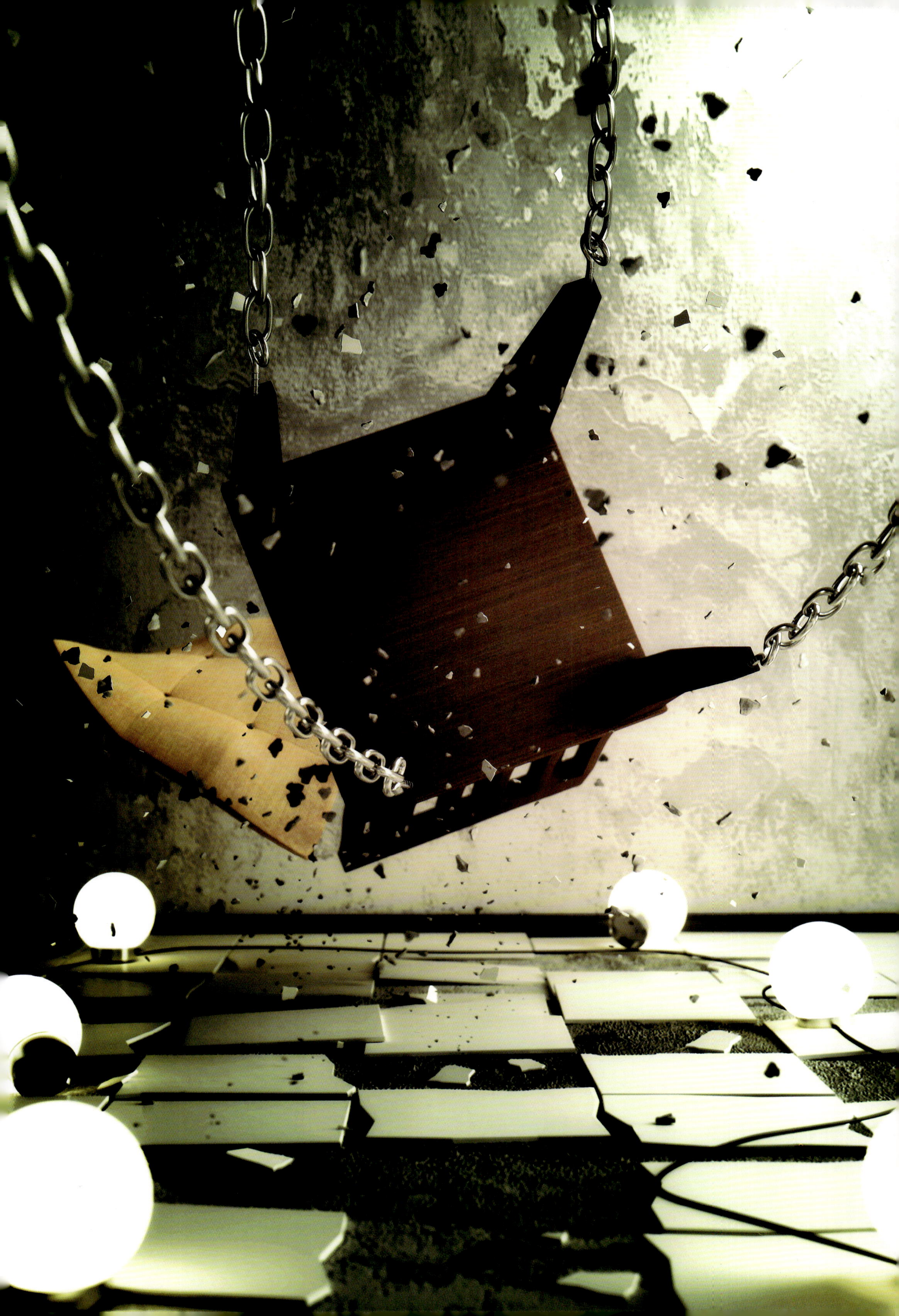

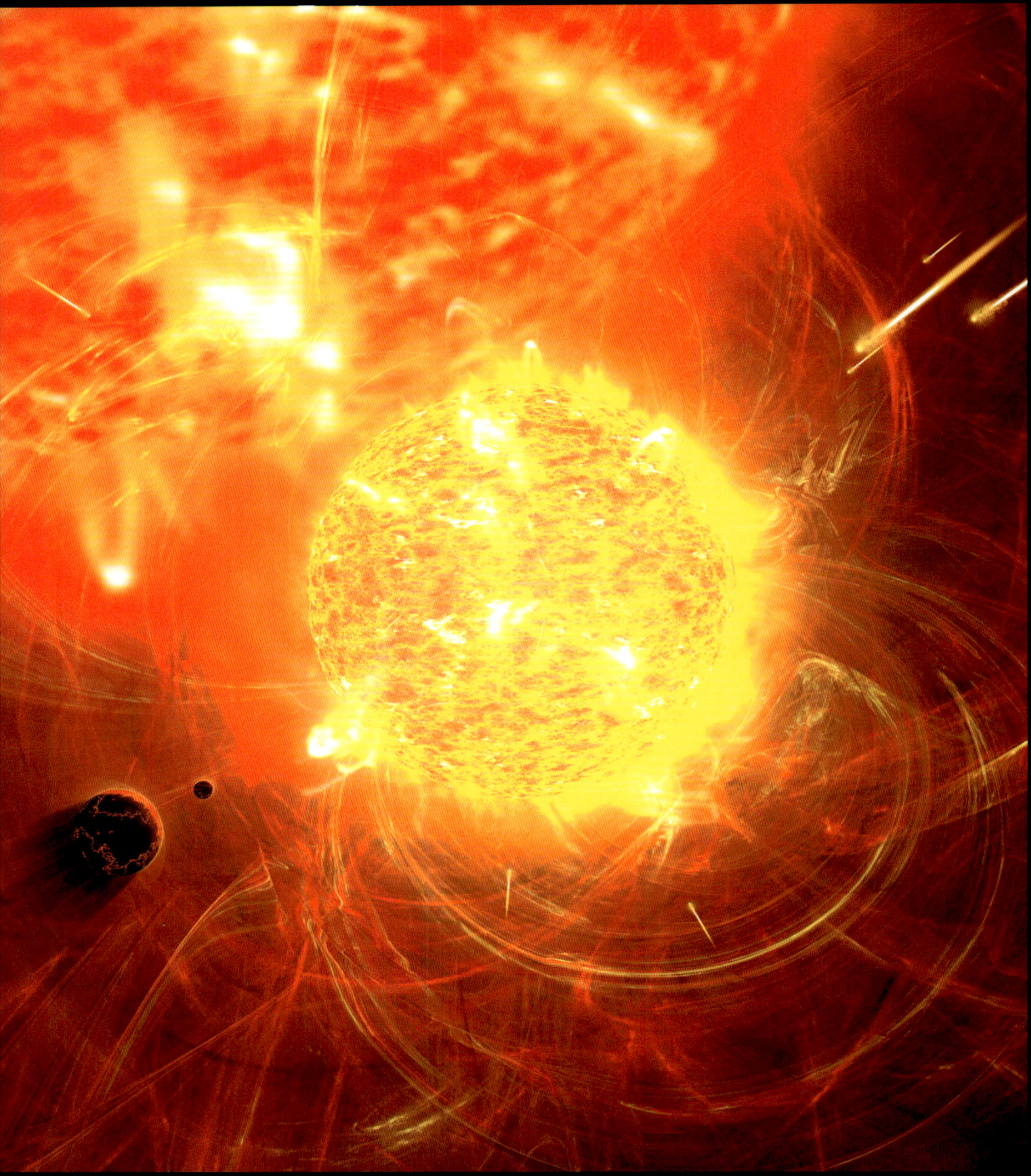

Dwarf star
Maya, Apophysis, Photoshop
Adrian Smith, GREAT BRITAIN
[left]

Nuclear Fission
3ds Max, V-Ray, Photoshop
Karuna Karan, Khan Global, INDIA
[right]

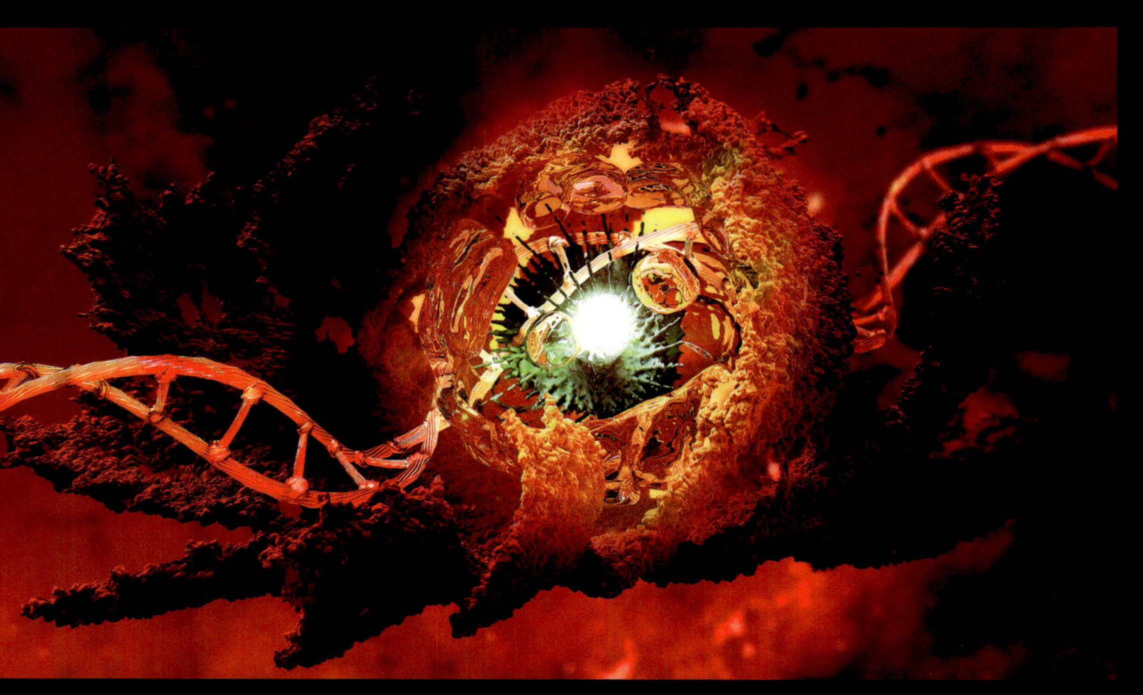

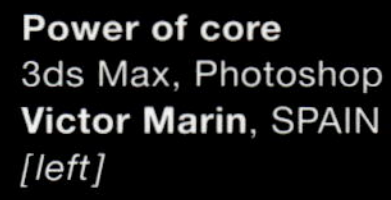

Power of core
3ds Max, Photoshop
Victor Marin, SPAIN
[left]

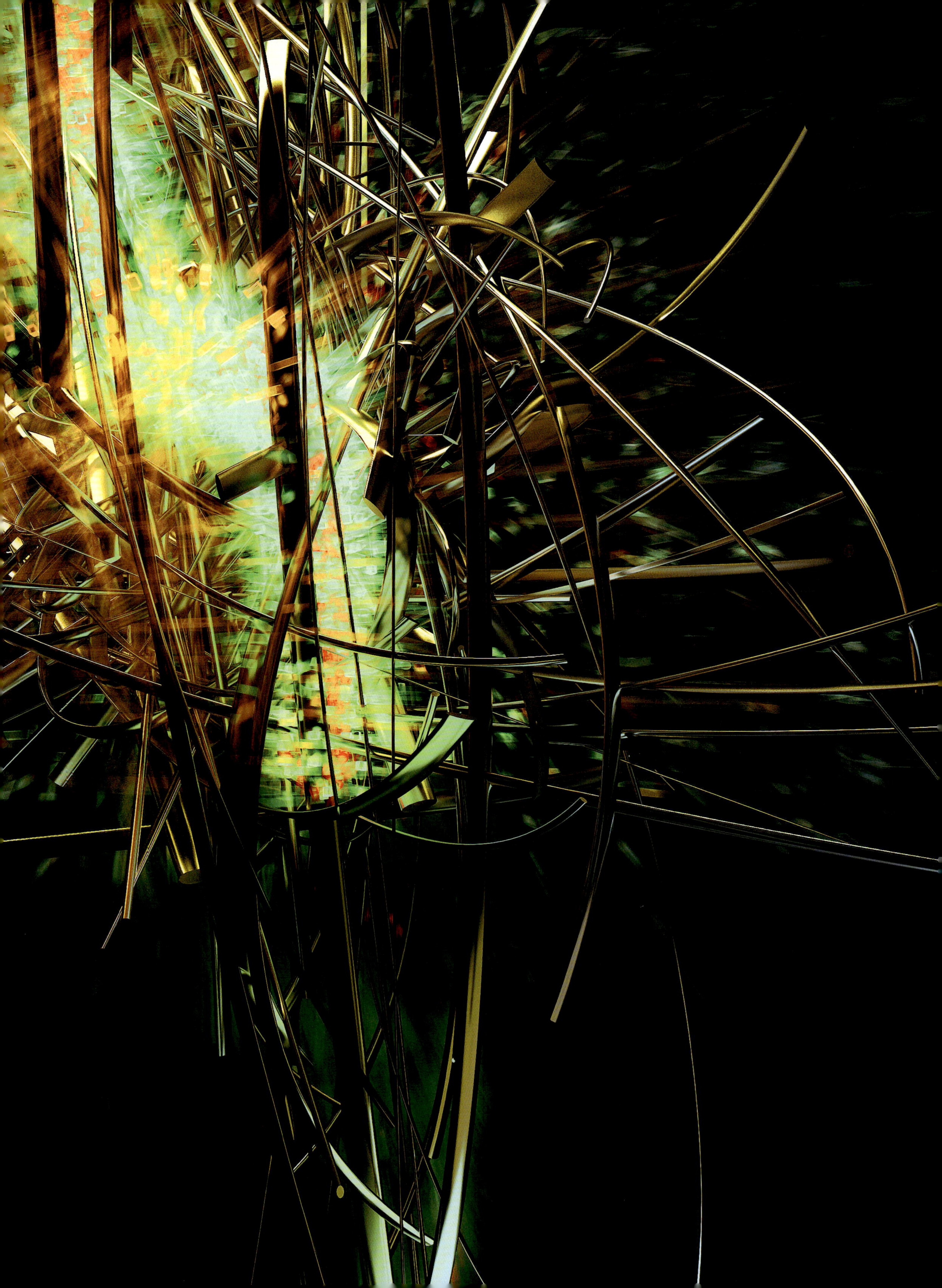

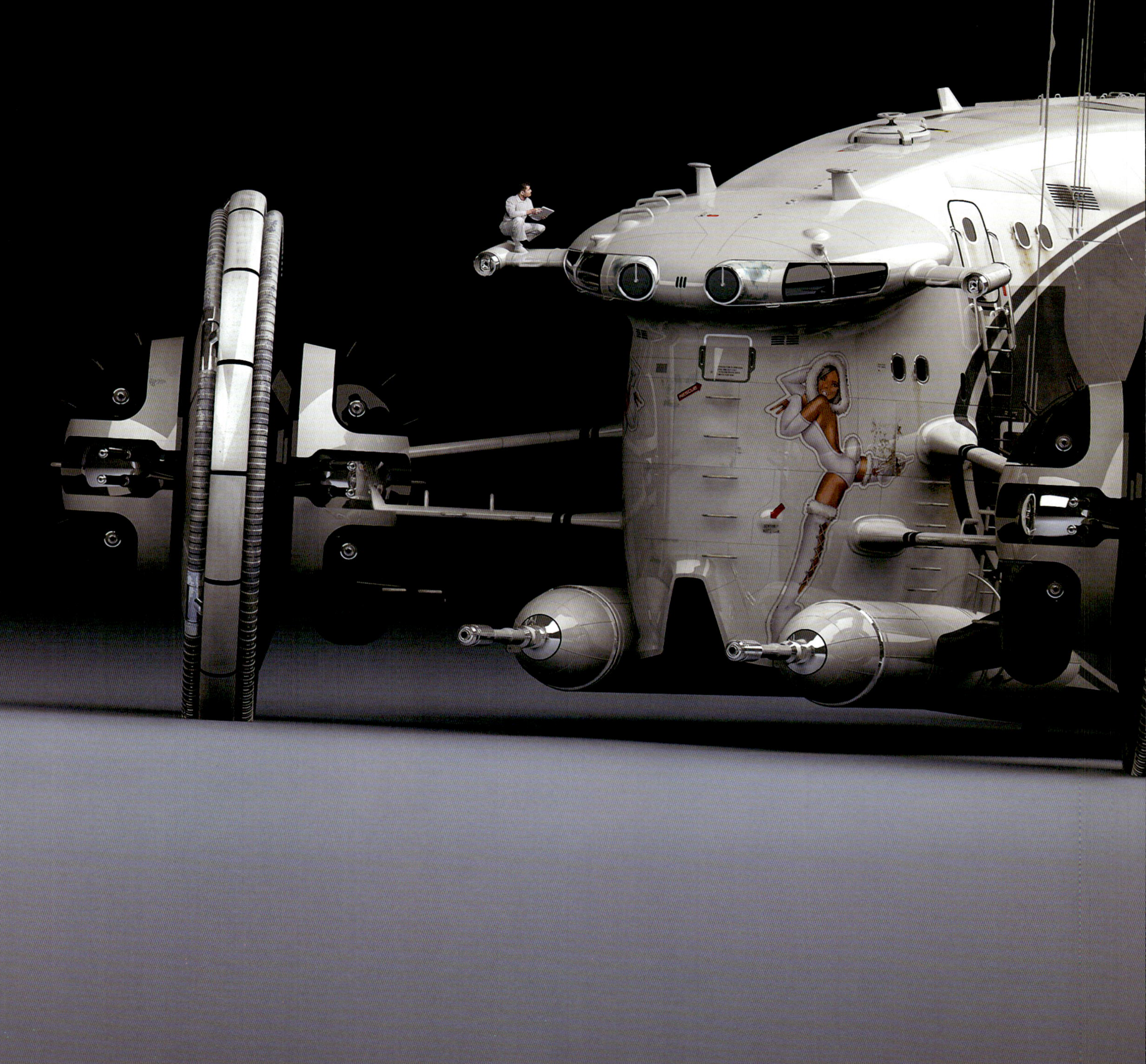

Master

Transport

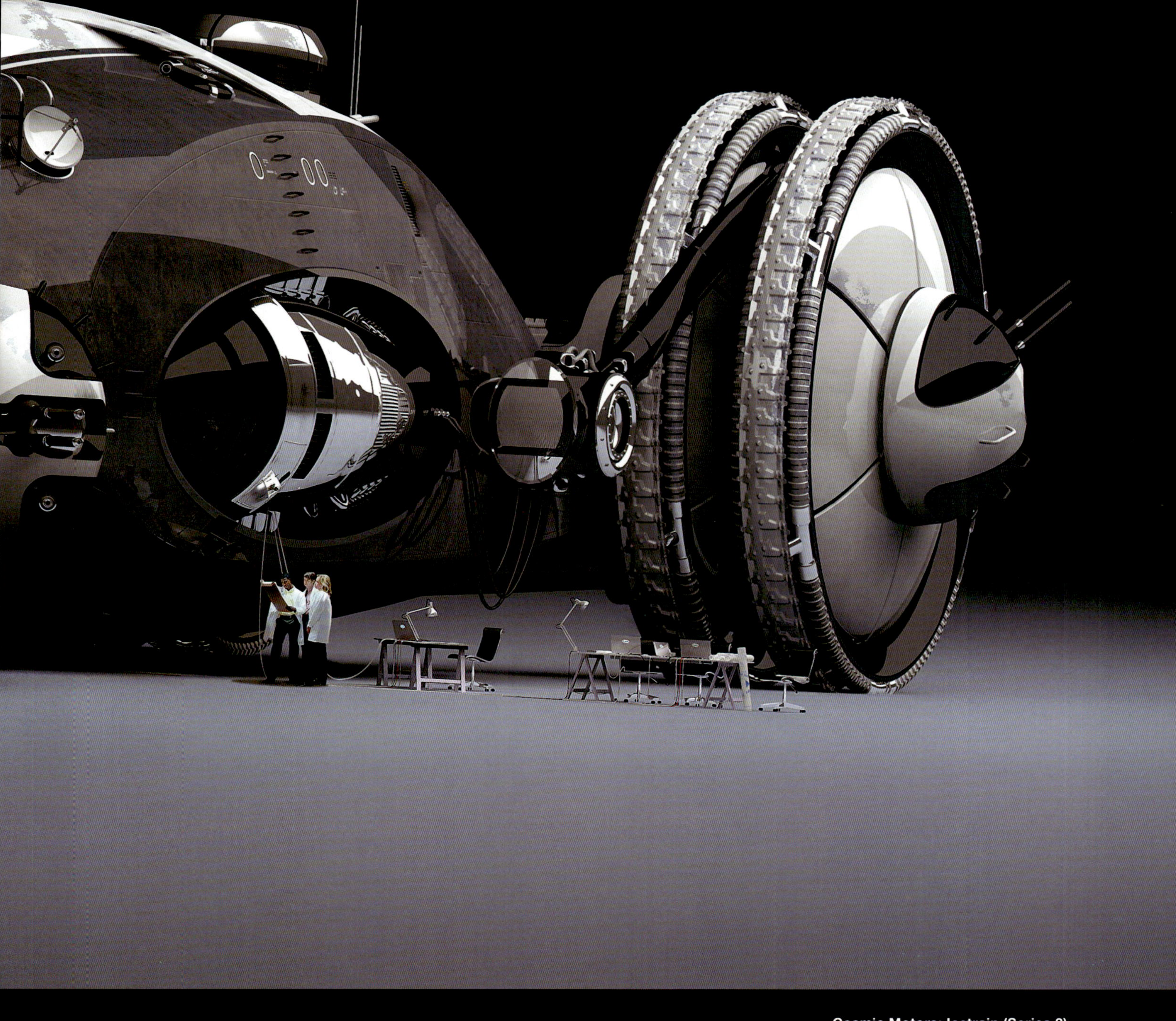

Cosmic Motors: Icetrain (Series 3)
StudioTools, Maya, mental ray, Photoshop
Daniel Simon, Cosmic Motors, GERMANY

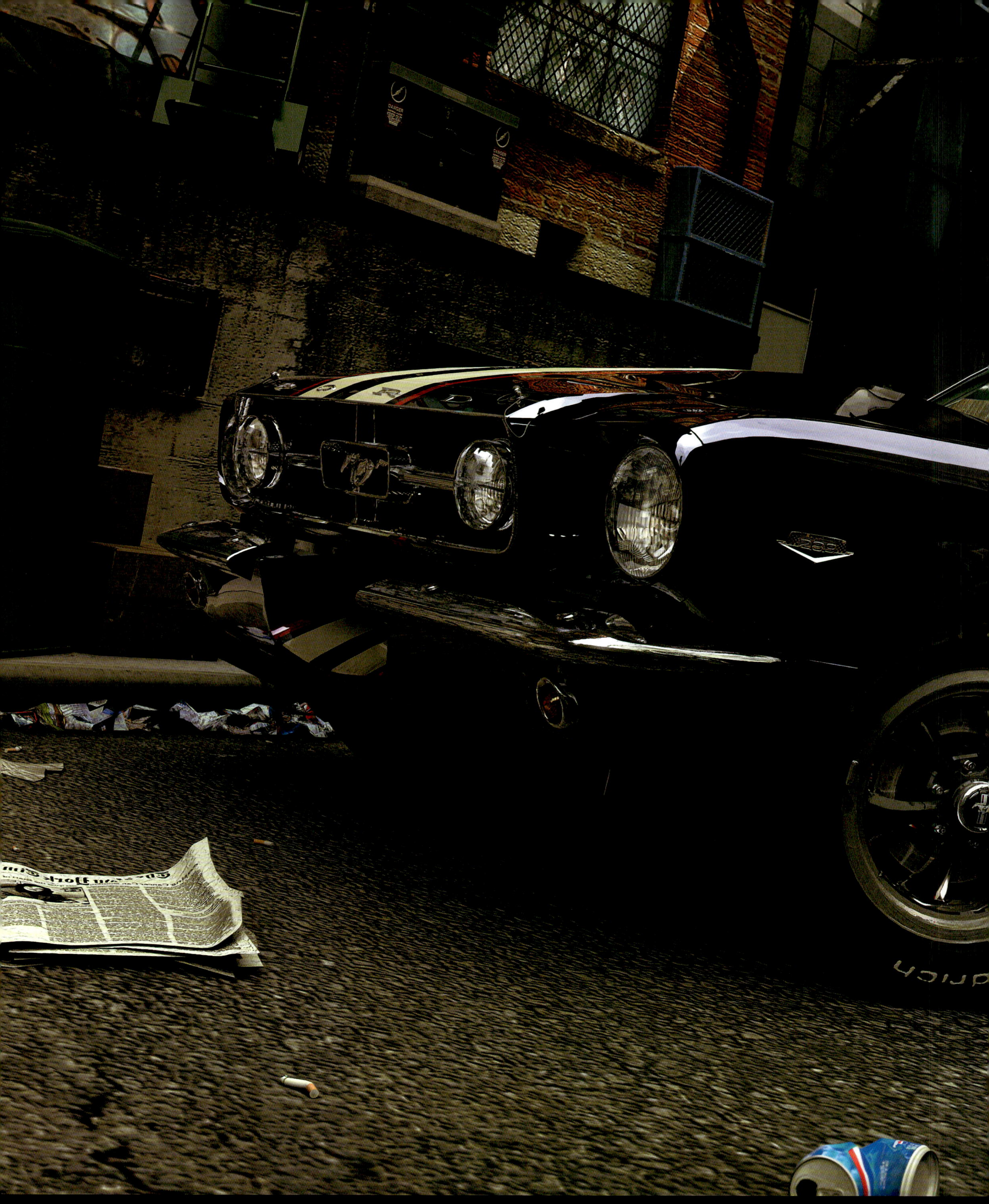

Excellence

Transport

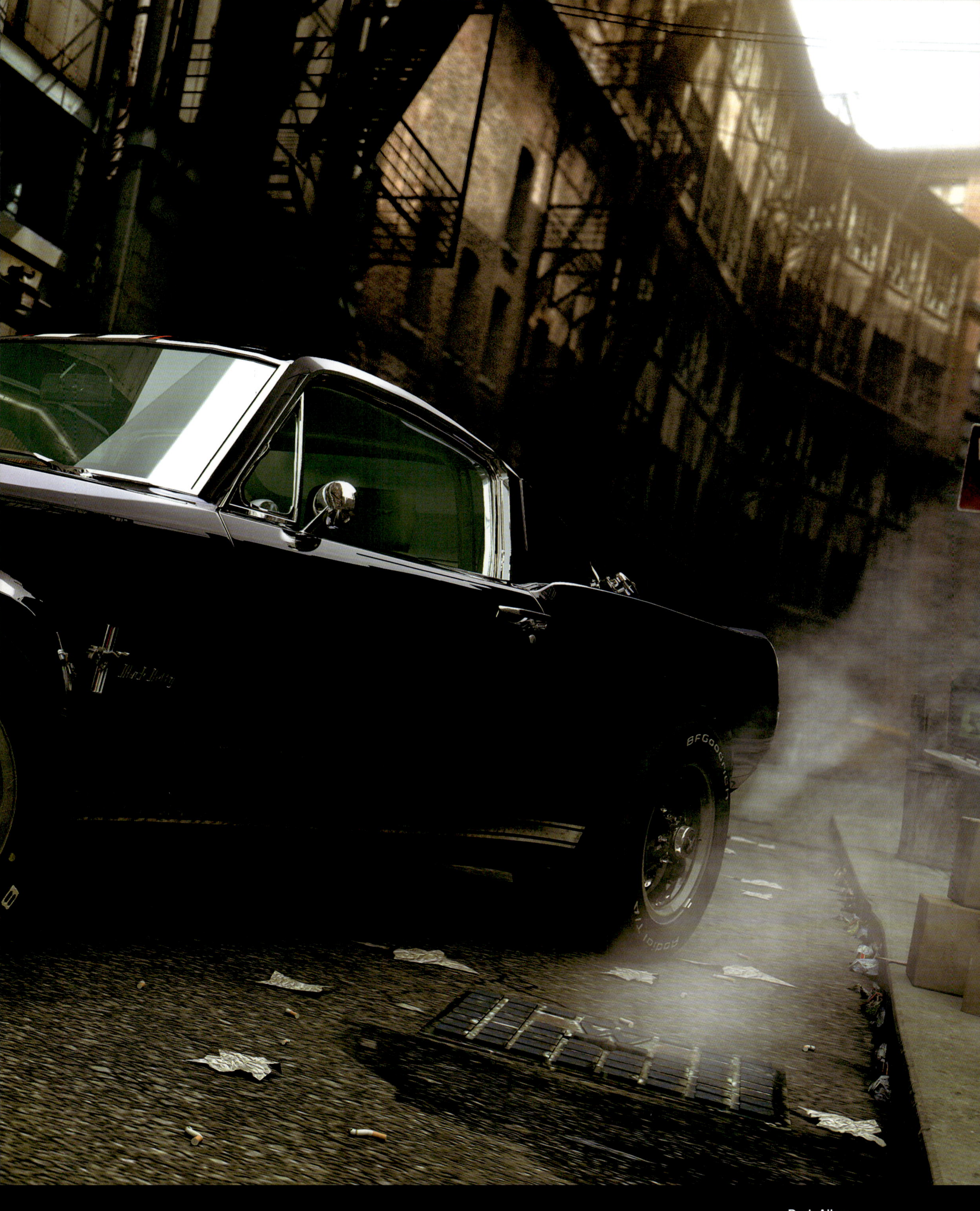

Dark Alley
3ds Max, Brazil r/s, Combustion, Photoshop
Andrea Bertaccini, Tredistudio, ITALY

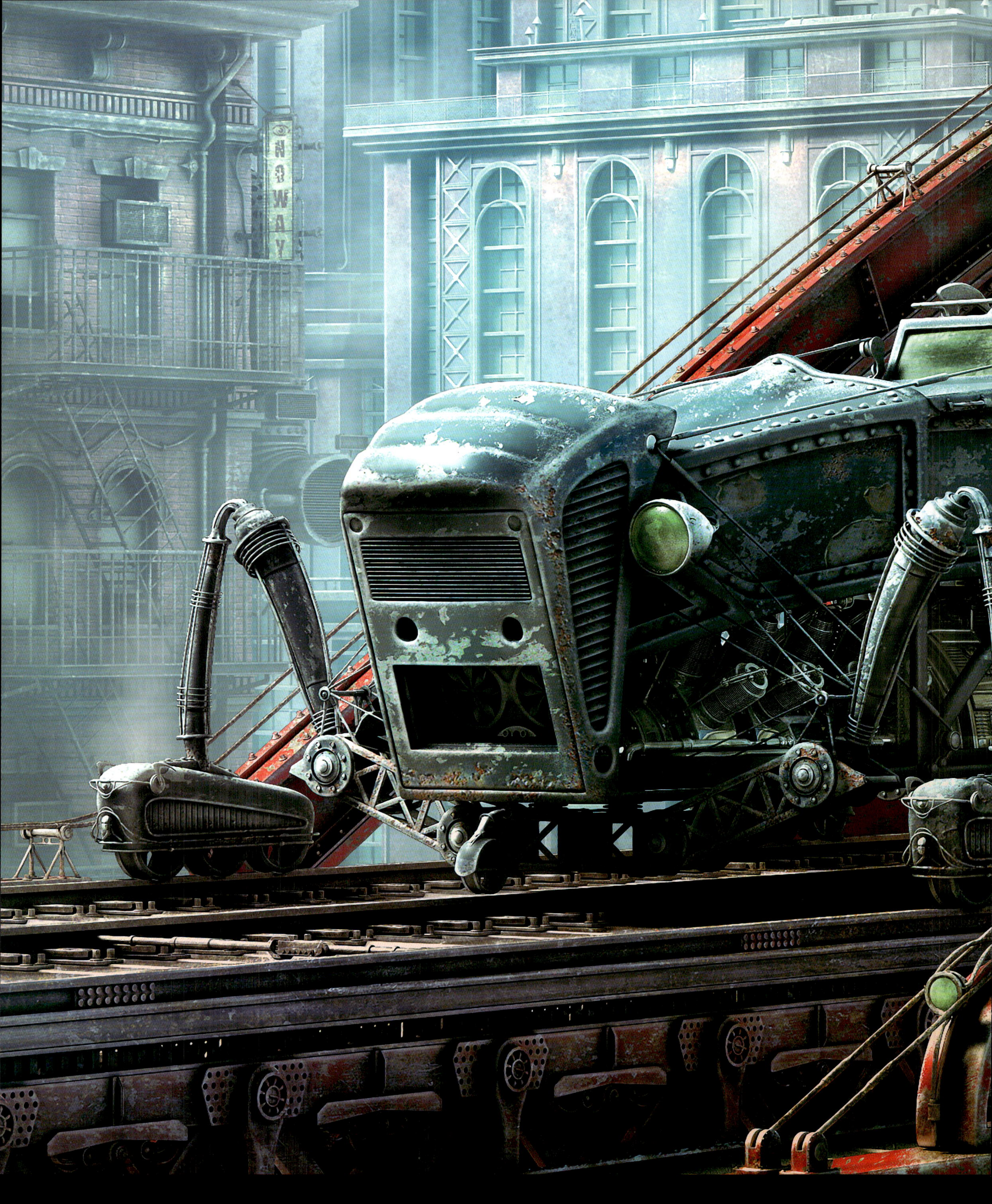

Excellence

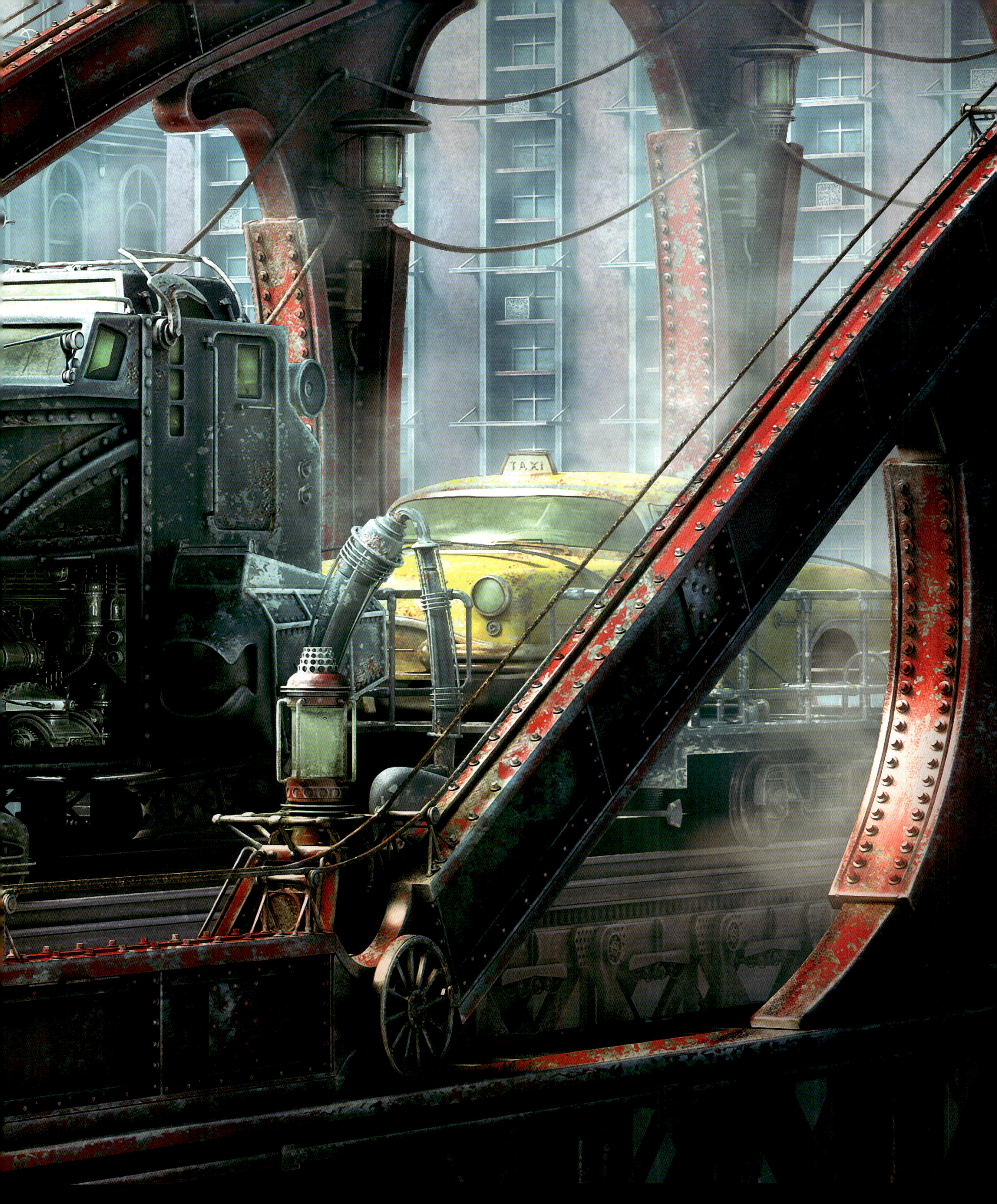

RusticMetal
3ds Max, modo, Photoshop, V-Ray
Jean Christophe Largillier, FRANCE

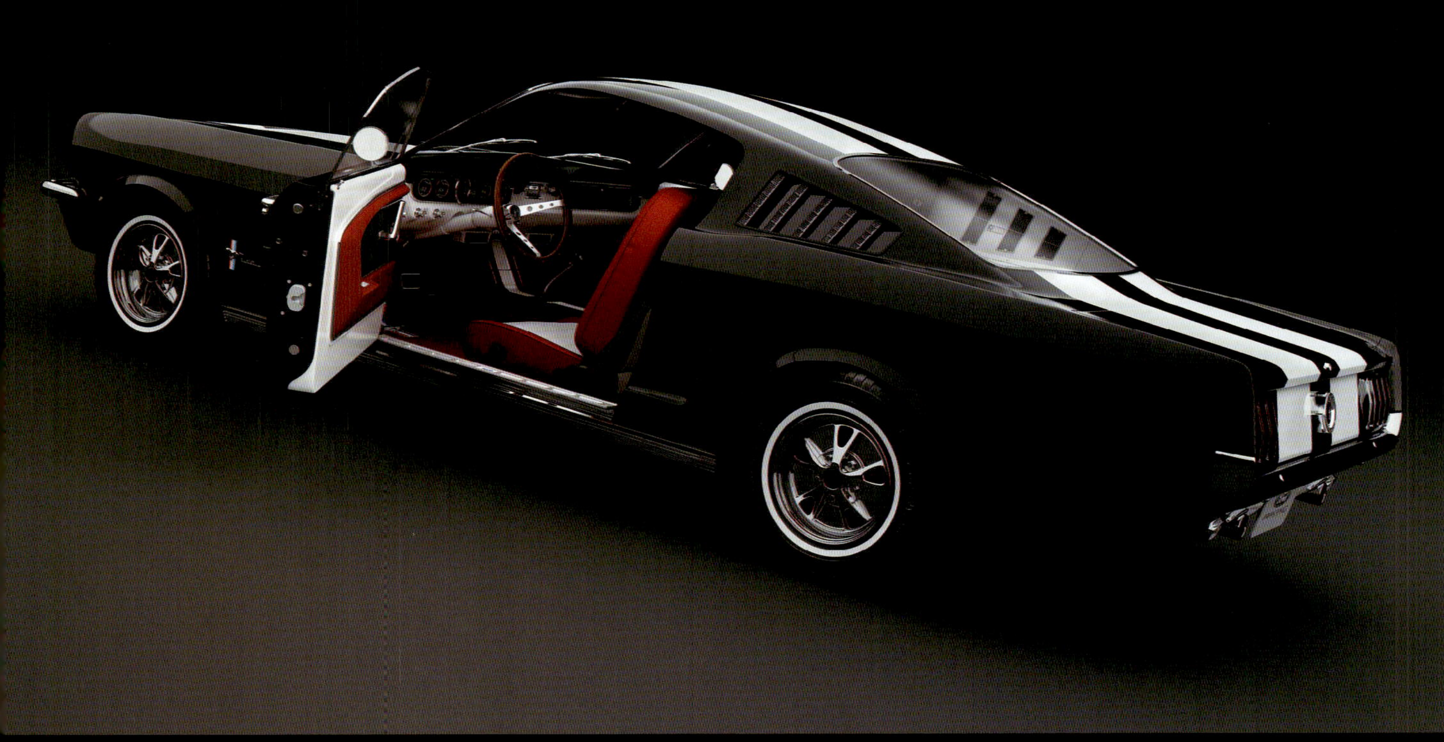

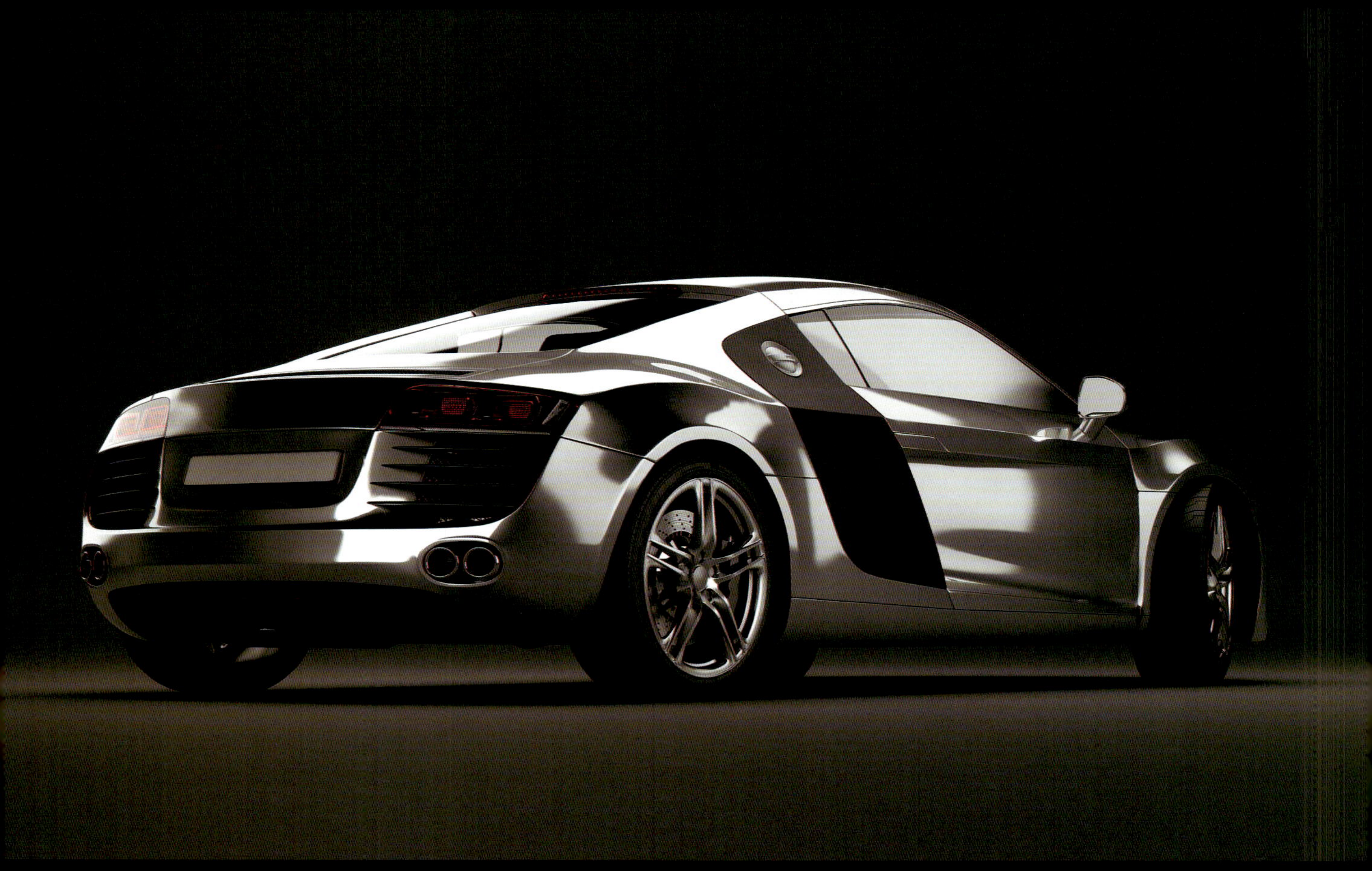

Ford Mustang Fastback '65
3ds Max, V-Ray, Photoshop
Paul Pâslea,
ROMANIA
[top]

Audi R8
3ds Max, V-Ray, Photoshop
Burzin Engineer, Elemental Crafts
USA
[above]

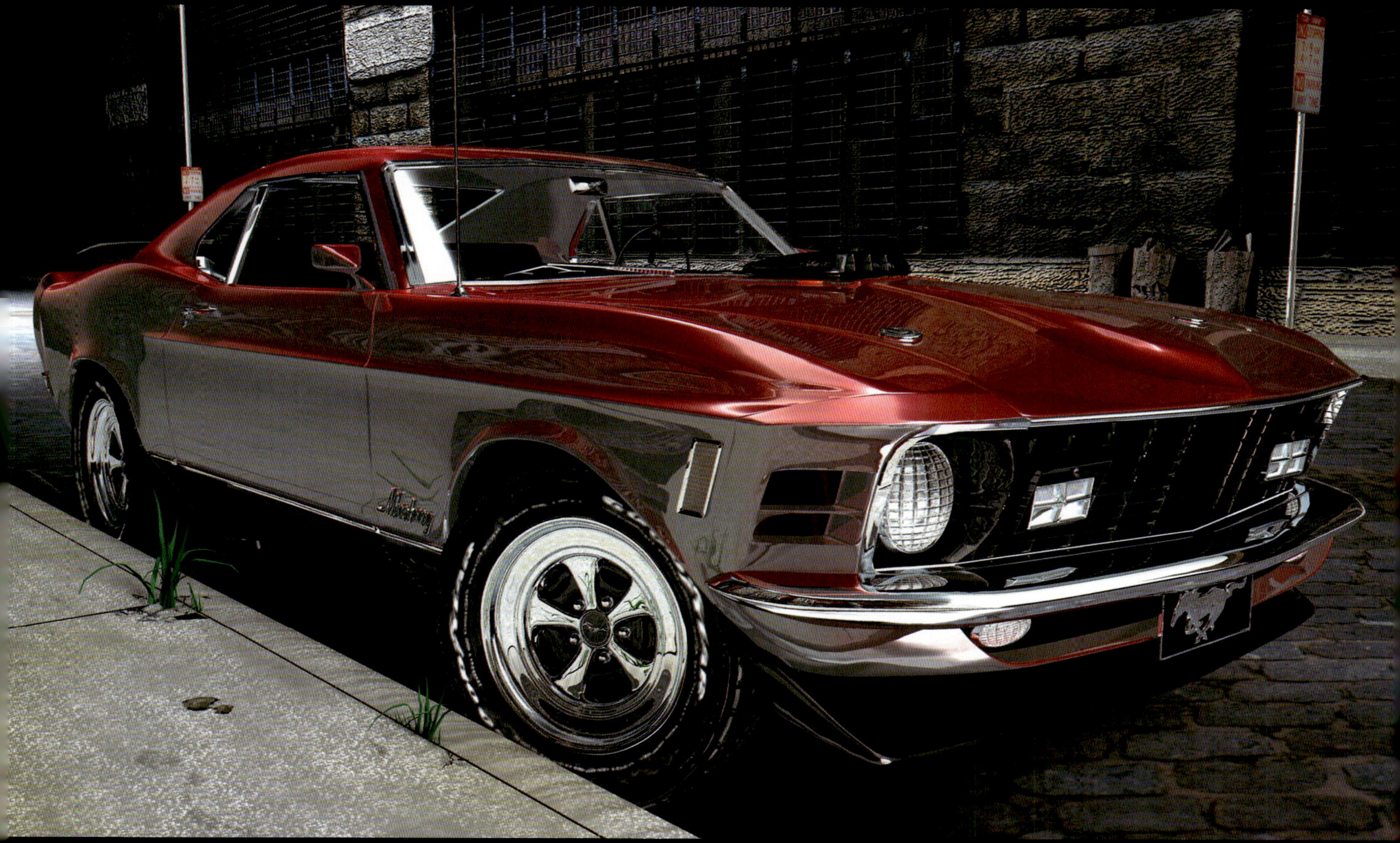

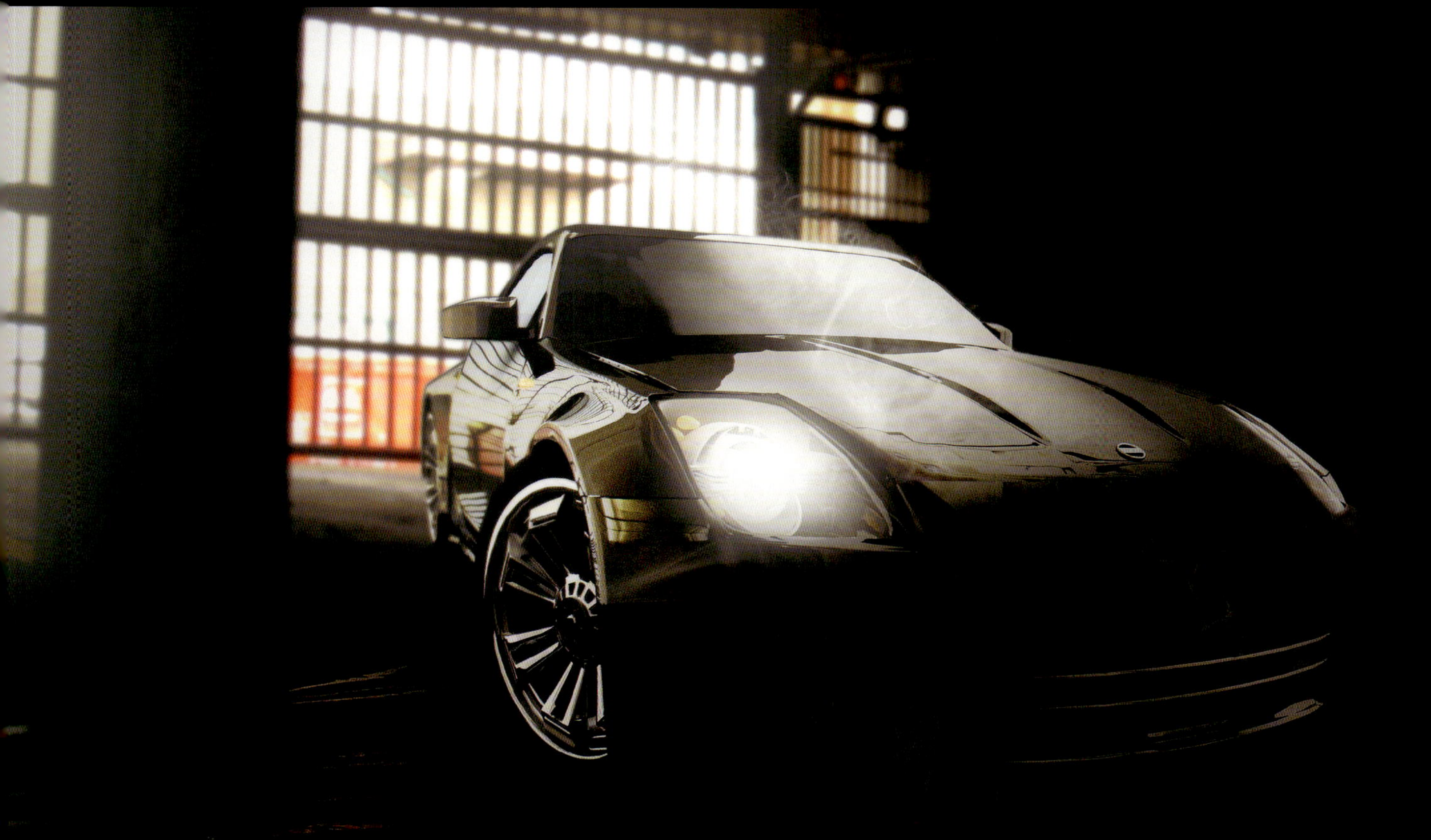

1970 Ford Mustang Mach 1
428 Super CobraJet
Maya
Ralph Manis, Infinitee Designs, USA
[top]

In the Shade
Maya, mental ray,
Photoshop, HDRShop
Brenda Li, CANADA
[above]

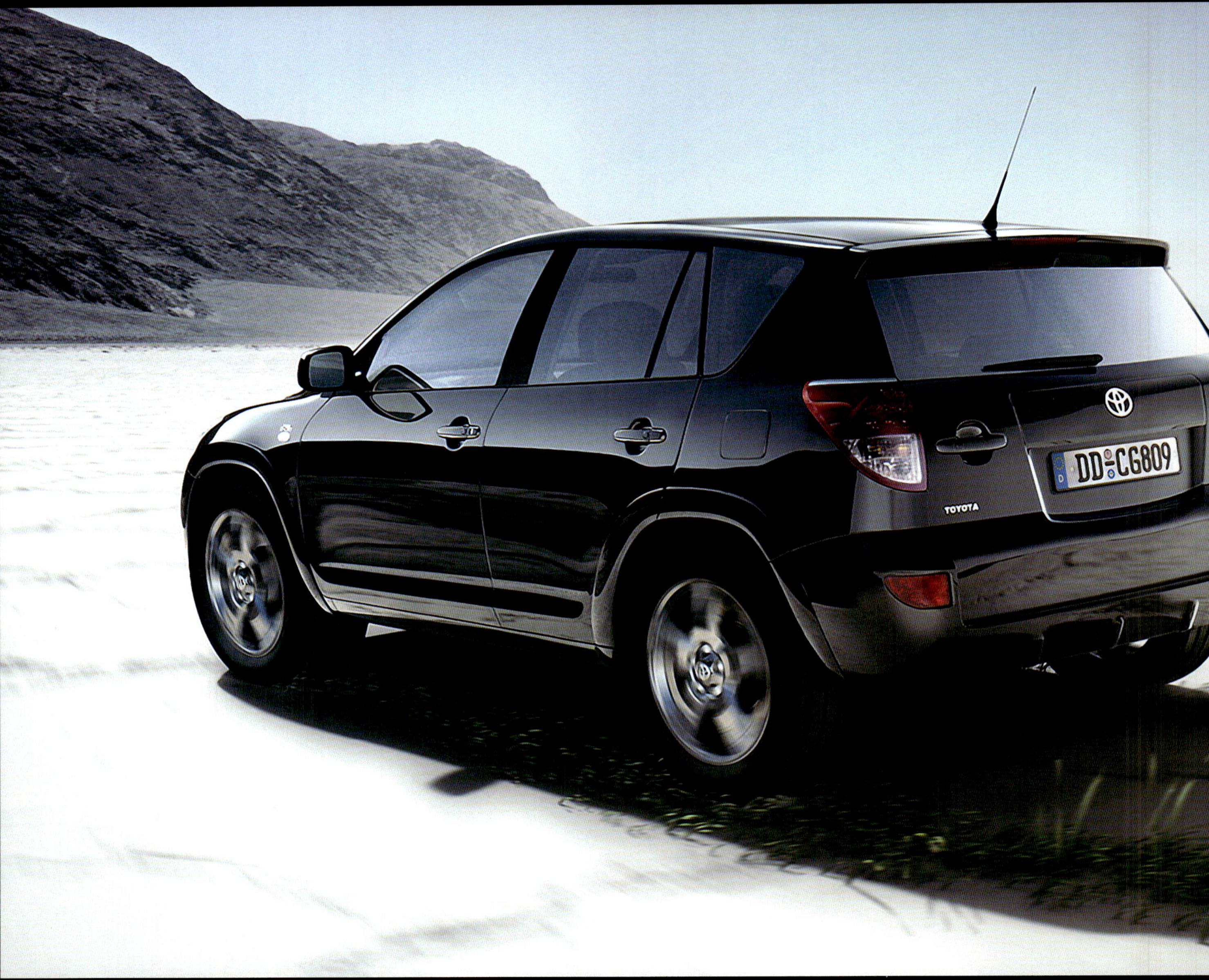

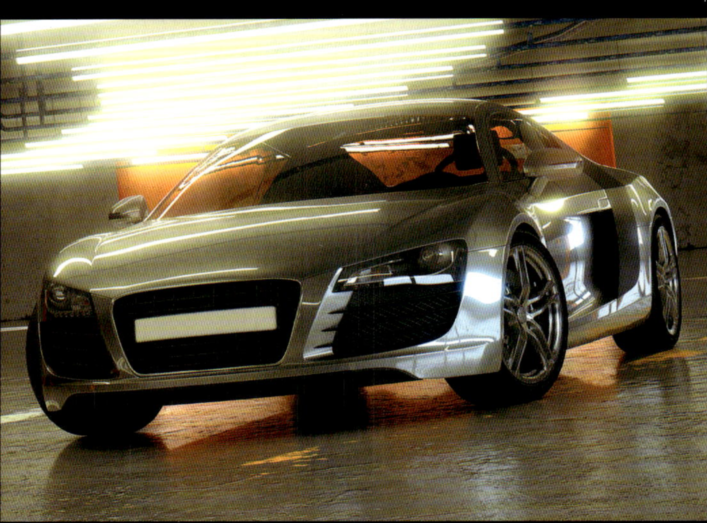

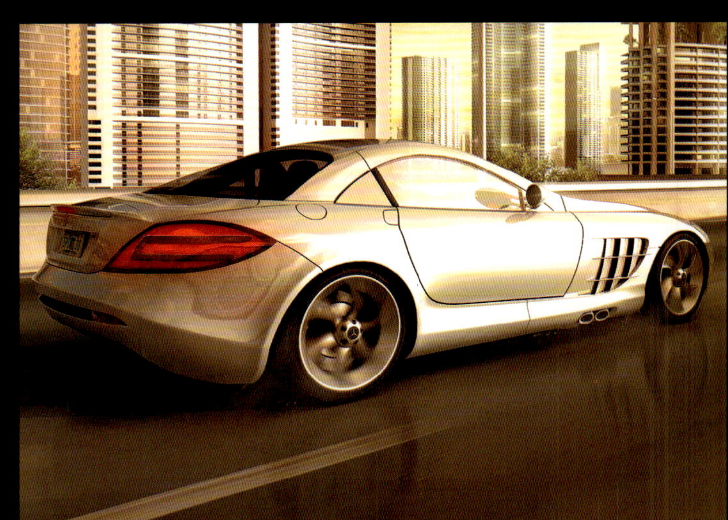

Badwater
Maya, mental ray, Photoshop
Dick Boot, 809cgi,
GERMANY
[top]

Audi R8 Artistic Representation
3ds Max, V-Ray, Photoshop
Burzin Engineer, Elemental Crafts,
USA
[above]

City Slicker
3ds Max, Photoshop
Spine3D,
USA
[above]

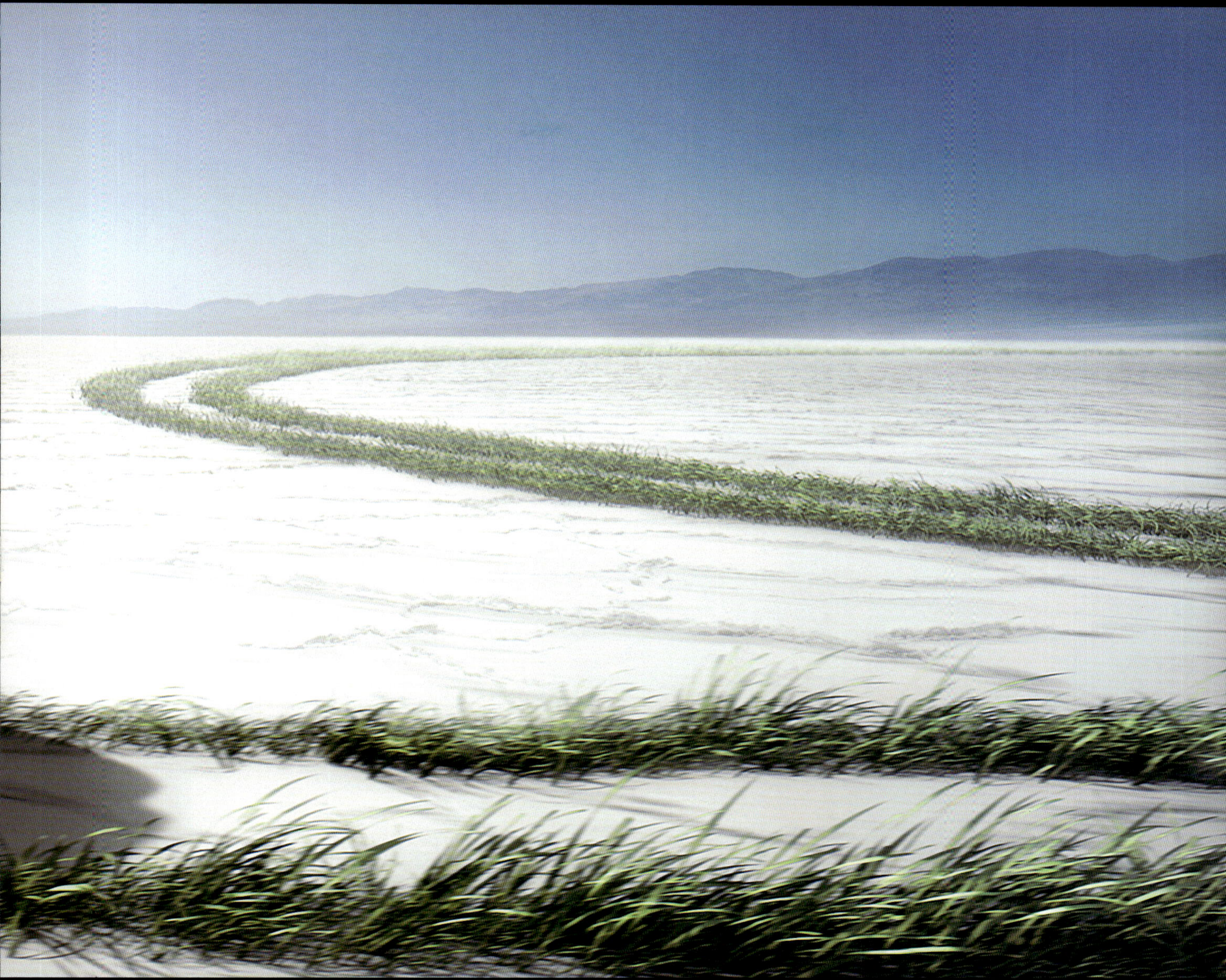

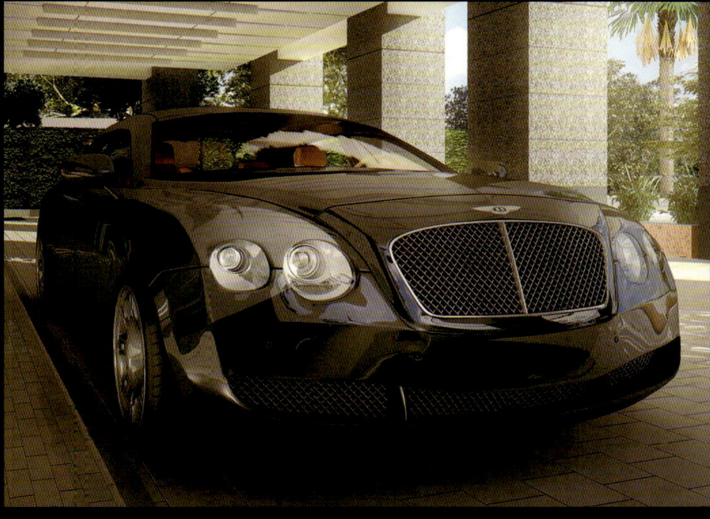

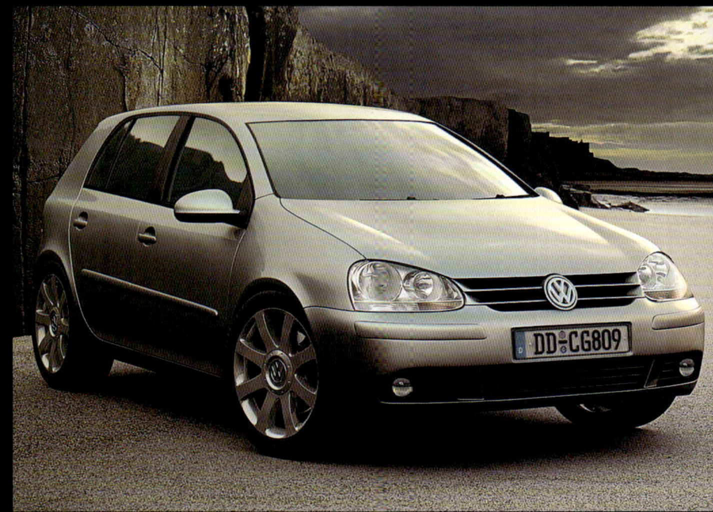

Clubview
3ds Max, Photoshop
Client: Fifield Companies
Spine3D, USA
[above]

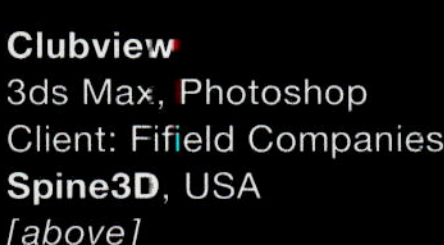

Bamburgh
Maya, mental ray, Photoshop
Dick Boot, 809cgi,
GERMANY
[above]

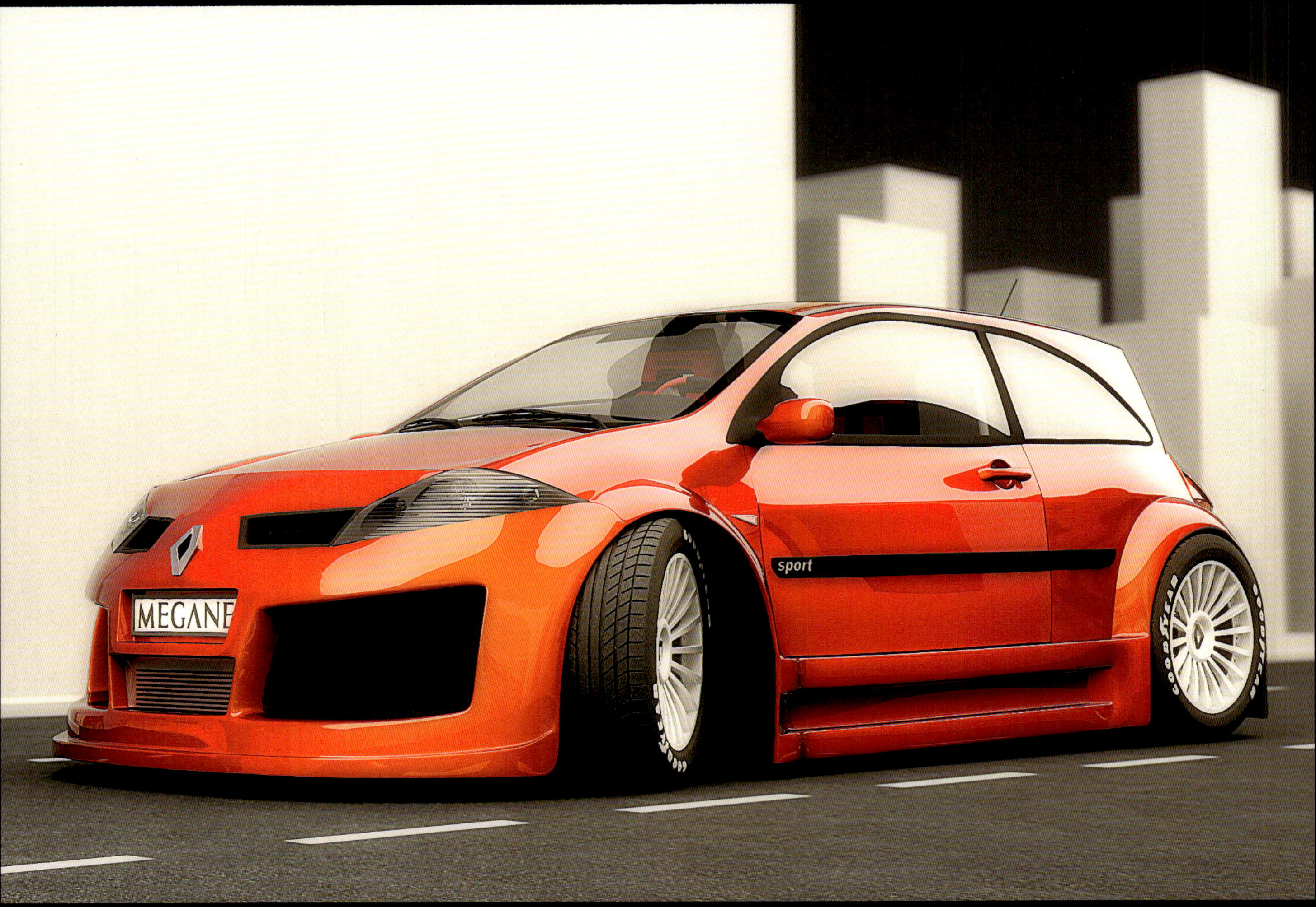

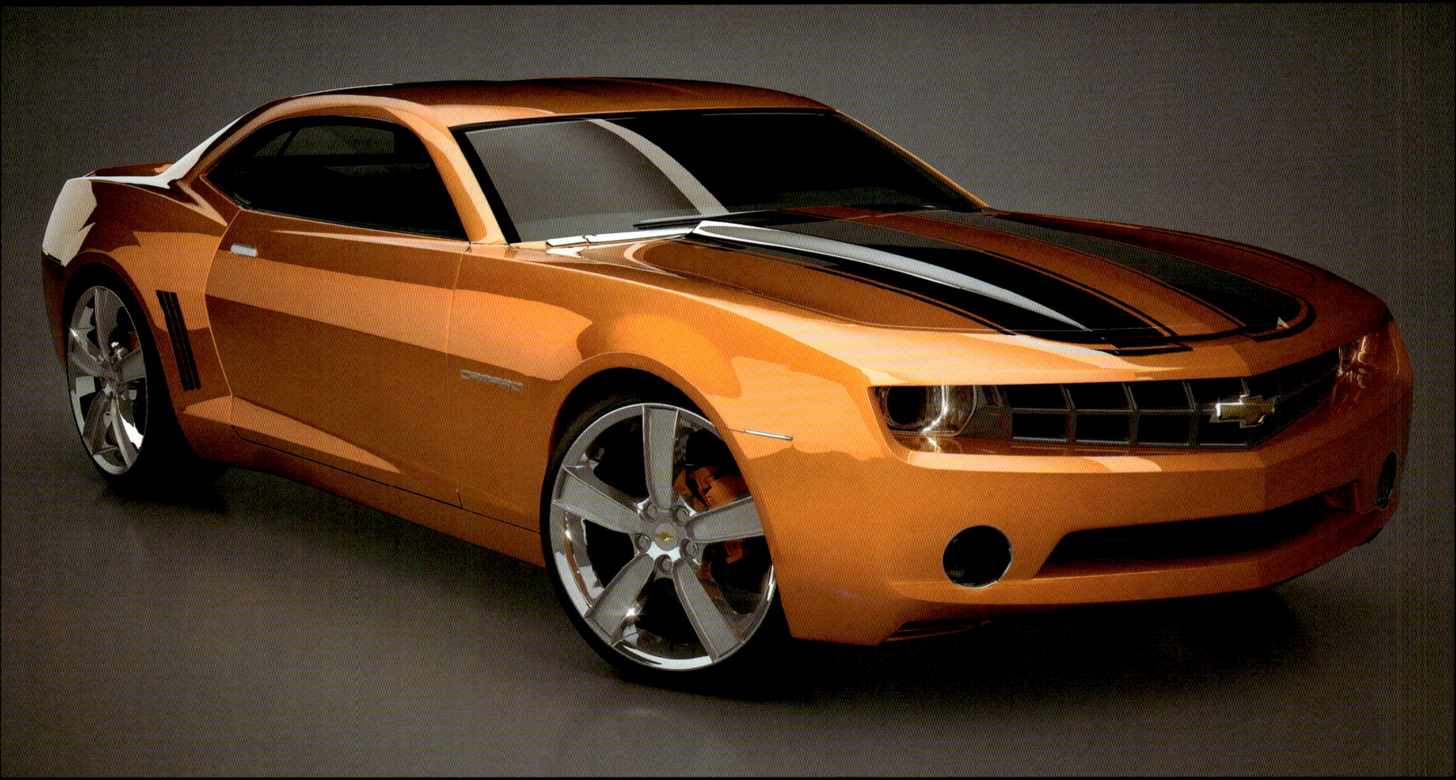

Modified Megane
3ds Max
Rafael Rubio Muñoz, SPAIN
[top]

Studio Car Render
3ds Max, mental ray
Joe Gunn, USA
[above]

Cosmic Motors: Icetrain (closeup)
StudioTools, Maya, mental ray, Photoshop
Daniel Simon, Cosmic Motors, GERMANY
[right]

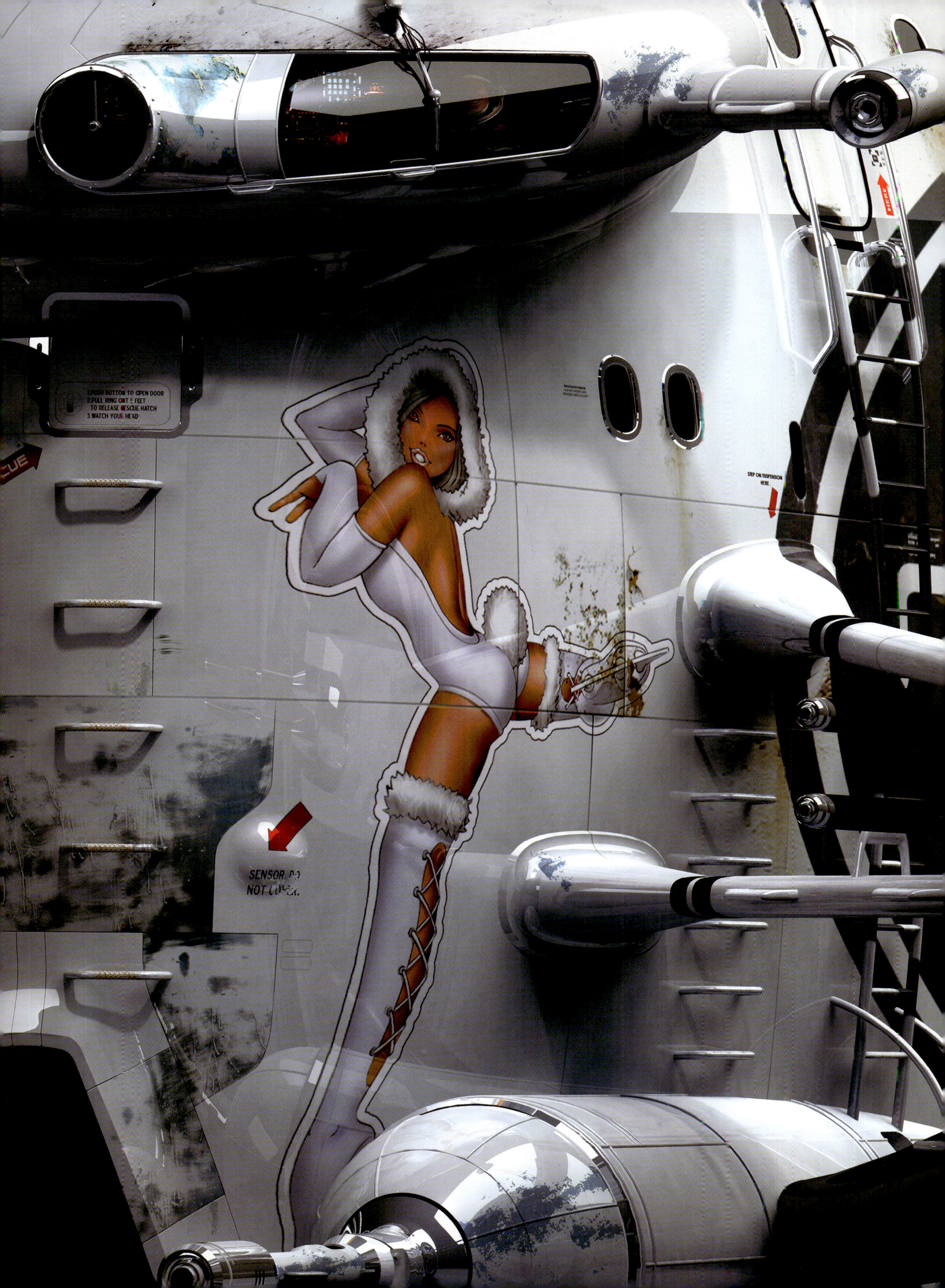
TO OPEN DOOR
2.PULL RING
FEET
TO RELEASE
HATCH
3.WATCH
HEAD
SENSOR
NOT

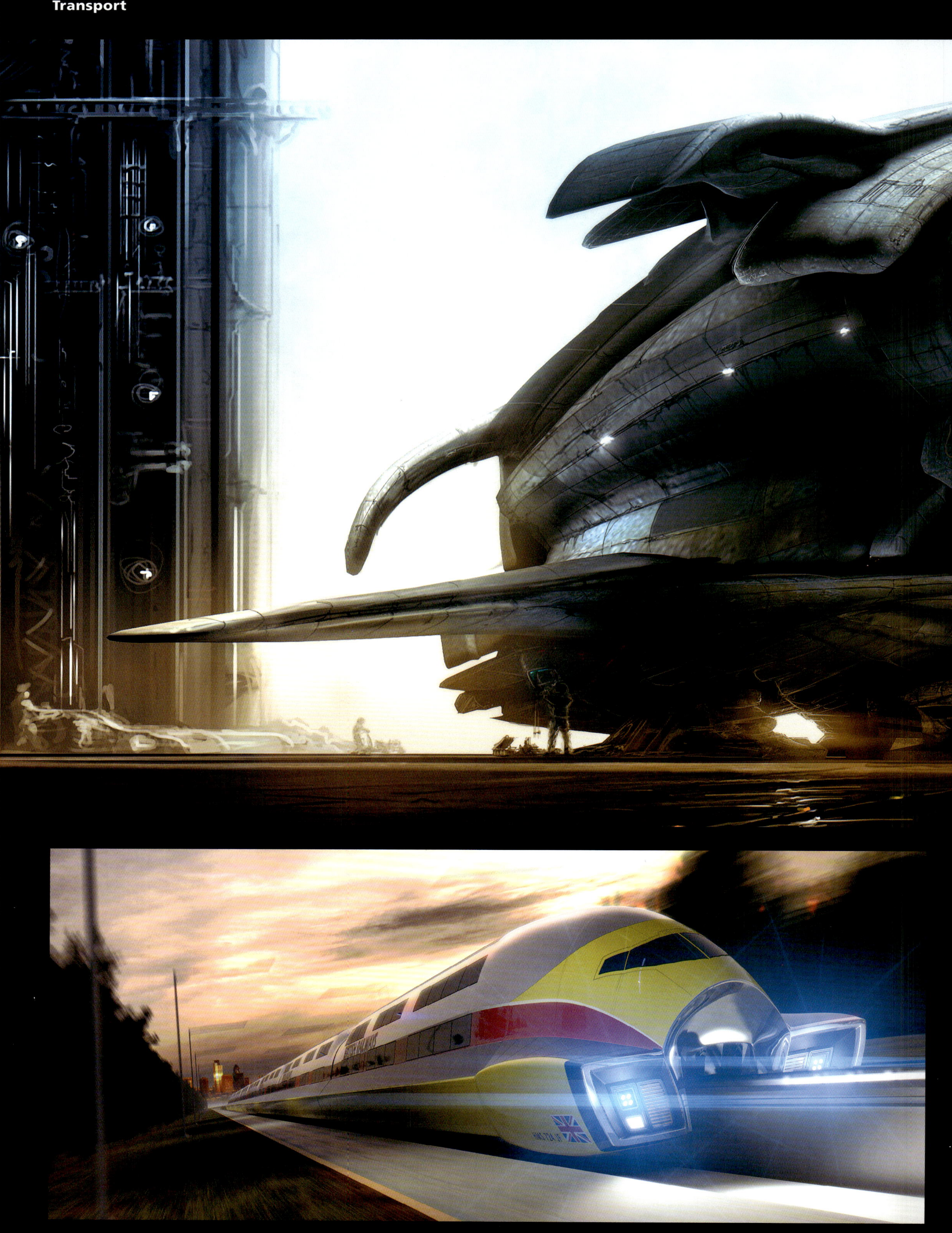

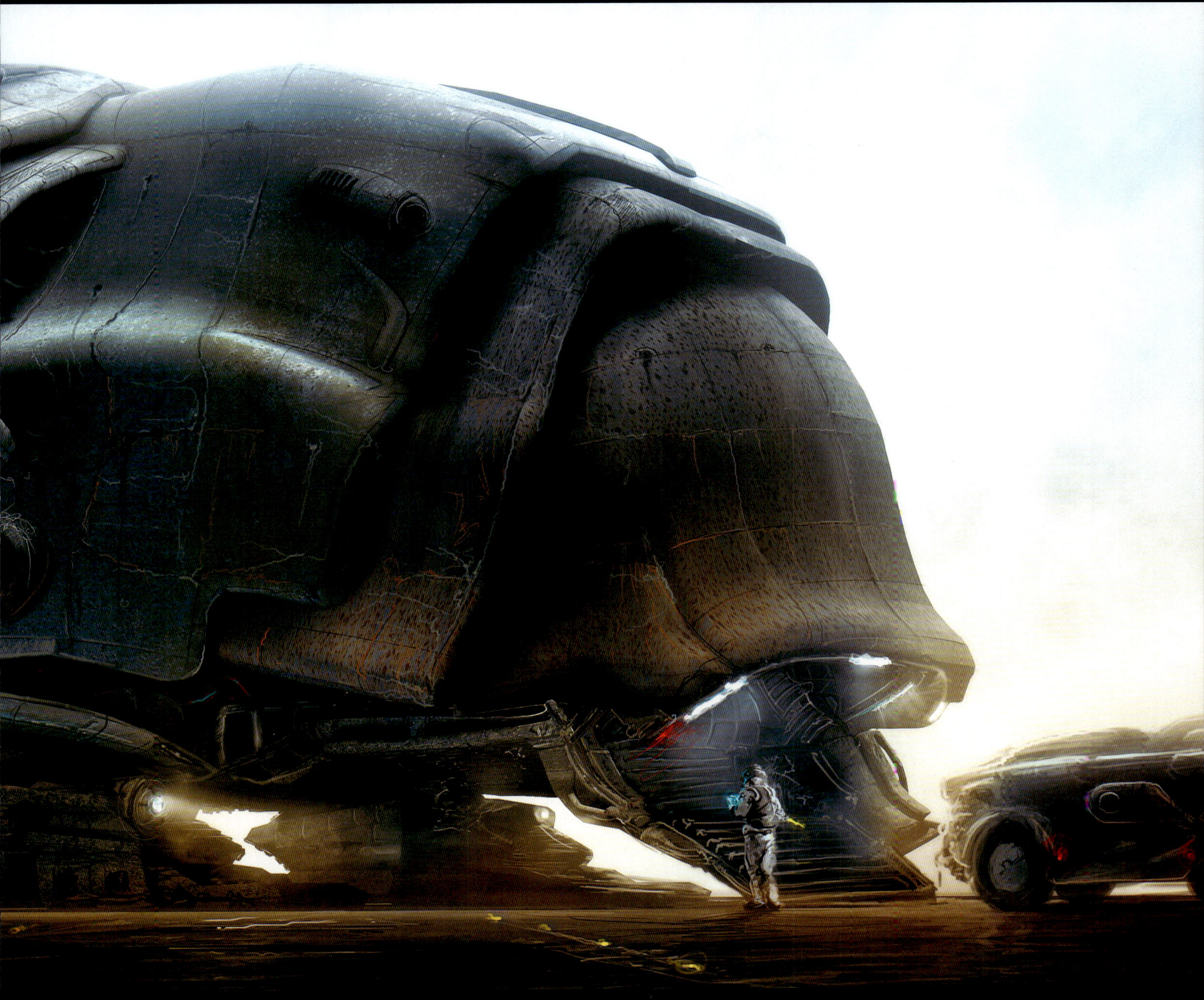

Cargo
3ds Max, Photoshop
Omur Ozgur, TURKEY
[above]

Future Train
3ds Max, V-Ray, Photoshop
Tom Shannon and **Glen Loyd**,
Parsons Brinckerhoff Project
Visualization, USA
[left]

Shiprock
Maya, mental ray, Photoshop
Dick Boot, 809cgi, GERMANY
[right]

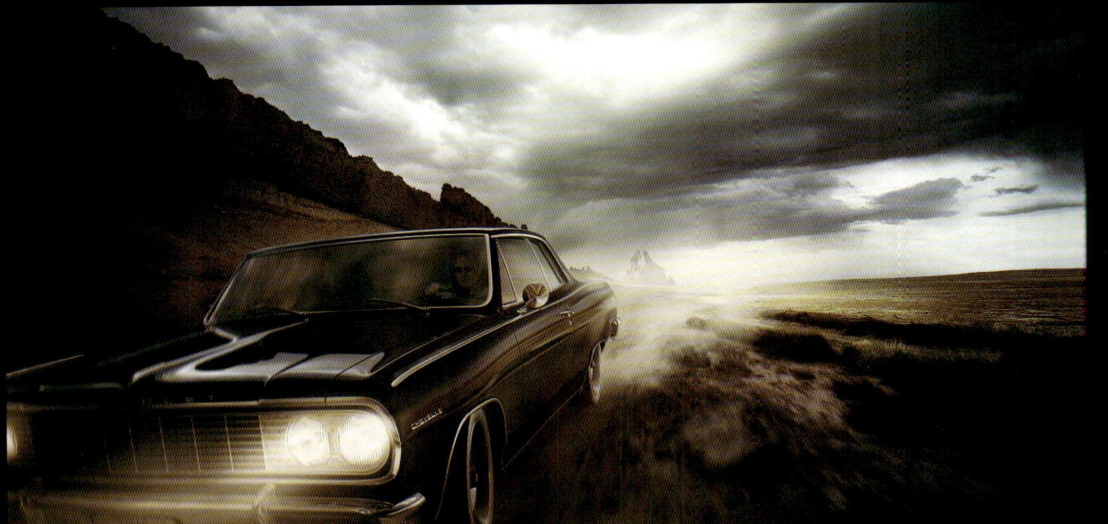

Index

SOFTWARE INDEX

Products credited by popular name in this book are listed alphabetically here by company.

Company	Products	Website
Adobe	After Effects, Photoshop	www.adobe.com
Apple	Shake	www.apple.com
Autodesk	3ds Max, AliasStudio, AutoCAD, Combustion	www.autodesk.com
	Maya, Mudbox, StudioTools, VIZ	www.autodesk.com
Cebas GmbH	finalRender	www.finalrender.com
Chaos Group	V-Ray	www.chaosgroup.com
Corel	CorelDRAW, Painter	www.corel.com
Google	SketchUp	www.google.com
Luxology	modo	www.luxology.com
Mark Townsend	Apophysis	www.apophysis.org
MAXON	BodyPaint 3D, CINEMA 4D	www.maxoncomputer.com
McNeel	Rhino	en.na.mcneel.com
mental images	mental ray	www.mentalimages.com
Orbaz Tech.	pFlow	www.orbaz.com
Parametric Tech. Corp.	Pro/ENGINEER	www.ptc.com
Paul Debevec	HDRShop	www.hdrshop.com
Pixologic	ZBrush	www.pixologic.com
Smith Micro Software Inc.	Poser	www.smithmicro.com
Softimage	SoftimageIXSI	www.softimage.com
SolidWorks	SolidWorks	www.solidworks.com
Splutterfish	Brazil r/s	www.splutterfish.com
The Foundry	Nuke	www.thefoundry.co.uk